Strengthening the U.S.-Japan Library Partnership in the Global Information Flow

グローバルな情報流通に向けての
日米大学図書館協力の強化

Strengthening the U.S.-Japan Library Partnership in the Global Information Flow

グローバルな情報流通に向けての
日米大学図書館協力の強化

Fourth U.S.-Japan Conference
on Library and Information
Science in Higher Education

Racine, Wisconsin
October 3–6, 1988

Editors

Theodore F. Welch　　　　Haruo Kuroda
Warren M. Tsuneishi　　　Eiichi Kurahashi
Mary F. Grosch

American Library Association

Chicago and London
Maruzen International Co., Ltd.　　1990
Tokyo

Designed by Charles Bozett

Composed by Ampersand Publisher Services Inc.
in Galliard and Helvetica on an Itek IGX
7000 Imagesetter

Printed on 50-pound Glatfelter, a pH-neutral
stock, and bound in B-grade Arrestox cloth
by Braun-Brumfield, Inc.

The paper used in this publication meets the minimum requirements of American National Standard for Information Sciences—Permanence of Paper for Printed Library Materials, ANSI Z39.48-1984. ∞

Library of Congress Cataloging-in-Publication Data

U.S.-Japan Conference on Libraries and Information Science in Higher Education (4th : 1988 : Racine, Wis.)
 Strengthening the U.S.-Japan library partnership in the global information flow : fourth U.S.-Japan Conference on Libraries and Information Science in Higher Education, Racine, Wis., October 3–6, 1988 / editors, Theodore F. Welch, Warren M. Tsuneishi, and Mary F. Grosch.
   p. cm.

ISBN 0-8389-3378-5

 1. Libraries, University and college—United States—Congresses.
2. Libraries, University and college—Japan—Congresses.
3. Libraries and education—United States—Congresses. 4. Libraries and education—Japan—Congresses. 5. Information science—United States—Congresses. 6. Information science—Japan—Congresses.
I. Welch, Theodore F. II. Tsuneishi, Warren M. (Warren Michio), 1921- . III. Grosch, Mary F. IV. American Library Association. V. Title.
Z675.U5U52 1988
027.7'0973—dc20   89-18141

Copyright © 1990 by the American Library Association. All rights reserved except those which may be granted by Sections 107 and 108 of the Copyright Revision Act of 1976.

Printed in the United States of America.

94 93 92 91 90   5 4 3 2 1

Liaison with Japanese Libraries
ad hoc subcommittee of the
International Relations Committee
American Library Association

Kazuko M. Dailey
Hideo Kaneko
Hisao Matsumoto
Warren M. Tsuneishi
Allen B. Veaner
Theodore F. Welch, chair

Contents

Preface	ix
TWO DECADES IN REVIEW: U.S.-Japan Conferences on Libraries and Information Science in Higher Education, 1969–1988	
by Theodore F. Welch	1
A Report on Planning for THE FOURTH U.S.-JAPAN CONFERENCE ON LIBRARIES AND INFORMATION SCIENCE IN HIGHER EDUCATION	
by Hiro Yamasaki	11
UNFINISHED BUSINESS: Computers, Libraries, and East Asian Studies	
by John W. Haeger	17
JAPANESE BIBLIOGRAPHIC DATA FILES	
by Toru Sugawara	24
THE NATIONAL DIET LIBRARY AND ITS PRESERVATION PROGRAM	
by Kazuo Takahashi	55
OPTICAL DISC FILE SYSTEM AND MATERIALS PRESERVATION	
by Masatoshi Shibukawa	72
THE PRESERVATION OF KNOWLEDGE: Strategies for a Global Society	
by Patricia Battin	90

DATABASE FORMATION AND SERVICES FOR
SCHOLARLY INFORMATION IN JAPAN
    by Jun Adachi   100

THE ESTABLISHMENT OF A UNION CATALOG
DATABASE IN JAPAN: Current Status and Problems
    by Eiichi Kurahashi   114

ISSUES SURROUNDING DATABASE DEVELOPMENT
IN THE UNITED STATES
    by Henriette D. Avram   129

ISSUES SURROUNDING NETWORK DEVELOPMENT
IN THE UNITED STATES
    by Rowland C. W. Brown   139

NETWORKING AS AN INFORMATION RESOURCE IN
JAPAN
    by Hisafumi Tanaka   145

THE EFFECT OF SCIENCE INFORMATION SYSTEMS
ON JAPANESE UNIVERSITY LIBRARIES
    by Kimio Ohno   158

SCIENCE AND TECHNOLOGY INFORMATION AND
COOPERATION WITH SPECIAL LIBRARIES
    by Takayasu Miyakawa   165

DISCOVERING THE BASIS FOR FUTURE
COLLABORATION
    by Haruo Kuroda   172

REFLECTIONS ON THE FOURTH U.S.-JAPAN
CONFERENCE ON LIBRARIES IN HIGHER
EDUCATION
    by Theodore F. Welch   174

Appendix: FINAL COMMUNIQUE   177

Editors and Contributors   179

Japanese text follows page 182

Preface

The U.S.-Japan library conferences, generically known as the U.S.-Japan Conference on Libraries and Information Science in Higher Education, began in 1969, when the first meeting was held in Tokyo. The second (Racine, Wisconsin) and third (Kyoto) followed at three-year intervals, in 1972 and 1975, respectively. A period of eleven years lapsed before the series was resumed in 1986, with a one-day seminar in Tokyo. This meeting was followed by the fourth full-scale conference in 1988, held in Racine, Wisconsin.

For the purposes of this introduction to the proceedings that follow, I have gathered the first three conferences into one grouping and the seminar and fourth conference into another. The overall character of each set of meetings contrasts significantly one group to the other. Spanning two decades, this contrast is due in large part to the changes in the way Japanese have approached their role in international meetings, which in large part reflect their increased role in global affairs. Since the first grouping when the Japanese participants showed a hesitancy to speak out, there has been a marked increase in candor on their part, especially since the 1986 seminar. This is viewed as a very positive step towards maturation of the relationship.

The 1986 Tokyo seminar was held to discuss library technology in higher education in both countries. It also offered the opportunity to assess the record of the first three conferences. After more than a decade-long recess, the conference planners needed a chance for review before developing a rationale for a fourth conference. Speaking as a participant who had attended all prior conferences, Allen Veaner offered a paper at that time, "Japan-U.S. Librarianship: Impact of the Binational Experience, 1969–1975," in which he recorded the major changes in librarianship that had occurred since 1969. He recounted what was, to him, twelve "clearly visible, obviously discernable impacts" of the previous meetings:

1. The Japan-U.S. binational experience revolved around many distinguished, learned librarians on both sides of the Pacific. Now, in both Japan and the United States, a whole new generation of leadership has emerged.
2. Attendees of the first conference were mostly high-level administrators who gave papers outlining research library problems in broad, abstract terms. In contrast, at subsequent conferences a significant number of middle-level managers presented papers on very practical day-to-day operational issues.
3. The entire educational environment has changed radically in seventeen years:

    An era of unprecedented expansion in U.S. colleges and universities has come to an end.
    The strong student unrest which characterized both countries in the late 1960s has disappeared, replaced with a seriousness of attention to academic matters. Today's students recognize that the world is far different from what it was barely two decades ago.

4. The potential of library networks was well recognized at the first conference.
5. The development of decentralized or distributed computing has actually presented us with a new problem: there is now some danger that the ready availability of computing power may bring back the narrowness of focus and inefficient use of personnel that formerly characterized so many libraries.
6. Important bibliographic tools that were in the development stages in the late 1960s have now been completed.
7. The personal computer was virtually unknown in 1969—merely a gleam in the eyes of some designers. Now it has come virtually to dominate both business and education in every advanced country, with Japan and the United States the leading producers.
8. At the 1969 conference there was a great deal of exciting talk and planning about Japan's MARC program. Today the National Diet Library (NDL) has fully implemented its MARC distribution program; NDL itself assures a timely flow of accurate bibliographic data to Japan and the rest of the world.
9. Aside from MARC, other vital international standards, such as the ISBN and the ISSN, have been widely adopted by Japan, the United States, and nearly all major producers of publications throughout the world.
10. The suggestion by one speaker at the 1969 conference that pros-

pects for the transmission of full text were "rather distant" demonstrates how rapidly technology advances. Both the storage and transmission of very large volumes of full text are now a commonplace.
11. The Japan Information Center of Science and Technology (JICST), founded in 1957, has grown into the largest and most comprehensive science information service in all of Japan.
12. Throughout the three conferences it was apparent that rendering Chinese characters in computer-readable form so that they could be processed by library networks was a major technical obstacle for North American libraries. Building upon fundamental work accomplished in Japan and other countries, the Research Libraries Group, which was formed during this important period of binational collaboration, solved that formidable problem and is now sharing the results worldwide.

It is very interesting to compare Veaner's list of achievements with the stated goals shown in each of the conference resolutions (final communiques) before 1986.

There are calls in each of the first three communiques for appropriate Japanese and U.S. committees to provide leadership and serve as channels of communication, as well as to provide a central clearing house (first communique, 1969). It was also envisaged that small working committees would be formed to implement specific projects (second communique, 1972); and forming a joint U.S.-Japan standing committee was seen as a need in planning for networks in both countries (third communique, 1975). None of these resolutions has yet to become a reality. Nevertheless, various calls for specific cooperation have occurred: exchange of personnel, including consultants and advisers; collection development and management assistance; and bibliographic cooperation (all conferences). Also unrealized to date has been the urge to enlarge the scope of the conferences to include other nations (second conference, 1972). In all, however, the comparison between conference aspirations and actual achievements is a favorable one. With a few exceptions, the stated goals were realized. It is important to note that the conferences, themselves, had no power to implement any of the goals other than to hold subsequent conferences. This is still true. The conference planning organizations in both countries are vastly different. In Japan, the coalition of public, private, and national academic libraries, known as the University Library International Committee, has been better positioned to foster the activities called for in the resolutions, although not necessarily always successful in achieving implementation. In the United States, the American Library Association is the parent body of the Committee on Liaison with Japanese Libraries, which co-plans and implements the conferences with Japanese counterparts. It has no administrative jurisdiction or any budget whatsoever to implement the resolutions emanating from these conferences.

The second group of meetings, beginning with the 1986 seminar in Tokyo and ending with the 1988 fourth conference in Racine, showed a remarkable progress in the area of cross cultural communications. In terms of improved dialogue, compared to the past conferences, these two meetings enjoyed widespread delegate participation, a high level of mutual understanding of the other country's way (and why) of doing things, open and specific dialogue, determination to identify and resolve issues, and the wholesome maintenance of an unshakable confidence in one's own culture. These two meetings were milestones in achieving perfection in the conference format and set high standards for future conference agendas.

Clearly, the resolutions of the second group of meetings, when compared with the first group, are more realistic in their aspirations with reference to other agencies' and organizations' help in implementing goals in each country, and because funding agencies are not shown by name, the reliance on the widespread effort of others is implicit. The reader will find evidence of this in the tenets of the conference final communique, herein. The wide range of binational activity in the information arena is so complex and multifaceted that fourth conference planners could only recognize this fact and give their open-ended blessings to all who would actively engage in library and information exchanges.

The urge to delegate some work to committees of the organizing bodies is still evident in the final communique of this conference, but a subtle recognition is made that groups can meet without first clearing their agendas with the parent or conference planning body. The inclusion of successor generation or younger participation continues to be a challenge, as it was to earlier conferences, but the age-level composition of delegates to each of the past two gatherings is encouraging. Of some delicacy, still, is the issue of inclusion of nonacademic subject specialists who comprise a major partner in the information or knowledge industry—that is, special librarians. As seen in the communique of the fourth conference, both sides are seeking ways to incorporate special library activities into the ongoing dialogue.

My colleagues and I on the U.S. Committee (as well as the Japanese Committee) have been deeply committed to the publication of these proceedings, in keeping with the important precedents set, beginning with the first conference in 1969. Each of the previous conference proceedings has marked a milestone in reflecting the stability of the relationship. Since 1969, 99 speakers have shared directly with some 525 participants their thinking on 21 different topics. All the proceedings to date have been published, including the one-day seminar held in 1986, thereby considerably expanding the audience for these essays. The records of these four conferences are in every major library in the world, and we feel grateful that a bilingual edition of the fourth conference is now available. I would like to thank my co-editors of this publication, Warren M. Tsuneishi and Mary F. Grosch, for their industry. Also, for their talent and selfless contribution, I want to thank the major translators of these pages from Japanese to English, Hisao Matsumoto and Warren Tsuneishi.

THEODORE F. WELCH
Chair, Liaison
with Japanese Libraries

TWO DECADES IN REVIEW
U.S.-Japan Conferences on Libraries and Information Science in Higher Education, 1969–1988

by Theodore F. Welch

The Fourth U.S.-Japan Conference on Library and Information Science in Higher Education has as its theme "Strengthening the U.S.-Japan Library Partnership in the Global Information Flow." The conference is conceived primarily as a dialogue to reach an understanding of the issues which confront the two nations' systems of scholarly information flow and exchange. With emphasis on identification of current activities, mainly of libraries, which facilitate the sharing of information, the conference seeks definitions of and solutions to major problems surrounding the development of databases which can be shared both within and between our countries; the unique problems faced by those institutions who seek to develop Chinese, Japanese, and Korean (CJK) files; the problems surrounding the networking of such databases, regardless of the language or peculiarities of the technological environment; and, perhaps most fundamentally, the challenge of preserving and conserving the information, in whatever format it resides, for effective future use.

The Conference Format as a Means of Assessing the Flow of Information between America and Japan

An article in the *Yomiuri Shimbun* in late 1977 appears to be as true now as it was a decade ago. Its author, Alan Miller, stated, "Those familiar with both America and Japan frequently speak of an 'information imbalance' between the two nations. Japanese newspapers and weekly magazines are flooded with stories on the United States, ranging from President Carter's wardrobe to women's liberation. American bestsellers from *All the President's Men* to *Roots* are quickly translated into Japanese and read avidly throughout the country. In Tokyo, American films far outdraw movies made in Japan. In school, students learn about American democracy in depth and any high school youth could name the American President . . . ." He goes on to say that, on the other hand, only a handful of Americans, including students, know that Tokyo is the capital of Japan and that Miki was (then) and Takeshita is now the Prime Minister.

But the knowledge gap doesn't stop there. Perhaps the disproportionate amount of ignorance about Japan in the United States is related to a general lack of interest in the outside world and a growing isolationism, especially since the end of our wars in Asia. But the world grows more complex daily, and no country can afford to ignore its complexity. We have been somewhat shaken out of our cloak of indifference by recent events in the Middle East. With these events has come a realization of the consequences we pay for our disinterest and ignorance. Within the context of this general setting of world awareness, I would like to focus on America's biggest overseas trading partner and most important Asian ally. For, in recent years, tensions between us have heated and cooled and heated again. The source of the problems we face lies in great part in America's lagging productivity, inflation-recession nightmares, dollar devaluation, and the emotionally charged perception that Japan is causing many, if not most, of these crises we face.

Japan's economic growth, even when oil prices were on the rise since the early 1970s, seems unfair. Her high technology is on the verge of putting us in a role reversal that would have been hard to anticipate a half century ago. The United States has seen itself as a tutor to Japan in the areas of democracy and modernization. And Japan has been more than willing to keep alive the notion that she has had much to learn from us as well as others. As well she might. The information door to the West has been wide open. Information has been easy to access, both in terms of on-site visits, and through the bibliographic networks that the United States, United Kingdom, and other Western countries have created. If one accepts the premise that knowledge is power and that information is the electricity that energizes and drives technological research, hence, advancement, then one must also consider them precious commodities in the scheme of international economic competition. With access to the world's most sophisticated and thorough information systems, the United States has seen itself as among the best informed nations in the scientific and technical areas of research. In recent years, however, we have heard the cry that Japan has something to teach us all. Whether or not Japan is bound toward the spurious glory of being Number One, the question has also been raised: "What does the West know about Japanese scientific and technical information?" The answer has come from recent research and U.S. congressional inquiry: "Precious little." Only twelve university libraries in America have minimal research capacity in the field of Japanese studies, according to a report made by the government-sponsored U.S.-Japan Conference on Cultural and Educational Interchange (CULCON).

Japan has been characterized by her strongest allies as an information-gathering rather than information-sending country. The one-way flow of scientific information from advanced nations into Japan has sparked intense studies and action by the U.S. Congress, calling attention to this information deficit. Japan anticipated the enactment in 1986 of Senate Bill 1073 (the Japanese Technical Literature Act of 1986, House Bill HR 3831) and its call for continued United States efforts to combat the information imbalance. In response, the Japan Information Centre of Science and Technology (JICST) has established a file on science, technology, and medicine in Japan available in English. JICST has displayed its online system at both international gatherings in Tokyo and elsewhere, calling its database JOIS—Japan Online Information System. The English version of JOIS, at its first appearance in August 1986, covered some 250,000 entries for the year 1985; about 15 percent of the citations were annotated. The majority of the items covered represented periodical literature, technical reports, and papers in chemistry, biochemistry, life sciences, and medicine. The Japanese are beginning to aid Western and other countries' researchers in finding answers to some fundamental questions, including how much is spent there for scientific and technical research.

Investment in research and development in Japan in 1983 was $27.384 billion, representing 2.95 percent of the national income. Twenty-two percent of this amount was funded by public sources. By comparison, in 1983, the United States committed an estimated $87.678 billion to research and development, representing 2.99 percent of national income, 46 percent of which came from public funding. The U.K. figures available to me are dated 1981 and amount to U.S. $12.219 billion or 2.76 percent of national income, of which 49.8 percent was public money. (U.S. dollar figures are calculated at the 1983 annual average rate quoted by the International Monetary Fund (IMF), International Financial Statistics, at Y237.5 = U.S. $1.00.) While the total dollar amount varies significantly, the percentage of national income for the three countries cited are very close, just under 3 percent for each.[1]

We need to know more of the composition and quality of the research labor force. What literature exists there that documents these research efforts? How much do we really know about the research being conducted in Japan? In what form is the literature available to Western or non-Japanese researchers? For an excellent and timely analysis of the availability of Japanese technological information, both within Japan and abroad, the landmark work to consult has been, *Japanese Scientific and Technical Literature: A Subject Guide* by Robert W. Gibson and Barbara K. Kunkel (Westport, Conn.: Greenwood Press, 1981). To this writer's knowledge, this book offers the best overall analysis of Japanese scientific and technological information availability. In their concluding chapter, Gibson and Kunkel point to the ways in which Western researchers can ensure a greater degree of use of Japanese scientific and technical efforts. One recommendation reads:

> Increased dialogues between Western and Japanese librarians, similar to those reported in the proceedings of the Japan-United States Conferences on Libraries and Information Science in Higher Education, by emphasizing especially the need for greater Japanese emphasis on bibliographical control as well as more effort towards indexing and abstracting journal articles and reports. [page 63]

The Gibson-Kunkel study was undertaken after the first three U.S.-Japan conferences were held, and the climate favorable to the gatherings of vital data (which exposed the weaknesses in accessing Japanese scientific information) in part can be attributed to the goodwill and personal contacts resulting from these conferences. (Another excellent source of information, especially dealing with the scientific flow of information between Japan and the United States and Western Europe, is to be found in the proceedings of the first International Conference on Japanese Information in Science, Technology and Commerce, co-sponsored by the British Library Japanese Information Service and the University of Warwick, held in Warwick in September 1987. Portions of this progress report were presented at that conference.)

While a number of important exchanges have occurred during and after the period of these conferences, some of them can be related directly to the programs fostered by these conferences, and others must be considered independent of the formal meetings. It is, however, the major assumption of this paper that these binational conferences have helped to shape the positive relationship that U.S. and Japanese librarians enjoy today. Perhaps the greatest indication of the personal involvement American librarians have enjoyed with Japan is found in the six Imperial awards given by the Japanese government to American librarians who have contributed to the binational relationship in the field of librarianship. Those honored include the late Verner Clapp, Daniel Boorstin, Andrew Kuroda, Robert Gitler, Robert Downs, and Foster Mohrhardt.

(See *Japan Honors America* by T. Welch; Dublin, Ohio and Tokyo: OCLC, 1988.)

The 1986 One-Day Seminar in Tokyo

Three previous landmark conferences on libraries and information science in higher education have contributed significantly to the history of U.S.-Japan academic library relations. The first was held in Tokyo (1969), the second in Racine, Wisconsin (1972), and the third in Kyoto (1975). Since the third conference, the regular interval of three years between conferences was suspended, and over thirteen years have elapsed since the convening of the fourth conference. Each conference continued for a period of several days to allow for a full discussion of the issues.

Thus, it was a significant event when, for the first time since 1975, American and Japanese university and research librarians met formally to discuss common concerns facing library service to researchers in both countries. The theme of the one-day meeting was, "Japan-U.S. Library Technology in Higher Education." The seminar was held on August 24, 1986, at the Gakushi Kaikan in Tokyo, and was attended by 22 U.S. delegates representing primarily universities, but included senior officials from the Library of Congress, the Association of Research Libraries, the Research Libraries Group, and the Online Computer Library Center (OCLC). Senior representatives of national, public, and private universities in Japan, as well as government leaders, rounded out a very well constituted Japanese delegation. As chair of the American Library Association International Relations Advisory Committee on Liaison with Japanese Libraries, I was chairperson for the American delegation and co-chair of the seminar. The Japan University Library International Relations Committee, made up of representatives of national, public, and private academic libraries in Japan, was chaired by Hiro Yamasaki, Director of the Library System, University of Tokyo. Dr. Yamasaki served as official host for the seminar.

In the belief that a one-day seminar in Tokyo would help fill the decade-long void resulting from lack of formal contact, the event was timed to coincide with the annual International Federation of Library Associations and Institutions (IFLA) conference schedule for Tokyo in August 1986. The main theme of the seminar addressed mutual concerns for and interest in the development of technology in library functions and services. In the beginning of planning for the seminar, it was presumed that about 30 to 40 American delegates would attend. However, owing to the dramatic rise in value of the yen against the dollar, participation was tipped in favor of the Japanese, two to one.

The seminar assessed past, present, and future areas of bilateral exchange of importance to library administrators and practitioners in both countries. Issues discussed included non-use of Japan MARC in the United States, the implications of bilateral versus multilateral negotiations over copyright, database ownership and pricing policies and practices in the United States, composition of Japanese databases, and how to identify (as well as access) the some 50 databases in the National Center for Science Information System (NACSIS). Finally, much of what was discussed centered on the need to establish national and international approaches to development of effective policies on information sharing, which must go well beyond the university boundaries. The public and private sectors of both countries must be involved in a cooperative way. The group also grappled with a sense of the priorities that should exist when attempting to respond to a multitude of information access-related concerns. In this forum, delegates from both countries were, in a short time, able to catch up on some fundamental issues not dealt with in over a decade. From the second half of the 1970s, there has been a remarkable change in the technological innovations introduced into libraries, with a commensurate dramatic impact on the nature of library activities during the same period. The level of candid discussion, in addition to the frank exchange of views in the six papers presented (three from each side), did much to address the nature of the dialogue that must continue in the future. During the period of informal contact through the conference medium, there had been a noticeable amount of friendly exchange, including many visits by librarians between the two countries.

The one-day seminar was financially sponsored by the Japan-U.S. Friendship Commission (Washington, D.C. and Tokyo), and the Shimazu Foundation for the Promotion of Science and Technology. Both assisted in the provision of local travel for Japanese delegates, overnight lodgings and per diem for all delegates, and costs related to the seminar itself, including simultaneous interpretation costs, meals, and coffee breaks. Funding for the Friendship Commission in the United States is controlled by Congress. The direct role of government spending to mount these conferences has decreased to almost nothing since CULCON discontinued library and information science in its formal agenda. The present fourth conference has benefitted from the financial support of the Johnson Foundation and the Japan-U.S. Friendship Commission. A special note of appreciation is mentioned here because of the encouragement, interest, and support afforded this gathering by these two highly committed agencies of international understanding. The future funding for these conferences is extremely uncertain, and will, at best, be realized on an ad hoc basis from the private sectors of philanthropy and corporate giving.

One-Day Seminar Recommendations

The following recommendations were formally adopted at the 1986 seminar in Tokyo.

> The Japanese and American delegates who participated in the Japan-U.S. Seminar on Library Technology in Higher Education today highly appreciate the results of the seminar and make the following recommendations in the hope of maintaining and enhancing the close cooperation between university libraries in Japan and the United States:
>
> 1. In view of the past three Japan-U.S. Library Conferences for Higher Education (held in 1969, 1972, and 1975), and in consideration of the rapid changes and developments within university libraries in Japan and the United States since 1975, it is desirable that a fourth conference be held in the near future to discuss and share widely the issues facing university libraries in both countries.
> 2. In consideration of the development of bibliographic utilities in Japan and the United States, national-level machine-readable records as well as specific subject-area computerized union catalogs should be exchanged between the two countries and made available by the bibliographic utilities for use by university libraries. Also, library networking should be promoted on a binational basis.
> 3. In light of the development of the optical disc and other technology, the proper means towards standardization in library use should be explored.
> 4. In consideration of the fact that the past interchange of professional librarians between Japan and the United States has made a significant contribution not only to the development of professional librarianship but also to the understanding of the culture of both nations, continued effective personnel exchanges and binational educational opportunities should be promoted in the future.
> 5. Research conducted at universities has benefitted greatly through cooperation with non-academic and special purpose organizations. Since university library activities will share increasingly more issues and concerns with the special libraries of such organizations in the future, means to enhance necessary cooperation between these types of libraries in both Japan and the United States should be explored.

The last recommendation represents a significant departure from past practice. Although the national libraries of both countries have been involved in the conference series from the beginning, and large public as well as specialized smaller private libraries, such as the Newberry Library, have had representation, no particular effort has been made to include special libraries. Such inclusion presents some unique challenges to both the Japanese and American sides. It has been a major accomplishment in Japan to create an umbrella organization that brings to the planning table representatives of national, public, and private academic libraries. Although the Special Libraries Association of Japan has its secretariat in the National Diet Library, and maintains close personal ties with parts of academia (some special libraries are, indeed, part of academic institutions in both countries), still, the challenge remains to bring them into close enough affiliation so that they will see the conference agendas as part of their own concerns. One of the primary motivations, beyond the kinship that naturally exists, is the relationship that special libraries have to corporations—a substantial source of future funding for bilateral initiatives. This holds true for both countries.

Another innovation, introduced during the planning of the one-day seminar but not formally a part of its recommendations, is the notion of the age factor of conference participants and the need to identify a successor generation. The current American Committee is made up of senior members of the profession who have been involved since the first conference in 1969. In Japan, the mainstay of the planning committees have been senior administrators as well. Both sides now realize that younger members of the profession must be involved in future conferences to assure continuity. Planning for the Fourth Conference has taken place with this thought firmly in mind: that new blood must have a role in the deliberations as well as the planning.

Efforts to Correct the Information Deficit

One factor which promises to provide the basis for equal partnership in this and future conferences is that Japan has started to answer the questions posed concerning the information imbalance. Through the Ministry of Education, a nationwide series of databases are being created within the framework of NACSIS. Although nothing similar to the U.S. National Technical Information Service publication and indexing program yet exists, an effort toward a network of networks is being widely discussed. JOIS abstracts in English provide a start. It will be some time before something on the order of 90 percent coverage of essential indexing is achieved, however. But the effort is long overdue, and it is significant, indeed, to see the Japanese commitment in this area.

In conclusion, I would like to indicate some possible avenues both countries could pursue in order to correct existing imbalances in the information flow. First, foreigners should study Japanese! It's not an impossible language. In this country Spanish is the foreign language most frequently chosen for study, followed by French, German, Italian, Russian, and Latin. Recent surveys show that Japanese is seventh, moving up from ninth, ahead of Hebrew and Greek. High schools are increasingly requiring foreign language, or making it a choice among several competitive electives for college entrance. It often competes with art and music for a required course for college entrance. It is yet to be seen as a mandatory component in the fundamental education of our citizens. We give lip service to studying foreign languages which are vital to our national security, our economic well being, and our cultural pride. We must correct the imbalance in language ability. From a child's earliest years, there should be a familiarity with foreign tongues, written and spoken, and students and practitioners should be required to know languages relevant to the areas of their professional fields. We cannot assume that either the best or the worst of Japanese research will find its way into English by way of Japanese initiative. Certainly, there is no evidence that the Japanese are screening their research results. There is no discernible pattern of careful selection, in either extreme, when Japanese scientists publish their findings for the benefit of the English-reading world community. However, how can we continue to make it incumbent upon the Japanese to communicate to us in our language? To complain about the quality or quantity is still another matter that Americans and English-language–reliant researchers must seriously reflect upon.

To the Japanese, I would say, please keep up your efforts to place into internationally available information networks the results of your scientific research. The money expended in Japan to assure communication with the rest of the world is in part justified. However, less spent on English translations should free up economic resources for abstracting and indexing services. The sophistication of the Chinese, Japanese, and Korean (CJK) vernacular files in the Research Libraries Information Network (RLIN) and OCLC suggests that Western entrepreneurism has responded to the challenge of computerized foreign scripts. Japan MARC versus USMARC issues are not so much technical concerns as policies and political matters. It should be of little consequence that these lists will represent works written in Japanese. While it is true that many of our scientists are intimidated by non-English articles, it is also true that if there is knowledge of potentially important information, users can find ways to have material translated. Without systematic indexing, there is slight chance for accessing information or even knowing that a piece of research exists. Japan can balance the equation by providing bibliographic information covering research performed there.

We live in a time of diminishing natural resources. Yet, information, a resource as precious and deserving of conservation as any that is naturally available, is unlike the other natural treasures of the earth. It increases with time. We must preserve it, avoid needless duplication of it, and share it for our common welfare if the well-informed and sensible global community we love, and love to talk about, is to survive.

NOTE

1. *Japan 1985: An Interarntional Comparison* (Tokyo: Keizai Koho Center, March 1986).

PUBLISHED PROCEEDINGS

Buckman, Thomas R., et al., eds. *University and Research Libraries in Japan and the United States.* Proceedings of the First Japan–United States Conference on Libraries and Information Science in Higher Education, Tokyo, May 15–19, 1969. Chicago: American Library Association, 1972. 299 p.

Stevens, Robert D., et al., eds. *Japanese and U.S. Research Libraries at the Turning Point.* Proceedings of the Third Japan-U.S. Conference on Libraries and Information Science in Higher Education, Kyoto, Japan, October 28–31, 1975. Metuchen, N.J.: Scarecrow Press, 1977. 240 p.

Tsuneishi, Warren M., et al., eds. *Issues in Library Administration.* Papers presented at the Second United States–Japan Conference on Libraries and Information Science in Higher Education, Racine, Wisconsin, October 17–20, 1972. New York and London: Columbia University Press, 1974. 181 p.

Welch, Theodore F., et al., eds. *Proceedings of the Japan-U.S. Seminar on Library Technology in Higher Education,* Tokyo, August 24, 1986. Tokyo: Maruzen, 1987. 211 p.

A Report on Planning for the FOURTH U.S.–JAPAN CONFERENCE ON LIBRARIES AND INFORMATION SCIENCE IN HIGHER EDUCATION

by Hiro Yamasaki

To provide a report on the Japanese efforts leading to this conference, it is necessary to look back.

The Three Previous U.S.-Japan Conferences

The first conference was held in Tokyo in 1969, and the theme was, "Promotion of Effective Binational Libraries Cooperation." The second conference, here in Racine, Wisconsin in 1972, was on "University Libraries and Research Libraries in the 1970s." The third conference in Kyoto in 1975 was on "Interlibrary Networks: Prerequisites for Sharing Resources." The proceedings of these three conferences have been published. Through these conferences, the Japanese representatives were exposed to and greatly enlightened by American library practices which had rapidly reached a highly sophisticated state in the postwar period, and as a consequence, they were able to put their knowledge to use in the subsequent development of university libraries in Japan.

During preparations for the first conference, the Japanese University Libraries International Liaison Committee (representing the libraries of seven national, five public, and seven private universities) was established. Since then, this committee has served as the Japanese liaison office to its American counterpart.

The scheduling of the binational conferences, supposedly to be held regularly, was interrupted after the third conference, some thirteen years ago. During this interim, many Japanese librarians, particularly of the younger generation, visited and studied in the United States and learned more about libraries in America. Many American librarians visited Japan, too, but there was no conference where representatives of the two countries could discuss common issues.

Among university librarians in Japan, not a few hoped to hold regular conferences. The Japanese University Libraries International Liaison Committee continued to exist on the premise that future conferences would be convened, but had no opportunity to bring the desire to fruition.

There is an old Japanese proverb which says: "Ten years is an epoch." This means that a generation change takes place, circumstances change, and conditions change completely in ten years. One decade in America is also a period in which broad changes occur.

During the past thirteen years, tremendous changes have taken place in the Japanese university library world. These can be summarized briefly as automation through computer and communications technology and network development. These changes first took place in the United States, with Japan in pursuit.

The Computerization of Japanese University Libraries and Network Development

As a university researcher, I wish to briefly explain the background of university libraries' changes in the constantly changing research environment.

The functions of a library can be summarized as acquisitions, preservation, and use. One can regard acquisitions as the spatial movement of information, and preservation as the time movement of information. Use may be regarded as the service system acting as the interface with users. Libraries have been confronted by many problems in all aspects of the fundamental functions of acquisitions, preservation, and use.

In the area of science information, which is increasing at a tremendous rate as seen in the explosive numbers of research papers being published, it has become, even in university libraries, economically impossible to acquire all needed research papers. Also, space to preserve these accumulating materials is insufficient. In addition, the shortage of highly qualified personnel to serve users and manage the rapidly increasing volumes of information has created numerous problems. In other words, we are faced with nothing less than the limitations of basic resources of funds, space, and people.

Computers can contribute substantially to ease these resource limitations. In the dimension of space and time, ways have been established through which information can be transmitted by electronic signal processing technology in high densities and at high speed. In other words, by applying communications technology to the spatial movement of information, and computer memories and high speed processing capabilities to the time movement of information, it has become possible to handle information at high speeds with less power and less space. Also, the use of high speed and low power computers has become an effective tool in library services, such as in retrieval of information and the circulation system. Therefore, computer network systems, in which computer information processing capabilities are linked with communications systems, are now indispensable to libraries.

The principal feature of a library network system is resource sharing. Network systems are a means of effectively using limited resources of funds, space, and manpower. In order to share the information resources held by individual university and research institute libraries as common resources, the idea of a science information system was developed in which bibliographic databases are constructed and linked by digital communication lines. The Ministry of Education's concept of constructing an infrastructure for science research has now been implemented. The National Center for Science Information System (NACSIS) was established in April 1986 in Tokyo to function as a national center. The present network system involves the participation of 68 university libraries and the large-scale computer centers of seven universities, all of which are interconnected. Participating libraries receive location information from the national union bibliographic database of the NACSIS, and they are required to input their own library's bibliographic data into the NACSIS database. The database of NACSIS also includes various secondary materials. NACSIS's communications technology permitted the implementation of an electronic mail system. University researchers can now access information stored in NACSIS's database from nearby terminals directly or indirectly through university libraries.

To solve common problems of libraries throughout the world, librarians and researchers in Japan have developed a system of fully using computer and communications technology. This system is still in the developmental stage. It is still premature to draw any conclusions as to its effectiveness, but we now have a vision as to the path we should follow. Fortunately, the phenomenal progress in recent Japanese computer and communications technology has helped us rapidly accelerate the development of automated university libraries and network systems.

Impetus to Convene the Fourth Conference

To fill the vacuum following the third conference, the Japan-U.S. Seminar on Library Technology in Higher Education was held in Tokyo in August 1986. Before the International Federation of Library Associations and Institutions (IFLA) general conference in 1986, Dr. Welch proposed holding the seminar, since many university librarians were to meet in Tokyo to participate in IFLA. The members of the Japanese University Libraries International Liaison Committee agreed with Dr. Welch's proposal, and the one-day seminar, hosted by the Japanese committee, was held as proposed.

The theme of the seminar was, "Library Technology in Higher Education." The seminar, co-chaired by Dr. Welch and me, was attended by 24 American delegates and 57 Japanese representatives, and the participants discussed issues presented in six papers. The seminar was beneficial to participants of both countries, and I suspect that the above-mentioned technological changes in Japanese university libraries might have had a refreshing impact particularly on the American participants. At the seminar, one subject of discussion was the downloading of databases. Because of wide variations in the speed of development of computer-related technologies, memory costs have dropped markedly in relation to network costs. Libraries are now able to use decentralized storage of much larger amounts of information than before by using rapidly progressing high-density information-storage technology, as seen in optical disc and CD-ROM technology. As a result, the demand for offline decentralized processing of specialized resources, as opposed to online access to information through the network system, has also been rapidly growing. Imbalances in technology may be the fate of progress, but this is an example of how technology has affected the future direction of libraries. This is an unavoidable problem in the course of the development of network systems.

At the end of the seminar, recommendations were adopted. One of the important recommendations was the desirability of a fourth Japan-U.S. conference in the near future. In accordance with this recommendation, the American organizing committee has been active in preparation for the fourth conference, and the proposal to convene in this Wingspread Conference Center under the sponsorship of the Johnson Foundation and the Japan-U.S. Friendship Commission was presented in April 1987.

The structure of the University Libraries International Liaison Committee, which is also the Japanese organizing committee, had been simplified and its activities had been limited for many years after the third conference, but the Japanese organizing committee, as a liaison committee, became active again at the time of the Japan-U.S. Seminar in 1986. The Japanese committee, in preparation for the fourth conference, was reorganized and revitalized to deal with its American counterpart. Further, in April 1987, the Japanese steering committee of the fourth conference was organized and devoted itself to selection of the conference theme, selection of papers, the budget, etc.

Also, the bilingual *Proceedings of the Japan-U.S. Seminar on Library Technology in Higher Education,* edited and compiled by Theodore F. Welch, Hideo Kaneko, Hiro Yamasaki, and Hisafumi Tanaka was published by Maruzen Company in September 1987.

The International Conference on Japanese Information in Science, Technology, and Commerce, sponsored by the British Library, was held at the University of Warwick, Coventry, England, in September 1987. Dr. Welch and I attended the Conference, and also discussed the agenda for the fourth conference and prepared a draft agenda.

We reviewed the results of the third conference, and we determined that the subjects for discussion in the fourth conference should have reasonably attainable objectives. The conference would be structured with major problems, possible solutions, and identification of best proposals, all of which would suggest concrete cooperative action programs. Also, we would have a forum to discuss the theme of the fifth and subsequent conferences.

The main theme of this conference is "Strengthening the U.S.-Japan Library Partnership in the Global Information Flow." The prepared draft was reviewed by both the American and Japanese committees, and after parts of the draft were modified, it was adopted.

The number of participants from each country was limited to 30, and six younger librarians from each country were added. The objective of including the younger librarians in this fourth conference was to help establish personal relationships, so as to be able to attain continuity for future conferences, as well as to train individuals for future leadership.

The selection of delegates, moderators, and speakers by the Japanese University Libraries International Liaison Committee began in late 1987. One of the difficult tasks was to secure travel funds for the Japanese delegation to the United States. A fund-raising subcommittee, chaired by Tetsuya Morita, Director, Hitotsubashi University Library, was established under the University Libraries International Liaison Committee, and the subcommittee actively solicited funds by explaining the significance of this conference. The Japanese delegation would not only participate in the fourth conference but would also study union catalog location systems in the university libraries in North America. As a result, the subcommittee was able to gain support from public and private universities as well as the publishing and electronic industries. Further, it was able to obtain special assistance from the Ministry of Education. In addition, the National Diet Library, NACSIS, and the Special Library Association provided specialists as moderators and speakers at the conference. The Japanese delegation is well represented and supported by the academic community. I wish to express my sincere appreciation for those who supported this conference.

In April 1988, Haruo Kuroda succeeded me as University Librarian of the University of Tokyo Library System. Accordingly, the responsibilities of chairmanship of the University Libraries International Liaison Committee were transferred to him. Also, Eiichi Kurahashi succeeded Hisafumi Tanaka as Associate University Librarian, University of Tokyo Library System. Accordingly, the responsibilities of the secretariat office of the Japanese Liaison Office were handed over to Mr. Kurahashi.

Under the leadership of Professor Kuroda, the Japanese delegation was officially organized, and the members of the delegation were given assignments. The delegation was divided into two groups and visited major university and research libraries in the United States for two weeks. We were able to successfully conclude our studies and accomplish the objectives of the visits. We are grateful to Dr. Welch, Warren Tsuneishi of the Library of Congress, and Kazuko Dailey of the University of California, Davis, for their kind assistance and arrangements for our visits.

Dr. Welch visited Japan in September 1988 for a final consultation with Professor Kuroda and other members of the Japanese committee, and arrangements were finalized. Again, we are grateful to the organizing committees of both countries as well as for the warm support provided by foundations and institutions. I hope this Conference will be a success. Finally, I hope this Conference will be useful to both countries, and I trust that the results of mutual cooperation will bring even closer cooperation between American and Japanese libraries.

UNFINISHED BUSINESS
Computers, Libraries, and
East Asian Studies

by John W. Haeger

Whether by accident or by clever design of the organizers, this bilateral conference marks the tenth anniversary of East Asian library automation in North America. In October 1978, Eugene Wu, Hideo Kaneko, Patricia Battin, and I, together with Frederick Mote of Princeton University and Robert E. Ward of Stanford, gathered in the New York offices of the American Council of Learned Societies (ACLS) to launch the East Asian Library Program of the ACLS, Social Science Research Council, and Association of Research Libraries. Automation was not the first thing on our minds. On the contrary, we were primarily concerned with the rising cost of acquiring and processing East Asian–language material in a period of declining extramural support for foreign area study programs in this country, with the looming problems of paper preservation, and with the difficulty of providing appropriate professional training for a new generation of East Asian library specialists. Mindful, however, that automation was affecting the operation of general research libraries in diverse and profound ways, the advisory committee to the joint program turned its attention rather quickly to automation, not as an end in itself, but as a means to address the economic, professional, and contextual issues which remained the ultimate focus of concern.

In June 1979 the committee sent a task force to Japan to investigate *kanji* processing systems, and organized an international conference on East Asian scripts and bibliographic systems later in the year. In 1980, the Research Libraries Group, with support from the Andrew W. Mellon Foundation, the Ford Foundation, and the National Endowment for the Humanities, began to develop the world's first online, network-based library processing and information retrieval system for East Asian materials. These East Asian enhancements to the Research Libraries Information Network were implemented in September 1983. In the years since, the Online Computer Library Center has implemented a similar capability; a local system has been established at the National Central Library in Taipei; the shared cataloging network of the National Center for Science Information System has been created in Japan, and UTLAS has announced its Japan-MARC cataloging system. The National Library of China has contracted with the Western Library Network to produce an automated Chinese, Japanese, and Korean (CJK) capability. Systems in use at the National Diet Library and the National Institute for Japanese Literature have matured.

At Research Libraries Group (RLG), the number of CJK records in the database has now grown to approximately 400,000—each record resulting from an online transaction executed by a member institution or the Library of Congress. Additional records, representing Japanese government publications held by the Hoover Institution and the University of California at Berkeley, Chinese rare books in the National Central Library (Taipei), Japanese serial titles in the National Center for Science Information System (NACSIS) union catalog, and article-level abstracts created by the Chinese Academy of Sciences in Beijing—as well as MARC resources records from the National Central Library, the National Library of China, and the National Diet Library—will be loaded from tape later this year and in 1989. There can be no doubt that this database, combined with CJK capability in Research Libraries Information Network's (RLIN) cataloging and acquisitions modules, has helped many institutions to contain or even to reduce CJK processing costs, despite the high price of the requisite hardware—precisely what the ACLS committee intended.

Cooperative approaches to other East Asian library problems have also been predicated on RLIN capabilities. With support from the National Endowment for the Humanities and the Henry Luce Foundation, six RLG institutions and the Library of Congress began a two-year project in 1986 to film brittle Chinese materials published between 1880 and 1949. Plans are underway for a subsequent preservation project that would include brittle Japanese and Korean materials as well. Decisions to film (queueing records) and bibliographic records for the resulting microforms are both recorded in the RLIN database. The RLG East Asian Program Committee (EAPC), composed of representatives from 26 RLG East Asian collections, has been active in cooperative projects to distribute responsibility for original cataloging and acquisition of costly materials. For example, the EAPC is exploring whether original cataloging responsibility can be distributed by LC class and language, and whether backlogs are sufficiently redundant to allow for cooperative cataloging of, for example, multititle sets. To offset the impact of the ever stronger yen on Japanese acquisitions budgets, the EAPC is compiling a list of expensive serials and monographic sets, discontinued or not acquired in the past two years due to insufficient funds, so that plans can be made to ensure that every title is maintained or acquired somewhere in RLG. Such institutional commitments can be indicated by entering local data in the RLIN records for those titles. Finally, a proposed cooperative retrospective conversion project would result in another 30,000 RLIN CJK records for selected subjects in East Asian studies, including Buddhism and Chinese economy.

Nothing has changed more dramatically since 1978 than our expectations about end-user access and data manipulation. In 1978 our world was firmly bibliocentric. We were concerned about library problems: acquisitions, processing, and preservation. We nurtured a fuzzy vision of so-called public access terminals hidden amidst card catalogs—ultimately replacing them—but we worried about the number of terminals we would need to provide and the size of the CPU to support them. The personal computer revolution of the early 1980s changed all that. Almost overnight, terminals became *passé*. A world of individual scholar workstations emerged: workstations equipped with powerful central processing units (CPUs), graphics, and windowing; running word-processing, database, spreadsheet, and desktop-publishing software; connected to university-based local area networks and gatewayed to one or more bibliographic utilities; able to access the utilities' databases to create interlibrary loan requests and electronic mail and to download data for subsequent manipulation in the workstation; able to integrate the imported data with nonbibliographic data (full-text, statistics, and image) from other sources in hypertext environments.

An astonishing percentage of this new vision is already in place. Certainly the first generation of affordable personal workstations exists. The Mac II running A/UX (for example) has the necessary functions. Broad band networks have been built at many universities. BITNET and networks offering terminal support like CSNET, ARPANET, and now NSFNET link mainframe nodes around the country and beyond. The development and marketing of powerful software for workstations is already a multimillion dollar industry.

Of course, scholars with personal computers (PCs) (much less workstations) are still a minority; network-connected PCs are outnumbered four to one by stand-alones used more or less exclusively for word processing; only a handful of universities have made local online public access catalogs available on campus networks; and end-user access to the bibliographic utilities is limited to a CompuServe gateway at OCLC and a pilot project using Telnet at RLG. But the velocity of change is dramatic. The functional prerequisites to scholar workstations all exist. There is no missing technology. What remains to be done, at least for the world of roman alphabets and arabic numerals, is to integrate the components.

Those of us whose data, bibliographic and otherwise, are represented in East Asian scripts, still face significant problems, however. The easy movement of East Asian vernacular data among software environments and the exchange of such data between disparate systems is at a rudimentary stage of development. This summer, RLG will introduce its third generation CJK hardware: the multiscript workstation (MSW). This workstation supports the processing of bibliographic information not only in Chinese, Japanese, and Korean scripts, but in Hebrew and Cyrillic scripts as well. The MSW is an IBM-PC/AT class machine equipped with a Wyse 700 high resolution monitor and a custom keyboard designed especially for East Asian character input. It incorporates software which allows it to function as an RLIN terminal. More important, the software embeds a comprehensive mapping of the three-byte codes used for East Asian characters in the RLIN database (and also in OCLC) to the proprietary two-byte code used for the same characters in products developed by JHL Research, Inc. of Anaheim, California. ChinaStar relies on JHL's unique system of character generation and display control (the JHL translator). These facilities also make it possible to insert CJK characters into data fields in commercial word processing, database, and spreadsheet programs such as PC Write, Lotus 1-2-3, and dBase III. The map between JHL codes (which interact with the commercial software) and the RLIN codes (EACC—East Asian Character Code Set for Bibliographic Use, a draft NISO standard) is the key to transferring data between bibliographic resource nodes like RLIN and OCLC and a wide array of commercial software.

This is good news only by comparison with our present predicament. It is still a long way from the seamless web of file transfer and data communication implied in the workstation-network-gateway vision. Far too much is device specific, code specific, nonstandard, or proprietary. Let me illustrate.

First, the JHL translator can work only with commercial software packages that manage the PC's display memory in a predictable, straightforward, and standard manner and do not use control characters that conflict with JHL's. That eliminates some very popular programs such as Word Perfect.

Second, the MSW is hardware specific with respect to the display controller. The JHL translator must be adapted to each display controller individually.

Third, RLG's chosen input system for East Asian script characters depends on a unique component-sequence analysis and a custom keyboard. We could switch input systems, but in the absence of a single, standard system analogous to the QWERTY keyboard for roman alphabetic characters (for which I harbor no hope whatsoever), it remains that *all* input systems depend on *some* attributes of the character: pronunciation, radical or stroke, etc. Shifting among input systems will require look-up tables, which someone will have to maintain.

Fourth, data sorting which is associated with the values of individual characters (the equivalent of alphabetizing in roman environments) turns rapidly into hexadecimal babble, since none of the existing East Asian character coding schemes—EACC included—orders characters in a single, lexicographically meaningful sequence.

Fifth, documents produced can be read and manipulated only by workstations with the same configuration and software. Each American vendor-marketed workstation that supports East Asian scripts uses proprietary internal codes that are incompatible with all others. An International Standards Organization (ISO) standard is currently being developed for character font information interchange that would allow documents containing East Asian scripts to be read and printed on disparate systems. If the proposed font registry maps the various East Asian fonts to the EACC code values, scholarly information flow would be greatly facilitated. But the standard, if adopted, must first be widely implemented, and it is unclear to what degree the proposed registry will represent bibliographic needs. We also must bridge the prevailing gap between the computer industry and the library community—each represented by different, and sometimes conflicting, ISO technical committees—if we are to integrate the data generated by both.

Finally, there are serious problems in the data communications area. Unlike standard ASCII, which uses the low order seven bits of each character code, character codes such as JHL's require all eight bits. Since most communication carriers normally recognize only the low order seven bits, the accurate transmission of a code such as JHL's will not be commonly supported. It is unlikely, therefore, that JHL code could ever be used for data communication purposes. From the North American perspective, the most likely alternative is EACC, once it has been registered with National Information Standards Organization (NISO) and ISO. EACC has the advantage of having been constructed in conformity with ISO standards honored in virtually all communications protocols. Unfortunately, it also has the disadvantage of requiring three bytes per character, which will make it unpopular in most workstation software. Translation to EACC for data communication and from EACC for data manipulation seems inevitable. In addition, since EACC will probably not be adopted in Asia, further translation between EACC and the standard character codes of Japan, China, and Korea will be required when data files are shipped across the Pacific, and some characters will emerge from the translation without valid values.

All this translation is conceptually simple but procedurally complex and, potentially at least, expensive. Given the linguistic history and the vagaries of orthographic development in East Asia, mapping national standard code sets to each other is a major intellectual enterprise. This work is complicated by the instability of the national standard codes, in part because, except for JIS, these codes are newly developed, and in part because East Asian character sets are inherently dynamic and never finite. Consequently, the translation tables need constant adjustment. The process of adjustment is not well understood by the standards agencies in East Asia—or by the user institutions—and there is no agreement regarding responsibility. In addition, except in Japan, where the Japan industrial standard is exactly what the name implies—a standard honored and implemented by the manufacturers of computer hardware—machine codes are likely to remain idiosyncratic and/or proprietary, requiring that data be translated to and from national standard codes for input and output.

Another manifestation of our predicament with East Asian scripts is local library systems. These are being implemented at a rapid rate in North America for circulation control, serials control, catalog maintenance, acquisitions, and online public access catalogs. Millions of records from the utilities are being loaded into local systems. Again, however, records which include CJK data present special problems. None of the popular local systems has developed the capability to handle CJK data. RLG is now examining those local systems which support PCs as terminals to ascertain whether the RLG-JHL character generator board can be used to enable CJK display in these systems, provided that appropriate modifications are also made to the local systems at the application level, but the outcome is uncertain given the expense which vendors and their customers will have to incur.

Enormous progress has been made in East Asian script processing for bibliographic applications over the last ten years. National MARC formats have emerged in Japan, China, and Taiwan, based on the UNIMARC standard. The USMARC format has been extended to accommodate nonroman data in parallel fields. The development of the Chinese Character Code for Information Interchange (CCCII) as a multiplanar, three-byte schema has established an architecture in which variant forms of the same character can be linked. The completion of the CJK enhancements to RLIN, the development of the CJK350 workstation by OCLC, and the emergence of the National Center for Science Information System network in Japan have provided an environment in which CJK bibliographic data can be created by numerous institutions. RLG's CJK Thesaurus has established a definitive mapping among national standard character codes. But we are still handicapped by the immaturity of the computer revolution in many parts of East Asia and the absence of industry-wide standards for codes and fonts. Intersystem data communications and file transfer are extremely cumbersome. Users of East Asian script data will be disadvantaged until these obstacles are overcome.

JAPANESE BIBLIOGRAPHIC DATA FILES

by Toru Sugawara

One major question in libraries is how to maintain Chinese, Japanese, and Korean (Han'gul) languages data files. The question in Japan is whether to mix in Chinese and Korean bibliographic data with the Japanese. It is a difficult question involving problems of language and access to Chinese characters. Problems of the reading and forms of Chinese characters in Japanese, Chinese, and Korean (South and North) must be addressed.

Problems of language and characters are especially marked between the Chinese and Japanese languages. This is because both are languages using Chinese characters. Chinese characters are ideographs, and information can be transmitted unambiguously only when the reading of a character matches its form. Take for example the book entitled: 現代中国之出版自由 (Freedom in publishing in contemporary China). Using Wade-Giles romanization, this may be rendered as: *Hsien tai Chung-kuo chih ch'u pan tsu yu;* using *pinyin*, this may be rendered as: *Xiandai zhongguo zhi chuban ziyou*. In romanized Japanese, however, the Japanese following their principles of reading Chinese characters, would render the title as: *Gendai chugoku no shuppan no jiyu*. On screen it is difficult to determine whether this is a Chinese or Japanese book. If this were a Chinese-language book, it would be wrong to read it in romanized Japanese, although the meaning of the words can be understood by the viewer. Further, the index term appearing on the screen will read:

中国之　出版自由

中国の　出版の自由

making it difficult to make a judgment that the first work is Chinese and the second is Japanese.

The identification of a book in Western languages such as English and German is relatively easy, but it is not so for works written in Japanese and Chinese. While the identical work in two Western languages may vary slightly, and its pronunciation (reading) may also vary, it is still possible to distinguish between the two, as in the following example: "anne" versus "anne´."

On the other hand, when one sees the two Chinese characters which are read "shuppan" (出版) in Japanese on the screen, it is difficult to determine whether this word (meaning "publish") is Chinese or Japanese. Many simplified Chinese characters are being used in China today, and it is possible in this case to differentiate between the two languages. Often the Japanese use simplified characters as they are (they are seldom used in writing books and articles, however). Thus, the identification of Chinese characters in written Chinese and Japanese in the same data file can be accomplished only by readings. But, is it possible to identify them in a data file by Japanese readings (standard pronunciation), by Chinese readings (pronunciation or romanized Chinese), and by Korean readings? In other words, is it possible when encoding Chinese characters to utilize the coding developed for one language—for example the JIS, Japanese Industrial Standard code for Chinese characters used in Japan—for the same characters used in China?

Let me touch briefly on Chinese character codes. As is well known, in information processing by computer the unit utilized is not the binary bit but the byte, where eight bits constitute a byte. When we refer to eight bits, we mean eight multiples of two, or in decimal notation in order of magnitude of 256. In other words, 256 different combinations can be expressed with one byte. In processing English-language texts, we need to accommodate 52 characters including upper- and lower-case letters and ten numeric characters; and in processing Japanese *kana* text including consonants we need a total of 50. These totals are well covered by one byte. However, because of large numbers involved in Chinese character sets, one byte is not sufficient so that two bytes are necessary to represent all characters. Two bytes mean sixteen bits or sixteen multiples of two, or a magnitude of 65,536 in decimal notation. The JIS character code is a system which accommodates Chinese characters, other characters, and symbols within part of the region of this magnitude.[1] In this way, in Japan we can accommodate not only Chinese characters used in Japanese, but also letters of the English alphabet and numerals.

However, Chinese characters in the Chinese language may be the same as those appearing in Japanese-language books, but their readings and meanings frequently differ in Japanese. Therefore, Chinese characters from Chinese texts, duplicated in the JIS code, lead to a degree of confusion.

Next, let us shift our focus to a comparison of English and Japanese. In the Japanese system, we utilize two bytes for Japanese *kana* and Chinese characters, and one byte for roman alphabet characters used in Western languages. However, the Japanese frequently write phrases or sentences using a mixture of Japanese- and English-language characters. An example is "VAN no rikai o motomeru hon" (VAN の理解を求める本). VAN is the abbreviation of Value Added Network. Even if it is an English abbreviation, when it is commonly used in a Japanese text and is embedded in the Japanese language, it is necessary to use the larger two-byte code. Therefore, when inputting, it is necessary to specify that the *V* in this case is a "Japanese V" (two byte). There are those who argue that regardless of whether the abbreviation occurs in a Japanese text, VAN is an English abbreviation and can be expanded in a one-byte code. In this case it is possible to distinguish between two- or one-byte codes, but because of the mixture of one and two bytes, the system is susceptible to mistakes in logic.

At the Waseda University Library, a consolidated bibliographical data file is maintained for the works in Japanese and in foreign languages—except for works in languages which are difficult to automate, such as Chinese, Korean, and Cyrillic alphabet languages. The language of publication is indicated by a fixed leader field. A widely used practice in Japan is, however, to have separate data systems for the Japanese language and for foreign languages, primarily English. It was possible to build a single bibliographical file of Japanese and Western-language works (except those in the Cyrillic alphabet), but we were forced to include also Chinese and Korean (North and South) works. Moreover, we do not know at present when we will be able to handle these languages for two reasons. First, whether or not we should adopt a two-byte or three-byte character code for Chinese characters used in China in order to avoid duplication of Chinese character codes used in the JIS code cannot yet be settled in Japan. Also, we have not yet solved the problem of appropriate input method. Second, librarians who handle works written in the Chinese and Korean languages have expressed their preference for handling them separately. This is closely related to the coding of Chinese characters. To build a system of Chinese texts and Sino-Japanese texts combined in one file means to create a new system which contains more than the present JIS character set.

Therefore, I see a big gap in the perception of this problem between the United States and Japan. In the United States, libraries seek to build a single CJK file, whereas in Japan such a development is unlikely. Quite apart from this issue, the coding of Chinese characters in texts remains to be investigated in the future in Japan.

Let me now move to the main topic of my report. First is the current status of Japanese MARCs and the method developed at Waseda University Library, where I work, to build a consolidated bibliographical data file for works in the Japanese and foreign languages (except Chinese, Korean—South and North—and the Cyrillic alphabet). I would especially like to address issues of data conversion. The second area is a historical review of CJK files in Japan. Also, I would like to comment on the coding of Chinese characters and building a CJK file, although they are not my major area of work.

The Status of Japan MARCs

Originally, MARC referred to Machine Readable Catalogs compiled and produced by a country's bibliographic agency. In Japan, several commercially produced MARCs are available besides the Japan MARC produced by the National Diet Library (NDL), the national bibliographic agency. These MARCs are produced by book distributors and will be referred to as private MARCs. Private MARCs are produced to fill the time gap caused by delays in the production of Japan MARCs by NDL. The delays average 90 days after publication, and occur for various reasons. The need for quick bibliographic data for new publications in Japan both for administrative control and for distribution led to production of other MARCs by the private sector. The time lag has been shortened to two to three weeks. Also, since Cataloging in Publication (CIP) information is not available in Japan, the private MARCs have been providing cataloging information similar to CIP and are widely used by public schools and university libraries for their cataloging, selection and book orders.

THE STATUS OF COMMERCIAL MARCS

Since the introduction of computers into public libraries, commercial MARCs have become popular in Japan. According to a survey by the Japan Library Association (JLA) in 1983, 33 out of 131 public libraries in Japan maintained computers and used MARC tapes for the purpose of (1) efficiency of processing, (2) retrieval of information, and (3) compilation of union catalog.

Public libraries have begun to use MARC tapes for automation of their libraries, and the use of commercial MARCs in public libraries has rapidly increased. The advantages of using commercial MARCs are as follows:

1. The use of computers in public libraries has changed from circulation to the management of bibliographic information. The library network system made possible by MARC has been developed, for example, with service points in the Urayasu and Suginami areas in Tokyo. The development of the interlibrary loan system has benefitted users by permitting borrowers to return books to convenient service points rather than to the libraries where the books were borrowed.

2. It is vital to input searchable bibliographic data in order to provide for the management of information and the unification of information. It is probably not possible for smaller public libraries to employ information management specialists. For these libraries, MARC tapes have been a welcome tool. Today many public libraries depend heavily on book processing companies to catalog and process purchased books; moreover, most such companies are affiliated with the large book distributors. These firms are required to process large quantities of new books as quickly as possible, and it is inevitable that they will use the same MARC system employed by the distributors. Consequently, there is the feeling that the ordering, accessioning, processing, and MARC servicing of books come together as a set.

3. Books purchased by public libraries are usually of current popular and practical interest, and recently a substantial number of books have been purchased at the request of readers. Such works requested of local libraries are usually popular books advertised in newspapers and other mass media. Users in public libraries generally demand quick service, so that NDL's Japan MARC is generally unable to meet their needs.

At present, there are three private MARC services available in Japan: (1) Nippan MARC (compiled by Nippon Shuppan Hanbai Tosho Senta, input by Dai Nippon Insatsu, and sold by Japan Computer Technology); (2) TRC MARC (compiled by Japan Library Association, input by Toppan Insatsu); and (3) Osakaya MARC (compiled by Osakaya and Film Looks, input by Toyo Information Service, and sold by Osakaya). Commercial MARCs were first developed by wholesale book distributors as a means of managing bibliographic data for books that they handled and later they were developed and sold as a means of expanding their services to libraries. Hence Nippan MARC is affiliated with the wholesaler known as Nippan; TRC MARC with the wholesaler known as Tohan; and Osakaya MARC with Osakaya.

There are some limitations to these commercial MARCs, however. One of the limitations is that cataloging information is not always accurate due to the need for speedy cataloging to meet commercial targets. For example, a given title may be treated as a series title or as the title proper, causing differences in data content, thereby adversely affecting retrieval. For example, a certain commercial MARC service coding *In Search of Ancient Japanese Culture: Horses* (日本古代文化の探求：馬) treated *In Search of Ancient Japanese Culture* as the title proper and *Horses* as the part title, as follows: Tag 251 $A In search of ancient Japanese culture $D Horses. When output in the system the display reads:

> In search of ancient Japanese culture : horses

When, however, In Search of Ancient Japanese Culture is treated as series title and *Horses* as the book title, the output system reads:

> Horses (馬) 1
> In search of ancient Japanese culture 9

Such differences in treatment are found in commercial MARCs. In numerous cases, moreover, there are differences in classification and subject headings because of differences in subject analysis.[2]

The preparation of reliable bibliographic data requires considerable time and effort. The large book distributors are unable to attain both speedy distribution of books and accurate bibliographic data simultaneously. In response to this problem, both Nippan and Tohan offer, in addition to Nippan MARC and TRC MARC, MARC data for current publications under such services as Shoseki Meigara Data [Book Brand Data] (Nippan) and Tohan Zero MARC (Tohan), for inventory control purposes. Included are brief entries providing title, author, publisher, date, ISBN, and book code number. These data are not equivalent to CIP data provided in the United States and England. As part of their services, 3-by-5 cards printed from commercial MARC databases are inserted in books and distributed to those public and school libraries with no computer facilities.

The coverage of books by commercial MARCs is limited because only current books handled by distributors and local publication centers are included. The total number of books covered probably amounts to 60 percent of the entries included in Japan MARC's annual total of 50,000 because these commercial MARCs exclude such materials as government publications and comic books.[3]

SUMMARY OF COMMERCIAL MARCS

Nippan MARC

As the pioneer of commercial MARC in Japan, Nippan began to compile online bibliographic data for publications in 1976, and introduced the Nippan Information System (NIPS) at its distribution center in Tokyo in 1978. The new automated system, Nippan Online Communication System (NOCS), began operation in 1984.

The database includes (as of January 1986) 350,000 entries entered since 1976. In addition, Nippan MARC includes incomplete bibliographic data for about 200,000 award-winning publications.

Bibliographic data for new publications are available two weeks after publication. Nippan can provide new publications to a library two weeks after receiving orders from a library.

Nippan has been preparing a kind of MARC called Shoseki Meigara Data [Book Brand Data] to control prepublication books up to the day before they appear on the market. This service is not offered to libraries. The data include title, author, publisher, date of book delivery, and Nippan book code number—all written entirely in *kana* or arabic numerals. The data are not for the purpose of retrieval but for inventory control of new publications to be sold.

Nippan MARC is linked with Shoseki Meigara Data through the Nippan Book Code Number, and both are automatically interchangeable. However, since the same numbers are used at three-month intervals as Nippan Book Code Numbers, it is necessary to key in both the code number and the year, month, and day of publication. Moreover, there is not 100 percent match between the two since, for example, data for publications handled by regional publications centers are added and there are no data for publications such as comic books that are not ordered by libraries.

Magnetic tape (600 feet) of Nippan MARC is distributed weekly (50 tapes a year). There are two types of tape specification formats: (1) 4096 byte format (similar to Japan MARC), and (2) 1024 byte unvariable format. The content of bibliographic data conforms to *Nippon mokuroku kisoku: shinpan yobihan* (Nippon cataloging rules, preliminary new edition). The Chinese character code used is JIS C6226 second level, while the roman alphabet and arabic numeral code is EBCDIC.[4]

TRC MARC

Toshokan Ryutsu Center (TRC) announced the availability of TRC MARC in 1981. Tohan, which had lagged behind its major wholesale rival, Nippan, in the provision of bibliographic data, joined with the Japan Library Association in 1982 in a venture involving TRC established by JLA in 1979. The Tohan Publishing Information Cataloging Retrieval System (Tohan PICS) was developed in 1983, and the Tohan Total Online Network System (TONETS) was introduced in 1984.

The TRC bibliographic database, as of August 1985, stood at 340,000 entries entered since 1974. TRC also includes data for some 150,000 items written only in *kana*. Newly added bibliographic data are for current books handled by Tohan and local publications distribution centers as well as for any books ordered by libraries which are not in the database. The annual addition to the database is about 35,000.

Tohan also prepares Tohan Zero MARC, covering new books up to the day before publication. The data are available to libraries, but there is some delay in delivery since the data are supplied in the form of floppy discs downloaded on a weekly basis. The data include title (twenty Chinese characters and twenty *kana* letters), author (ten Chinese characters), publisher (seven Chinese characters), delivery date, ISBN, G-code, and size. Tohan Zero MARC and TRC MARK are linked by G-code, and the data are interchangeable only to a limited degree because of differences in the scope of the two databases. It is necessary for TRC MARC subscribers to ask Tohan to input the G-code into the TRC MARC data because commercially sold TRC MARCs do not contain the G-code.

There are three types of record formats in TRC MARC:

1. III type: 300 byte unvariable. Simple retrieval system under title and author; used primarily for circulation control.
2. VI type: 1024 byte unvariable; can be used for retrieval.
3. V type: 256 byte in 1 block; attempts to assure required record lengths by providing only an arbitrary number of linkages.

Over 160 libraries in Japan are subscribing to one of the three types of TRC database services today.[5]

Osakaya MARC

Osakaya MARC, the latest entry into the MARC data market in Japan, was jointly developed by two companies with a long history of affiliation—Osakaya and the book processing firm Film Looks Co.—and was offered commercially in April 1983. The characteristics of Osakaya MARC are as follows:

1. Unlike Nippan MARC and TRC MARC, which include databases with books, the Osakaya MARC database can be subscribed separately from the books. In this sense it can be regarded as a pioneer in MARC marketing.
2. Osakaya MARC includes all new publications as a package. Hitherto, TRC and Tohan offered bibliographic data for individual titles accessed by JLA or NDL numbers.

3. Without dividing publications data into new publications MARC and trade publications MARCs. Osakaya compiles and sells a commercial MARC service timed to new publications. Hence, it is said that the data content is crude and inappropriate for retrieval. The reason for the adoption of this method is related to the following characteristic.
4. Osakaya MARC was produced to be used not by itself but in conjunction with NDL's Japan MARC.

Machine-readable data are available for some 130,000 post-1972 books, including pre-1982 titles listed in *Sentei tosho somokuroku* (Catalog of selected books) published by the Japan Library Association. The annual addition to the database is some 27,000 titles.

Subscribers have a choice of one of the following: MARC tape alone, tape with selected books, the entire set, or piece by piece.[6]

Shoseki Data Senta

The establishment of Shoseki Data Senta (Publications Data Center) has been announced. The new company is responsible for the production and distribution of Standard MARC—a goal toward which publishers and libraries have worked cooperatively through the Publications Control Code Committee of the Japan Publications Distributors Association. According to the announcement, the purposes of the new center are as follows:

1. to prepare standard bibliographic descriptions for new publications under the supervision of the JLA and provide the data produced by Tohan, Nippan, and TRC to the industry through book distributors;
2. to prepare and provide "Book Distribution Information MARC" (Distribution MARC) for individual titles based on Standard MARC; and
3. to manage ISBN code numbers for the development of the publication industry's network.[7]

The relationship of the new center to existing commercial MARC is still ambiguous on the basis of reading of the literature. According to one of the producers of Standard MARC, the data in Standard MARC will be transferred to commercial MARC after the completion of standardization of the 40 MARC data elements. The Standard MARC (this name is ambiguous) will not be provided to libraries, and commercial MARCs will be provided to libraries as in the past. The competition among major commercial MARC products will no doubt continue.

Analysis and Output of Japan Book MARC (Japanese Language MARC)

Approximately 40 to 50 percent of the total collections of most university libraries in Japan consists of foreign books. Therefore, Waseda University Library developed and now maintains a single bibliographic database of its Japanese and foreign books, having introduced the total system as a package, DOBIS/LIBIS (Dortmunder Online Bibliothekssystem/Leuvens Integraal Bibliothek Informatie System). Seinosuke Narita (associate director) and Akira Saito (development team) of the University Library presented a paper at the sixth DOBIS/LIBIS user group meeting held in Nice, France, in September 1987, summarizing Waseda University Library's system. My discussion is therefore focused on the problem of data conversion of Japanese book MARC.

In order to maintain Japanese book MARC and LC MARC in a single file, it is necessary to analyze the descriptive contents of both MARCs and to develop a conversion program to unify format. Fortunately the format of DOBIS/MARC is virtually identical with LC MARC, and so we converted Japan MARC to LC MARC format. At this time, we set up a blank for the control field (tag 0) which LC MARC has but Japan MARC does not. Variations in descriptive cataloging rules are connected with cross-references. Since then all issues which cannot be resolved through references are handled when the two MARCs are uploaded to a bibliographic file (a file loaded only with MARC data) and corrections are made when books with appropriate MARC data are added to the collection, copying through the system.

One of the major variations of descriptive cataloging rules between Japanese rules (preliminary new edition) and *Anglo-American Cataloguing Rules*, second edition, is the treatment of access point of main entry and of multivolume sets. In the Japanese rules, the physical unit (book unit) is the unit of description, and therefore the volumes are treated individually; whereas *AACR2* and ISBD treat the volumes as a set. Therefore, *AACR2* and ISBD adopted multiple level description on multivolume sets. This difference is reflected in both MARCs. The Japanese rules have been revised, however, and the *Nippon Cataloging Rules* 1987 edition permits treatment of multivolumes sets to follow ISBD. However, "the output work from MARC data can easily be adjusted in various ways"[8] so that the multiple-level description has been adopted. Because the merits of both rules are taken into consideration, rules have become complex.[9] It is unpredictable at this time whether the format of Japan MARC or other commercial MARCs can be changed to follow ISBD.

The procedure for retrieval of Japanese-language books is usually by "readings" through phonetic rendering of the script—and not through graphic analysis. Chinese character retrieval is practiced only in isolated libraries in Japan. Even where retrieval is by Chinese characters, one needs to know the reading of the characters used as search keys. Hence in Japanese book MARCs, there exists a field for readings. This is one of the major differences between Japan MARC and foreign alphabet MARCs. In order to resolve these two points, a single file system must be constructed or some other approach is needed. Let us now turn to a general explanation of Japan MARC, an analysis of its elements, and conversion of elements.

JAPAN MARC

Since the introduction of computers in 1971, NDL has developed various automated systems and has conducted various studies on Chinese character processing by computer. NDL began inputting data for Japanese publications into its databases in January 1977 and began distribution of the database Japan MARC on a weekly basis with the first week's issue in April 1981 of *Japan National Bibliography Weekly List*, no. 13, formerly *NDL Weekly Acquisition List*.

The input work on retrospective data has been steadily progressing to expand public access to earlier publications. Records for January–December 1981 were completed in August 1981; for 1979–80 in April 1982; and for 1977–78, after some revision, in April 1984.

Furthermore, NDL has continued to input retrospective records for works in the *Kokuritsu Kokkai Toshokan shozo mokuroku* (NDL catalog). Some 220,000 entries from 1969 to 1976 are being input by subject and are being distributed to subscribers by subjects. The entire ten volumes of *NDL Catalog* are scheduled to be completed in February 1990. The input operation for 1943–68 bibliographical data began in 1988 and is scheduled to be completed in March 1992. NDL is also planning to input serials published in Japan (excluding serials in Chinese, Han'gul, and other Asian languages) and to publish the product as Japan MARC (Serials). By way of illustration the records in Japan MARC produced in 1983 numbered 53,553 titles; government publications numbered 13,357 titles and nongovernment publications 40,196 titles.

Characteristics

Specifications of Japan MARC are as follows:

1. The bibliographic record format of magnetic tape is based on ISO 2709.

2. The arrangement and structure of various elements of magnetic tape are according to UNIMARC.
3. Logical record or the format structure comprises: record label, directory, and bibliographic data.
4. Character set is as follows:
   (a) EBCDIC or JIS C6220
   (b) Chinese character code is JIS C6226. NDL uses its own Chinese character code internally but converts the data when publishing the data in Japan MARC format.
   (c) Chinese character code control is JIS C6225.
   (d) A reserve area is set aside for character codes other than JIS C6226.

Characteristics of Japan MARC deserve special consideration. First, I would like to say a word or two about standardization of character representation. For Japan MARC, the treatment of Chinese characters was standardized. Because Japanese usually retrieve bibliographic data by readings, readings were assigned to Chinese characters, with the readings being represented in *katakana* (letters of the Japanese syllabary) or in roman letters (according to the *kunrei-shiki* or Cabinet decree system of romanization).

Second, care was taken because of special characteristics of the Japanese language as follows:

1. Written Japanese offers various forms of the same character, and printed characters are quite complex. Accordingly, new print forms were adopted, and old forms are converted to new.
2. There are numerous syllables in Japanese words with identical sounds but with different written characters. This problem can mean "electronics" (電気) or "biography" (伝記). Since characters cannot be distinguished by reading alone, the system is so devised to pair readings with Chinese characters so as to identify specific Chinese characters.
3. There is no practice of word division in written Japanese. In English, for example, a space is used to separate words, as in "University Library." In written Japanese, on the other hand, the five Chinese characters denoting *daigaku toshokan* (大学図書館) are written without a space separating *daigaku* (university) and *toshokan* (library). Thus, in Japanese there is no differentiation of words as units, and consequently it is not possible to retrieve key words. To cope with this problem, there is provision for spacing of readings so that key words can be isolated from the mixed Sino-Japanese character titles. But since keyword in context (KWIC) indexing is only possible from the readings, this causes problems in indexing. Moreover, distinguishing between homophones is not possible with KWIC indexing.

In Japan MARC, in addition to the field where mixed Sino-Japanese texts are recorded, there are two other fields. Therefore, three fields are readied for the title, author, and subjects fields, and are connected with tags as shown in figure 1.

Description Block	Access Point Block
Tag 251 Title and statement of authorship	Tag 551$a Kana reading $X romanized reading
	Tag 771$a Author in kana $X author romanized
Tag 291 Title and statement of authorship of individual volume of multivolume publication	Tag 591$a Title in kana $X romanized
	Tag 791$a Author in kana $X author in romanization
Tag 280 Series	Tag 580$a Series in kana $X series in romanization
Tag 650 Personal name used as subject heading	Tag 650$a Personal in kana $X personal name in romanization
Tag 658 General subject headings	Tag 658$a Gen. subj. heading in kana $x gen. subj. heading in romanization $b Chinese character

Figure 1. Tags used in Japan MARC.

Conversion and Output of Multiple Structures

Japan MARC has two tags corresponding to LC MARC tag 245. This is derived from differences in the cataloging rules for units of description in Japan and the United States. According to *Nippon Cataloging Rules*, preliminary new edition, a multivolume set is cataloged individually with the physical unit used as the basis of description. This practice has led to the unit concept of the volume title. *AACR2* provides for multilevel description of multivolume sets. Therefore, when the title encoded for a volume title in Japan is unique, we find tag 251 of Japan MARC corresponding to tag 245 for the overall level LC MARC, and tag 291 of Japan MARC corresponding to tag 245 for individual volume records. To resolve this difference, we at the Waseda University Library have developed several conversion devices.

First, the mixed Sino-Japanese texts (tag 251) and its reading (tag 551$a) were put in the same field. Second, since there is no practice of word division in written Japanese, it is not possible to retrieve a key word. So we attempted to make word division in both Sino-Japanese texts and reading forms by adapting Automatic Japanese Keyword Extraction Program (AJAX) and KMATCH (Keyword match) developed by Waseda University Library.

Bibliographic Data Field Output

A brief explanation of the output system for the bibliographic data fields is as follows:

Title Field Output (tag 251 and tag 751). Japan MARC uses tag 251 for descriptive information for the title and tag 751 for the access point. For the volume title, Japan MARC provides tag 291, and tag 791 for access. In experiments, we have found that 70 percent of data input as volume titles are identified as title without ambiguity. Here, I would like to explain that two title fields are available, and that we must develop patterns based on a variety of cases. Let me note further that the title field includes the following subfields:

> $A Title (Main title)
> $B Sub-title (Other title information.
>   No such field in tag 551.)
> $D Volume numbering, etc.
> $F Statement of authorship. (*Its reading is in
>   tag 751.)
> $W Category of material (No such field in tag 551.)

1. Case 1: Monograph

    Data input in Japan MARC occurs through tag 251 $A (: $B) $F and tag 551 $A (*kana* reading), $X (romanized reading), and also tag 751 $A (*kana* reading of authorship), $X (romanized reading of authorship), $B (Chinese character of authorship).

    For example, in Japan MARC the book entitled *Unfinished Progress: Fifty-Year History of American Football in Japan*, edited by Touch-down Co. Ltd., is recorded as follows:

Tag 251$A 限りなき前進 [Unfinished history] 日本ア メリカン フットボール $B 五十年史 [Fifty year history of American football in Japan] $Fタッチダウン株式会社//編 Touch-down Co. Ltd., editor] [description of main title and subtitle]

Tag 551$A カギリナキゼンシン $XKagiri naki zenshin$B#251 [*kana* and romanized reading of title; no such reading of subtitle]

Tag 751$A タッチ ダウン カブシキ カイシャ//ヘン $XTatchi daun Kabushiki Kaisha//hen$B タッチ ダウン 株式会社//編 [*kana* and romanized reading of authorship]

Therefore for outputting:

Title: tag 251$A (':'$B) '@' tag 551$A (':' $B-reading supplemented by AJAX) to title field [corresponding to tag 245].
Intellectual responsibility: "Other title information/intellectual responsibility" [tag 245 #C-at the head of note in the system]

The above example is shown as output in Japan MARC in figure 2.

Further, there is no reading tag in Japan MARC corresponding to tag 251 $B (subtitle) (reading tags are available in TRC), and so it was supplemented automatically by AJAX.

2. Case 2: Multivolume and continued publications

This is a case of a multipart title of two or more volumes where the volumes do not have unique titles. This should correspond to multilevel descriptions to be treated below. However, in Japan MARC descriptive tags are input only in tag 251$A ($B), $D, $F and access points in tag 551$A, $X, $D, $B and in tag 751 $A, $X;

Cataloging
Correct entry
Entry summary   System

1 First code   statemt
2 Second code   not applicable
3 Entry   限りなき 前進 ： 日本 アメリカン フットボール 五十年史 @ カギリナキ ゼンシン ： ニホン アメリカン フットボール ゴジュウネンシ
   Diacriticals

Figure 2. An example of Japan MARC.

Source: *Japan MARC Manual*, 2nd ed. (Kokuritsu Kokkai Toshokan (NDL); dist by Nikon Toshukan Kyokai (JLA), 1987), p.4–5.

there are no multiple level descriptions. On the other hand, DOBIS recognizes the existence of the volume record as a record type.

Japan MARC sometimes loads not only the volume number but also the frequency number in subfield D of tag 251 data in excess of 18 bytes. For example:

$D Showa 51-nenban fujin to shakai hosho [$D 1976 edition. Women and social welfare. 昭和51年版　婦人と社会保障].[10]

In this case the title *Fujin to shakai hosho* (Women and social welfare) is an individual title given to the annual referred to as the *Showa 51-nenban*, 1976 edition. Accordingly, should it be repeated as a partial title in tag 252 $A or input in tag 291? Moreover, in 1975–76, we find *suisan-hen* (marine volume), where we encounter cases where definitions are unclear, thus requiring further study.

3. Case 3: Multivolume sets

A multivolume set can have data on tag 251 and tag 291 in Japan MARC. For example, the title *New Selections on English Grammar*, edited by Akira Ota and Suguru Kajita; v.5. *A Phrasal Verb,* by Yuji Shimada was recorded as follows:

On tag 251:$A Shin Eibunpo Sensho $D dai 5-kan $F Ota Akira, Kajita Suguru // sekinin hennshu [$A New English grammar series $D vol. 5 $F Ota Akira, Kajita Suguru // editor]

On tag 291:$A Kudoshi $F Shimada Yuji // cho [$A Phrasal verbs $F Shimada Yuji // author]

In these descriptions, title and authorship are separated. The authorship description of *Shin eibunpo sensho* is Ota Akira and Kajita Suguru, but because of the interposition of *dai 5-kan,* they appear to be the authors of volume 5, though they are not.[11]

Sometimes in Japan MARC when the data input in tag 251 is lengthy, residual data are recorded in tag 291 $A. Therefore, the volume title recorded in tag 291 is not always a distinctive title. Consequently, we should automatically look to see whether the volume title recorded in tag 291 is a distinctive title or not (i.e., whether or not the reading of volume title is recorded in 591, tag 291 $F is recorded, and so on). If a volume title is recognized as a distinctive title,

*The data are transferred in the form "tag 251$A [i.e., description of main title] '@' "tag 551$A [i.e., *kana* reading of main title] ';' $D [i.e., volume no].

Tag 251 $A as output in title-series field (in tag 440 of LC MARC

Tag 251 $D in output in the volume number of title field

and also

Tag 291 $A as output in "title proper" (in tag 245 of LC MARC) in the form:

Tag 291$A [i.e., title statement of individual volume of multititle sets] '@' tag 791$A [i.e., *kana* readings].

In addition,

Tag 291 $F [i.e., author statement of individual volume of multititle sets] is used as output in both "remainder of title fields=responsibility" (field of tag 245$C of LC MARC) and "heading of main entry" (tag 110 of LC MARC)....

4. Case 4: Series output
   The subfields in Japan MARC for works in series (tag 280) are as follows:

   $A Series title
   $B Volume numbering
   $D Name of part
   $F Numbering of part

The principles governing output are as follows:

a. The series title is output in first position in the title series field (tag 440). The output form is:

Tag 280$A '@' tag 580$A ';' tag 280$B

There are cases, however, in Japan MARC where a publisher's series is further divided into several subseries and where the description (tag 280) and the reading (tag 580) do not match. For example:

Tag 280$A Kyoikusha shinsho $D Sangyokai shirizu# [tag 280$A Kyoikusha books $D Industrial world series#]

Tag 580$A　サンギョウカイ　シリーズ　$XSangyokai shirizu $B
産業界シリーズ　[12]

In cases of multiple level descriptions, judgment is needed about whether to create three-level descriptions or not. In Japan MARC, however, *Kyoikusha shinsho* (Kyoikusha books) is not treated as an access point by policy, and hence the readings of only access points are recorded. This is a choice each library should make, and in the Waseda University Library, since readings are automatically assigned to those items without readings by AJAX, we are able to provide output even in this case, as follows:

Tag 280$A '@' tag 580$A [added reading according to AJAX] ';'
tag 280$D '@' tag 580$D

As is evident, the title series field (tag 440) is repeated.

    b. Priority is placed on tag 280 over tag 251 in cases where tag 251 is used as title series field (tag 440). This indicates that three-level descriptions are possible.

Intellectual Responsibility Output. Japan MARC's tag 251 $F (author statement) is linked with tag 751. Moreover, tag 291 $F (statement of authorship of single volume-level) is linked with tag 791. Therefore, the data are combined with the Chinese characters and their readings and are output according to the following principles.

1. Tag 251 $F is output in the page=tag 245#C=at the head of note in the system.
2. In the name field=tag 100, Japan MARC's tag 751$F-tag 759 $F, tag 791 $F-tag 799 $F are output in that order; e.g., tag 751 $B (*kanji*=Chinese character) '@' 751 $A (*kana* reading). For foreign names, Japan MARC's tag 751 $A has the *kana* reading and $B has the original in roman alphabet with double brackets. We at the Waseda University Library use the original form ($B) without the brackets.
3. LC MARC's tag 100 (name field) designates the kind of name indicator 1, but Japan MARC does not have this feature. Our system's name field designates (1) first name only, (2) single family name only (common family name), (3) double names, and (4) surname only (family name); whereas Japan MARC's tag 751 $B gives individual names in *kanji* by the designation of (1) name only and (2) double names. Generally speaking, single names are given to Japanese in Japan, but this presents some problems for retrieval. Since the names in the database are usually of well-known indivi-

duals, we have adopted the use of double names for the Japanese for ease of access.
4. Japan MARC inserts double slash marks (//) between the first name and surname, but our system uses one space.
5. In *AACR2* the role of an individual ($C) in the name field is not indicated. In Japan MARC, however, the role of the individual is shown in the author statement. A table is provided as the name relator code. A profile combining the author statement of Japan MARC and the table can be therefore made into a set.

Publishing Data Output. Japan MARC's tag 270 (publishing) has subfields $A (place of publication), $B (name of publisher), and $D (date of publication), but there are no corresponding readings. Since the names of publisher under authority control serve as access points in our system, the output work is handled in the following manner:

> Conversion form: tag 270 $B (publisher in *kanji*) ':' $A (place of publication in *kanji*) '@' $A (readings according to AJAX) ':' $A (reading in AJAX)

Furthermore, when there are two or more publishers or there is a distributor, such information in Japan MARC is input through tag 350 $A (general) and this data can be extracted and output as publishing data.

Subject Output. Japan MARC has two fields for subject access points: tag 650 (personal name as subject heading) and tag 658 (general subject headings). Our system has a single field distinguishing between subject headings by type—personal names (by type), corporate names (by type), geographical names, and general subject headings, and provides also subject heading tables (subject heading sources). Therefore, when outputting subjects from Japan MARC the type of subject heading is automatically applied. The subject headings are based on National Diet Library General Subject Headings.

UTILIZATION OF COMMERCIAL MARCS

In addition to Japan MARC, the Waseda University Library has been subscribing to one of the commercial MARCs, TRC MARC. Here are a few comments on this point.
1. The basic question in utilizing two MARCs in a library is whether a library should maintain two systems or a single system converting one MARC to the other. We have no definitive answer as yet.

However, since we would like to separate searching for materials held by the Waseda University Library from information searches (MARC data searchers), we decided to output all purchased bibliographic data into a bibliographic pool (data file).
2. When we maintain this bibliographic pool (data file), it is necessary to have a key to identify bibliographic data for the same publications stored in the two different MARC databases. The Japan publishers (JP) number is used as a unique identifier for Japan MARC, and the JLA number serves the same function in TRC MARC. These are nothing more than numbers used to sell necessary data to librarians. Thus the most effective key to distinguish between duplicate bibliographic data is the ISBN. However, often two different ISBNs are assigned to one book, or a single number is assigned to all volumes of a three-volume set, so that ISBNs are not always a reliable key to identify duplicate bibliographic data. The only certain way of distinguishing the two is by some manual method. In the absence of the actual object, the method, strictly speaking, can be said to include the problem. Here, we decided to clearly indicate the authority (MARC source) so as to distinguish between the two MARCs as the source of the data without unifying the two sets of data.
3. TRC MARC has the identical content identifier (tag) and subfield unit ($) as Japan MARC. The output specifications are basically the same as Japan MARC. However, TRC MARC has developed individual additional fields. (The table of TRC MARC fields and subfields are shown in appendix 1.) In addition to the above, tag 780 has reading of publisher, and this has nineteen subfields.

CJK FILES

At the Waseda University Library, we developed a single bibliographic data file of Japanese- and Western-language materials with conversion and output features for MARC data for Japanese books. This means that we are adapting *AACR2* for description of Japanese monographs. Japan has its own *Nippon Cataloging Rules*, but we have not yet been able to establish unified cataloging rules for both Japanese- and Western-language works.

The maintenance of a single bibliographic data file was also suggested for the National Center for Science Information System, the only national bibliographical utility of Japan. However, the nature of the center—cooperative cataloging is a part of its functions—has prevented it from constructing an integrated system of Japanese- and Western-language files, and separate files are maintained.[13]

As mentioned earlier, the key to building an integrated system is to have the descriptive area (Chinese characters, *kana*) and the access points (reading in *kana* and romanization) in the same field. In machine records, it is possible to input in separate fields but output in the same field by providing linking numbers. This procedure has been achieved in the data files of the National Center for Science Information Center and the CJK file of OCLC. This can be said to be the future trend for online descriptive cataloging.[14]

Although the future of descriptive cataloging is evident, we have not yet reached the stage when we can input Chinese and Korean (North and South) bibliographic data into existing files. The reason for this lies in the establishment of Chinese character codes. The current policy of the National Center for Science Information system is as follows:

1. Works in Chinese and Korean (North and South) can be registered in the Japanese books file in Chinese characters (*kanji*) or in Japanese translation.
2. Works in Chinese and Korean (North and South) can be registered in Chinese characters (*kanji*) with Western-language file.
3. Works in Chinese and Korean (North and South) can be registered in translation (regardless of method of translation) in the Western-language file.

Each participating library may decide on which method to use. In all cases, simplified characters used in Chinese will not be used; instead corresponding characters found in the character set for cataloging purposes will be substituted.[15]

As we have seen, no definite policy has been decided upon in Japan about the treatment of Chinese- and Korean-language materials and whether bibliographic data for such materials are to be integrated into Japanese-language or Western-language files. The reasons for this indecision are as follows:

1. Japan, located in the *kanji* culture sphere in Asia, has been strongly influenced by continental Chinese culture in the formation of its civilization. A variety of standardized styles for writing Chinese characters flourished and declined during the course of Chinese history. Woodblock print technology developed during the Sung Dynasty (960–1279), but there was no standardization of characters in China. It has been said that standardization was achieved with the compilation of the *K'ang-hsi tzu tein* (*Kang-hsi* dictionary) during the reign of Emperor K'ang-hsi (1661–1722). During the third century, Chinese characters and their

pronunciations were introduced to Japan. The pronunciations, called *on* (the original Chinese sounds), were Japanese approximations of the sounds of the original Chinese. Furthermore, other readings called *kun* were developed in Japan, *kun* being written with a character that originally means "to interpret the meaning."[16]

Books were imported to Japan from China along with the written languages. Books written in Chinese were generally called *kanseki* (Chinese classics).[17] These books were essential reading materials for the Japanese. They read these classics with the pronunciations of *on* in combination with *kun*.[18]

Ever since, the Chinese classics have become indispensible materials for the Japanese. This tradition formed the single concept of the *Wa-Kan-Sho* (Japanese-Chinese classics) in Japanese libraries. Libraries with long histories and traditions in Japan have shelved these Chinese classics together with Japanese materials and processed them together without any problems. There should be no discomfort in finding data for Chinese works in the same file containing Japanese bibliographic data.

2. On the other hand, the reform of Chinese characters as a basic problem of Chinese culture has been debated for many years among the Chinese themselves. The romanization of Chinese characters began in China in the early seventeenth century, in the late Ming Dynasty.[19] It was, however, not until the enlightenment and language reform movement in the years following 1915 that the Chinese themselves began to seriously debate the reform of their writing system. In 1928 the government of the Republic of China announced its statement on the romanization of the national language. In 1912, however, the *Hsun yin t'ung i hui*(Foundation Unification Society) studied the need for the standardization of pronunciation and produced tables known as *Chu yin tzu mu*. The modernization of pronunciation went through several phases, and the definitive version is known today as *Pin yir tsu mu*.

Chinese books published pre- and post-1912 are treated separately in many Japanese libraries today. In Japan, the reform of character readings in 1912 in China was a point of separation for Chinese books in Japanese libraries. The pre-1912 Chinese books have no readings. Alphabetic scripts like English can be read without reading marks; Japan has *kana*, which can be used as reading marks for idographic Chinese characters, thus providing pronunciations to such characters. The readings of Chinese characters were traditionally transmitted by word of mouth in China in the absence of reading marks. Although *Fan chieh* (the use of two Chinese characters to indicate pronunciation for a single character—a method devised in the Han dynasty, 220–206 B.C.) was developed in China. It was not popularized among the masses.[20] Therefore, in Japan, there does not exist the concept of Chinese books as found in the West, and this is the source of the practice of treating post-1912 Chinese books as foreign (Western) books.

3. Korea is another country in the *kanji* cultural sphere in Asia. Sejong Taewang, the fourth king of the Yi Dynasty in the middle of the fifteenth century, was the originator of the Han'gul alphabet. During his time only a limited number of upper-class nobles had access to Chinese characters and Chinese books, and the masses did not have access to writing. The Han'gul alphabet was used as a tool for communicating in writing in lieu of Chinese characters. However, the use of Chinese characters, especially in public documents, continued until the late nineteenth century. The movement to use the Han'gul alphabet, in combination with Chinese characters, began in the early twentieth century and was popularized.[21] Today, there are two kinds of Korean books: those written entirely in Han'gul and those written using Chinese characters, called Korean classics.

As to the establishment and prospects for character codes, consider the following:

1. Japan has established JIS X0208 (formerly JIS C6226), the Chinese character code for information exchange. This code specifies the combinations of characters and readings commonly used for reading and writing. These include arabic numerals, roman alphabet letters, and *kana*. The Chinese character set contains a total of 6,349 characters, of which 2,965 are in the first level, and 3,384 are in the second level. Included in the first level are those characters of *joyo kanji* (Chinese characters for daily use and JIS C6220 regional local codes); the remainder are in the second level.[22] This code will be revised every five years.

How many Chinese characters are required to cover all characters used in Chinese and Japanese books? *K'ang-hsi tzu tien*, the first Chinese standard dictionary, contains 47,034 characters. Compiled by Tetsuji Morohashi, *Dai Kan-wa jiten shuuteiban* (Comprehensive Chinese-Japanese dictionary), the largest Chinese-Japanese dictionary in Japan (13 volumes) contains 49,964 Chinese characters, including those created in Japan.[23] Also compiled by Tetsuji Morohashi is *Ko Kan-wa jiten* (Extensive Chinese-Japanese dictionary, 1981–82, four volumes), which has 20,000 characters. In order to build a bibliographic file of contemporary literature, Japanese classics, and Chinese classics, more characters than are provided by the JIS code are needed.

2. Chinese characters used in Chinese books cannot be treated the same as in Japanese books. The reason is that simplified Chinese characters in China are constructed in eight different ways whereas the new Japanese characters are constructed to save strokes.[24] Also, the way in

which a character is inscribed is different so that the same character used in China and Japan should be assigned two different code numbers. The number of characters to be coded will be some 10,000 characters. *T'ung yin tz'u tien*, published by Shomu Inshokan in 1956, contains 10,503 characters,[25] and *Chu-Nichi dai jiten* (Chinese-Japanese dictionary), compiled by Aichi Daigaku Chu-Nichi Daijiten Hensanjo in 1986, contains 7,876 (including 2,238 simplified Chinese characters).

3. Is coding of the Han'gul alphabet possible? Because it is based on a phonetic system, it can be treated in the same way as the Japanese *kana*. Han'gul has ten basic vowel sounds and fourteen basic consonant sounds. In addition to the basic sounds, eleven sounds are added to the vowel sounds and five to the consonant sounds, with a total of 40 sounds in the Han'gul alphabet.[26] Accordingly, the Han'gul has 140 letters, which is about three times more than the number of Japanese letters.[27] The Chinese characters used along with the Han'gul alphabet should be treated separately with the Chinese characters used in Chinese and Japanese books. The total of such Chinese characters in Korean books is about 1,800 characters.[28]

Conclusion

Japanese have the concept of books being written in either Japanese or Chinese but not Japanese, Chinese, and Korean. That is, Chinese and Korean classics are all represented by the initials "CJ" and we don't refer to them as "CJK." Here, I will examine the background to the above-mentioned concepts and the possibility and prospects of inputting books in Chinese and Korean mingled with Chinese characters into the bibliographic data file. As I described before, I think there is difficulty in coding only Chinese characters used in Japanese, Chinese, and Korean (South and North) languages and in the development of new software. I cannot offer a concrete suggestion about the problem of the coding, and developing software is far beyond my capabilities as a library worker, but I will describe my vague idea in the following:

1. My first suggestion is to build another system, using MARCs made by each country, that is, the Chinese character code set by a particular country.
2. The second suggestion is to code in a way which meets all of the conditions as a basic character for common use in comparison with Chinese characters coded in Japan and those in China (GB 2312). The Chinese characters peculiar to each country are to coded separately. It is to be desired that Chinese characters be coded in an area of two bytes.

However, it is not only the code of Chinese characters in China and Korea that is necessary for systematizing cataloging in Japan. Though the theme in this chapter is restricted to CJK, we should study the code for other oriental characters, Cyrillic characters, and so on. Cyrillic characters are applied to the roman alphabet in the United States, but in Japan are given a JIS code, thereby avoiding the necessity of transcribing them into the roman alphabet in Japan. It takes a long time to proceed to the next stage as many things should be coded in two bytes as mentioned above.

Coding Chinese characters requires an enormous amount of work, but I think it will be possible. When I think of the CJK file, there is a bigger problem than the coding for characters. This is how to input. In Japan the conversion input of the Japanese rendering of a Chinese character into the Chinese character, that is, the conversion of *kana* into *kanji* and that of *romaji* into *kanji*, have been realized, and the conversion of every articulation is also available. Only special characters are input using character code (*kanji* code). But, Chinese characters in China or Han'gul have no established method of input. For example, the present *Pin yin tsu mu* to convert the reading into *kanji* has not been popularized in China, and the method of using the Wade system of *romaji* was for foreigners. Therefore, in Formosa, *kanji* is now input by the method of making up a Chinese character by synthesizing the character divided into some sections; that is, single *kanji* conversion.

The systematization of bibliographies in Japan is being promoted not only for the construction of bibliographic data files, but also for rationalizing cataloging work. Therefore, input method such as single *kanji* input in which a Chinese character is converted by synthesizing the sections, used now in RLIN, for example, or the code conversion done after checking each *kanji* code will meet resistance from job sites in libraries. Therefore, I cannot but declare that it is difficult to construct the CJK file in Japan as long as the problem of the input method for *kanji*, as well as that of the CJK concept are not solved.

Finally, I will touch on the code for Chinese characters. It has been done at the responsibility of each country. Japan has JIS code and the Republic of China has its own character code, too. And MARCs have similarly been made at the responsibility of the bibliography-making institutions of each country. In addition, MARC users have been thought to be responsible for constructing databases using MARCs made by each country. Therefore, I think that, in principle, MARC users should introduce the character code of the country that made the MARC if the character code is needed or make the common character set according to the content of the database to be constructed. I can understand that a future problem is a common character set for exchanging bibliographic information, which is necessary so that MARCs with different *kanji* codes can be used under the same conditions. But this common character set may cause problems in another respect if nations in advanced information providing services, such as United States or Japan, take the lead in generalizing such sets among East Asian countries. To solve this problem, including the problem whether or not we or they should have the CJK file, it is necessary to establish a standing committee on East Asian bibliographic information in some form as Hiroshi Tanabe proposed at the IFLA preconference in Tokyo.[29] In the committee, the nations in advanced information processing should listen fully to the remarks of the East Asian countries.

Appendix 1. TRC MARC Profile

Block	Tag	Field	$	Subfield
0	080	JLA number		
2	251	Title and statement of authorship	$T	Edition of subtitle
	265	Edition	$F	Author of edition
	270	Publishing statement	$T	Place of publication
			$R	Publisher
3	350	Note 1	$R	Edition's general note
	360	Note 3	$J	Special price
			$L	Set price
			$T	Price note
	365	Note (individual)	$A	Targetted user
			$B	Circulation code
			$D	Distribution number
5	551	Reading of title	$T	Single entry indicator mark
			$R	*Kana* reading of $T
			$H	Romanization of $R
	560	Reading of subtitle (individual)	$A	*Katakana*
			$X	Romanization
			$R	*Katakana*
	561	Volume number (individual) reading	$A	*Katakana*
			$X	Romanization
			$B	*Kanji*
			$D	Volume number
	562	Reading of subtitle of edition (individual)		No data
	565	Reading of edition (individual)		No data
	580	Reading of series	$R	*Katakana*
			$N	Series code
	581	Reading of subseries (individual)	$A	*Katakana*
			$X	Romanization
			$B	*Kanji*
			$R	*Katakana*
			$D	Series number
			$K	Series code
	591	Reading of single volume level of multivolume work	$R	*Katakana*
			$H	Romanization
	567	Reading of notes of ed.		No data
	570	Reading of title of author's note		No data
6	665	Subject heading (individual)		No data
7	751	Reading of author	$T	Sign for single entry
			$R	*Katakana*

Source: TRC

Appendix 2

Mixing One- and Two-Byte Character Codes

The mixture of one- and two-byte character codes in one field can be supported by Release Seven of CICS version one and later release numbers. Although it is possible to express all data in the database using two-byte coding, the materials handled by Japanese university libraries are not limited to Japanese alone—nearly half are in foreign languages, making collections linguistically similar to those of Western libraries. When simply calculated, a two-byte coding of all these materials would require twice the computer resources. Since this system would be an obvious waste, we decided to use the EBCDI system for the standard roman alphabet.

Mixing two different character codes in one field requires the use of a control code or codes for discriminating them. We are presently using two control codes: a shift-out code (X'OE') for indicating the beginning of the two-byte code and a shift-in code (X'OF') for indicating the end.

Example: 日本 IBM .... Data

 OE4562 4566 OFC9C2D4 ...... Database

that is:
- OE → Shift out
- 4562 → 日
- 4566 → 本
- OF → Shift in
- C9 → I
- C2 → B
- D4 → M

This is how code discrimination is carried out with a mixture of one- and two-byte character codes, but this alone does not solve all problems. In the DOBIS/LIBIS system, processing is often conducted to move some of the first bytes of one field to another field.

In the above example, if we move the first four bytes to another

---

Extracted from DOBIS/LIBIS with Multi-Language Processing by S. Narita and A. Saito, Waseda University Library (Papers presented at the Sixth Annual Meeting of the DOBIS/LIBIS Users Group, Nice (France), September 8–11, 1987).

location, we will move data 0E45624566. However, the system does not understand what this means. The two OE and OF codes together make a set that constitutes meaning. If one of the control codes appears independently in data, its task will cause an abnormal end. The DOBIS/LIBIS Japanese-language version is, of course, able to cope with this situation.

MAP CODING

If two different character codes are mixed, their correspondence becomes essential in map coding as well. To be more specific, MAPATTS = SOSI must be added to the operand in the DFHMSD (macro instruction). Even in the DFHMDF, SOSI = YES must be added to the operand, if it is an input area on the map (fig. A1).

In map and character coding, fixed values should be defined using the OE and OF control codes, as shown in figure A2.

```
*+ EXEC DBSHAPTR, N = ECA03
ECA03B      DFHMSD CTRL = FREEKB, LANG = PLI, MODE = INOUT, MAPATTS = SOSI
ECA03       DFHMDI
*     SUBFIELD CODES AND FIELD CODES OF A SINGLE NOTE
*     USED BY DBSCA09
            COPY      EKEYIN
            DFHMSD    TYPE = FINAL
            END
*+  EXEC DBSMAPTR, N = ECA03
*+  EXEC DBSMAPGN, N = ECA03, M = B

*+  EXEC DBSMAPTR, N = EKEYIN
*     USED BY DBSCA02 PROGRAM
*     CURSOR POSITION SET IN PROGRAM
*     INCLUDE IN ALL ADDKEY MAPS
SUBCD1  DFHMDF POS = 0320, LENGTH = 1, ATTRB = (ASKIP)
ENTRY1  DFHMDF POS = 0332, LENGTH = 77, ATTRB = (UNPROT, BRT, FSET), SOSI = YES
SUBCD2  DFHMDF POS = 0400, LENGTH = 1, ATTRB = (UNPROT, BRT, FSET)
ENTRY2  DFHMDF POS = 0402, LENGTH = 77, ATTRB = (UNPROT, BRT, FSET), SOSI = YES
SUBCD3  DFHMDF POS = 0480, LENGTH = 1, ATTRB = (UNPROT, BRT, FSET)
ENTRY3  DFHMDF POS = 0482, LENGTH = 77, ATTRB = (UNPROT, BRT, FSET), SOSI = YES
SUBCD4  DFHMDF POS = 0560, LENGTH = 1, ATTRB = (UNPROT, BRT, FSET)
```

Figure A1. Example of map coding

```
括哭    ---DEMO. MAP. SOURCE (JC0200S) = 01.11------------------ COLUMNS  001  072
コマント ===>                                                            ===> PAGE
000023          DFHMDF    POS = 480, LENGTH = 15,                              X
000024                    INITIAL = ' 1検ж ',                                  X
000025                    DBSPOS = 010, DBSCODE = A2858199,                    X
000026                    DBSTEXT = ' DBSSE01 '
000027          DFHMDF    POS = 580, LENGTH = 18,                              X
000028                    INITIAL = ' 2 発注・受入 ',                           X
000029                    DBSPOS = 020, DBSCODE = 818398A4,                    X
000030                    DBSTEXT = ' DBSSC01 '
000031          DFHMDF    POS = 640, LENGTH = 25,                              X
000032                    INITIAL = ' 3 逐次刊行物管理 ',                       X
000033                    DBSPOS = 030, DBSCODE = 97859989,                    X
000034                    DBSTEXT = ' DBSPE01 '
000035          DFHMDF    POS = 720, LENGTH = 16,                              X
000036                    INITIAL = ' 4 目録 ',                                X
000037                    DBSPOS = 040, DBSCODE = 8381A381,                    X
000038                    DBSTEXT = ' DBSCA01 '
000039          DFHMDF    POS = 0800, LENGTH = 15,                             X
000040                    INITIAL = ' 5 貸出管理 ',                            X
000041                    DBSPOS = 050, DBSCODE = 83899983,                    X
000042                    DBSTEXT = ' DBSC101 '
000043          DFHMDF    POS = 0880, LENGTH = 15,                             X
000044                    INITIAL = ' 6 x - r ',                               X
```

Figure A2. Defining fixed values

NOTES

1. Hiroyuki Kaiho, ed., *Kanji o kagaku suru* (Scientific consideration of Chinese characters), (Yuhikaku, 1984), p.76–77. (Yuhikaku sensho).
2. Toshiki Nagashima, "Japan MARC to TRC MARC: hikaku kento to mondaiten no seiri" (Japan MARC and TRC MARC: comparison and problems), in *Daigaku toshokan kenkyu* (Journal of college and university libraries) no.26 (1985 [5]): 21–28.
3. Akira Toda, "nihon de shihan sareteiru maku" (Commercial MARC in Japan), in *Maku o umaku tsukau niwa: kikai kadoku mokuroku nyumon* (How to better use MARC: an introduction to machine-readable cataloging), edited by Masahiko Kurosawa and Tetsu Nishimura (Sangyo Shuppan Boeki, 1985), p.93–104.
4. *Nippan tosho kanri shisutemu* (Nippan library control system), (Nippan Shuppan Hanbai Kabushiki Kaisha [1986]), p.17–39.
5. TRC eigyo no goannai (TRC guide on services), (Toshokan Ryutsu Senta [1986]), 13p.
6. Toda, p.103–105.
7. *Toshokan zasshi* (The library journal), 82, no.1 (1988 [1]): 4.
8. *Nippon mokuroku kisoku, honpan dai 3-ji an.* (Nihon Toshokan Kyokai [JLA], 1986), 150p.
9. Ikuko Mayumi, "*Shoshi joho oyobi toshokan mokuroku no hyoujunka*" (Standardization of bibliographic data and library cataloging), in *Toshokan mokuroku no genjo to shorai* (Current

status and future of library catalogs), edited by Nihon Toshokan Gakkai kenkyu Iinkai (Nichigai Associates, 1987), p.81. (Ronshu: Toshokangaku kenkyu no ayumi, dai 7-shu)

10. *Japan MARC Manual*, 2nd ed. (Kokuritsu Kokkai Toshokan (NDL); dist. by Nihon Toshokan Kyoukai (JLA), 1987), p.20.

11. *Shin Mokurokuho to shoshijoho* (New method of cataloging and bibliographic information), edited by Shojiro Maruyama (Yuzankaku Shuppan, 1987), p.4–5.

12. *Japan MARC Manual*, p.7.

13. Gakujutu Joho Senta (NACSIS). *Mokuroku Shisutemu Riyo Manyuaru: database-hen* (User guide to NACSIS cataloging system: database), (Gakujutu Joho Senta, 1986), p.7.

14. *Ibid.*, p.10; p.57; *User Guide for Creating/Editing OCLC CJK Records* (OCLC, March 1987, 19p.

15. Gakujutu Joho Senta, p.24.

16. Tetsuo Endo, *Kanji no chie* (Knowledge of Chinese characters), (Kodansha, 1988), p.34–48. (Kodansha gendai shinsho)

17. Masana Kusano, ed., *Saishin toshokangaku Jiten* (New dictionary of library science), (Gakugei Tosho, 1974), p.41.

18. Shuji Suzuki, *Kanji: sono tokushitu to kanji bunmei no shorai* (Kodansha, 1984[c1978]), p.159–161. (Kodansha gendai shinsho)

19. Nobumitsu Kanegae, *Chugokugo no susume* (Advice on learning the Chinese language), (Kodansha, 1986[c1964]), p.63–64. (Kodansha gendai shinsho)

20. *Ibid.*, p.59–62.

21. Kaiho, p.165–169.

22. Kaiho, p.41.

23. Kaiho, p.2.

24. Kanegae, p.54–55.

25. Kanegae, p.48–49.

26. Yong-gown Kim, *Hanguru Shoho No Shoho* (Nan'undo, 1986), p.15.

27. Ktsuyo Watanabe, Takao Suzuki, *Chosengo No Susume: Nihongo Kara No Shiten* (Kodansha, 1988[c1981]), p.135–136. (Kodansha gendai shinsho)

28. Kaiho, p.168.

29. Hiroshi Tanabe, *Higashi Ajia ni okeru shoshi joho no koukan* (Exchange of bibliographic data in East Asia), in IFLA publications 38, edited for the Section on Information Technology by Christine Bossmeyer and Stephen W. Massil. Papers from the Preconference: 21–22 August, 1986 (Yushodo-Shuppan, 1988), p.264.

THE NATIONAL DIET LIBRARY AND ITS PRESERVATION PROGRAM

by Kazuo Takahashi

It is said that the publications of a country serve as a barometer of its cultural level. It is said also that paper is a symbol of culture. One acquires knowledge through paper, records it on paper, transmits it by paper, and preserves it on paper. Paper is an indispensable commodity for daily cultural and intellectual life, and it is the source of civilization. As the sole depository library of Japan, the National Diet Library (NDL) is responsible for the comprehensive acquisition of publications published in Japan, the maintenance of the collections, and the service and preservation of the collections permanently—as well as their transmission in so far as possible. It is generally recognized not only by Japan's national library, NDL, but also by all national libraries in the world that their countries' publications are their cultural properties, so that it is their mission to preserve them in original format and to transmit them to the next generation.

In recent years, because of advances in photoduplication technology and the widespread diffusion of photocopiers, the number of requests for photoduplication of materials held by NDL from readers and by mail has increased rapidly each year, and surpasses the 4.5 million mark today. Although it is gratifying to find that the library is being used heavily, it is true that library materials are being damaged by frequent use. The discovery, moreover, of the deterioration of books caused by acid paper shocked all librarians, and for all of us it is today's most serious library problem.

In Japan, only a handful of researchers had recognized the seriousness of the acid paper problem, and the research was very limited. Up until the early 1980s not many librarians had shown interest in the problem. However, interest has been generated during the last few years, and countermeasures and preservation problems are frequently discussed.

This is due primarily to librarians in Japan who have learned more about the research on preservation from their counterparts in the United States, such as librarians at the Barrow Laboratory, Library of Congress, university and research libraries, and the Council on Library Resources. Today many libraries in Japan, including archival libraries, have begun to take serious measures to preserve their collections and records. One of the concrete results in Japan was the enactment of the public archives law in December 1987.

The preservation of materials is not restricted to the domain of bibliographical studies, but is now a dynamic discipline involving physics and chemistry as well as other academic disciplines, and is now of course a matter of worldwide concern. International Federation of Library Associations and Institutions Conference of Directors of National Libraries as well as its Preservation and Conservation (PAC) core program are engaged actively in a program to protect all publications wherever published. As a member of the world library community, NDL, with high expectations as well, has decided to cooperate actively with other nations to help solve the problem.

Deteriorating Library Materials at NDL

As of March 1988, the total collection of NDL numbered 4.8 million volumes. Of the total, it was estimated the paper of some four million volumes, other than traditional Japanese old books made of handmade Japanese paper, *washi*, was acidic.

THE COLLECTION OF TRADITIONAL OLD JAPANESE BOOKS

The first Western-style paper manufacturing company was established in Japan in 1874. The regular production of Western paper from wood pulp began in 1895. It was around the year 1912 that the production of Western paper exceeded that of handmade Japanese paper. Until then, elegant and durable traditional handmade Japanese paper had met the domestic needs of paper in Japan. It had met the demands in Japan for over 1,000 years, and it had helped support Japanese culture.

The earliest known paper extant in Japan is *Hokke gishi* (Commentary on the lotus sutra) written around 606 A.D., and the oldest known paper documented through a postscript is the *Kongojo daranikyo* (Diamond enlightenment prayer) used from 685 A.D. There are numerous other paper treasures produced from 606 A.D. to 700 A.D. held in Shosoin in

Nara. These materials have been transmitted from generation to generation for over 1,200 years and are rare materials as well as valuable properties which can be seen today. It is well substantiated in Japan that books produced from hand-made paper can be preserved not for several hundred years but for over 1,000 years, if the books are properly maintained avoiding damage by insects or fire.

NDL holds in its collection, *Hyakumanto darani* (One million prayer charms) dated 765 A.D. and *Juissai fukutoku zanmaikyo* (Sutra of meditation on all virtue) dated 740 A.D. Although library materials written from the Heian and Kamakura periods (about 600 to 1,200 years ago) are small in number, those materials written from the Muromachi and Edo periods (about 300 to 600 years ago) are plentiful in the collection. We found that the quality of these papers has not deteriorated, and the paper is still strong. We anticipate that these materials will continue to last for an extended period of time as long as they are properly maintained in an appropriate preservation environment.

All Japanese old books are kept in special cases called *chitsu* at NDL. Among old books, those identified as rare are further placed in boxes made of paulownia wood and are housed in cabinets. The cabinets are placed in stack areas which are air conditioned. Usually, all lights are out in the stack area leaving only safety lights. All possible precautions have been taken to ensure their preservation.

SURVEY AND SYMPOSIUM ON MATERIALS DETERIORATION

Survey

About the time NDL found that it could no longer disregard physical damage to materials by photoduplication, the mass media introduced articles about the deterioration of acid paper. NDL accordingly decided in July 1983 to conduct a survey to determine the condition of the entire collection of books and nonbook materials, as well as to identify preservation problems and to develop countermeasures for the future. A task force with seven groups was established according to materials to be studied or cause of damage or deterioration: (a) rare books, (b) microfilm materials, (c) phonograph records, (d) magnetic tapes, (e) damage by insects, (f) damage by photoduplication, and (g) acid paper. After six months of investigation of the collection, each group submitted a report to the Librarian. In each group report, many valuable recommendations on preservation of materials were proposed.

Results of Survey

Publications Published in Japan. Compared with foreign books, Japanese domestic books showed less deterioration. They found that many foreign books were in very brittle condition, considerably worse than that of Japanese books. Perhaps this was due primarily to the widespread use of traditional hand-made paper in Japan. Production of Western paper from wood pulp in Japan was begun about 30 to 40 years later in Japan that in Western countries, and the dissemination of Western paper in Japan was delayed 30 to 40 years. However, publications issued between 1944 and 1960 in Japan were in a conspicuous state of deterioration. This was perhaps due to the effects of the war, which led to materials scarcity and poor quality paper. Books published during this period in Japan may not last for many years in the future. The report recommended expediting the transfer of these books to other media such as microfilm. (See Appendix Tables 1 and 3.)

Foreign Publications. Both monographs and periodicals showed remarkably similar results (see Appendix figures A2 and A4). Compared to books published from 1860 to 1899, books published later were progressively worse. NDL has found similar results to those reports in the West, that the paper of books held in libraries of the Western countries crumbles to pieces after 100 to 130 years. Our results were remarkably similar to those reported in surveys undertaken by the University of Michigan Library and the University of North Carolina Library. (See Appendix A2 and A9.)

Symposium

On November 9, 1983, NDL sponsored a symposium entitled Paper Deterioration and Preservation of Library Materials, inviting 40 representatives from various professional groups—such as librarians, archivists, museum workers, publishers, paper manufacturers, printers, binders, information scientists, and scientists engaged in papermaking.

The morning semiopen sessions featured the presentation of papers including NDL's survey of paper deterioration in its collection. Attended by 74 professionals, the afternoon sessions were divided into small panel discussions led by conference speakers, invited guests, and NDL staff members. As a result of this symposium, the problems of acid paper were reported by the mass media, and an awareness of the problem has developed not only in the library world but in the general public as well. At the 1984 All Japan Library Annual Conference, a session on preservation was held for the first time, and the session was well attended by librarians. NDL provided a keynote speaker at the session and had an exhibit with basic paper, photographs, and a panel demonstration corner.

Preservation Planning Committee

With the presentation of the final report to the Librarian of NDL by the task force based on the seven group recommendations in January-February 1984, the mission of the task force was completed. However, in order to continue to gather information from within the country and abroad and to continue research on preservation and countermeasures, the Preservation Planning Committee was established in June 1984. The Committee members consisted of one chairperson and fourteen members: eight individuals who had served as leaders of the former task force groups and five appointed members, who formed the Acid Paper Planning group.

Basic Policy on Materials Preservation Planning

POLICY AFTER COMPLETION OF NEW ANNEX BUILDING

The construction of the new annex building adjacent to the present main building began in 1981 and was completed in September 1986. (The entire floor area in both the main and annex buildings was enlarged to 145,000 square meters with a book collection capacity of 12 million volumes.) As to the NDL's basic policy on material preservation after the completion of the annex building, the Planning Committee for the Future prepared a report entitled "Library Materials Preservation after the Completion of the Annex Building" following thorough discussions and consultations with the members of the Preservation Planning Committee, and forwarded it to the Librarian in March 1985. This report comprises the guiding principles for the preservation of library materials at NDL. All NDL's activities on preservation are based on these policy guidelines. NDL's basic policies of preservation of library materials are:

1. As the nation's depository library, NDL has responsiblity for acquiring, maintaining, and preserving for posterity publications issued in Japan.
2. Utmost efforts will be made to preserve all domestic publications in their original format, taking into consideration user needs.

The policy states further that toward these ends duplicate copies will be made and that for those materials which have restricted circulation, such as rare books, books in an advanced state of deterioration, and books which cannot be retained in original format, NDL should expedite the production of microfilm copies or copies in other media. For administrative functions, two new offices, the Preservation Planning Office and the Preservation Division, should be created.

PRESENT STATUS OF MATERIALS PRESERVATION PLANNING

Organization

A new office, the Preservation Planning Office, was established in June 1986 at the time of the reorganization of NDL. Also, the former Binding Office was renamed the Preservation Division. As a result of the establishment of the new offices, the organizational structure responsible for the preservation of library materials was formally established. The Preservation Planning Office is responsible for planning and research of preservation, while the Preservation Division is responsible for the implementation of the technology of preservation. The functions of the two offices require close coordination in order to carry out NDL's preservation program.

Conservation Planning

The guiding principle for preservation planning at NDL is to make every effort to acquire, maintain, and conserve all publications published in Japan in their original format. One effective measure to maintain conservation of originals is deacidification, while another is conservation of originals. Still another possible effective measure is the deposit of two copies, or the preparation of duplicate copies.

Deacidification. The most effective measure to preserve present acid paper publications is to deacidify the publications, so that the books can be preserved in their original format. We have placed high hopes on mass deacidification facilities. In order to retain semipermanently the massive collection of acid paper publications held in NDL at present, it is imperative to install a deacidification facility. Furthermore, because acid paper is still being used today and will be used for many years to come, it is anticipated that the NDL's collection of acid paper publications will increase by several thousand volumes annually.

We are monitoring the development of mass deacidification research in other countries, acquiring documentation on existing facilities as well as those under development. At the same time, we are conducting our own basic research here at NDL and are considering the installation of a facility best suited for use in Japan. NDL is lagging behind the Western countries on this research and has just begun experiments with the single method and spray method. Many obstacles and trials await us, but we believe we have an obligation to overcome them all in order to discharge our responsibilities in the area of materials preservation.

Conservation. NDL's conservation program has long been carried out on the principle that publications must be retained as much as possible in their original format with high quality materials and creative methods used to ensure long life. The binding activities at NDL began in 1898 at the Imperial Library (which later became the Ueno branch library of NDL) and have continued for the past 90 years. During these years NDL has bound many books and has conserved many volumes, and techniques developed over the years are more than adequate to maintain NDL's future conservation program. However, the purpose of the past conservation program was primarily to bind publications to be strong and durable for many years and the conscientious preservation of books in original format was regarded as secondary and was often neglected. Today, it is NDL's objective to retain materials in their original format as much as possible.

New Two-Copy Depository System and the Maintenance of Duplicate Copies. Since its inception, NDL has implemented a single copy depository system. Twice in the past, in 1986 and 1987, NDL requested funds for a two-copy depository program, but the proposals were turned down because of severe budget curtailments by the government. The two-copy depository system is not only related to a funding problem but also to problems of legislative changes, so that it has not yet been resolved.

As to duplicate copies, some funding was authorized for the preservation of domestic publications in 1987, and plans are being pushed to work toward a preservation collection within the scope of the funds allocated for this purpose.

Conversion to Other Media

Library materials which cannot be preserved in original format, or are difficult to preserve for an extended period of time, can be converted to other media, thus preserving their intellectual contents. Today, NDL has implemented a policy that allows rare and valuable documents, as well as materials frequently circulated, to be converted to other media as service copies. The service copies are then circulated to readers and researchers.

Microfilming of Materials. It is the policy of NDL to produce two copies of all materials at the time of microfilming: an original film copy, and a service copy. The original work and the original film copy are preserved, while the service copy is served to readers and is also used for reproduction. At present NDL microfilms newspapers, periodicals, and monographs. As to monographs, priority attention is given to rare books or valuable documents, family records related to constitutional government, deteriorated books, and government publications for international exchange.

Other New Media. At present, NDL is not using optical disc technology for preservation. However, NDL has produced a CD-ROM of national bibliographical data, known as Japan MARC on Disk, which has been commercially available since April 1988. The CD-ROM is a compact disk which can store over a half-million bibliographic records produced by NDL over a period of ten years.

Control of Environmental Conditions

Although there are some variations in the conditions for preserving materials from medium to medium, the important requirements which cannot be lacking for purpose of preservation relate to temperature, humidity, lighting, and dust. The effect of environmental conditions on the deterioration of materials cannot be disregarded. NDL has taken the following countermeasures:

Temperature and Humidity in Stack Areas. The temperature in NDL stack areas is set at 22°C and the relative humidity at 55 percent (plus or minus 5 percent), with air conditioning. Efforts have been made to meet and to maintain the established requirements by the installation of air conditioning. The energy center for the electricity and air conditioning of the main annex buildings is monitored by computer 24 hours each day. The buildings are well maintained. However, it has been some 20 to 28 years since the construction of the main building so that it is inevitable that part of the equipment may be deteriorated. Needless to say, equipment in the main building and its general present conditions do not necessarily meet the latest standards compared with that of the annex building. In order to improve the environment in the main building, renovation of the stack areas has been considered.

Lighting. The stack areas of the main building (seventeen floors) have no windows and the stacks of the annex building are located underground (eight floors). These locations are ideal for maintaining library materials. The lighting in the stack areas is well designed to avoid direct sunlight. Equipped with a thermostatically controlled switchboard, the lighting in the stack areas is designed to save and preserve energy. Although special fluorescent lights should be installed to prevent ultraviolet rays from entering the stack areas, regular fluorescent lights are still used because of the restricted library budget. There is no automatic switchboard in the main building, so lights are controlled manually.

Dust. To control the dust that accompanies air conditioning, the stack areas are equipped with vacuum machines. However, the effectiveness of the vacuum machines in the main building has decreased over the years. The improvement of the machines has been planned for the next renovation of the stacks.

Fire Extinguishers. The fire extinguishing device in the main and annex buildings works by gas: by carbon dioxide in the main building stacks and by halogen elements in the annex building stacks. It has been known that halogen elements are safer than carbon dioxide for extinguishing fires.

Study on Use of Acid-Free Paper

Since the beginning of the Preservation Planning Committee, the committee, as part of the study, has been taking measurements of acid values of new books received by NDL during one week in August every year. Some 500 to 600 volumes are selected as samples and their acid values are measured by portable electronic pH measuring instruments. The committee hopes to find a clue as to how much acid-free paper has been used in books in the country. The results of the study conducted in August 1988 were as follows:

pH over	6.5	46.7%
pH	5.0–6.4	37.8%
pH under	4.9	15.5%

Highly acidic samples with pH values under 4.9 have decreased by 12 percent compared with the study conducted in 1986. Also, less acidic samples with pH values of 5.0–6.4 have increased by 10 percent compared with those of the previous year. Because a great deal of the paper used for publications was acid paper, with pH value around 4.0, four to five years ago, this study found that the publishing and paper industries have changed to using more acid-free paper. The study found that the private sector has used more acid free paper than the government sector. Incidentally, since April 1985, NDL has used acid-free paper for all its publications.

Conclusion

Many of the acid paper books held in NDL have been in the collection for 100 to 120 years since their publication. No doubt every one of them is deteriorating gradually, even at this particular moment. We must deal with this problem.

Five years ago in July 1983, a task force was formed to cope with the preservation of library materials at NDL. It was in July 1986 that the new Preservation Planning Office and new Preservation Division were established as part of the NDL's permanent organizations.

The full scale program to preserve library materials at NDL has been operational since then. Our work has just begun. We need to monitor carefully the developments of preservation in the United States and Europe. We need to conduct our own research, especially consulting with the pioneers in the United States, and we need to proceed with the implementation of policies which best suit NDL.

There are numerous actions that need to be taken: the construction of mass deacidification facilities, the promotion of microfilming materials, the maintenance and improvement of environmental conditions, the preparation of various guidelines, the national planning of preservation (as a national leader and as promoter), the dissemination of acid-free paper, and the improvement of photoduplication machines.

As a member of the world community, NDL may need to be one of the regional centers of the Preservation and Conservation Program of IFLA.* Needless to say, NDL needs to engage actively in any program on materials preservation by coordinating as well as cooperating with countries in Asia and the rest of the world. The question of materials preservation is an old problem, but a renewed concern for all of us. Uniting with other countries of the world, we are determined to deal with this giant problem of materials preservation.

---

*Editor's note: NDL in fact assumed responsibility as the Asian regional preservation and conservation center of IFLA in early 1990.

Appendix

Materials Deterioration Survey at NDL (Survey Date: September–October 1983)

Table A1. Subject of Survey

Materials	Date of Publication	Volumes
Japanese books (excluding traditional books)	1870–1969	2,067 v.
Foreign books	1810–1969	1,078 v.
Japanese periodicals	1870–1980	56 t. 1,026 v.
Foreign periodicals	1660–1980	42 t. 1,029 v.
Legal & parliamentary materials	1820–1980	10 t. 248 v.
Total		5,448 v.

Note: Among Japanese and foreign books, the following categories of books are excluded: (1) books in circulation in the NDL classification general collection; (2) oversized books.

Table A2. Paper Deterioration Standards

		Status of Paper Deterioration	Standard Grade
Degree of Deterioration	Excellent	Excellent condition	4
	Good	Flexible, folded but no mark left	3
	Fair	Folded and folding mark left	2
	Brittle	When folded easily broken	1
	Very brittle	In process of crumbling to pieces	0
Color	Color faded		0
	Color faded severely		-1

Source: Standard used by the University of Michigan Library Survey

Table A3. Results of Survey (Number of Materials in Volumes)

Degree	Fair	Brittle	Very Brittle	Total
Japanese books	286,500	33,600	0	320,100
Foreign books	90,600	24,500	1,200	116,300
Total	377,100	58,100	1,200	436,400
Japanese periodicals	66,000	2,800	300	69,100
Foreign periodicals	40,000	3,100	300	43,400
Total	106,000	5,900	600	112,500
Grand Total	483,100	64,000	1,800	548,900

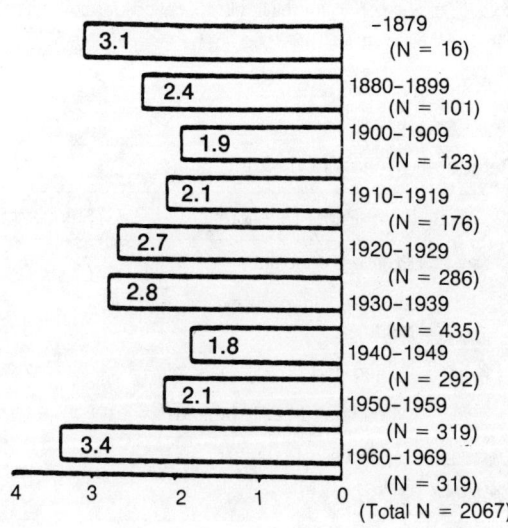

Paper Deterioration by Year (by Average Grade Points)

Grade	Period	N
3.1	–1879	16
2.4	1880–1899	101
1.9	1900–1909	123
2.1	1910–1919	176
2.7	1920–1929	286
2.8	1930–1939	435
1.8	1940–1949	292
2.1	1950–1959	319
3.4	1960–1969	319

(Total N = 2067)

Figure A1. Japanese books

Paper Deterioration by Year (by Average Grade Points)

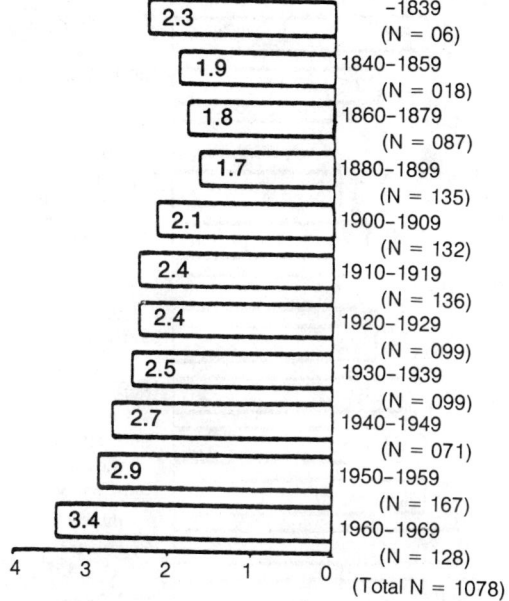

Figure A2. Foreign books

Paper Deterioration by Year (by Degree of Deterioration)

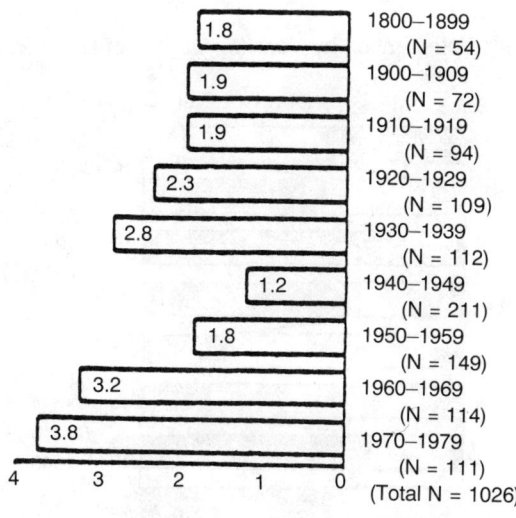

Figure A3. Japanese periodicals

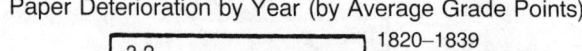

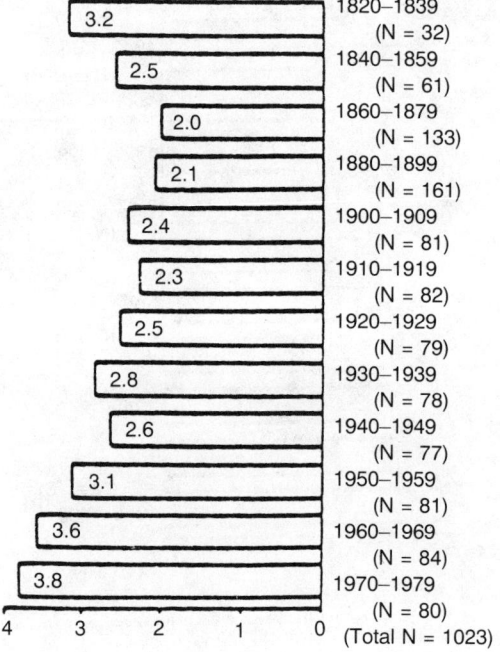

Figure A4. Foreign periodicals

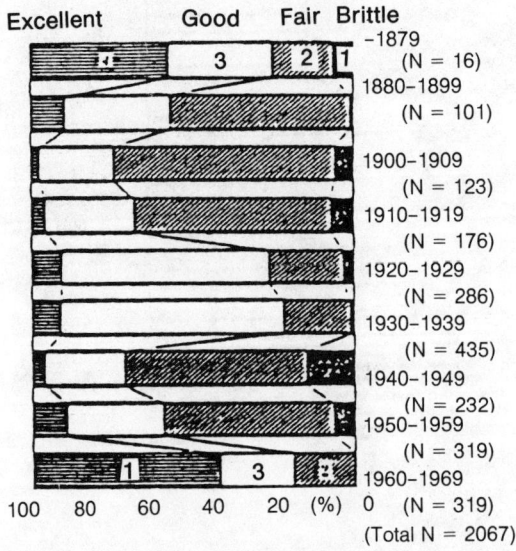

Figure A5. Japanese books

THE NATIONAL DIET LIBRARY   69

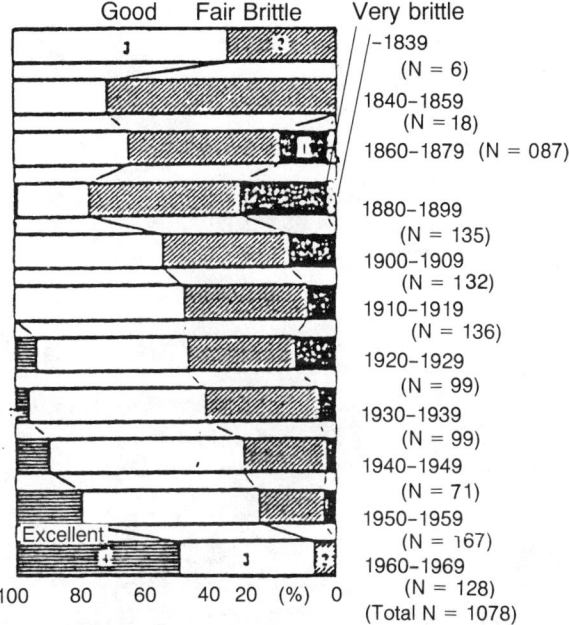

Figure A6. Foreign books

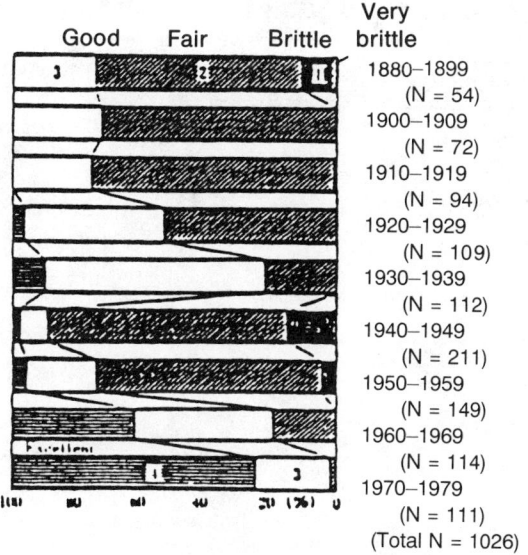

Figure A7. Japanese periodicals

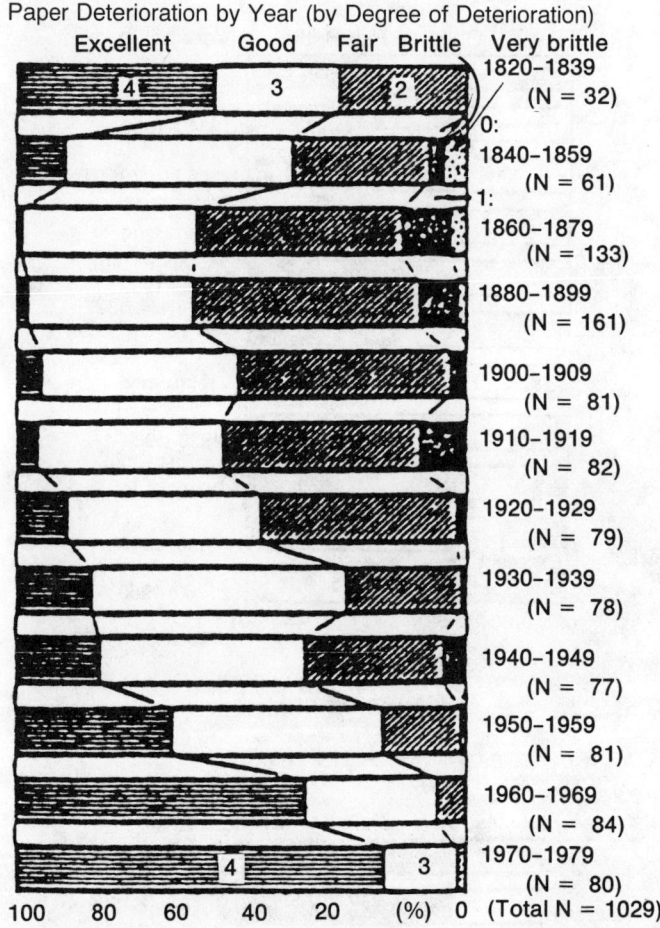

Figure A8. Foreign periodicals

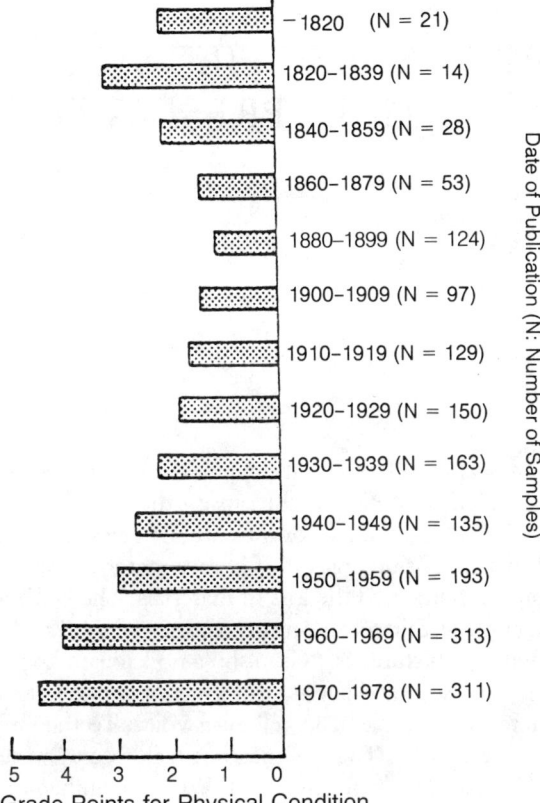

Figure A9. University of Michigan Library Survey

OPTICAL DISC FILE SYSTEM AND MATERIALS PRESERVATION

by Masatoshi Shibukawa

Until a few years ago I was indifferent to the problem of the preservation of library materials. Whatever the cause—the use of acid paper, or damage to books by frequent use, or the natural deterioration of materials—I believed that the disintegration of library materials was inevitable.

Of course, I lamented the loss of materials. The famous phrase at the beginning of the thirteenth-century classic the *Heike Monogatari* (The tale of Heike), which reads, "Gion shoja no kane no koe, shojo mujo no hibiki ari, shara soju no kane no iro, josha hissui no kotowari o arawasu [At the Jetavana Temple, The bell gives voice, To the impermanence of all. As it reverberates, That the pairs of teak trees, In the Hue of their Flowers]"* was always on my mind. Whether human or animal, every creature comes into being, lives, changes, and disappears. These four stages are the natural truths of existence for all beings, the only variations lying in the realm of time.

Librarians recognize the importance of the problem of preservation, and their efforts to retain library materials for future years are similar to those of doctors endeavoring to develop medical technology and disseminate information on the public health, so that the lives of human beings may be prolonged. As a member of the university-library community engaged in administration, I now take a serious view of the problem and give high marks to those who have been endeavoring to solve the problem. However, at present I cannot but hesitate on whether to invest substantial funds as well as to invest the wisdom and efforts of professional staff on this issue. University libraries are faced with a

---

*Translation in *The Princeton Companion to Classical Japanese Literature* by Earl Miner, Hiroko Odagiri, and Robert Morrell (Princeton, N.J.: Princeton University Press, 1985), p.163.

change of direction and are confronted by many problems today. Under these circumstances, it is difficult to obtain a consensus among university administrators.

As a librarian disengaged from the responsibilities of administration, however, I have a different view. As one who has received professional library training under the basic concept of "living with books" and has worked in the library for a quarter of a century, I have a strong sense of the mission of libraries. I am not certain, however, that I will be able to deal with the problem of materials preservation because it is not my area of primary interest, so I am lacking basic knowledge. Without a doubt, however, there are some librarians in Japan who are seriously engaged in this problem of preservation.

Individual efforts have played an important role in every aspect of the development of Japanese libraries. A collective power has solved numerous problems whenever large research and development projects were not possible.

Often small groups of individuals foster the awareness of a problem. These groups investigate and study the developments of problems in other countries. They apply the knowledge they gain to their own libraries. Although it may be a microscopic experiment in a library, it is not an easy task for them to solve. If the experiments prove to be successful, it may impact other libraries. Soon many libraries adopt the results of the experiment, and if successful, the original experiment may be established as a standard measure. In the development of preservation, such individual efforts have been an important factor in Japan.

I am delighted to note that there is every indication that a cooperative research project on preservation is being considered in Japan. The implementation by cooperation among university libraries is finally coming to being. Japan hopes to carry out preservation as a national policy. The National Center for Science Information System was established in accordance with national policy. Preservation is a national issue in the United States, and the preservation of materials has commenced not only in the library community but also among local historical societies and archives.[1] In Japan as well, preservation must be an urgent agenda for library cooperation, and must be considered a social concern by the general public. It is necessary for us to gain the cooperation from all groups concerned with this problem and also from the business and industrial groups.

New Media in Materials Preservation

We have had micrographics technology (microfilming) in which original materials are converted to another medium as one method of preservation. This is the traditional technology. Microfilming, in terms of information processing, is the photographic reproduction of writing, printing, and drawings page-by-page (or sometimes two pages at one shot). But this is not the kind of new technology that we wish to discuss at this conference. A new concept of collecting, classifying, storing, retrieving, and disseminating recorded knowledge in all of nature has been developed in recent years. Electronic engineering expedited this development. This advanced technology has made possible the preservation of materials as an alternative medium. Is this new technology better than the old?

Not very long ago, we at the Keio University Library had occasion to discuss the future of card catalogs. One of the reasons was our concern for space, and another was our expectations of switching to machine-readable catalogs. At the Keio University Library we had to discard the card catalog system as did many university libraries in the United States. One way to solve the problem of space was to switch from card to book catalogs such as those produced by G. K. Hall Company in the United States. In this process we microfilmed the cards, reproduced them, and bound the resulting volumes. However, we are in the new age. We needed to investigate the possibility of solving this problem electronically.

To build a catalog database by use of digital technology is logical for the future. However, in our judgment, the environment to switch to computer cataloging earlier was not appropriate for financial and technological reasons. While we were investigating alternatives, a salesman visited us to sell his company's optical disc filing system. There was, interestingly, a gap between the perceptions of the high-technology manufacturer's sales pitch and the consumer's sense at that time. It seems to me that the perception gap was especially conspicuous between the high-technology information processing devices and the actual equipment needed by the library.

The young salesman pursued the concept of high-technology equipment for the processing and maintenance of documents in the library's administration. While he was explaining the use of the equipment for office use, I mentally applied the high-tech equipment for the use of library services. He was not aware of what I was thinking of at that time. Needless to say, the manufacturer was not familiar with the library and its services or where high-tech equipment could be used.

Nevertheless, at that time I conceived the notion that optical disc technology could be utilized for cataloging purposes. Optical technology is primarily electronics technology and is different from machine-readable cataloging. It does not require the coding of data for the preparation of a catalog substitute; all that is needed is the inputting of the catalog card image itself into an optical disc. (In practice, we mounted four cards per page of A4 size paper to each image.) This is a different method from the experiment done by the Library of Congress.[2] This is a new idea of recording and storing information on this new medium, and I had hoped for its success.

However, the Keio University Library has not yet introduced the optical disc catalog. The major reason is simply the cost. An optical disc file system including the necessary minimum equipment costs at least Y21,000,000 ($168,000) to buy, and Y4,500,000 ($35,000) a year to lease. In addition, an estimated Y950,000 ($7,600) a year is required for maintenance. Furthermore, we were concerned with the initial cost including personnel cost of producing the optical disc catalog.[3] Whether this amount is high or low is premature to say because needs and efforts for the solution of the problem have to be taken into consideration. In addition, there are technical problems still to be solved, especially vital issues in the retrieval system.

If and when we change our card catalogs to optical disc catalogs, our basic assumption is that the optical disc catalog must be equipped with an easy and simple information retrieval system. In order to achieve that end, it is necessary to build a new retrieval system step-by-step. The traditional system was acquired through experience. Whether the method begins with author, title, or subject, it is recognized as a simple method. Therefore, it is a question of how to replace the old system with the new. It was a difficult task for us to explain the simple task of traditional retrieval systems to the manufacturers. Unless the system is understood by them, we could not expect the manufacturers to design the new system. I feared then that they would be unable to accomplish the task.

A few years have passed since then. I do not know how the technology has improved. During the intervening years, the general attitude of replacing the catalogs with computer products has improved at the Keio University Library. I am not sure of the future possibility of cataloging by optical disc technology. Given the theme of optical disc technology for this conference, I hope to change from photocopying and printed materials to optical disc materials. Following is a report of the findings of the preservation of materials by optical disc.[4]

Optical Disc File System[5]

OPTICAL DISCS

In general, nontechnical terms, optical discs may be described as follows.[6] First, the form of the optical disc is like a phonograph record.

The circular substrate is made from an alkyl resin or glass-coated film made of tellurium oxide or an amorphous metal. The metallic film is the memory core.

Inputting is accomplished by taking graphic images obtained by electronic text scanning and transferring the images to the metallic film through lasers. In principle, the images are fixed by creating points (pits) through the laser operation, digitizing the groups of points, and recording them as numbers. To read the images on screen the stored numbers are translated into images. There are three optical storage systems: the first two systems can be used only to read stored data and write new data; previously written data cannot be erased. The third system is the erasable optical disc. Though the storage capacity varies by size (discs are produced in diameters of 13, 20, and 30 centimeters), it is possible to store some 16,000 to 100,000 pages of 4A size paper documents, and data can be accessed rapidly.

Optical disc technology has numerous capabilities. It is capable of storing large quantities of information in a compact space. Nearly instantaneous retrieval and display of information are possible. It is capable of organizing data by designing an image-editing drive unit. Furthermore, the data stored in optical discs may be transmitted to distant places by linked facsimile transmission, host-computer, and local area networks. The technology may be used in a network of computers to store all kinds of forms and records which can be retrieved and reproduced on many different peripherals in the network.

This brief description of optical disc technology may provide a better assessment of the application of the new technology to library services and preservation. It may be that this optical disc technology, among many new technologies, may substitute for—may serve better than—microfilm as a means of preservation and providing access to a variety of collections.[7]

As I mentioned earlier, optical disc technology has three distinctive types of systems: *analog*, which is capable of reproducing information; *digital*, which is capable of adding digital information, and *erasable*, which is capable of erasing information. The first type, analog, is known to librarians as video disc or compact disk. The two are commercially available as well as acquired by libraries as library materials. Also, analog is widely known as CD-ROM (compact disk–read-only memory) for the purpose of storing voice and visual image by digital codification. CD-ROMs have also been recently sold commercially as electronic publications. It is the sign of future development that the optical disc may replace the use of commercial microfilm widely used for the preservation of newspapers, magazines, and old books.

Briefly, the second type, digital, is a system capable of adding information only once while in use, and information can be reproduced at any time. However, it has the limitation in that the reproduction must be done at a stationary position like that of the microfilm machine. As long as the machine is equipped with this feature, the optical disc machine can be utilized in the library for the reproduction of newspapers, magazines, and old books. The third type, erasable, is a type of optical disc system in which the information in the disc can be erased as from cassette tapes, video cassettes, or floppy disks that we commonly know. However, this type is not yet commercially available.[8]

In reviewing the development of new technologies relating to information processing, I believe that the optical disc can be a new medium to replace microfilms for the purpose of preservation of materials. Especially among the three types, the digital system, capable of adding information, shows promise as a medium because codification is not required and a full text can be transmitted.

ELECTRONIC FILE SYSTEM

The electronic file system is a compact work station similar to a personal computer which can be placed on desks. The application of this system varies widely, from office document management to complete electronic information processing systems. One of its special features is its ability to read letters of documents, diagrams, and images, and record them as images. The operation of this system is as simple as operating the existing photocopying machine. In other words, this is a convenient office machine for copying and filing images. Furthermore, the system accumulates information of several thousand pages by using the optical disc as a medium for the image file. At the same time, it has another special feature of quick retrieval capability, if necessary.

The promotional pamphlet of the electronic file system of Toshiba's TOSFile says that the system is, in principle, a simple operation.[9] Although major electronic products and office automation equipment manufacturers in Japan have produced optical disc file systems, as shown in figure 1, and have sold them commercially,[10] the systems are basically the same. All have identical designated operational parts on the equipment but with different names.

First, the system has a device which reads the graphic image, automatically transforms it into digital data, and inputs it into the optical disc. The device is called the phase scanner in TOSFile. It takes two steps for the reading of original documents: first is the book mode input and second is the automatic paper supply input. Regardless of the size of paper, A3, A4, B4, and B5, the document is automatically input in the same size or reduced size. At the time of input it is possible to allow for

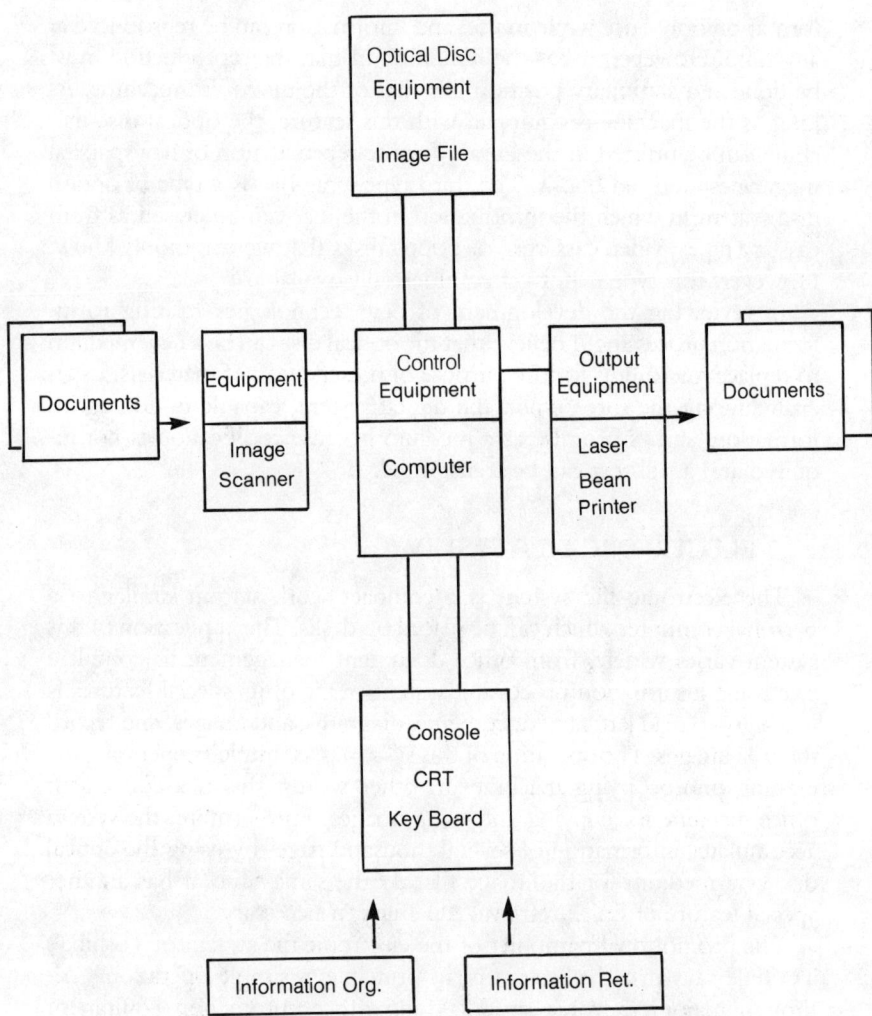

Figure 1. Structure of electronic file system.

variations in the darkness of the printed text by setting five gradations of darkness, as well as a setting for resolution.

The function of output equipment is to print the image stored in the optical disc, and the hardware is equipped with a laser printer capable of high definition printing. Paper in A3 and A4 sizes is standard; when larger papers are required for printing, adjustments can be made by replacing the part with optional hardware. The console is composed of display and keyboard devices used for image display and operations guide. The display is equipped with parts to read vertical legal document lettering. In the case of TOSFile, the 17-inch vertical part is equipped with monochrome adjustment and tilt swivel, which function to read the screen correctly. The keyboard is designed according to Japanese Industrial Standard (JIS) specifications.

The control hardware consists of a microprocessor system, image processing system, eight-inch floppy disk, and magnetic equipment. The control hardware is also equipped with a microcomputer so that it can be expanded to interface with outside systems, such as a host computer and a facsimile transmitter.

The optical disc is the heart of this system, and its capabilities are to input an image into an optical disc and reproduce it through a retrieval system. Because the image is recorded by electronic signals, it is possible to transmit the image by facsimile communication as well as to engage in remote operations. The optical drive unit in TOSFile uses an optical cassette which is a part of the optical disc. When the drive unit is inserted into the system, the system is automatically set.

ELECTRONIC FILE OPERATION

The operation of transmitting printed texts to optical disc in the electronic file system is a simple one like operating a photocopier. Moreover, once you become accustomed to the system, it is as easy to retrieve information stored in the optical disc as it is to obtain microfilm information through a microfilm reader printer. The basic operation is done in the following manner:

Input of Image Information

First, the optical disc is inserted into the optical-disc drive in exactly the same way one would insert a compact disk into a player. Next, the image information input mode is set. For instance, in inputting large volumes of images as in the case of books and periodical articles, one can set the device for continuous feed of the text being scanned.

In order to systematize information to be stored on optical disc, one must select the predetermined menu frames where the images are to be stored. There are four frames in TOSFile: cabinet, binder, document, and page. Following the file distribution system, necessary data in the form of key words are input at this stage. (For example, in the case of materials input, bibliographical data, classification number, and subject heading are input.) The special feature of the electronic file system in which images are transferred to optical disc electronically lies in this step and differentiates it fundamentally from a microfilm system.

Once the input of the retrieval key is completed, the rest of the operation is easy. The image which is information—namely, materials to be printed—is set on machine-readable equipment and is stored on optical disc. Finally, the images are registered according to the established procedures and the input operation is completed.

Retrieval and Output of Image Information

First, an optical disc containing image information is set on the optical disc player. This is like setting microfilm reels in microfilm readers or microfilm printers. Next, the operator selects the retrieval mode from the menu. In TOSFile, direct retrieval, multiple retrieval, and general note directory modes are all preset. Next is a special step which is not necessary for microfilm readers. The steps for the electronic file system are a bit complicated. Be sure that the retrieval key is correctly set and follow the next step properly. It is guaranteed to retrieve needed information. Follow instructions which appear on the screen, selecting appropriate frames accordingly—such as "cabinet" in the case of TOSFile. Once the necessary image code is found, it is displayed on the screen in order to search for the needed image. The image on screen is monitored and the needed image is selected. When the needed information is found, it is printed in hard copy.

POTENTIALS AND PROBLEMS

Whether or not the optical disc as a medium for conversion and preservation of materials can replace microfilm or microfiche will become clear when the special features of both methods are studied.

Simple Input Operation

As has been seen, the operation of transferring the original materials to optical disc is easy and simple. In principle, in microfilming operations, various steps are needed in taking photographs by setting for exposure and focus and then developing the film. These steps are not necessary in the case of the electronic file system. However, it is necessary to register information in appropriate frames at the time of input. One of the most attractive features of the electronic file system is that data is automatically digitized so that manpower is not necessary at the time of input.

It may be true in the case of microfilms that no skill is required to operate a microfilm reader. However, I have experienced anxiety until I see the clear screen while operating a microfilm reader. In the case of the optical disc file system, I simply insert a disc in the disc drive, and the operation becomes routine, although some basic knowledge of procedure is required. Once it becomes routine, one need not fear. At the time of information retrieval by electronic file, one need not overshoot a needed screen or adjust the margin of the screen as one would a microfilm reader.

Image Retrieval

In order to understand the simplicity of operation for the retrieval of needed information in the optical disc file system, one needs to understand the structure of the system itself. The structure of TOSFile model 3200 is mentioned in the manual as follows:

For the purpose of handling a large amount and a large variety of materials, the model 3200 file system adopted the graduated document management system. The classification system is cabinet, binder, document, and page—the system commonly used for general paper files and here adopted intact. It is a user friendly and easy system. Six different classifications are designated for each key word (title) in TOSFile. The identification of each key word can be designated to fit the user's need.[11]

If the file structure is regarded as being organized as described, the definition of the four tags may be specified with some modification on its use and operation to transfer the contents of rare books and back issues of periodicals to the optical disc. The contents can easily be retrieved, and the texts can be reproduced and read.

How easy is it? I shall give you an example. Waseda University has just begun a project to microfilm Meiji period (1868–1912) publications which are deteriorating in its collection and to publish them in microform.[12] The collection was estimated to contain some 100,000 volumes. The number is about 20 percent of the total books published during the Meiji era. These books will be grouped by subjects. The project is planned to be completed in ten to fifteen years.

Now, suppose this project were to be carried out using optical discs and the electronic file system. The first priority is to determine the file structure in the electronic file where the texts are to be stored page-by-page by the project. As mentioned earlier in this paper, when discussing file structure, the key word for a given cabinet in which a group of materials is organized by subject is the output itself. The binder key words are the titles of books or periodicals. In the document the table of contents or the title of an essay or article in the book or periodical are input, and with page the pagination of the article or essay is input.

I suppose the establishment of the key word in the case of library materials would not be an easy task, but it is the first priority in proceeding on a project. Once the key words are set, each material is input accordingly into the databases of respective key words through keyboards. Information is stored in respective data frames, and the bibliographical information can be seen on screen, and the texts can be reproduced, as needed.

Thus, the full text of Yukichi Fukuzawa's *Buzen bungodo fushin no setsu* is stored in the cabinet whose subject is *shinbun hodo ronsetsu* (newspaper news, editorials), in the binder labeled *Kotsu* (transportation), in the document labeled *Yubin hochi* (postal service), and paginated as *Meiji 7-nen 11-gatsu 17-nichi* (November 17, 1874).

Image Editing

It is possible to make the inputting and outputting more convenient by connecting TOSFile model 3200 with an image editing terminal. This terminal is optional but equipped with the unique capability of editing and processing images and creating a new document from clippings and extracts of newspaper articles and periodical texts which are stored in optical disc. It is said to have the following features.

Fukuzawa Yukichi's *Buzen bungodo fushin no setsu* was written in the early Meiji period. In this short essay, he suggested a concept of information very similar to the use of the term today. He was the first Japanese to advocate understanding information correctly and to provide a variety of ways to distribute information, since information was vital to building a modern nation.

He translated the Japanese word *joho* as "information" and explained the nature of the word in various ways. If we are able to design the image editing terminal just described equipped with appropriate file components, which store all data of his works on information, we would be able to see them on screen and store them in a new database. Likewise, if we input all relevant data on information from his other works such as *Meiji 7-nen 6-gatsu 7-ka shukai no enzetsu* (Speech delivered at a meeting held on June 7, 1874), *Gakumon no susume, shohen* (An encouragement of learning, first edition), *Gakumon no susume, 2-hen* (*An encouragement of learning,* second edition), and *Minjo isshin* (The revitalization of the people's mind), then we would be able to read his many texts on screen and study his thinking on information.

Retrieval and image editing capabilities are special features of optical disc files, which have computers at their very core. These special features provide new conveniences which traditional microfilm machines cannot provide.

Information Accommodation Capability

How much information can be stored on an optical disc? In the case of 35-millimeter (mm.) microfilm, it is generally known that the length of a reel is 100 feet, containing 800 exposures. Normally a reel may contain 1,600 pages if each exposure covers two pages. On the other hand, one 12-inch optical disc would be able to record 80,000 documents of A4 sized paper. It can accommodate about 50 times more documents or pages than microfilm.

Now, the microfilming project of Meiji books involves some 100,000 volumes of books. Provided an average number of pages per book is 200 pages, the total would be 20 million pages. If the project is done on 35mm. microfilm it would require some 12,500 reels. If it is done on 12-inch optical discs, the project would require 250 discs. Space needed to store these microfilm reels or optical discs is self-evident—clearly the optical discs are advantageous compared to microfilm reels.

According to the recent brochure of TOSFile, the accommodation capacity of the file system to which the basic system can be linked with at least two drive units is not enough to cover 250 discs. A high-speed automatic-changer optical-disc drive unit that can accommodate 25 discs has recently been developed. Therefore, ten high-speed drive units linked with the expanded system to control the host computers would be able to cover an electronic library holding the 100,000 books of the Meiji collection. Needless to say, appropriate funds are needed to build such a library. This is a trend for the future, not only for the purpose of materials preservation, but also for the purpose of collection development, maintenance, and services.

Costs

As I have discussed earlier in this paper, the estimated cost of an optical disc system including necessary hardware (file controller), two single disc decks, two 80-megabytes (MB) expanded retrieval hardware, two 17-inch retrieval terminals, floppy scanner, and a laser beam printer is Y21 million ($168,000), (and Y4.5 million [$35,000] a year for a five-year lease). In addition, Y950,000 ($7,600) a year is needed for maintenance.[13]

There are thirteen manufacturers in Japan who sell optical file systems commercially today. The cost of a small system is about Y4 million ($32,000) and of a medium-scale system, Y13 million ($104,000). In England, for instance, the product manufactured by Philips costs £69,000 ($34,850), and by Tandem £142,600 ($72,000).[14] Except for a large-scale system, the cost of commonly sold systems internationally is around $30,000 to $100,000 per set, and the price of the system is gradually declining. The cost of a disc, varying in sizes, is between Y25,000 and Y35,000 ($200 to $280).

If it were possible to store the entire Meiji book collection on 250 optical disc, how much would it cost? All systems producers have hesitated to provide estimates. However, our estimate based on the price list of TOSFile 3400 H series is Y200 million ($1.6 million), including all needed equipment such as basic hardware, ten high-speed automatic-changer optical discs, and some optional equipment. In addition, some Y8 million ($54,000) is required annually for maintenance.

Standards, Permanence, and Image Clarity

To discuss the possibility of optical discs serving as a medium for materials preservation, one has to take into consideration certain aspects of the new medium—establishment of standards and permanence, for example—as well as hardware requirements for the optical disc file system, with special attention to the user friendliness of the scanner, console, and printer.

The standardization of optical discs may not be so grave a problem if generalized input and output systems are used—for example, if the TOSFile or some other system is used for the Meiji collection project. The important point is for the library acquiring the collection to purchase the same equipment. When another collection is produced through Panafile, for example, and is commercially distributed in the form of optical discs the standardization issue immediately arises. No library is willing to invest large sums of money to purchase equipment to use the data produced by, in this case, Panafile. Also, if a library uses a medium only for the purpose of material preservation—for example, one library using the TOSFile and the other library using the Panafile—the purpose of library cooperation would be defeated.

The standardization of optical discs has been discussed recently at the International Standards Organization and agreement has been reached on the physical elements of optical discs such as size and mechanical features. However, the essential elements of optical disc drives are still left up to the manufacturers of optical discs[15] and these manufacturers have no definite answer to that question as yet. This development of technology reminds us of the problem we have had with the sizes of videocassette recorders: Beta vs. VHS. If we are unable to develop standards, it is possible that someone will come up to make an effective converter to link both systems together.

The other concern is the question of permanence of the optical disc. This is crucial for materials preservation. It has been said that microfilm (silver halide) can be preserved semipermanently. Although the optical disc cannot last as long as the microfilm it can last over ten years according to the brochure prepared by TOSFile. The life of discs is, however, tested and calculated under severe use conditions. According to TOSFile, it will last 40 to 50 years under normal conditions. Also, the data on optical discs can easily be transferred to other discs, so that the purpose of the materials preservation can be achieved. If that is the case, can the clarity of the image be maintained? The manufacturers of the optical disc assure us that the technological quality of the image will not decrease, because the technology of transfer from one disc to another is different from that of copying by photocopying machine.

Special devices for the maintenance of image clarity are provided on scanners, displays, and printers. However, I am not completely convinced from my personal experiences. For example, I have seen specks of dust and fold lines of papers on the images. These defects may have been caused by the optical processing technology. We do not know whether they are caused by the high performance scanners or are inherent in the optical disc recording principle. I also have noticed varied degrees of clarity of images on screen. The problem is noticeable, especially for farsighted people, on those images stored in reduced sizes. Although this problem is partially solved by using the enlarged screen, it must be answered by an improved scanner or a larger screen display.[16]

Conclusion: Prospects and Problems

The optical disc file system was originally intended for effective office management (space saving and economy by quick and effective retrieval) and is sold commercially. Therefore, when we introduce the system into a library as a medium for preservation we must understand the office documents management system and incorporate this understanding into our own thinking on how to utilize the disc file system as a preservation medium.

The idea of an optical disc file in libraries began as a casual idea, so that it is necessary for us to discuss thoroughly whether it is an appropriate or justifiable concept. However, I will not go into the discussion in detail here. Assuming that the concept is appropriate, I would like to discuss the possibility of the application of optical disc to the library.

SOLUTION OF TECHNICAL PROBLEMS

The development of a file system by optical disc is still in its beginning stages. Therefore, the possible application to a library must be considered while examining the future trends of technical improvement.

Permanence and Standards

Improvements of optical disc equipment and accessory units are necessary. Questions of permanence and standardization are the most important elements insofar as library applications are concerned. Although I have had opportunities to discuss these matters with the manufacturers, I was not able to get any definite answers.

Before we decide to adopt the new technology in libraries, we must first consider the cost. However, the most important factors are permanence and standardization of the optical disc system. Unless the preserved data on discs can be used by all libraries, we will not be able to make intelligent cost effective analyses. This is even more the case if optical discs become the prevailing tool around the world. The amount of material to be preserved is unlimited, and consequently individual libraries must share the burden of creating preservation discs of their own materials.

If these requirements are technically possible, we would seriously consider the replacement preservation of library materials by optical discs, even though the cost might be high. If my estimates for the costs of installing an optical disc system in a library are correct, we need some Y200 million ($1.6 million) initially and an additional Y8 million ($54,000) for maintenance. Then, we can determine the cost of building anew and operating a library in which 100,000 volumes can be preserved and accordingly make comparisons with traditional methods.

Retrieval Systems

Permanence and standardization are the primary requirements for the preserving materials but also a way in which we can proceed with are the conditions for judging cost effectiveness, the first priority in the application of optical discs to libraries is the retrieval system. Unless needed information is obtained effectively, quickly, and simply by the system, it will not be acceptable to users.

Practically no retrieval system is available in a traditional microfilm reader. Retrieval of the data in the microfilm reels usually depends on supplemental tools such as checklists, bibliographies, and indexes prepared for the microfilm collections. On the other hand, if we are to credit sales talk, it is possible to develop an adequate retrieval system for optical discs. However, the retrieval of the term "information" from a vast body of Fukuzawa's works and his many other papers stored on discs is very complicated and requires a sophisticated retrieval system. As I have said earlier in this paper, a file structure composed of cabinets, binders, documents, and pages is inadequate to meet the needs in such cases.

Librarians are responsible for at least one half of the development of technology related to library services. Since the years of Charles Cutter (1837–1903), or perhaps before that, librarians have endeavored to develop methods to organize and maintain library materials effectively.[17] We are still searching today to find a way to improve our methods by computer. I am confident that we know how to succeed. What we have to do with our wisdom now is to develop an effective retrieval system in cooperation with optical disc manufacturers.

MANUFACTURERS AND LIBRARY COOPERATION

If our objective is the preservation by proxy of printed materials, existing file systems are inadequate in terms of the permanence of the medium, standardization, and retrieval. We must first solve the technical problems.

Libraries are powerless in the solution of technical problems. We depend entirely on the ability of the manufacturers. However, their primary concern is whether their investment in the technical developments for libraries is profitable or not. In other words, the question is whether their purpose and ours are identical or not. Would it be profitable for them? I have no answer to that question. I would, however, have to say to them today that it would not be profitable. What we have to do now is to inform them of the needs and significance of preservation by the use of the new medium and to gain their cooperation. We should ask them for their cooperation as partners not only for their technical assistance alone but also for the common purpose of preserving cultural properties.

If cooperation in preserving materials involving manufacturers and libraries can be developed at such a basic level, I believe it would be possible to undertake the joint development of new methods with cutting edge technology on the one hand and know-how in materials use on the other.

WHAT AND HOW TO PRESERVE

The preservation of library materials is our primary concern. There are other professionals who are engaged in the preservation of materials, but the librarians are responsible for the preservation of books. Therefore, we need help concerning new technological aspects of materials preservation, but again this is primarily to be our problem and must be solved by us.

One of the problems is what is to be preserved and how to preserve it. What is to be preserved means to identify books to be preserved among many materials which will disappear after an extended period of time. There are items which need not be preserved or can be discarded. Therefore, our first priority is to identify those materials to be preserved among a large quantity of library materials. How books are to be preserved means not only finding new technologies for the development of preserving materials but also a way in which we can proceed with preservation cooperatively with all libraries.

Yet, an even more important task for librarians is to promote the need for preservation in the public at large. This must stem from our belief that our mission is to preserve our cultural heritage, especially at university and research libraries where books of value to scholarship are held. The public would understand this point. However, understanding alone does not make any progress. Whatever we do requires financial resources. We must continue to seek the understanding of others with the practical assurance of financial assistance.

Finally, I must answer the question of the possibility of materials preservation by optical disc. Should I convert the present Keio University's collection of scholarly journals to another medium and should I propose a project to adopt optical discs to my colleagues and university administrators?

In order to answer that question, I need definite comments and assurance from the manufacturers on points raised in this paper. It may be premature to move from microfilms to optical discs, but I find I cannot discard the concept and consider other possibilities. In fact, some libraries in Japan have already changed their systems to optical discs for the preservation and maintenance of their library materials.[18]

NOTES

1. J. Berry, "Preservation, Priorities, and Politics," *Library Journal*, 112, no.20, (1987):6.
2. B. Aulpor, "An Optical Disc System That Will Allow the Library of Congress to

Print 5.5 Million Catalog Cards 'On Demand'," *International Journal of Micrographics and Video Technology*, 2, no.4 (1982):281–285.

3. W. O. van Arsdale, "The Rush to Optical Discs," *Library Journal*, 111, no. 16 (1986):53–55.

4. Surprisingly, many materials are published in the United States; many works are found in the recent issues of *LISA*. On the other hand, in Japan few works on optical disc as a medium of library are found, although many technical works are on optical disc. (See note 18).

5. Takashi Saito, *Denshi joho kanri shisutemu nyumon—hikari desuku fuairu shisutemu no katsuyo* (HBJ Shuppankyoku (1987)), 202p., "Hikari desuku fuairu shisutemu no genjo," *Nikkei Data Puro OA*, vol. 1, p.1–186, Nikkei Magurohiru, 1987.

6. *Gendai yogo no kiso chishiki* (Jiyu Kokuminsha, 1987), p.905, 939.

7. A. Bender, "Optical Disc Technology for Records Management: A User Perspective," *Electronic Library*, 5, no. 5 (1987): 276–281; C. Chen, "Libraries in the Information Age: Where Are the Microcomputer and Laser Optical Disc Technologies Taking Us?" *Microcomputers for Information Management*, 3, no. 4 (1986): 253–265; D. Finlay, "Archives: Old Records Meet New Technologies," *Administrative Management*, 47, no. 12 (1986): 37–40.

8. *Gendai yogo no kiso chishiki*, 1987.

9. *TOSFile 3200 H shirizu* (Toshiba Denka OA Shisutemu Jigyobu, 1986), p.9.

10. Special contribution article: "Teikakakuka de shintenkai o mukaeta hikari desuku fuairu shisutemu konputa to netto waku," *LAN*, 5, no. 4 (1987): 104–111.

11. *TOSFile 3200 H shirizu.*

12. "Meiji shiryo maikuroka jigyo keikaku no igi to sono keikaku ni tsuite," Waseda Daigaku Toshokan Meijiki Shiryo Maikuroka Jigyoshitsu, *Waseda Gakuho*, 41, no. 10 (1987): 42–45.

13. "Teikakakuka de shintenkai o mukaeta hikari desuku fuairu shisutemu;" "Hikari desuku fuairu shisutemu no genjo," p.3.

14. "Philips Upgrades Document Storage System," *Communication Technology Impact*, 9, no. 11 (1988): 11; "Tandem Announces Optical Storage System," *Communication Technology Impact*, 9, no. 4 (1988): 4–5.

15. Tomio Yoshida, "Hikari desuku memori," *Joho Kanri*, 27, no. 6 (1986): 636; "Hikari desuku kikaku-zukuri ni chakushu," *Nihon Kogyo Shinbun*, (October 27, 1987); "13-senchi tsukigata hikari desuku ISO kikaku kettei," *Denpa Shinbun* (January 4, 1988); "Hikari desuku gokansei kakuho juyo," *Denpa Shinbun* (January 11, 1988).

16. Koichiro Kurahashi, "Daigamen desupurei," *Joho Shori*, 27, no. 7 (1986): 711–717.

17. Masatoshi Shibukawa, *Mokuroku no rekishi* (Keiso Shobo, 1986), 212p.

18. "Sekai de hajimete no kokoromi kobunsho o hikari desuku de hozon e: Funabashi-shi nishi toshokan," *Toshiba TOSFile no Katsuyo shirizu* (July 1986), p.11; "Sekai de hajimete konputa ni yoru bijutsu kenkyu to bijutsuhin no deta banku o kochiku," *Toshiba TOSFile no Katsuyo shirizu* (September 1986), p.11; "The Paperless Plan of the Japanese Patent Office," *World Patent Information*, 8, no. 3 (1986): 210–217; Akira Ito and others, "Tokkyo seido to tokkyo kanri tokkyo joho sono rekishiteki kosatsu," *Joho Kanri*, 29, no. 1 (1986): 73–74; Hiroo Ohara and others, "Kikai kensaku," *Joho Kanri*, 28, no. 11 (1986): 991–1012; Shigeji Sugita, "Kokuritsu minzoku hakubutsukan ni okeru maruchi medea deta besu," *Joho Kanri*, 30, no. 12 (1988): 1131–1141.

THE PRESERVATION OF KNOWLEDGE
Strategies for a Global Society

by Patricia Battin

Responsibility for the preservation of knowledge—the obligation of stewardship for our printed record—is perhaps the most highly revered tradition of librarianship. And that traditional service today, though long taken for granted by our society, is in great jeopardy because of the frailty of acid paper. The threat of slow fires consuming from within the knowledge of our shared cultures is a topic of equal and immense importance to both our countries, as well as the rest of the world.

Probably every medium we have used to record the creativity of the human spirit, since we moved away from stones, is subject to deterioration. Indeed, it seems that the more sophisticated our technology becomes, the flimsier the medium we employ for storage. In our fast-paced throwaway society today, we too often fall into the trap of devaluing the experience of the past—of believing that the explosion of new knowledge is happening so fast it makes the wisdom of yesterday irrelevant to tomorrow.

The importance of our cultural heritage to civilized societies was described recently by Lynne Cheney, Chairman of the National Endowment for the Humanities (a government-funded agency dedicated to the support of the humanities in American society). She emphasized the importance of Alfred North Whitehead's concept of a symbolic code, a shared common knowledge, to the cohesiveness of our society. In Dr. Cheney's words: "While that knowledge must reflect the experience of each new generation, it must also be linked to the tradition that has formed the society.... Without this link to the past, we are unmoored, lacking the awareness of where we are and who we are, which is essential to determining what we, as an American community, shall be. As Whitehead put it, 'Those societies which cannot combine reverence to their symbols with freedom of revision must ultimately decay.'"

The deterioration of acid paper, upon which much of our symbolic code has been printed for the past 150 years, presents us with a crisis of historic and international dimensions. And because we now live in a global village, such a crisis demands global attention.

The fragility of acid paper has created both a disaster and an opportunity of monumental proportions. On the disaster front, we are losing at an alarming rate an enormous portion of our knowledge base—a crisis probably as difficult for the human mind to comprehend as the losing of half a trillion dollars in a few cataclysmic days on Wall Street. Of the 305 million volumes in American research libraries, we conservatively estimate that 25 percent, or 78 million, are brittle and turning to dust because of the alum sizing introduced into the papermaking process around 1850. The alum reacts with the moisture in the air to break down the cellulose wood fibers that give paper its structural strength.

The opportunity lies in the potential of the new technologies, including hard-copy publication on demand from digitized text, not only to access knowledge heretofore unevenly available, but also to utilize new formats to enhance and facilitate new research directions. In a sense, the preservation crisis can serve as a test for reaffirming the importance of broad access to the recorded knowledge of our civilization, for assessing the archival properties of the newer storage media, and for linking our traditional knowledge base to the needs and habits of future scholars in order to protect the symbolic code, the language that is so essential to a cohesive society. In essence, the preservation challenge forces us to redefine our notion of the research library.

If we view our solution to the preservation problem narrowly only as a reformatting operation without regard to the fundamental changes occurring in research and publishing, then we will have failed in our obligations of stewardship. The past will be as lost to the future as if we permitted it to decay. In so many ways, the case of preservation represents a paradigm for the broader set of issues that demand our attention in redefining the library in a society increasingly dominated by information technology. These issues include effective collaborative efforts, knowledge of disciplinary research methods, choice of format, selection criteria, bibliographic control mechanisms, use of new technologies, copyright implications, network standards, compatibility and access, management of systems of distributed access, the role of the private sector, and new financing strategies.

The primary issue in preservation today, it seems to me, is not the exciting potential of the new technologies—and it does appear that to date, the excitement is more about potential than affordable reality—but the critical need to develop and execute the global strategies to use those technologies productively and in a cost-effective manner to provide enhanced access to the knowledge of the past.

During the past thirty years, the American library profession has compiled an impressive record of achievement in issues related to the conservation and preservation of library materials. These efforts include research on paper chemistry and conservation, the establishment of education and training programs for preservation experts and conservators, cooperative filming projects for newspapers and brittle books, the conversion of the National Register of Microfilm Masters into machine-readable format, the development of the online capacity to record both the film and the master negative, and a self-study survey for the assessment of the preservation needs of individual collections. Reflecting the pluralistic nature of American society, these activities have been carried out by a number of independent organizations and research libraries. The list is too long to recount here, and most of the progress has been recorded in the library literature. A few examples will give you a sense of the wide range of efforts and funding sources.

The Library of Congress has provided valuable leadership to the research library community through its National Preservation Programs Office and three program initiatives: (1) commitment to a major microfilming effort of 750,000 volumes over a ten- to twenty-year period; (2) extensive investigation of a process for mass deacidification of acidic but not yet embrittled volumes; and (3) a pilot project for storing and retrieving journal literature on optical disc.

The National Library of Medicine has outlined a program in cooperation with the network of medical libraries across the nation to microfilm the brittle volumes of journals indexed in *Index Medicus* as well as unique collections of historical materials important to medical research and practice. The National Agriculture Library is investigating the potential of electronic-imaging technologies for the preservation of research materials in the field of aquaculture.

With grants from the Mellon Foundation and the National Endowment for the Humanities, the Columbia University School of Library Service created a pioneering educational program for preservation administrators and technicians. The program has graduated 33 individuals to date, 33 more are completing their studies, and 19 new students have been accepted into the program. The success of this program is reflected in the growing number of research libraries with preservation operations, from five in 1978 to 54 in 1988.

The National Endowment for the Humanities has funded a coordinated, decentralized program for filming United States newspapers. The Research Libraries Group, a consortium of 36 research institutions, supports, through private foundation and member institution funding, a series of cooperative microfilming projects to preserve distinctive collections held by the membership. The American Theological Libraries Association has supported, from member subscriptions, a long-term program to film 400,000 deteriorating manuscripts and books in American theological libraries.

For the past fifteen years, the Association of Research Libraries (ARL) has actively promoted an awareness of the problem and the development of preservation activities in its member libraries through its sponsorship of self-studies, emphasis on the need for education and training programs, and recognition of the need to convert the bibliographic records of microfilm master negatives into machine-readable form to permit decentralized filming programs without costly duplication.

In 1984 the ARL membership, in recognition of the increasingly national and international implications of the preservation challenge and the need for coordinating the broad spectrum of existing activities, passed a resolution urging the Council on Library Resources to establish a national strategy for preservation. For the past 30 years, beginning with the support of the Barrow Laboratory's investigations into paper chemistry, the Council on Library Resources (CLR) has actively supported a wide range of preservation activities. In response to the encouragement from ARL, the Commission on Preservation and Access was established in 1986 on the recommendation of the Committee on Preservation and Access after an eighteen-month study sponsored by the Council on Library Resources. The governing body of the Commission, which was initially funded by a number of universities and private foundations, includes university officers and librarians. The goal of the Commission is to foster, develop, and support systematic and purposeful collaboration among all libraries and allied organizations in order to ensure the preservation of the written record in all formats and to provide enhanced access to scholarly information.

It is the intent of the Commission to maintain a small staff and to work through existing organizations wherever possible in order to facilitate and encourage the institutionalization of preservation as a vital component of library and archive operations on a continuing basis. In addition to administrative support, the Commission's program will seek funding of approximately $5 million to $6 million over a five-year period from several sources to support a range of research and demonstration projects, consultants, technical advice, and scholarly expertise necessary for the development of a massive preservation effort with high visibility and widespread societal support. The Commission will promote and encourage efforts to generate approximately $200 million from federal, state, and local governments, universities, and foundations to support the coordinated large-scale production operation necessary to preserve by microfilming or by other technologies the contents of as many as three million seriously embrittled volumes.

We believe that the concept of the Commission on Preservation and Access, a small agency dedicated to the development and coordination of a nationwide program building on the broad range of existing activities of autonomous institutions, is the appropriate strategy for a pluralistic society. We further believe that our strategies for the future must be based on a series of new recognitions, recognitions which challenge our traditional assumptions underlying research library services:

> that the book is an excellent dissemination format for the user and a fragile storage format for the archival steward
> that we will need to accommodate both functions for decades to come
> that enhanced access to knowledge formerly available in geographically distant locations is justification for the federal support of preservation of collections previously financed by public and private universities and research libraries
> that traditional funding formulas are strained and inadequate to support libraries and services as in the past
> that the preservation effort represents an opportunity to begin to change the way we provide information services in our society
> that the redefinition of information services offers an unparalleled opportunity for strategic planning in each institution; there is no longer a university library template which says this is how it should be done.

The magnitude of the costs, the vastly increased torrents of published information we must cope with, the changing requirements of scholars, and the constantly changing technical capacities are such that we need a cooperative effort by institutions which have long valued their autonomy. The technology exists to create a national and international infrastructure that will provide cost-effective and efficient means, although in very different ways, for the storage of, and enhanced access to, our accumulated knowledge. We must now create the international policies and cooperative structures to exploit that technology.

I would like to emphasize the principle of diversity of approach, of the need to develop a national coordinated effort that permits a great number of local options. Because of the diversity of need, the technological volatility of our society today, and the constantly changing information requirements as our researchers continue to extend the frontiers of knowledge, our best strategy in conceiving a national plan is to develop:

- a set of basic principles to ensure the long life of and broad access to the human record
- a set of accepted standards for format, for bibliographic control and retrieval, and for preservation and archival practices
- a series of options for local institutions in determining the shape and character of the local collection depending upon the institution's academic mission and financial resources.

The Commission on Preservation and Access has a dual objective:

1. Establish an international context for a greatly expanded coordinated, collaborative effort to preserve our written record in general and the brittle books problem in particular as a specific initial effort
2. Institutionalize the preservation process in local institutions through the establishment of:
    disaster programs
    climate controls
    training of staff and patrons
    repairs, binding, conservation techniques
    survey and knowledge of the collection and procedures for continuing maintenance
    development of strategies for the shape of the collection in a technological society within the context of a jointly owned "national collection" of master copies in a variety of formats

The Commission's primary objective at present is the establishment of a nationwide collaborative, large-scale filming program to capture the intellectual contents of brittle books in a new master copy format and to create a central distribution center to provide enhanced access to this new national collection. To date, microfilm technology is the only stable technology with internationally accepted technical standards for longevity and access. The important point to remember, for those who do not like microfilm, is that the format of storage is not necessarily the format of use. We expect that the developing capacity to digitize microfilm will be affordable and standardized within a few years. However, I would not be at all surprised if photographic technology, rather than electronic technology, will continue to be the format of choice for archival purposes for quite some time. The costs, rate of change, and lack of standards for hardware, software, and networking capacities necessary for broad access to electronic information may take decades to stabilize.

The Brittle Books program has three major components:

convince publishers to change to alkaline paper
explore the feasibility of deacidification
capture the intellectual contents of a substantial number of brittle books in an archival master copy format

The ultimate vision is the existence of a collective knowledge base, in digitized format, from which individual institutions and individual scholars can obtain a variety of formats to serve their scholarly objectives and programs. Initially, this national collection could take the form of a centralized depository of microfilms with access through online services and efficient 24-hour delivery mechanisms with the expectation that storage, access, and service enhancements will evolve with the increasing use of technology by scholars and expanded availability of network capabilities to the research community.

Because we see the preservation of knowledge as a social issue, not one confined to libraries, the Commission's activities will also include the following:

mobilize the higher education community to recognition of the problem and the need for action
convince publishers to use acid-free paper
involve the technology corporations in developing cost-effective applications of new and emerging technologies
develop productive international connections in order to establish a common database of microfilm masters and programs to share filming responsibilities
support research and demonstration projects to explore the capabilities of the new technologies, reduce preparation and filming costs through automated techniques, and transform our current cottage industry approach to mass production, high-volume microfilming facilities
make preservation a household word and enlist broad grass-roots support in a major national effort to save our heritage and reaffirm our belief in unfettered access to information

At first glance, the prospect of developing a national plan for microfilming millions of volumes in an environment where few institutions are preserving more than 1,000 books a year seems to pose an impossible challenge. However, if we assume that of the estimated 78 million brittle books in our nation's libraries, approximately 68 million represent duplicate copies, we have then reduced our problem to ten million. If we further assume that of those ten million, approximately three million represent an essential core collection to be saved, we have reduced our problem to solvable dimensions. The solution requires a new level of cooperation among public and private universities and research libraries, federal, state and local governments, private foundations, the corporate sector, and individual citizens to combine forces and funds to preserve three million volumes over a twenty-year period.

The national strategy would encompass the following basic principles:

1. Twenty large institutions with comprehensive research libraries would commit initially to filming 7,500 volumes a year for twenty years for a total of three million volumes.
2. The federal government, through the National Endowment for the Humanities, would provide a per-volume subsidy of $60 to cover preparation and filming costs.
3. Participating universities would provide the additional resources necessary through their own budgets and fund-raising from local governments, foundations, corporations, and citizens. Support would also be solicited from nonparticipating institutions that would benefit from the product—a national collection of three million microfilms.
4. Participating institutions, in return for the federal subsidy, would subscribe to the following principles:
use of a simple, standardized online capacity to indicate commitment to reformat
use of a simple, standardized online capacity to indicate existence of master copy
agreement on technical standards for specific format
agreement on minimal standards for bibliographic control
deposit of master negative and printing master with central distribution facility
5. The Commission would oversee the development of a central distribution facility which would provide rapid retrieval in a variety of formats—paper, film, fiche, CD-ROM, magnetic tape, etc. —for purchase or loan. The facility would be supported by all who need access, with customers sharing both overhead costs and transaction fees.
6. A series of disciplinary advisory committees composed of scholars and librarians would be established to review selection criteria and format options.

Although there have been a number of cost studies during the past five years as well as samplings of duplication overlap and inventories of our collections on a national scale, we still lack precise data in many of these areas. We would expect to learn a great deal during the first five years of the project. This knowledge would shape the directions of the second five years. Although cost estimates from the experience of existing microfilming operations in individual libraries range from $40 to $100 per volume, we believe we can reduce that higher figure to $60 by establishing cost-effective regional filming facilities, eliminating the traditional but unproductive "bells and whistles" from preparation procedures, and creating improved online sources for bibliographic searching to eliminate duplicate filming. In addition, we expect to gather more precise data about the overlap in our collections as well as the gaps in our large comprehensive collections, gaps which might well be filled by specialized collections in smaller institutions.

Because of the National Collection Inventory Project, initiated by the Research Libraries Group and expanded by the Association of Research Libraries, we have an excellent tool on which to base our initial selection decisions. We would expect to refine those decisions as we proceed with the help of researchers in the specific disciplines. Again, diversity of approach is essential. In some instances, because of disciplinary needs, the book as artifact must be considered although the Brittle Books program seeks primarily to preserve the intellectual content. Filming projects currently underway have explored the viability of approaches through (1) subject and chronology; (2) title by title; (3) frequency of use; (4) Great Collections; and (5) identification of genres and exemplars. Because our program will take twenty years to complete, it is important that the format we choose will support the information needs of researchers in the 21st century.

For example, a set of specific problems exists in those disciplines, such as art history, biology, and medicine, where knowledge is contained in both text and image. No satisfactory solution exists today; yet we must agree on a choice among unattractive alternatives before the books disintegrate on our library shelves. This issue and other similar dilemmas are typical of the research and demonstration projects to be pursued by the Commission.

And finally, the options provided by a national collection of preserved materials accessible to all will permit individual libraries to develop strategic plans for the shape and services of the local operation. Dependence upon a shared national collection will alleviate increasingly severe space problems, as the rate of publication continues to grow and the availability of building space shrinks. The consequent nationalizing of knowledge will provide the broad, unfettered access to information we see as essential in a global society. Intellectual resources heretofore accessible only in a few limited locations will now be broadly available across the nation as our universities move toward expanded network capacities for students and faculty. The cost of housing rapidly growing but often infrequently used book collections can be effectively reduced through cooperative support of a national collection and the funds reallocated to the support of electronic information resources, the strengthening of distinctive, heavily used local collections, and expanded preservation efforts.

Our success in executing this unprecedented national strategy for a global society will require a high degree of leadership and statesmanship from the library profession as we seek to transform our traditional habits and conventional wisdom to conform to our new realities. We must learn to live comfortably with ambiguity, because insistence on setting specific goals in a constantly changing environment will constantly limit our progress. Over the years, the library profession has developed admirable and enormously productive systems to support international scholarship—we must now take care that we do not permit those systems, of which we are so justly proud, to strangle our strategies for the future.

DATABASE FORMATION AND SERVICES FOR SCHOLARLY INFORMATION IN JAPAN

by Jun Adachi

This paper gives an overview of activities concerning database formation and services in Japan, focusing on activities in Japanese universities. First, recent database-related business in Japan is outlined, then database activities for scholarly information are explained. Finally, issues for expanding the international flow of information are discussed. The flow of information from abroad has surpassed for years the export of information originating in Japan. Recent progress in advanced information and telecommunication systems and the rapid global expansion of business focus our attention on issues of international flow of information. International issues may sometimes be regarded as domestic problems derived from local conventions in each country, such as the immaturity and diversity of information services and systems inside Japan. Thus, those who insist that making domestic systems more systematic is the first and foremost means to resolve international issues may indeed be offering the best solution.

In these circumstances, as far as scholarly information is concerned, the activities to establish a new comprehensive information system have already started in Japanese universities. This is generically called the Science Information System project, and a prominent feature is that university libraries are included as important components. Thus, the philosophy of this project is expected to dominate the future of Japanese university libraries. After explaining overall trends, this paper describes the activities and concepts of the Science Information System. Then, with this as a basis for mutual understanding, this paper offers some topics for discussion from an international point of view in the hope that our activities can become more cooperative and comprehensive.

Database Services in Japan

STATISTICAL OVERVIEW

Although Japan has reached one of the highest positions in the world in terms of electronic hardware production techniques, the level of its activities and services for supplying and disseminating information is said to be ten years behind the United States.

Here I would like to outline Japanese information services in 1987, based on the report of the Database Promotion Center.[1] In 1987 database service revenues amounted to about $880 million, accounting for 6 percent of the total $15 billion of information-related industry sales. This amount is about eight times larger than that of 1975, which translates to an average yearly growth of 20 percent. The sales of database services in the United States were about $4.5 billion in 1987, or approximately five times larger than Japan's.

Commercial databases in Japan numbered 1,483 in 1987. About 80 percent of these were foreign databases and this rate has continued almost unchanged over the years. Until a few years ago the percentage of business databases was on an even par with sci-tech databases. But the number of business databases has grown gradually and is now 50 percent of the total, of which 23 percent are Japanese. The number of sci-tech databases, however, is decreasing, currently to about 30 percent, and of this 14 percent are Japanese. The number of databases in the humanities and social sciences accounts for 4 percent, with only one database in these fields made in Japan.

The percentage of bibliographic databases had been high, but in 1987 it dropped below 50 percent and was exceeded by fact and full-text databases. Although the number of foreign databases in Japan accounts for 80 percent, the percentage of Japanese-made database sales is 66 percent. The three most frequently used databases in Japan are Japan Information Centre of Science and Technology (JICST) science and technical file, Japanese patent information file, and Nikkei economic databases. Popular systems are JOIS, DIALOG, NIKKEI, ORBIT, STN, and BRS in order of precedence, clearly showing that Japanese firms are doing fairly well.

JICST started its commercial services of MEDLARS and its bibliographic database in science and technology on the JOIS system in 1976. Then the Japan Patent Information Organization (JAPIO) began a patent information service on the PATOLIS system. An English version of this patent database is now provided on ORBIT. Database services are most active in business fields and there are many firms like Nikkei (Japan

Economic Journal Corp.) that provide economic and stock market online services.

TREND OF DATABASE SERVICES

An acknowledged characteristic of database services in Japan is their high dependence upon foreign databases. In the United States, the database industry benefited from large government subsidies in the 1960s. When Japan came on the scene later, database services began by using databases that were already commercially available in the United States. The compilation of a database generally requires large initial investment and stable operating funds. However, the lack of initial investment in the database business in Japan resulted in the high dependence on foreign databases that has continued unabated for years.

A notable example of this tendency is the inactivity of database formation in the humanities and social sciences. In advanced technologies and sciences, however, the formation of several databases has been brought about by active research and development. A recent trend is the expansion of the database market into business and securities. This trend is considered to be the result of the rapid global expansion of business. The market for full-text databases, some of which are actually newspaper articles in machine-readable format, is gradually expanding with the development of telecomputing networks.

Because of the lack of large and continuous investment in database formation, online databases in Japan are often provided by small and medium firms. And as these firms offer only a few services, users are forced to select several systems to accommodate all the fields they want to search.

The expansion of database services is supported by the rapidly increasing use of personal computers (PCs) and the advance of telecommunication services. It should be noted, though, that prevailing PC architecture in Japan is different from the de facto standard in the United States. The necessity of Japanese-language capability hinders U.S. software from being distributed in Japan "as is." As to the telecommunication services, the deregulation in 1985 dissolved the monopoly of the telecommunication business by a public corporation and opened the market to competition. Although Nippon Telegraph and Telephone Corp. (NTT) was put under private management, its dissolution was not as complete as in the United States. As a result, telecommunication charges are still rather expensive, compared with the United States. This is a crucial factor which suppresses the expansion of online database business and other value-added communication services. NTT started commercial ISDN services in April 1988. But the increase of ISDN stations has not been rapid, since its service areas are still limited. Thus, the future commercial success of ISDN is unpredictable at present. The deregulation of international telecommunication services is also going on in parallel, and the development of international telecomputing services is expected to expand the use of online databases.

Gateway services for online databases are also not available in Japan although user expectations are high. Meanwhile, domestic telecomputing services for PCs are spreading very rapidly, and the users of several major networks exceeded 100,000 in 1987. Experimental and commercial manufacture of CD-ROM is also going on, but most of it is for dictionary databases at present. In the U.S. market, it is estimated that a considerable portion of online databases will be transferred to CD-ROM in the future. One estimate says CD-ROM will account for 7 percent of the database market in 1991. Since U.S.-made databases are very popular in Japan, the trend of CD-ROM in the United States may be repeated in Japan, but software transplantation may face some difficulties because of the difference of PC architectures.

Database Use in Japanese Universities

The use of databases in universities is rather different from that of business. Database usage in universities is reported in the NACSIS survey of 1987.[2]

Approximately 20 percent of researchers in universities use databases. The percentage of database users is highest in medical fields, where 30 percent of medical researchers use databases. Engineering and science rank second. As to the types of databases, bibliographic databases are most popular, used by 50 percent of users. Fact and full-text databases are not used as frequently as might be expected. Popular databases are CAS, MEDLINE, and INSPEC, in order of usage frequency. Popular systems are DIALOG and JOIS. It should also be noted that many researchers use database services provided by university computer centers. Forty-four percent of database users access online databases for themselves. Thirty-eight percent request retrieval services at libraries. Terminals at libraries are used for access by 49 percent; 38 percent use terminals at their offices. Half of them use PCs.

Nonusers' reasons for not using databases are lack of terminals, of knowledge, of need, and of funds. On the other hand, most database users complain of insufficient funds for database use, and some express dissatisfaction at the quality of databases. The NACSIS survey reveals that the biggest problem hindering use of databases is the shortage of research funds. It can also be noted that database use must be oriented for potential users and researchers unfamiliar with computers. The survey also shows that a large portion of database use in universities is still for the acquisition of bibliographic materials.

Activities for Scholarly Databases

The statistics in section 2 of the survey are primarily concerned with commercial databases and exclude activities in universities. Hereafter, I would like to describe database-related activities by university researchers, university libraries, and academic societies.

FORMATION OF SCHOLARLY DATABASES

Many researchers in universities pointed out the necessity of promoting the formation of Japanese scholarly databases needed for scientific research and instruction. In response to these requests, the Ministry of Education, Science and Culture (MESC) has been supporting researchers' activities and making an effort to increase budgets for database formation.

The MESC policy for database formation has two phases of execution. The first phase is financial support with Grant-in-Aid for Scientific Research for the research group intending to make a scholarly database. Table 1 shows a brief classification of Grant-in-Aid projects in 1988, with a total budget of $2 million. Approximately 70 percent of applications are adopted and the criteria for adoption are as follows:

1. a database that is necessary due to the lack of major databases in the field of research

Table 1. Number of Databases Formed with Grant-in-Aid (1988)

Field	Total	English	Fact
Humanities	12	4	4
Sci-Tech	11	5	10
Medical	8	5	2
Other	14	7	6
Total	45	21	22

2. a database in a field where remarkable scientific progress has been achieved in Japan
3. a database in a field where a Japanese research group or institute is playing a leading role in the world.

Typical examples are a full-text database of Chinese classics, a database of high-polymer material properties, and a speech wave database. In the Grant-in-Aid database project, database formation is closely related with research. This is apparent from the high percentage of fact databases.

Some databases can be completed in a certain period, but most require continuous maintenence. Formation of a large comprehensive database generally require continuous, well-organized activities. However, in the Grant-in-Aid project, a small research group is usually responsible for activities. Therefore, it is rather difficult to form a large database only with Grant-in-Aid support.

MESC understands well the necessity of continuity and comprehensiveness in database formation. Therefore, the second phase of database formation support is conducted with the ordinary MESC annual budget. Table 2 shows the classification of twenty database projects, with a budget totaling $2.5 million. This budget is appropriated to the continuous and steady database formation activities in universities and research institutions. For example, a deoxyribonucleic acid (DNA) database is being made by the National Institute of Genetics, which is one of the international centers cooperating with Genbank of the United States and EMBL in Europe.

Table 2. Number of Databases Formed by MESC Budget (1988)

Field	Total	English	Fact
Humanities	6	1	2
Sci-Tech	9	8	7
Medical	2	1	
Other	3	3	
Total	20	13	9

Database formation at the National Center for Science Information System (NACSIS) is categorized into MESC phase 2 projects as well. NACSIS is expected to make comprehensive or large databases that are difficult to make at an institute in a specific field. The projects at NACSIS as of 1988 are listed in table 3.

Table 3. Databases Formed by NACSIS (1988)

Name	Size
Union catalog of foreign periodicals	90,000 titles/ 620,000 holdings
Union catalog of Japanese periodicals	40,000 titles/ 1 million holdings
Japanese dissertation abstracts	21,350 records (from 1984)
Scholarly database directory	Approx. 500 records
Abstracts of Grant-in-Aid research	13,340 records (from 1985)
Preprint database	Approx. 2,000 records (from 1987)
Full-text database in chemistry	Not yet in service
Disease case database	Not yet in service

ENVIRONMENT FOR DATABASE FORMATION AND SERVICES

The MESC policy for the establishment of a Science Information System promotes research activities in diverse fields through database formation and use in national, public, and private universities. The participants of this system are university libraries, interuniversity research institutes, and computer centers at universities. (There are about 500 universities in Japan, including 95 national universities.) NACSIS, which was established in 1986 as the nucleus organization of the system, will coordinate and plan the whole system.

Projects for library computerization and networking are also included in the Science Information System. Powerful supercomputers are installed in the interuniversity computer centers of seven major universities, and 46 national universities have computer centers for their research and education activities. NACSIS is now constructing a nationwide telecommunication network to interconnect university libraries, computer centers, and other institutions. This network, called the Science Information Network, is actually a dedicated packet-switching network that employs T1-like high-speed fiber optic circuits.

Functions provided on the Science Information Network are as follows:

1. remote login services between computer centers
2. online database access
3. library network applications for cataloging and interlibrary loans
4. electronic mail.

In the near future a medical information network will also be implemented on the Science Information Network to interconnect university hospitals.

The Science Information System is the fundamental framework for database-related activities and services in universities. Researchers engaged in database formation use university computer centers and NACSIS. Compiled databases are put into service at computer centers or NACSIS. The appropriate service location is chosen for ease of maintenance and by characteristics of the database. Figure 1 shows major databases in service at the interuniversity computer centers. Some are foreign databases purchased on magnetic tape and others are made by university researchers.

The implementation of campus information networks is continuing along with the development of the nationwide computer network. Technically, such networks are classified as local area networks (LANs) which interconnect mainframes, workstations, and PCs on campus. These networks also provide facilities on terminals located at researchers' offices for effective and enhanced access to scholarly databases outside the university.

Since the databases compiled at universities are academic by nature, they are supposed to be open to all researchers. However, several restricted databases like medical databases that contain private information are not open to all researchers.

TREND OF DATABASE FORMATION IN UNIVERSITIES

According to the NACSIS survey in 1987,[3] more than 750 databases are being compiled at universities. As to financial support, 74 percent are being compiled from university funds, and 33 percent from Grant-in-Aid. (Multiple answers were permitted in the survey.) Other means of financial support for research also contribute to the formation activities. As to the fields of databases, 63 percent are science, engineering, agricultural, and medical databases. The largest database type is numerical, accounting for 52 percent. English is used as a description language in 67 percent of databases. Databases that are open for researchers are 51 percent, but in many cases, use is restricted to a closed research group or people inside the university. As to computers used for database formation, 43 percent are PCs and 42 percent are mainframes.

FEATURES OF DATABASE-RELATED ACTIVITIES IN THE SCIENCE INFORMATION SYSTEM

The features of the activities under the Science Information System are summarized as follows:

1. The activities are directly related with advanced research in universities. Computer centers and libraries are the facilities which effectively support researchers' database formation activities.

Kyoto University

CHINA-1	Fact, Chinese history
ERIC	(US)
IDEAS	Fact, DNA, and protein
INSPEC	(US)

And 34 other DBs

Osaka University

PROTEIN-DB	(US)
GEODAS	Fact, Earth sciences
JSR	Bibliographic, Scientific films
BIOSIS	(US)

And 8 other DBs

Nagoya University

SVDBANK	Bibliographic, Vibration
PLATE	Bibliographic, Plate theory
FEMBANK	Bibliographic, Finite element method
SECND	Bibliographic, Material sciences

And 18 other DBs

Hokkaido University

FRM	Bibliographic, Derivatives
HGEN	Fact, Genetics
NRDF	Fact, Nuclear reaction
SESS	Numerical, USSR economic

And 9 other DBs

Tohoku University

METADEX	Bibliographic, Metallurgy, (US)
C-13NMR	Numerical, ^{13}C NMR
SEDATA	Numerical, Solvent equilibrium
QCLDB	Bibliographic, Quantum chemistry

And 3 other DBs

Kyushu University

Japanese word dictionary	Dictionary
Thomas Mann file	Full text
GENEDB	Fact, Nucleic acid
RAMBIOS	Bibliographic, Molecular biology

And 7 other DBs

University of Tokyo

CASearch	(US)
MOL	Fact, Chemical material dictionary
XDC	Bibliographic, Crystallography (UK)

And 13 other DBs

NACSIS

Life Science Collection	Bibliographic, (US)
MathSci	Bibliographic, (US)
COMPENDEX	Bibliographic, (US)
Ei Engineering Meetings	Bibliographic, (US)
Harvard Business Review	Full text, (US)
ISTP & P	Bibliographic, (US)
EMBASE	Bibliographic, (Netherlands)
SciSearch	Bibliographic, (US)
A & H Search	Bibliographic, (US)
Japan MARC	Bibliographic, (Japan)
LC MARC-Books	Bibliographic, (US)
LC MARC-Serials	Bibliographic, (US)
Union List of Japanese Periodicals	
Union List of Foreign Periodicals	
Grant-in-Aid Report Abstracts	
Japanese Dissertation Abstracts	
Preprint Database	
Scholarly Database Directory	

Figure 1. Databases available at Japanese universities. DBs without country name are made by Japanese researchers.

2. The whole system is intended for the integration of diversified information services. Instead of installing one service system for each database, various information services like database, library computerization, and electronic mail are being integrated into one comprehensive academic system.
3. The system aims at resource-sharing among universities. One of the purposes is to store information as resources shared among researchers, not only in scientific and technical fields, but also in the humanities and social sciences. For this reason, several foreign databases are introduced in the Science Information System to provide information as inexpensively as possible for common use by university researchers, instead of using expensive commercial services.

The Science Information System supports research activities in various fields by sharing scholarly information and materials and effectively disseminating information. Networking is one of the crucial factors in achieving this objective.

SERVICES PROVIDED BY NACSIS

NACSIS is the main institution for the formation and dissemination of scholarly information in Japan. Here, I would like to briefly describe the major database activities executed by NACSIS.

Database Directory and Other Reference Databases

NACSIS compiles databases commonly needed by various research fields. A typical example is a database directory. This gives profile information of scholarly databases being compiled or in service at universities and assists researchers in getting information about various activities of the Science Information System. The database of abstracts of Grant-in-Aid research gives the latest information concerning research supported by MESC Grant-in-Aid, which includes an outline of the research, paper references, and names of researchers. MESC Grant-in-Aid is the largest financial support for research in Japanese universities and covers all research fields. This database includes reports of ongoing research and English information as well. The *Japanese Dissertation Index* is also compiled by NACSIS and includes abstracts of doctoral dissertations presented at Japanese universities. All these NACSIS databases are quite useful for getting information on the actual status of research activities at Japanese universities.

Union Catalog Databases

One of the features of the Science Information System is that database services are carried out in regard to university library activities. Union catalog databases formed by the NACSIS cataloging system on the library network are provided online for researchers as well. These databases are fundamental information resources for accessing materials stored in university libraries and are especially helpful when used with other bibliographic databases.

Cooperation with Academic Societies

Another feature of NACSIS activities is database formation in cooperation with academic societies. In Japan a large academic society covering several related research fields has not developed, unlike the United States. Instead, many small and medium societies exist in a narrow field. In these circumstances, NACSIS started to compile databases requested by researchers in cooperation with several groups of academic societies. For example, in the chemical field, a full-text database of English papers of scientific periodicals is being compiled, applying computer-typesetting data. In computer science, electronics, electrical engineering, and control engineering, NACSIS is trying to provide the latest research information by compiling a preprints database of annual meetings and symposia. People in medical fields plan to form a fact database of disease cases. MESC has been supporting for years the activities of academic societies in various ways to promote scientific research. These activities are one way in which MESC gives support to academic societies.

International Telecommunication Link for Database Services

NACSIS will install an international telecommunication circuit to the United States in January 1989 to interconnect information systems in both countries. The U.S. access point is located at the National Science Foundation (NSF), Washington, D.C., where interconnection of electronic mail and database services are provided. The details of the services are not yet defined precisely, but this link will certainly become an important path between academic communities in Japan and the United States. NACSIS has plans for international links to Europe and Asia as well.

Database Service Issues from International Viewpoints

Interest in Japanese information has been growing in foreign countries. This tendency brought about the international conference on Japanese information that was held in Britain last year. At this conference, issues on the acquisition of information concerning Japanese research and development were discussed, focusing on science, technology, and commerce. The summary report of questionnaires collected at the conference, however, reveals that the biggest problem in information flow is the Japanese language itself. Since the atmosphere of the conference was not political, it was very successful, making it possible to exchange practical analysis and suggestions, including the language problem.

In Japan, foreign languages exert considerable influence over scholarly information in various situations. For example, a library catalog is compiled separately for Japanese and foreign materials. Of course, English is the most necessary tool in all research, and most researchers have taken some measures to obtain foreign information in their school days. Therefore, researchers engaged in database formation consider how to give their databases international characteristics, since academic activities are more or less universal and should not be impeded by languages and national boundaries. This is confirmed by the high percentage of bilingual databases compiled at universities. Meanwhile, there has not yet been any general trend to do supplementary work such as English translation for foreign users in the Science Information System. Instead, it is considered urgent to make Japanese databases more accessible from abroad to the fullest extent. This philosophy appears in the plan for implementing the bilateral link to the United States in 1989. As languages affect not only mutual understanding in cultural matters, but also the coding schemes of data and electronic equipment for character input and output, it will take more time and effort to resolve this difficult problem.

The second problem is the lack of an advisory body to assist potential foreign users in accessing the appropriate Japanese information. This is partly because Japan has no institution with comprehensive information resources like DIALOG and many small and medium database firms exist in each field. Thus, it seems very difficult for foreign people who have little understanding of this situation to access Japanese information. It is very unfortunate for Japan that this has created the misunderstanding that Japan does not have open access to its information services from abroad. It should be noted that an effort has begun to simplify information access for the academic community. For example, NACSIS activities to implement a nationwide information network and compile the database directory, the Grant-in-Aid database, and the union catalog databases are all regarded as providing comprehensive means for accessing Japanese information. However, it should be mentioned here that the Science Information System primarily considers academic communities as its service targets, and it has no commercial services. There will likely be some restrictions on user qualifications in the development of international services because of the different interpretations of academic protocol. It is expected, however, that some practical measures will be taken to avoid such constraints to extend international cooperation between academic communities.

The third problem is that MESC policy tends to focus database formation on some specific research fields. It is also rather difficult to form a large comprehensive database, since a scholarly database is formed by researchers who have research to do. Meanwhile, such research information can be attractive for foreign researchers in the same field. This kind of information is often a numerical or fact database, having universal characteristics without the language problem. Establishment of international communication links will improve the exchange of such research information. In the formation of a large database, redundant activities in the same field should be avoided and the emphasis put on establishing a complementary relationship of practical work. One example is a Japanese group taking part in collecting information originating in Japan for integration with another country's information. In some database projects, such a system has already been adopted.

The last problem is price setting for information services. International telecommunication charges in particular can be the highest barrier because they are expensive. As to services in the Science Information System, where all services are available on a nonprofit basis, a minimum charge is paid by users, since the whole system is provided as a shared facility among academic researchers. Therefore, telecommunication charges are the only barrier to inexpensive services. I expect that competition among communication companies will reduce charges after the deregulation.

Conclusion

Among various database-related activities, the plan for the establishment of the Science Information System is very unique since it comprehensively includes the entire process for the acquisition of original materials, formation of scholarly databases, and dissemination of information. A university library is in a very important position as the body for acquiring information, providing information services, and compiling union catalogs. The Science Information System is a network environment in which a university library develops a new information service for academic researchers. Efforts are accelerating for the achievement of integrated services in accordance with MESC policy. At the same time, checks and review from an international point of view are now required to facilitate the effectiveness of the Science Information System.

NOTES

1. "1988 Database White Paper" (Database Promotion Center, March 1988).
2. "Survey of Database Usage" (NACSIS, July 1987).
3. "Survey of Scholarly Database Formation" (NACSIS, July 1987).

THE ESTABLISHMENT OF A UNION CATALOG DATABASE IN JAPAN
Current Status and Problems

by Eiichi Kurahashi

National Center for Science Information System*
Cataloging System

FUNCTIONS

With the development of DDX (Digital Data Exchange) for data communication in the early 1980s, it became possible not only to interconnect different types of computers located in university computer centers but also to transmit data between computers located far from one another.

It was in this kind of environment that a future-oriented science information system for Japan was studied, and a plan was developed for a system in which the entire country's national, public, and private university libraries and computer centers would be linked in a data communications network.

Driven by the concept of resource sharing, the National Center for Science Information System (NACSIS) was assigned responsibility for three major activities: (1) the collection and servicing of primary information; (2) the establishment of an information retrieval system; and (3) the establishment of databases.

In order to carry out these activities efficiently, NACSIS, established in 1986 as the core facility for the entire country, focused on five major

---

*In the name of the center, and throughout this paper, the Japanese term *Gakujutsu* (officially translated into English as "Science" in the name of the center) is to be understood in the broad sense of "knowledge," since the center provides information services to scholars in all fields of knowledge and not just those in the field of "science" narrowly defined.

functions: liaison and coordination; planning; database services; research and development; and education and training.

Database services, one of the five functions, include (1) information retrieval service, and (2) cataloging support service. The former, called NACSIS-IR, provides information retrieval services to researchers in universities and other organizations using specialized domestic and overseas databases. The latter, which provides cataloging support services to participating university libraries, has begun work on the compilation of a national union catalog.

OBJECTIVES

The responsibility of a university library is to acquire, store, and serve science (i.e., scholarly) information needed for research and teaching. However, the production of information has increased tremendously in recent years, and it has become very difficult for individual university libraries to collect all required information. The purpose of the NACSIS cataloging system is to assist in the cataloging of monographs and serials collected by university libraries nationwide while at the same time developing a national union catalog database through cooperative shared cataloging operations, thereby promoting the shared use of primary information located in the nation's university libraries.

In order to carry out its responsibilities, NACSIS subscribes to LC MARC, Japan MARC, and to as many other bibliographic databases as possible, and utilizes the information found in these MARC databases, thus seeking to lighten the burden of cataloging operations by reducing the amount of original cataloging required in the participating libraries. Even where original cataloging is required because of the absence of MARC records, the cataloging burden for participating libraries is reduced once an original record is input into the system.

Furthermore, participating university libraries do more than merely cooperate in the creation of the NACSIS national union catalog database. They can extract their own bibliographic records from the union catalog and integrate them into their own library's system, and can thus provide service to researchers and students through local OPACs (Online Public Access Catalogs). Thus, the cataloging system of NACSIS can serve two purposes simultaneously: the compilation of a national union catalog database and the reduction of the cataloging burden on individual university libraries.

FOUNDATIONS FOR NATIONAL UNION CATALOG DATABASES

In the past, Japan's national union catalogs were represented by two major printed works: *Gakujutsu zasshi sogo mokuroku* (Union list of periodicals) compiled by NACSIS and *Shinshu yosho sogo mokuroku* (New union catalog of foreign books) issued by the National Diet Library (NDL).

Because of the magnitude of the task, *Gakujutsu zasshi sogo mokuroku* was formerly published in three parts: *Wabun hen* (Japanese-language serials), *Jinbun kagaku o-bun hen* (Western-language serials in the humanistic sciences), and *Shizen kagaku o-bun hen* (Western-language serials in the natural sciences). At present, however, the latter two parts have been combined into a single *O-bun hen* (Western-language serials) volume with machine compilation scheduled for completion in 1988. The bibliographic records of *Wabun hen* (Japanese-language serials) have already been loaded into the database. Hence it can be said that insofar as serials are concerned the work of creating a union list database has been completed and no additional work to construct the database is necessary.

However, the *Gakujutsu zasshi sogo mokuroku* database must be supplemented and revised regularly. In order to make these revisions, a large-scale nationwide survey of holdings and of title and location changes is required. Since this is a very substantial undertaking, in the future NACSIS will gradually move toward a system of online cooperative shared cataloging as university libraries are connected to NACSIS.

On the other hand, the National Diet Library (NDL) has been collecting foreign book catalog cards from Japan's major libraries, compiling and publishing since 1954 ifs *Shinshu yosho sogo mokuroku* (New union catalog of foreign books). This catalog has thus served an important role as a tool for interlibrary loan among university libraries.

However, NDL decided to discontinue the compilation of *Shinshu yosho sogo mokuroku* after the 1987 edition because of the heavy burden on staff time required to compile it manually. NACSIS will therafter assume this responsibility using its national union catalog database.

NACSIS's task of compiling a national union catalog has been well received with high expectations by all members and is expected to play an important role in interlibrary loan among university libraries. It is aimed at developing an online cooperative shared catalog to meet needs in the network age.

In order for the centralized NACSIS cataloging system to operate smoothly, the system must first of all, be designed in such a way that librarians in the participating libraries will find it easy to use. It must, second, be a system wherein participating libraries can efficiently use records produced through cooperative shared cataloging operations.

To create a national union catalog database, the development of a user friendly cataloging system by NACSIS and of efficient university library systems are both vital—the two standing in relation to each other like the two wheels of a cart. The sound development of a national union catalog database is achieved only when both systems are developed simultaneously.

Improvements in NACSIS Cataloging System

CHARACTERISTICS OF THE CATALOGING SYSTEM

The cataloging system was inaugurated by NACSIS in December 1984, thus commencing quite recently when compared to similar services provided by the Online Computer Library Center (OCLC), Research Libraries Group (RLG), Western Library Network (WLN), and UTLAS in North America. Thus it was only natural that NACSIS would aim for the development of technologies and systems newer than those found in pioneering agencies. NACSIS studied the systems of existing information services and introduced the concepts of bibliographic levels* and authority control in order to maintain quality records.

The concept of bibliographic levels provides for the linked cataloging of monographs published in series, with the series title treated as the higher-level bibliographic record and the monograph title treated as a subordinate record. Independent bibliographic records are created for both series and monographs, and the two records are linked. Accordingly a particular volume in a series is linked to that series by its level number, and, theoretically, the records can be infinitely stratified.

In the past, university libraries in Japan normally did not produce multiple bibliographic catalog cards for a single title, and therefore the concept of bibliographic level has led to new experiences in cataloging.

---

* "Level" is used here in an entirely different sense from its meaning in American writings on "full level" and "minimum level" cataloging, where "level" refers to differences in the number of different items recorded for bibliographic entries.

With respect to authority controls, participating libraries are now required to establish the names of authors in standard format and also to link authority and bibliographic records so that all the works of a single author can be displayed through a single search. This again is a new experience for many university libraries since hitherto they have had virtually no experience with authority records.

FACTS ON CATALOG SYSTEM USAGE

As is evident from the foregoing discussion the NACSIS cataloging system, developed on the basis of the experience of pioneering agencies elsewhere, places emphasis on bibliographic precision. However, many participating libraries voiced dissatisfaction over the long periods of time required to catalog individual titles.

The greatest problem, however, has been the low rate of increase in the number of records input into the NACSIS database despite the gradual rise in the number of participating libraries. The reasons may be (1) because catalogers in the participating libraries were not yet accustomed to the new system which had just commenced operations, and (2) since the number of records in the NACSIS database was initially small, the payoff for shared cataloging was not fully evident. It must be said that basically the operational burden borne by catalogers in the system has been substantial.

University libraries in Japan, moreover, had no experience whatever with the stratification of bibliographic records, and practically no experience with authority control. The result has been an increase in catalogers' workload in all libraries.

CHANGES IN THE CATALOGING SYSTEM

In order to improve the system, representatives of the participating libraries consulted with the staff of NACSIS and decided to take two measures to increase efficiency beginning in 1987: (1) bibliographical levels would be limited to two; and (2) authority control work would be optional.

Although the concept of bibliographical level was introduced to the system with much attention—the first time ever in the world—because of heavy workloads created in the participating libraries it was decided to limit the levels to two.

On the question of authority controls, NACSIS adopted a practical method of dividing libraries into two categories: libraries capable of authority control operation, and those unable to do such work.

With these changes, the cataloging time lag was greatly reduced. Together with other favorable circumstances involving the system, the number of bibliographic records input into the NACSIS database has greatly increased. Today, the number of participating university libraries exceeds sixty, the cataloging system has become stabilized, and NACSIS has assumed in name and in fact the appearance of a bibliographic utility.

At the beginning of its operation, NACSIS experienced minor changes in the cataloging system, and it is expected that it will continue to make improvements in order to provide a system easy to use by the participating libraries while it maintains bibliographic precision together with equality in the sharing of workloads.

University Library Systems

PROBLEMS IN THE COMPUTERIZATION OF LIBRARIES

In order to build a national union catalog database through the NACSIS catalog system, it is important to develop efficient university library systems that can make effective use of catalog data created by shared cataloging.

The automation of university libraries in Japan began in the 1970s. Computers of the period were capable only of processing upper case letters of the roman alphabet and *katakana* (one form of script of the Japanese syllabary) so that it was impossible to automate cataloging operations which are at the heart of library operations. Automation then was primarily focused on accessioning, lending, and serial maintenance activities.

With the 1980s, came data communications, the arrival of the network age, the establishment of NACSIS as a bibliographic utility, and the advance of UTLAS and OCLC into Japan.

The greatest difference between the 1970s and the 1980s in library automation was the development of automated cataloging operations. Cataloging was now possible in collaboration with other libraries, and networking became a possibility.

The automation of university libraries in the new age is thus centered around cataloging operations, and linkages between university libraries and NACSIS and the development of OPACs are priority needs. However, library automation concepts planted in the 1970s are deeply rooted in university libraries, and the tendency is still strong to emphasize the lending, accessioning and serial control functions, leaving the automation of cataloging to the very last. The urgent task today is to change this kind of thinking to concepts appropriate to the new age of networking.

One of the characteristics of university library automation, moreover, is the tendency for each library to develop its own automated system.

The reason is that individual libraries, which had developed their own distinctive operational patterns based on their separate histories and scale, simply sought to automate existing manual operations without change.

Accordingly, in automating university libraries, requests were made for major systems changes, or for the development of new projects, as was done by pioneering libraries. Recently, however, computer distributors have not responded to such requests, and have proved unwilling to provide major modifications.

Computer systems should change, reflecting developments in society and technology. But if the current practice of individual libraries requesting individual improvements continues, we will wind up with the creation of a complicated university library system with a host of minor modifications. There is the danger, therefore, that it will become impossible to make fundamental improvements to the system.

Hereafter, in order to create an environment in which the burden of systems development by university library staff members is reduced, and in which systems can be easily improved, it will be necessary at the very least to organize users groups for computer manufacturers, to agree upon common requests, and to construct a common—that is a package—system for all libraries to adopt.

FROM CARD CATALOGS TO ONLINE PUBLIC ACCESS CATALOGS

The card catalog was an epoch-making innovation in the history of libraries since it overcame the deficiencies of its predecessor, the book catalog—that is, lack of currency and difficulties of consultation.

However, in an age characterized by a flood of publications, the card catalogs of large research libraries rapidly increase in size, ease of consultation worsens, the cost of filing cards rises, and because of filing arrearages, it becomes impossible to maintain currency.

The first attempt to overcome these shortcomings was the Computer Output Microform (COM) catalog. The need to compile supplements and the periodic issuance of revised versions were characteristic problems of COM catalogs, but with the introduction of OPACs to libraries as a consequence of advances in computers, it was possible to overcome the deficiencies of COM catalogs. Compared to card or COM catalogs, the

OPAC does not involve waiting for filing or updating. Moreover, for the reader, the OPAC permits retrieval through multiple entries in contrast to the card catalog. It can be said that the dream catalog has arrived.

However, among university libraries where cataloging operations have been automated, many still use catalog cards printed from the database. This is the case even among many university libraries that have already adopted the OPAC system. They continue to print catalog cards for users in their libraries and also for other purposes, and are unable to disassociate themselves completely from catalog cards.

In extreme cases, moreover, some libraries have not adopted the OPAC system and use their computer terminals solely for the production of catalog cards, utilizing the computer solely as a substitute printer. As a result, the burden on computer resources for the output of catalog cards has increased. And since labor costs for output operations cannot be avoided, the whole point of introducing OPAC is defeated.

The greatest advantage of OPAC is the elimination of the cost of filing. So long as libraries continue to use traditional catalog cards, the benefits of automation will not be achieved. It is necessary for libraries to devise ways in which cards will not be used.

COMPUTERIZATION OF UNIVERSITY LIBRARIES

The basic concept undergirding the university libraries network centered on NACSIS involves treating cataloging operations, which are very costly in terms of computer and human resources, as a collaborative shared activity; automating other operations in the individual libraries relating to acquisitions, lending, and serials control, as well as providing OPAC facilities; and integrating a centralized system (cataloging) with dispersed systems (university library system). Taking these actions will bring about realization of an efficient, automated university library network.

The computerization of university libraries must be accomplished in order to successfully establish a national union catalog database through the NACSIS cataloging system. As has been seen, however, the computerization of university libraries today is characterized by (1) priority attention to the automation of loan, acquisition, and serials control operations; (2) the development of unique systems; and (3) an adherence to card catalogs.

Related to these problems are antiquated concepts of library computerization. In Japan the concept of computerizing university libraries on the assumption that they are part of a network centered on the NACSIS cataloging system has just begun to take hold, and librarians remain strongly influenced by concepts of the 1970s.

University libraries of today exist on the basis of accumulations of the past, but in an epoch-making revolutionary age dominated by the computer and telecommunications technology, we cannot simply continue past practices, we must proceed by incorporating the new concepts of the day in order to fulfill the mission of libraries.

Problems of Creating a National Union Catalog

SCOPE

The greater the number of participating libraries the greater is the value of a national union catalog. The number of libraries participating in NACSIS is still small because the center has been in operation only a short time. Several of the major university libraries which contributed to NDL's *Shinshu yosho sogo mokuroku* (New union catalog of foreign books) are not yet participating in the NACSIS program. To increase the number of participating libraries is thus a major task.

Another problem is the fact that participating university libraries are only partially involved—typically with the main library and only some of the departmental libraries participating. This tendency is especially marked in the largest universities and it is the task of NACSIS to encourage entire library systems to participate.

A further question relating to scope is language. The present NACSIS catalog system is unable to handle the Chinese and Korean languages, and it has not yet been decided whether Russian-language data are to be entered in the original Cyrillic script or in romanized form. The treatment of these languages differs from library to library, and some libraries are not registering their works in the NACSIS database. It is necessary for NACSIS to clarify the linguistic scope of the database as well as input (romanization) methods.

There are, moreover, cases in which bibliographic records for books in other languages are not yet being registered in the NACSIS database by participating libraries.

The computerization of cataloging operations is based on the use of the NACSIS cataloging system to create bibliographic records which are downloaded into local OPACs. However, in many university library systems, it is possible to input original cataloging records directly into local OPACs.

Accordingly, we have a system where, if there is little or no consciousness of the importance of participating in the work of creating a national union catalog, the NACSIS cataloging system is treated as a mere tool to produce catalog records for local use, and is used for copy cataloging of simple records, while the product of the burdensome work of original cataloging is input directly into local OPACs.

Since it has been the practice for Japanese university libraries to create catalog records solely for their own use, some time will be required to switch completely from this traditional thinking to the new concept of cooperative shared cataloging. A national union catalog database becomes valuable only when bibliographic data for all materials held in participating libraries is recorded. In order for this to happen, participating libraries must change their mindsets from individual cataloging to cooperative shared cataloging.

RETROSPECTIVE INPUT

The value of a database increases through the acquisition of data on a comprehensive basis. Usually university libraries participating in NACSIS begin by inputting bibliographic records for newly acquired materials. Once the foundation has been laid, however, the input of retrospective records becomes a problem.

The inputting of retrospective records is extremely burdensome if individual libraries attempt to do the job alone. Hence the most economical way to achieve this task is usually to input all the records of a large-sized library, or to input all the records of a union catalog in book form as in REMARC, with participating libraries using the records.

In the case of Japanese monographs, NDL is scheduled to input all records retroactive to 1948 in Japan MARC, with the project to be completed soon. The number of pre–World War II Japanese monographs is not enormous, and so when the retrospective conversion of these records is completed, university libraries will find it relatively easy to convert their older Japanese monograph records to machine readable form.

About one half of all Japanese university library collections consist of foreign books, and it is an enormous task for the libraries to input these retrospective records into the national database.

At present, the major national university libraries have begun to study ways in which they can efficiently input the retrospective records in cooperation with other libraries. They are also studying automatic-card-reading and voice-input methods, but the application of these new technologies may require some time.

On the other hand, a few major university libraries have begun to input retrospective records of their own collections into the national database. It will not be possible for them to complete their projects in a short period of time, and this is one of our major concerns for the future.

DUPLICATION OF BIBLIOGRAPHIC RECORDS

In the process of building the bibliographic database during the last three years of NACSIS, inevitably the problem of duplicate records has emerged. In principle, NACSIS does not permit the existence of duplicate records because the basic idea is to use an already existing record when cataloging into the system, but in reality a number of duplicate records have been input into the database.

It is estimated that about 1 percent of the records are duplicates, and whether or not this percentage is actually higher or lower depends on the method of evaluation. There are several reasons for duplication: (1) carelessness on the part of catalogers, (2) intentional duplication on the part of catalogers, and (3) the cataloging system itself. It would appear that in most cases carelessness is the cause.

Duplication may be considered inevitable, or a necessary evil. But countermeasures to correct the problem are being studied, such as programs to automatically detect duplication, methods of communicating with libraries involved to correct duplicate records, methods of coordinating between inputting libraries, etc. If the number of duplicates increases too greatly, the editing workload will rise to unacceptable levels, and it is therefore absolutely necessary to devise measures to prevent duplication in the first place.

At present, however, since the cause of duplications is primarily the carelessness of catalogers, there are no effective countermeasures except for the continuing education and training of cataloging staff.

CD-ROM and Union Catalog Database

CATALOGING

LC MARC data in CD-ROM form has been widely distributed in the United States for many years under the Bibliofile tradename. Recently, CD-ROMs for language dictionaries, biographical dictionaries, newspapers, magazines, etc., have come into daily use in Japan.

Under these circumstances, the conversion of Japan MARC data to CD-ROM form was studied and then commercialized in the spring of 1988 under the name JAPAN-BISC. JAPAN-BISC is a single optical disc containing a half million bibliographic records produced during Japan MARC's ten-year life. It is possible to conduct Boolean searches through numerous indexes, copy, edit, and add records, to create and download original cataloging records, and to output records. Bibliographic records in the disc are updated regularly four times a year with a new disc arriving every three months.

At about the same time, Bibliofile produced by the Library Corporation, Inc., in the United States, has been marketed in Japan. It contains some two million bibliographic records in a single optical disc and its functions are not inferior to those found in JAPAN-BISC.

NACSIS, UTLAS, and OCLC are all bibliographic utilities providing cataloging services for the Japanese library world in competition with each other. They have a very shallow history of operation and the reality is that they have not yet left the starting gate. Before these utilities have had a chance to establish themselves, they have been challenged by the new CD-ROM technology and must now deal with an entirely new situation.

It can be said that the history of computerization in Japan began in the age of dispersed processing of the 1970s, continued through the 1980s, challenged by coexisting centralized processing (cataloging) and dispersed processing (operations other than cataloging) systems, and now has entered a phase characterized by a split in cataloging into coexisting systems: centralized processing (bibliographic utilities) and dispersed processing (CD-ROMs).

BIBLIOGRAPHIC UTILITIES

The advantages of JAPAN-BISC and Bibliofile are that they are relatively inexpensive and can be used independently. On the other hand, their shortcomings are the limited number of terminals that can be accessed simultaneously, the delayed updating of records, the high rate of original cataloging, and the fact that they are unsuitable in the compilation of union catalogs.

Therefore, it is possible that CD-ROMs will be widely used in small libraries which have low budgets, or which do not rely heavily on the resources of other libraries, or which are primarily interested in the production of catalog cards of their own holdings rather than in the creation of a union catalog.

There are about 490 universities and colleges in Japan. Among them, many libraries are more interested in cataloging their own collections than in the creation of a union catalog, and many are more interested in card catalog operations than in OPACs. The CD-ROM, then, is a convenient tool for them to use to perform their work.

Therefore, it is possible that where the sharing of library resources is not a prerequisite, university libraries will adopt the CD-ROM, and where the sharing of library resources is essential, libraries will participate in the NACSIS system and will contribute to the creation of the national union catalog database.

Bibliographic utilities, challenged by CD-ROM, will have to improve cataloging operations and lower utilization costs, emphasizing the advantage of interlibrary loan and other functions which CD-ROMs cannot provide.

COOPERATIVE SHARED CATALOGING

It can be said that bibliographic utilities and CD-ROMs represent polar opposites: centralized cataloging versus dispersed cataloging, and cooperative shared cataloging versus individual cataloging. CD-ROMs, therefore, are suited basically to the task of cataloging the holdings of a single library and are not suited to the production of a national union catalog database.

In theory, if catalog record formats and cataloging rules are standardized, it would not be impossible to produce a national union catalog database by collecting records created by individual libraries from CD-ROMs. Because of delays in the updating of CD-ROMs, and because of the inability to utilize the original records of other libraries, the duplication of bibliographic records occurs, and it becomes necessary to devise means to eliminate such duplicates.

One such means to be considered is the development of a software program to automatically detect duplicate bibliographic data. The fact is, however, software which would search individually created records and detect and eliminate duplicate records may be impossible to create.

At a time when the concept of cooperative shared cataloging is not widely accepted by librarians in Japan, it would be an extremely difficult task to devise a program to evaluate computer records bearing innumerable idiosyncrasies. It is therefore likely that the use of CD-ROMs for the compilation of a national union catalog database will result in the creation of many duplicate records.

Thus, the construction of a national union catalog database can only be achieved by cooperative shared cataloging through a bibliographic utility.

Future Problems

INTERLIBRARY LOAN SYSTEM

The objective of establishing a national union database is not to create the database as an end in itself but to use it as a tool for interlibrary loan.

For interlibrary loan of books and serials to be a true convenience for researchers, it is necessary that loan arrangements be conducted speedily and that the time from the request for loan to delivery of materials be shortened as much as possible.

The traditional interlibrary loan service, from sending of requests to dispatch of books, has been conducted by mail, in many cases inviting extraordinary delays in delivery of books sought by readers, especially when the requested material cannot be found in the lending library. The NACSIS interlibrary loan system was created to eliminate this kind of reader dissatisfaction. Through this system, participating libraries can request interlibrary loans through terminals, and recipient libraries can respond immediately as to availability through terminals.

In the initial phase of operation of the NACSIS interlibrary loan system, national university libraries have requested prepayment for photocopying because of financial regulations applying to government agencies. Changes permitting postpayment are being studied in order to provide quick service to researchers.

The number of the participating university libraries in the NACSIS system is still small, and the NACSIS interlibrary loan system is not yet in operation. But a prototype system has been completed, and participating libraries have high hopes for its future performance. Once the system begins to operate, interlibrary loans should show marked improvement in terms of speedier service.

FACSIMILE TRANSMISSION

Even if the communication of requests and responses through the NACSIS interlibrary loan system is expedited, only half the problem of increasing the effectiveness of the interlibrary loan system is addressed if too much time is taken to transmit books or photocopied journal articles. It is probably inevitable that the sending of monographs on interlibrary loan by mail and motor vehicle will continue as in the past, but the most efficient method of transmitting journal articles is through facsimile technology. At present, the government is implementing an annual plan in which major national universities are designated as node universities, connected by dedicated telecommunication lines installed across the Japanese Archipelago. There are also plans to develop in selected universities campuswide LANs which can be linked with each other.

At the same time the transmission of photocopied texts by facsimile communication (fax) between university libraries using the dedicated lines is being implemented. Fax machines were installed in thirty national university libraries in 1988, with facsimile transmissions of texts to begin in 1989.

This does not mean that all transmissions of photocopied material between university libraries will be done by facsimile technology because the number of university libraries with facsimile facilities is still small and dedicated telecommunication lines have not yet been extended to all university libraries. But we can say that progress has been made in the speedy transmission of photocopied materials between university libraries.

The sending of photocopied materials by fax is expected to gradually increase as dedicated lines are extended to other university libraries and as the number of fax machines rises in these libraries.

INTERNATIONAL COOPERATION IN INTERLIBRARY LOAN

The purpose of creating a national union catalog database is to promote the interlibrary loan of books and periodicals. Interlibrary lending is not, however, limited to domestic service but can be extended abroad, with foreign researchers searching our national union catalog database, requesting loans online, and receiving photocopied materials by facsimile transmission. When this happens, it will be possible for libraries to make enormous advances in the provision of information to readers.

Of course, worldwide interlibrary loan transactions are being carried out by mail today. But when and if it becomes possible to use electronic telecommunications facilities, then international interlibrary loan service will also make extraordinary advances.

In order to bring such a system into existence, it will be necessary to rationalize international communications protocols. However, I understand that NACSIS is taking concrete steps to establish communications linkages with the U.S. National Science Foundation, and so it can be concluded that an important first step has been taken in addressing this problem.

Furthermore, the international linkage of databases presents a whole host of additional systems problems, all of which require substantial study before they can be resolved. Communication technology is changing rapidly and the technology of international communication is also developing rapidly. It may not be long before we will be able to conduct international interlibrary loan services with this new technology, but our first priority must remain the establishment of a truly useful and reliable national union catalog database.

ISSUES SURROUNDING DATABASE DEVELOPMENT IN THE UNITED STATES

by Henriette D. Avram

In 1976, I had the pleasure of taking my first trip to Japan. The purpose of the trip was to meet with my colleagues at the National Diet Library and work with them on the development of an information exchange for the Diet Library based on the then emerging UNIMARC format. By this time, the American Library Association (ALA) character set for roman alphabet languages was practically a de facto international standard and those involved in national and international standards activities began to ponder on the problems of nonroman character sets. And so it was during that trip to Japan that the emphasis was more on how to input, represent, manipulate, and output the Chinese characters and less on the problems of exchange.

Much has happened since that time, and I note with interest that formats and character sets are still high on our list of issues in the United States when we consider methods to take advantage of the machine-readable bibliographic records created in Japan as well as other countries all over the world. The issues of formats and character sets are just two among many more today that challenge not only the database developers in the United States but the database developers worldwide with an interest in more effective resource sharing.

This presentation concentrates on bibliographic databases and in particular, two kinds: the machine-readable version of a library catalog

---

This paper is based in part on a presentation given by the author at the U.S.-U.S.S.R. Seminar on Access to Library Resources through Technology and Preservation, entitled "Databases: Issues in the Bibliographic Control of Information in a Computer Environment," July 6, 1988.

representing the items in its collection and the database maintained by a bibliographic utility. The latter is a resource database of bibliographic records, contributed to by many organizations and which is used by a library to select records for inclusion in its own catalog, representing items to be added to its collection. This function of the bibliographic utility is known as shared cataloging or resource sharing.

Consistency[1]

The majority of libraries in the United States today do follow standards developed for the exchange of bibliographic data in machine-readable form. In fact, it has frequently been stated that libraries are the only major segment of the information community that has successfully established and adopted such standards. Thus, as networks have evolved in this country, with each phase of advancing technology, implementation of new means of exchanging data has been facilitated by adherence to such standards as cataloging rules and practices, formats, character sets, etc. As significant an accomplishment as this is, when selecting records from bibliographic utilities for inclusion in their individual catalogs, many libraries still modify the access points (names and subject headings) of these records to make them consistent with their catalog. This modification for consistency, albeit far cheaper than performing original cataloging, is nevertheless costly.

Among the primary functions libraries perform are acquisitions, classification, indexing, storing, and providing for the retrieval of information. These functions are taken care of by collection policies, classification schemes, cataloging codes, and storage and retrieval systems. The resulting bibliographic records become the catalogs of libraries, where consistency becomes critical.

No matter in what format the library catalog is compiled (i.e., book, card, or machine-readable), the function of the catalog does not change. It is a finding tool by a variety of access points, for example, author, title, subject, location on the shelf; and it serves to bring together the works of one author, and all materials on a given subject. Having a consistent database is to guarantee successful management of data. It also promotes cost benefits in the long run, increasing the usefulness of data by reducing expensive duplication in acquisitions and allowing users to get to information quickly and easily.

Sufficient attention must be paid to the maintenance of a catalog so that the principal access points, names and subjects, chosen coincide with those already in the catalog. Such front-end maintenance has the effect of producing a coherent file and the authority record embodies the conventions and mechanisms that provide this desired agreement among access points in the file. If consistency is not maintained, then the user of the catalog will only be aware of what was retrieved but never know what existed in the library which was not found because the catalog was lacking in consistency.

Because maintaining consistency in a catalog is expensive, many libraries are questioning the economics of doing so. Records are selected from the resource file of a bibliographic utility and added to a library catalog without the research needed to ensure their compatibility with records already in the catalog. The ability to search the machine-readable catalog in ways not available in card or book formats is often given as the reason for the lack of attention to the consistency attribute of the catalog.

To data, to the best of my knowledge, there have been no conclusive studies to prove this point. However, to achieve this consistency more readily, without costly individual library modification, it follows that the records on the bibliographic utilities (or any other organization which provides bibliographic products and services) should represent items which have been cataloged against a single database. Naturally, in a large country like the United States this is difficult to achieve.

Two projects are underway, however, aimed at increasing consistency and which, it is hoped, will additionally decrease the costly duplication of cataloging, increase timeliness of the availability of cataloging records, and increase the number of standard records available for shared cataloging.

But before elaborating further on these projects, I shall mention the cooperative venture undertaken by the Library of Congress (LC), the Research Libraries Group (RLG), and OCLC to link their computers so that the huge files of bibliographic data residing on each system can be shared directly and expeditiously. I am referring to LSP or the Linked Systems Project.

As the bibliographic utilities emerged in the late 1960s and early 1970s and their databases grew, it became apparent that, along with the LC database, there existed large separate files housed on disparate systems with no means for them to be shared except through LC's distribution of its database via its MARC Distribution Service. Taking advantage of protocols based on the International Standards Organization (ISO) Open Systems Interconnection (OSI) Reference Model, the LSP partners developed the Standard Network Interconnection, a communications facility, to forge a national bibliographic network in the United States. In the LSP environment a member of one utility (e.g., Research Libraries Information Network [RLIN]) can search the database of another partner (e.g., LC) using the search commands of his or her own utility or local system. LSP protocols will allow records to be transferred from one system to another, eliminating the need for tape loading to exchange data. By using LSP links, immediate and direct access is gained, thereby reducing duplication.

Since 1977 machine-readable records for authority data have been created by LC and participating libraries to build a national database maintained by LC through its National Coordinated Cataloging Operations (NACO) program. These records are made available to the library community via the MARC Distribution Service and LSP. This past year 50,000 records, or approximately 25 percent of the name authority records added to the LC authority file, have been contributed by the present 43 participating libraries, and the number of participating libraries continues to increase. Maintenance of this database, in light of its national level characteristics, has been the responsibility of the Library of Congress.

The second project, called the National Coordinated Cataloging Program (NCCP), is designed to increase the availability of national-level cataloging as well as authority records. This project is presently in a pilot phase and the participating university libraries are Chicago, California at Berkeley, Harvard, Illinois, Indiana, Michigan, Texas, and Yale.

In both projects, NACO and NCCP, institutions follow LC cataloging practices when creating records. Records are to be integrated into one database maintained by the Library of Congress, and made available to all subscribers of LC's data. The database therefore is no longer only the catalog of the Library of Congress, but a resource of consistent bibliographic records that extends far beyond the walls of the Library of Congress. These other institutions likewise have opened up their databases from being available only to the members of the utility that they belong to or a register of their individual collections by being resource records for a much larger group of libraries.

Since both the NACO authority records and the NCCP bibliographic records are available on the bibliographic utilities to be used for original cataloging as well as shared cataloging, over time, the probability exists for increasing consistency nationwide.

Copyright

Intellectual property rights in the technology-driven environment have become one of the most critical issues that libraries and information processors face today. The issue is so complex that much time and energy will have to be devoted to unraveling the intricacies to ensure that appropriate protection under the copyright law is accorded to the producers of data and builders of databases. Over the past several years in the United States considerable attention has been focused on the problem;

much more attention will be needed to achieve satisfactory results, however. Let me set the stage for this discussion of copyright issues by reviewing some of the activities undertaken in the United States related to these concerns.

The federal government has recognized the importance to be attached to the topic by the publication in 1986 of *Intellectual Property Rights in an Age of Electronics and Information*, issued by the U.S. Office of Technology Assessment (OTA). This was a report requested by the U.S. Congress which examines the impact of information technologies on intellectual property rights, including databases. The international context is also explored.

In April 1987 and March 1988,[2] the Library of Congress Network Advisory Committee (NAC),[3] held two program sessions on this topic. Presentations at the 1987 session centered on: (1) a general and legal overview of the OTA report; (2) a review of the purposes of the 1976 Copyright Act; (3) the position of a U.S. congressional subcommittee regarding intellectual property rights; (4) a librarian's view of bibliographic database ownership; and (5) presentations of real-life property rights situations in the private sector. This meeting only underscored the need for further delving into these murky waters, and so a follow-up meeting was planned for 1988.

At the 1988 session, a background paper was prepared to provide NAC members a starting point for grappling with issues pertinent to intellectual property rights in an electronic age. Among the current issues identified were: (1) what is and is not protected and for how long; (2) what is and is not infringement; and (3) what mechanisms are used for enforcement. Approaches for dealing with these issues were offered, such as continued dependence on contracts and the copyright system as it stands, with some possible revision and more reliance on compulsory licenses.

The goals of the conveners of these sessions were (1) to further the knowledge of NAC organizations in this area; (2) to propose solutions to the issues that were identified; (3) to share the outcome with constituent NAC groups; and (4) if deemed appropriate, to forward the recommendations as the NAC conclusions via the Librarian of Congress to the appropriate congressional committee.

Most resource sharing databases have, until the recent past, contained bibliographic records and not traditional copyrightable works such as printed materials in machine-readable form. Rights and use have generally been determined by contract; copyright law has not played an important role. The scene is changing now and the copyright law is assuming greater significance, although the full extent of its applicability remains to be determined.

Under the U.S. copyright law, databases are considered compilations and are protected under its section 103. In this context, compilations are defined as works resulting from the selection, coordination, and arrangement of preexisting materials. A work must be *original*, which means there must be human involvement, to be copyrightable; a minimum amount of selection, coordination, or arrangement must be involved.

Whether individual bibliographic records are original and thus copyrightable is a question that may have a unclear answer. The separate records may not contain sufficient original creative authorship because cataloging rules are designed to produce similar records no matter which cataloger does the cataloging of a particular item. This would probably make the individual records themselves noncopyrightable, while the aggregate of the records, i.e., the compilation or database, might be protected.

Another question concerns rights and what constitutes infringements of those rights. Rights include authority for the organization that creates the database to control reproduction and public display of the compilation. Infringement occurs when a right is violated. In the case of the reproduction right, the infringement might be to reproduce the database in whole or in any substantial part.

As one illustration of how copyright of records in a database has implications in the international arena, I cite the example of LC. It has sought to protect its database of records while commercial vendors and others at the international level have used and disseminated them. Beginning April 1, 1985, all MARC tapes of LC records that were distributed by LC domestically and abroad carried a copyright notice. This step resulted from the work of LC's Processing Services department, its Copyright Office, and its General Counsel's Office to clarify the copyright status of Library of Congress records internationally. As a national library, in the United States our records are in the public domain, but beyond our borders they are not and we desire protection for the data we create. The notice reads as follows: "Records on this tape originating with the Library of Congress are copyright © 1985 by the Library of Congress except within the U.S.A."

On the basis of adherence to the Universal Copyright Convention, the United States and Japan respect the copyrights of each other. For LC's MARC tapes, this means that if a tape of LC MARC records is loaded into a Japanese database, use of those records is fully protected. The license or other agreement between the receiving agency and LC would determine the extent of use to be made of the records. The use that could be made of the records could involve searching the records to identify an item, with no changes made to the record retrieved; or, the use permitted could include printing the record as part of a subject bibliography; or, the use allowed could be to manipulate the data in the records to derive cataloging records. Copyright, as reflected in the copyright notice, further prohibits the distribution of those records by the receiving agency to any other institution or organization in Japan.

Similar restrictions obtain for the Japan MARC records that LC has negotiated with the National Diet Library (NDL) to convert and distribute in the United States beginning some time next year. NDL, through its distribution agent, the Kinokuniya Company, has drafted an agreement stipulating the parameters of use. LC will be the sole distributor of the tapes in their *complete* form; other customers of the tapes can make use of and redistribute records from the tapes as long as the tapes themselves are not duplicated, copied, or published.

Clearly, ways of compensating the creators of bibliographic databases and contributors to those databases will have to be formulated for future networking activities. Voluntary licensing agreements or legislatively enacted compulsory licenses are two ways that can offer compensation. The courts may be called on to make definitive rulings as to what comprises copyrightable subject matter as formats and configurations of data changes. The implications become even more complicated as records are exchanged in the international sphere.

Local vs. Centralized Processing

The widespread use of local systems has been a boon to libraries in carrying out many of the traditional functions that heretofore have been done in a manual mode or performed using a central processing facility. The power and efficiency that mini- and micro-computers afford libraries are tremendous. The boost that their use has given libraries should not obscure the deleterious effect that could result if the library community does not remain diligent in monitoring the impact local systems can have.

It is an inarguable fact that certain activities can more effectively be performed at the local level, where they can be geared to the needs of the institution; serials check-in, acquisitions, and circulation come readily to mind.

Cataloging, however, is the most expensive operation performed in a library and therefore contributed cataloging data to a national or regional database is a natural for resource sharing. Likewise by the very act of cataloging, original or copy, the library's union catalog designation is stored with the item cataloged and makes possible, in addition to the cost and benefits of sharing cataloging data, the cost and benefits of sharing the items themselves through a system of interlibrary loan.

As noted above, the technology has made possible effective local systems and the same technology has also made possible the linking of systems, computer-to-computer, to both upload cataloging and location data from a local system to a national resource or download data from a national resource to a local system. Fiber optics and other technological advances will, over the long run, reduce the costs of telecommunications.

Librarians in the United States in this period of economic uncertainty are questioning the role of the bibliographic utilities because of the cost factors involved. Library of Congress MARC data is available from LC and other sources and the use of a local system for cataloging would substantially reduce the costs for telecommunications when compared to using the services of a bibliographic utility. Additionally, if records cataloged locally are not to be shared, then the institution has no requirement to follow cataloging or format standards, again reducing costs. This latter advantage is often described as maintaining local autonomy.

It would be extremely shortsighted to run the risk of undermining all the progress made over the years in resource sharing. Although it must be acknowledged that the costs of telecommunications and following standards are high, it is more costly in the aggregate to have original cataloging repeated every time an item is cataloged. The sheer cost of the cataloging process is the strongest argument for continuing efforts to ensure that locally created records adhere to established standards and are contributed to a national pool and interchanged without great modification.

A Unified Information Network?

An issue of relatively recent concern is that of building a unified information network. I have described how the library community is harnessing LSP to establish a viable network for resource sharing. The LSP network, however, is not the only network being configured to gain access to information. An academic and research network is now in the formative stages, supported by large organizations such as IBM, AT&T, and within the U.S. government, the National Science Foundation—all capable of wielding considerable influence in the networking environment.

The goal of these builders is to link supercomputers across this country to create what can be characterized as a supernetwork. This link will form the backbone of the NSFNet (the National Science Foundation Network), which in turn will link the many component networks nationwide. These include ARPANET, BITNET, and NYSERNet,[4] which form part of the Internet, an infrastructure governed by a set of protocols known as TCP/IP (Transmission Control Protocol/Internet Protocols) developed by the Department of Defense to support ARPANET. Because TCP/IP is not OSI-based like the LSP/SNI protocols, there is the danger that two separate network structures will emerge, unable to communicate with each other. It will be for the good of all the nation's information seekers that this not be allowed to happen. There should exist one logical information network for the nation's diverse information needs.

The builders of the academic network include, in addition to NSF, EDUCOM (a consortium of over 500 higher education institutions). The network aims to connect these institutions of higher education to enable research information to be shared among campuses. Naturally academic libraries are a part of the university campuses that are being linked, and they are also likely candidates to join the library community's LSP network. No matter which network they belong to, the framework should be in place for them to communicate.

Currently what is being planned for the network is a pilot where a scholar, positioned at a workstation, will have access to information on the network, including information residing in libraries. Beyond this, however, the major application appears to be electronic mail. As indicated above, LSP, on the other hand, is a production-oriented network that can support resource sharing and other library functions.

Overtures have been made in both directions to help bridge the two networks being developed so that interoperability with each other, or the ability to communicate, will be possible. Interaction among representatives of the various groups has occurred in several settings and is continuing to take place. There are ongoing discussions among personnel from LC and representatives of TCP/IP networks. These forums have been used to share information about what each group is doing and the implications of what is being planned. As a result, the proponents of the academic network can take advantage of the vast experience that librarians have amassed in areas critical to successful networking; for example, copyright, governance, and standards.

NSF has forecast that it intends to move or migrate to OSI protocols by the early to mid-1990s. Until that happens several options for linking OSI/LSP and TCP/IP networks are being explored by the LSP partners. RLG and OCLC are looking into possibilities of TCP/IP networks interfacing with their systems. LC is investigating having a NACO institution that is a node on NSFNet send its authority records over the TCP network to be added to the Authority File on the LC database. Further interaction is slated for later this year when NAC and EDUCOM will hold a joint meeting in December.

Conclusion

Cooperation must touch upon all the elements that go into database development in order to achieve optimum access. Most importantly for this discussion, there must be cooperation in the way databases are created. Database managers must take the time to be informed and cooperate with other database managers. Being informed begins by making others aware of what you are doing. If everyone makes an effort to inform others of what advances have been made, duplication of effort can be avoided and standardization for consistency can be promoted.

Our ultimate goal should be to bring to fruition the concept of Universal Bibliographic Control; that is, that an item should be cataloged but once, ideally in the country of publication, and that it should be produced in machine-readable form as thoroughly, as accurately, and as soon as possible for worldwide use.

NOTES

1. The dictionary definition of *consistency* is "the condition of holding together . . . agreement with what has already been done or expressed; conformity with previous practices." (*Webster's New World Dictionary of the American Language*, David B. Guralnik, editor in chief (New York: World Pub. Co., c1970), p. 303).
2. The proceedings of the 1987 meeting have been issued as Library of Congress Network Planning Paper no. 16, *Intellectual Property Rights in an Electronic Age* (1987). The proceedings of the 1988 meeting are to be published as *Network Planning Paper* no. 17.
3. NAC was begun in 1976 and is chaired by the Library of Congress. It is an umbrella group composed of representatives of major library, archival, and information industry professional and trade associations, regional and nationwide library networks, bibliographic utilities, database vendors, national libraries, and other information service agencies. Its principal functions are to: (1) advise the Librarian of Congress as to the role of the Library in an nationwide network; (2) promote the development of nationwide networking of library and information services and serve as a focal point for such activities; (3) provide input to the Council on Library Resources on its networking activities; and (4) serve as a sounding board and a forum for the National Commission on Libraries and Information Science. In the past twelve years, NAC has addressed and made recommendations on a wide range of networking issues.
4. ARPANET is one of the first wide-area packet switching networks, built in 1969 by the U.S. Department of Defense's Advanced Research Projects Agency (DARPA). In 1984 ARPANET was divided into two components—MILNET, to serve the operational needs of DOD, and a second part as a research network, which retained the name ARPANET. BITNET is a large, general-purpose computer network in higher education, currently connecting over 1200 computers on almost 400 campuses. NYSERNet is the New York State Education and Research Network.

ISSUES SURROUNDING NETWORK DEVELOPMENT IN THE UNITED STATES

by Rowland C. W. Brown

The Foundations

Library cooperation in the United States has a long tradition and was flourishing before the term "networking" became a part of our vocabulary. Interlibrary loan, serials union listing, and circuit van delivery of materials were thriving library consortial activities before anyone had thought of or heard of MARC or OCLC. OCLC, the Research Libraries Group (RLG), and the Western Library Network (WLN), with the concurrent leadership of the Library of Congress in the development of MARC, applied technology to the next logical step and brought unprecedented networking library bibliographic processing with its shared cost, shared benefit, and shared resources on a scale almost impossible to envision. That activity resulting from the combined forces of collaboration and technology is largely made possible by economies of scale—a theme I will return to later in this paper.

The United States has seen the concurrent development of OCLC, RLG and WLN in what has been described as the Golden Age of Library Cooperation. However, library collaborative networks range from consortia of libraries simply providing access to their own online catalogs through some linking process to highly structured and professionally staffed multiservice organizations like OCLC, RLG and WLN that serve hundreds or thousands of libraries. Networking has taken many different forms. Some organizations are government-sponsored, some are membership not-for-profit, and some are commercial-service based. Growing technological options are likely to increase the diversity, and the opportunities for linking will be increased.

Where libraries have a strong commitment to collaboration, the introduction of technological support has enabled them to pursue their commitment to resource sharing, union catalogs, serials union lists, cooperative collection development, and preservation activities. The effectiveness of electronic networking among such libraries is based on strong foundations and is not likely to waiver as technological innovations provide varying alternatives. It is the cultural support for networking rather than the particular technological approach that is the real foundation for effective networking. The technological opportunities and economic benefits only reinforce the collaborative efforts. However, the reverse is also true. Where there are not strong ongoing collaborative traditions and goals of resource-sharing that are somewhat independent of cost, constantly changing technological options tend to sacrifice the networking concept on the alter of institutional cost justification.

When the large bibliographic networks began, the primary economic benefit was shared cataloging based on access to the significant volume of bibliographic records available initially from national libraries, soon followed by cataloging from similar institutions. The cost of original cataloging delayed access for users to acquired materials, making national cataloging preferable. Delay in receipt of national cataloging is now no longer the significant problem it once was. While original cataloging is still an expensive process, the amount done by individual participating institutions has been dramatically reduced. The costly task of retrospective conversion has also been dramatically affected.

An almost immediate by-product of shared cataloging was the effect on interlibrary loan. As holding symbols were attached to bibliographic records during cataloging, librarians no longer had to guess where an item was located. Librarians of all types and sizes became active participants in borrowing and lending rather than relying so heavily on the large libraries in a state or region. The sophisticated online interlibrary loan system with electronic messaging was a natural progression in networking on a regional, national and, increasingly, international scope.

It is interesting to note that despite tapeloading and the addition of cataloging of many national libraries into the huge and rapidly growing OCLC international database of over 18 million records, the contribution of national library cataloging information accounts for only 25 to 30 percent of the current OCLC cataloging, as well as the cumulative OCLC database. This fact indicates how effective shared cataloging can be on a massive scale, a point frequently lost sight of today as libraries examine various local options which ignore reciprocal data entry obligations. These activities have been assisted by federal and foundation support for retrospective conversion and local system support. The availability of electronic networking and collaboration has resulted in a broad range of national programs, like CONSER, the U.S. Newspaper Program, collaborative major microform cataloging efforts, and in the future, collaborative preservation efforts.

The work of the Library of Congress, RLG, and OCLC in the Linked Systems Project, particularly as it migrates towards an international Open Systems Interconnection (OSI) standard, may in time prove to be one of the most far-reaching developments in the bibliographic networking area. By the same token, the development of academic networking on a regional and eventually a national and even international basis will broaden the ongoing efforts of organizations like OCLC to extend library networking for bibliographic purposes to scholarly networking and electronic text delivery. Indeed, in the future the principal activities of networks like OCLC may fall primarily into facilitating information access and transfer as they move beyond bibliography.

Another item to take note of is the increasing activity at the state level wherein various state agencies are providing various forms of online and distributed resource-sharing through state databases. One of the challenges will be to integrate state-developed activities with the de facto national network.

The Future

In the environment in which the major bibliographic networks now operate, the roles of the main players are changing. This new environment requires changes in relationships, in patterns of distribution and support, in membership concepts and, possibly, in governance. These changes affect networks, libraries, and their patrons. There are special issues in the academic world, involving the changing relationship of the library with the campus computing center and their collective relationship with the broader educational community as it explores the implication of electronic access and manipulation of information in learning and research. This dynamic is further complicated by emerging national and international academic and research telecommunications networks. The major bibliographic networks are affected by and are themselves changing forces in these areas.

In our environment, we tend to focus on the implications of technological change. There are some underlying assumptions in considering technology:

technology is only a tool—a means to the end

- technology is changing at a steadily increasing rate, making obsolescence a major factor in the planning and economics of automation
- as telecommunications and local processing and electronic storage rapidly change the economics of how networking can most effectively be carried out from the standpoint of both capital and operating costs, the approach towards online and local networking will change significantly from time to time
- the library community and networking will be faced with the gap between the technological haves and have nots
- the development, adoption and implementation of new technologies can change relationships between the participants in networking
- new technology can effect changes in power, status, and control
- new players are entering the information market, making the environment more competitive and offering more choices.

The large bibliographic networks have flourished, but each is undergoing change that is not atypical for organizations in a rapidly changing environment. The library world has experienced some major changes that significantly affect OCLC, RLG, WLN, and UTLAS. These major changes include:

- the evolution of distributed systems and personal computers
- linking capabilities of system to system, machine to machine
- increased knowledge of automation among library staff
- commercial competition in the information and library environments
- new players or older players, such as state agencies, information providers and national libraries, seeking new roles
- growing interest in international or global library cooperation.

The major networks are all experiencing a stage where their traditional products and services have become mature based on technologies, needs, and relationships that had served them and their members or customers well in the past.

The evolving environment would seem to call for flexibility to cope with accelerating change at every level. Systems now focus at the local level—the campus network, the vastly expanded local online library catalog which is transformed into a campuswide information network, and the individual or scholarly workstation which itself can be networked directly with other users. Individual users are increasingly the focus of software and interfaces, designed to be used by the individual in an easier and less complicated manner. Global networking is at the other end of the spectrum with potential for international databases and worldwide resource-sharing on a monumental scale and calling for centralized planning and sophisticated networking among national institutions. Linking of systems is a key for all levels of information users and information providers.

The major bibliographic networks were formed and have flourished through collaboration and a membership concept. Those basic commitments and values are increasingly under question as local options multiply and libraries face economic challenges. There is a basic paradox as shared cataloging and national resource sharing are questioned at the same time that international databases provide the promise of global programs for traditional services, document delivery, preservation strategies and archiving, collection development, full-text access, and scholarly networking.

Indeed, there are numerous paradoxes, ambiguities and dichotomies in regard to the major bibliographic networks:

> membership and collaboration in counterdistinction to the network as a vendor with customer relationships
> governance and the marketing and distribution roles of affiliated networks
> conflicting agendas of networks and libraries
> national and international contention
> databases that were built to serve cataloging or technical service needs, now supporting reference and resource sharing
> technical services orientation and public services orientation
> libraries and library users
> libraries and sponsoring institutions (academic institutions, governments, parent firms)
> library environment and information environment
> price based on cost and price based on market value.

These ambiguities do not necessarily require resolution as they are not totally incompatible. However, they do point up the varying perspectives that networks must acknowledge and deal with. Management and members of the networks must be prepared to deal constructively with the changes and ambiguities of the environment.

Conclusion

The most profound changes for library networking in the future, I believe, will come from three broad developments. The first is the growth in power, application and use of microprocessors or desktop workstations, combined with rapidly increasing use of high density and volume optical or other storage devices that will create new challenges in forms of networking. Another is the increasing availability of digital fiber-optic and satellite telecommunications, which will facilitate international exchange of not only bibliographic records but documents and other forms of full-text delivery. Last, but by no means least important, is that library and information systems have become increasingly accessible to the public—the library user, scholar, researcher, educator, and others. These users will increasingly dictate the form, content, structure, and limits of both national and international library and scholarly networking. We have just begun the journey.

NETWORKING AS AN INFORMATION RESOURCE IN JAPAN

by Hisafumi Tanaka

The term "library network" refers to different concepts. It has meant in most cases a web of libraries for various cooperative activities. The best examples of its traditional activities was interlibrary lending service, shared collection development, or others. Today the word is understood mostly as a library information network, which connects online a bibliographic utility and libraries via a telecommunication carrier. In any case, the term implies actual methods for the upbuilding of information resources or the sharing and mutual use of resources regionally or nationally. The integration of these various methods leads to the establishment of a system, which might be called a library network in a real sense.

The Network Project for National Collection Development

BACKGROUND

It can be said that library materials as national resources in Japan have been held in library groups of the following three categories: (1) college and university libraries (CULs), (2) public libraries, and (3) the National Diet Library (NDL), which is the country's unique national library. The total holdings amount to about 300 million volumes (in 1986), a half of which CULs hold. In Japan very few public libraries hold research collections, and NDL is viewed, above all, as the library which should bear a hereditary function for all of the country's publications and also serve as the bibliographic information center.

CULs have a characteristic different from the other library groups in that they are primarily facilities for specially enrolled clientele. They have a user group—students—who use basic and popular publications on various areas. The major part of CULs' holdings however are formed by materials which have been collected for the needs of research workers in highly advanced and specialized fields. Today publications are being published in more various forms and in much greater numbers, while budgets are being comparatively reduced. Under such circumstances a collection of each CUL tends to lack completeness or wholeness, which causes them to be far from well balanced and to be quite distinct one from another. In that sense each CUL shows characteristics of a special library.

Scholarly research has advanced into multiple interdisciplinary fields, while library collections have been unable to follow such advances. As a result a measure was needed to establish complete library resources nationwide.

Japan is located as an isolated island in the Far East, distant from modern civilization until a hundred years ago; it seems a paradox that she has been eager to acquire information from overseas—especially in the field of scholarly study and research.

After World War II each country established national measures for information service to meet its various conditions, political and social. For example, in the United States, the Farmington Plan was started in the 1940s and National Program for Acquisition and Cataloging (NPAC) in 1960. In the United Kingdom, the National Lending Library of Science and Technology was founded in 1962; in West Germany, the Special Collection Field Plan was started in 1949 and a Central Specialist Library in 1959. Japan started late, in 1977.

A CONCEPT FOR FORMING NATIONAL INFORMATION RESOURCES

Acquiring Materials

An executive of a national library said at a meeting that his library should collect library materials of "all ages and countries, and the whole universe." This idea would be conceivable only as a kind of rhetoric, and the high spirits should be admired. But what would the possibility be? It might not be easy even for a mighty national library to satisfy every domestic demand, even if limited to scholarly fields. We don't know that there exists a successful example in any country of the modern age. On the contrary, it could be said that such an endeavor has been becoming much more difficult in recent years. Is there any possibility such a collection could exist?

What's the situation of resource formation in regard to Japanese domestic publications? New publication titles in Japan are reported at

37,000 books and 10,000 serials in 1986. Besides these there are many local publications in small circulation, which would be estimated more than 20 percent of the above number. It is said NDL acquires 70 to 80 percent of all the domestic titles. This fact is to be admired and we feel reassured that NDL is carrying on the role as a guardian of Japanese culture. The majority of publications which have never been acquired by NDL are considered to be held at local CULs or public libraries. Therefore it can be said almost all Japanese domestic publications are collected somewhere in public institutions, even though a system should be established for making use of those collections as a national resource.

Bigger problems lie in foreign publications. In order to collect all publications worldwide, even if limited to scholarly fields, tremendous money and labor would be needed, and it would not be practical. Even if it was possible, one set of the collection at a single library would not be enough to meet nationwide needs. It might be possible to collect all the publications of a certain form in a narrow specific field. But to collect everything, including the humanities and the social sciences would be impossible. What might be possible is that each user or their group collects materials they need, as many materials as possible within the given conditions. This method would not result in a systematic collection, and there would be many duplicates among groups. Those duplicates however might be considered to be necessary.

Would such a *laissez faire* approach work? Users perhaps would enjoy *laissez faire*, but they would not always be satisfied completely with the results at a local level. The results of *laissez faire* might be a fairly high degree of completeness as a whole nationwide, however. Therefore a measure should be taken at the second stage to establish a system for using jointly those local collections as interdependent resources. A third measure which should be considered would be to complete those local collections. This process would eventually need international cooperation. Thus a hypothetical pattern for resource formation emerges: in regard to domestic publications, each country tries to collect all materials at its national central library and at its backup libraries; in regard to foreign publications, each user group collects according to its primary needs; a national measure prepares a system for mutual use and for collecting supplementary materials. Finally each country cooperates at the international level.

Methods for Resource Formation

Two approaches are possible for a national formation of library resources: a concentrated formation (at a single library) and a decentralized formation (at several sharing libraries). The selection of either type would depend upon the state of existing resources, the administrative (or governmental) system relevant to these problems, and other various conditions.

One of the most successful examples of the concentration type is the British Library Document Supply Center, while a model of the decentralization type is the Central Specialist Libraries. BLDSC started as a lending library mainly for serials in science and technology. The most remarkable feature of the library is the uniqueness in its processing and service system, which is far from that of a traditional library. It is similar to a goods distributing center rather than a library.

In West Germany the educational administration is handled by the local governments, and there is no national educational institution. Among the existing state university libraries, therefore, four libraries were nominated as a Central Specialist Library for each of the four special fields: technology, medicine, agriculture and economics. They were given the mission of building up the collection in each field and provide supraregional lending service. It is said that France also is taking such a decentralized system.

It is meaningless to dispute which is a better selection between the two types. It is more important how those libraries bearing a particular mission achieves it. Japan has adopted a decentralized system, but its practices are different in various aspects from those in West Germany. In Japan the higher education system has been highly advanced, and institutions, which are equipped fairly well, are located all over the country. Viewing this situation as a whole, the state of library resources is at a high level, and the establishment of supplementary functions is the next measure to be taken. The backup libraries will fill the gaps in BLDSC, but Japanese central libraries will fill the gaps among the existing libraries.

THE STATE OF COLLECTIONS IN JAPANESE COLLEGES AND UNIVERSITIES

The ratio of higher education students to the general same-age population in Japan is 36 percent, which is lower than in the United States. National four-year colleges and universities number 96 and they are located evenly over the country. Private institutions, where 74 percent of the total students are enrolled, number 350.

The number of teaching staff and other research workers are 124,000, and it was calculated in FY 1985 that each of them spent in a year roughly Y248,000 ($2,000) for purchasing books and Y153,000 ($1,180) for serials. As far as foreign publications were concerned, Y129,000 ($1,000) for books and Y123,000 ($950) for serials within each amount above were spent, which corresponds to ten to eleven volumes of foreign books and two to three titles of serials.[1] Despite dissatisfaction of each professor, are these expenditures considered low for joint use?

Each institution includes 270 professors and research workers and library holdings of 310,000 volumes, acquiring each year 11,000 volumes of books (3,000 foreign) and subscribing to 2,500 title serials (850 foreign) on the average.[2] Those foreign publications can be said to be mostly research materials.

These numbers are presumably lower than those in the United States, but it is supposed that the ratio of foreign publications might be rather higher. Especially in the field of science and technology, foreign serials occupy a higher ratio, 49 percent of sci-tech serials (60 percent among all foreign serials), but 20 percent of the humanities and the social sciences serials. Reviewing these points, it can be seen that much attention has been paid to collecting foreign materials and it may be said that foreign information resources as a whole, thus, have improved.

THE ESTABLISHMENT OF THE FOREIGN PERIODICALS CENTERS AND ITS EFFECT

Starting the Centers

It was after 1977 that an intended measure for collecting foreign publications (serials in this case) systematically was taken in Japan. Seeing that national CULs had been forced to cancel many foreign titles due to decreased budgets and high prices of serials, the Monbusho (Ministry of Education, Science, and Culture), which is responsible for national institutions, set up the new additional budget for purchasing foreign serials. The amount of the budget was not large at the initial stage, so that NACSIS officials decided not to allocate the funds to each CUL, but provided them to some selected libraries on the condition that they expend the funds for subscribing to serials which no CULs acquired at that time. The first designated libraries were as follows:

- physics, chemistry, technology and related fields—Tokyo Institute of Technology Library
- bio-medical fields—Osaka University Nakanoshima Medical Library, and as the backups Kyushu and Tohoku University Medical Libraries
- agricultural fields—University of Tokyo Agricultural Library, and as the back-up Kagoshima University Agricultural Library.

After that the officials proceeded to discuss at the Science Council (an advisory organ to the Minister of Education, Science and Culture) general problems of a dissemination system of scholarly information in the country. The Council submitted a report to the Minister in 1980, recommending the following points:

1. to promote systematic collection development of primary literature
2. to form a database of nationwide catalog and location information and to set up a network for disseminating the information
3. to provide a system and network for secondary information databases needed by academic research workers
4. to build original databases for domestic needs
5. to establish a science information center for carrying a pivotal function of facilitating these measures.

In regard to systematic collection of primary literature, the officials took up foreign serials as an urgent problem and raised it from a mere budgetary measure to a policy issue. Thereafter, the social sciences and a part of the humanities were also included. Kobe University was designated in 1985 and Hitotsubashi in 1986. In 1987 Kyoto University was designated as a backup to Tokyo Institute of Technology. As a result, today this policy involving foreign periodical centers is carried on by nine libraries.

The Authority has been providing special funds for binding and other expenses, and also personnel. These libraries are all national institutions, but needless to say they are serving broadly other public and private academic and research institutions.

Holdings of the Centers

The Foreign Periodicals Centers (FPCs), which started with five libraries and increased to nine, are subscribing now to 17,604 titles in total. (This number, of course, does not include titles which each of them is acquiring as an individual university library.) How did they select those titles? What the titles have in common with one another is that they were selected from titles which had been adopted in international secondary literature, but did not exist in Japan.

In the bio-medical field, the survey sources at the first stage were *Index Medicus* and *Current Contents* (CC), afterwards, *Excerpta Medica, Biological Abstracts, Chemical Abstracts* (CA), and *Science Citation Index* (SCI).[3] In the physics-chemistry-technology area, *CA, Ulrich's International Periodicals Directory, Journals in Translations (BLLD), Index to Scientific and Technical Proceedings (ISI)* and others were used.[4] In the agricultural field they used *SCI, CC, Commonwealth Agricultural Bureau Database, Aquatic Science,* and *Fisheries Abstracts*, and also they surveyed citations in some journals of the agricultural associations.[5] In the social science field, *Ulrich's, Social Science Citation Index*, and others were issued.[6]

Selection by each FPC led to many duplicates. Those duplicate titles were reduced to one copy of each through coordination among FPCs. The total subscriptions in 1987 are shown in figure 1. Due to the process of selection, those titles are not core journals, but rather those rarely used. In this sense those journals are supplementary in substance. This means that each FPC is not designed to be a central library of self-perfection. A FPC subscribes to more titles than a regular library, but it is also substantially a research library which has to depend on other libraries in order to respond to demands from users inside its parent institution. This is a point that distinguishes FPCs from West German Central Specialist Libraries.

Current State of Service

As mentioned above, each FPC does not hold a complete collection of serials, and it shares one special field with other FPCs. Therefore, in order to provide broad service of those collected serials, it is indispensable to make known which FPCs holds what titles. *The Union List of Scientific Periodicals in European Languages* was published by the National Center for Science Information System (NACSIS) in 1980 and the

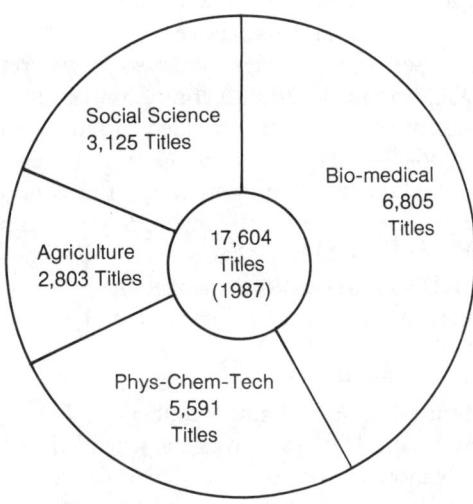

Figure 1. Number of titles subscribed by FPCs in each field.

new revised edition will be published in February 1989. Such a nationwide union list is issued after a long interval in the nature of things, and it is not sufficient for current information. For those reasons, FPCs have published the joint subscription list through their cooperative efforts since the beginning. As of today five editions have been issued between 1980 and 1987. They include all titles acquired, and the lists have been distributed to all colleges and universities in the country.

How much service are they providing? Total copy requests accepted by nine FPCs amounted to about 400,000 in 1987.[7] This number represents the total sum of acceptances at FPCs, and it is not clear what the proportion of FPCs' "supplementary titles" within all items they copied was. According to a report, their proportion corresponded to 48 percent of all copies; "the use of those titles was higher than expected."[8]

The state of service at FPCs is fairly different from center to center, due to the character of each research activity and information use. Among FPCs in the four fields the most heavily used centers are those in bio-medical science. This is predictable, judging from the state of academic medical libraries. There exists no national center medical library, and major sites of medical research are medical schools and their hospitals, and, generally speaking, medical schools have been comparatively eager to foster their libraries. In the fields of technology and agricultural science, nonacademic institutions also have actively fostered research and study and have collected information needed for their use. Therefore from a nationwide point of view, the dependence on academic libraries seems to be comparatively low in these fields.

The British Library Document Service Center (DSC) gained a good reputation for its service to foreign libraries. It was reported that in 1978–1979, DSC provided 520,000 copy services outside the United Kingdom, 7 percent of which was provided to Japan, namely 36,000.[9] Thereafter, in 1986–1987 Japan became the largest user.[10] In the meantime DSC improved the distributing method of its coupons so that any library in Japan could get them easily through private dealers; this convenience might contribute to broadening use. I, myself, always have had high respect for DSC's well-refined management, and I would like to hope that Japanese authorities and libraries could adopt such a flexible system.

Could FPCs contribute to decreasing Japanese libraries' dependence on overseas libraries? The declining numbers in figure 2 provide an answer. Japanese medical libraries have been provided with copy services from the U.S. National Library of Medicine for many years. (Many medical librarians know it well and appreciate it very much.) Recently libraries of many kinds have been using DSC. Anyway, as far as academic

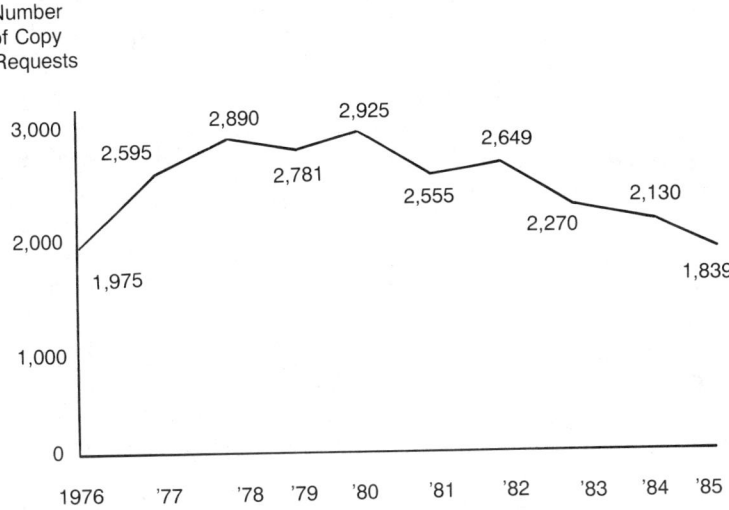

Figure 2. Transition of copy requests to overseas libraries by Japanese medical libraries.

medical libraries are concerned, it can be said the FPC system is contributing to building up domestic information resources.

FUTURE PROBLEMS

Ten years have passed since the FPC system started. It was said that before then the appropriate authorities had an idea of establishing a national science library, but such a library has not been supported broadly and has never been realized. Under such circumstances, as a pragmatic measure for enhancing the country's scholarly information resource, the administration selected a way of establishing a function supplementing the existing resources. The funds of Y464 million ($3.6 million) were appropriated for the subscriptions by nine FPCs in 1987. These expenditures might be said to be extraordinarily economical for an administrative measure of this kind. I am convinced that it has produced many more benefits than what the amount of money would normally provide. The fact should not be forgotten that those libraries which were designated as FPC have devoted many resources to a new additional mission.

That there exist some problems in this supplementing function cannot be helped. A premise for establishing a supplementing function would be a stable fundamental function. The increasing cost of subscriptions with a level or decreasing budget has forced each library to cancel many subscriptions; the foundation, thus, becomes unstable. In this situation the FPC group had ordered many additional titles in 1986 after surveying the cancelled subscriptions at other national universities.[11] As far as carrying on a supplementing function such checks and review may be inevitable, and as a consequence there would be some fears of lacking consistency in the collections of FPCs. In the future, therefore, in the long run, it would be necessary to expand from supplementing to a more complete collection.

A supplemental or shared collection system will be completed by the power of all constituent organizations, and information about materials they hold is an absolute prerequisite. NACSIS is storing and providing such information. NACSIS's final aim is a nationwide online service, but it needs much time to complete a whole library network. The online information retrieval and cataloging service of the Union List of Scientific Periodicals is now in use. An effective interlibrary lending system is also expected to be realized. The more developed such a system, the more sufficiently FPCs could carry on their function.

When domestic holdings increase to a high degree, does the need for international cooperation decrease? Presumably not. Domestic publications in most cases could not be collected sufficiently except in the publisher's country. In the situation where a national central specialist library does not exist, as in Japan, nationwide location information (a union catalog) is necessary for enhancing international, interlibrary lending service. If databases of information could be developed, a bibliographic utility could provide service for domestic use. International telecommunication networks have been developed technically to facilitate access to a counterpart database. Information technology will advance to augment possibilities of many kinds.

Sources of information are getting more varied. Apart from the topic of electronic publications or other new technology, the so-called gray literature augments traditional main information media at libraries. Very few libraries are trying to collect systematically such fugitive materials that exist throughout the world. Is it possible to collect such materials systematically? Even if possible, much attention would have to be given to build the location information databases for those materials.

Characteristics of the Library Information Network in Japan

DEVELOPMENT OF THE NETWORK

A library information network in Japan started far later than similar systems in general society and in commerce and industry, and it has been in existence only a few years. It has, however, been developed by different local systems. The reason might be that technical aspects of library service have not yet become standardized. Cataloging, for example, has been omitted from the menu of automation because of the difficulty in processing Chinese characters in a small local system. As a consequence, areas of automation have been mostly clerical services such as circulation, acquisition, and accounting procedures. It can be said that since NACSIS (and its predecessor) started with the function of a bibliographic utility, cataloging, which is the most basic work in library service, has been automated.

DEVELOPMENT OF SCIENCE INFORMATION NETWORK

NACSIS was founded as a multipurpose utility for scholarly information dissemination in the Japanese academic community in 1986. Therefore, the service as a bibliographic utility is one of the major functions of NACSIS. Moreover as it is an integrated information service center, it performs information retrieval service via databases in many fields and manages production of original databases as well. A research worker (or a reference librarian) can search for the existence of a research report through the secondary information retrieval service; then he or she can find the location (a holding library) of the publication, through the reports of the NACSIS union catalog service; and thereafter he or she will able to request the document delivery to the library through interlibrary loan (ILL) service. In the near future he or she can get copy service by high-speed facsimile. NACSIS is designed as a utility to provide these information services to the academic community.

NACSIS also provides a network carrier service which facilitates this information transmission via a nationwide leased telecommunication line. This network links seven large-scale computer centers (including supercomputers), other computer centers, and, in the near future, several university local area networks (LANs). The NACSIS network provides as a value-added service an electronic mail (message exchange) among research workers, librarians, and other academic people. This network has been developing as a trunk line with packet switching nodes from north to south in the Japanese islands at the first stage, and it is planned to expand branch lines into each region of the country at the second stage.

The cost of telecommunication in Japan is higher than in the United States. In this case an integrated leased-line network is estimated to be less expensive than the total sum of individual payments. Then through this network each research worker can economically use supercomputers that are located in other regions, or exchange messages with colleagues, or access databases, including the union catalogs of serials and books installed at NACSIS and other computer centers. And also through this network each university library can build up its cataloging system, including online public access catalogs (OPAC), and join ILL service by high-speed facsimile, free of anxiety about telecommunication costs.[12]

Another characteristic of this network is its capacity to link computers made by different manufacturers. In Japan several main-frame computer manufacturers, including IBM, share the market in similar proportion. Therefore an interinstitutional network has to be capable of interconnecting among these systems.

The library information network in Japan, which so far is unique within the country, is not independent, as is one formed by a single bibliographic utility and its member libraries, but is a subnetwork based on type of use of the multipurpose network. It is designed to be a utility used jointly by libraries and their clientele, a characteristic feature in the Japanese library network.

In North America and Western Europe there exist some domestic and international academic research networks. NACSIS-NET is to link up with these overseas networks, and in January, 1989, it was extended to the National Service Foundation (NSF) in Washington, D.C. At the first stage this line facilitates access to the NACSIS databases by the terminals installed at NSF and also provides an electronic mail service between binational research workers via CSNET. And in the near future, via this line, it will be possible to access NACSIS databases directly from academic institutions in the United States.

NOTES

1. Ministry of Education, Science and Culture (Monbusho), Science and International Affairs Bureau, Science Information Division. *Library Statistics of Colleges and Universities, 1986.* March 1987.

2. *Ibid.*

3. Hiroshi Iwamoto. "Report at the Workshop on Medical Librarianship," 1986. (Unpublished)

4. Toshio Imagawa et al. "Ten Years of Foreign Periodical Center in Science and Engineering; Its Current State and Problems." *Daigaku toshokan kenkyu* (Journal of college and university libraries), no. 30 (1987): 91–94.

5. Tatsusuke Ozaki. "The Current State of Foreign Periodicals Center in Agricultural Science." *Daigaku toshokan kenkyu*, no. 30 (1987): 84.

6. Yukihiko Yamada. "On Acquisitions at Foreign Periodicals Center in the Humanities and Social Sciences: Current State and Problems at Hitotsubashi University Library." *Daigaku toshokan kenkyu*, no. 29 (1986): 63–65.

7. The Meeting of the Foreign Periodicals Center Libraries, March 1988. Reports submitted from each Center. (Unpublished)

8. Ozaki. "The Current State of Foreign Periodicals Center in Agricultural Science." 85–86.

9. *The British Library Annual Report*, 1978/79.

10. *The BLDSC Annual Report*, 1986/87.

11. Takeshi Fukutome. "Activities of the Foreign Periodicals Centers." *Text for the Workshop of Academic Librarianship* (1987), p.58.

12. The current status of NACSIS Cataloging System as of December 1988 includes 78 member universities (62 national and 16 private); input records: 1,250,000 books (bibliographic records: 650,000) and 1,230,000 serials (bibliographic records: 140,000).

THE EFFECT OF SCIENCE INFORMATION SYSTEMS ON JAPANESE UNIVERSITY LIBRARIES

by Kimio Ohno

My regular position at our university is professor of quantum chemistry in the Faculty of Science. At the same time, I am the director of the university library and have been holding this position for the last three and a half years. I am a physicist by training and am a complete amateur in library science and library management. You can imagine how difficult it is for me to address this audience of experts in library science. The report, or rather, remarks I am going to make are, therefore, based mainly on a user's viewpoint rather than that of a librarian's. I hope you will tolerate me if my views are not well founded or well balanced.

Until several years ago, Japanese university libraries had been doing their daily business more or less independently. A notable exception was interlibrary loans (ILL). The practical means of ILL were, however, not modern, to say the least. A librarian had to find out which library held the literature of interest by leafing through printed catalogs which were often several years old. When the librarian found a book or journal's location, he or she had to write and ask for it. The pertinent book or journal was sent by mail. As the previous Japanese speaker told you, about ten years ago, several university libraries were designated by the Ministry of Education as foreign periodical centers. Thus, systematic collection of foreign journals began. However, even now, the means of ILL remain essentially the same.

When the explosion of science information came about in the middle of the sixties, the individual university library could not meet the necessities of their academic staff. The explosion was characterized by a vast increase in the quantity of information and a great diversity in its form. All who were concerned thought of making use of the then rapidly developing computer and communication technologies. A network of university libraries and computerized library functions was naturally discussed. However, reactions from university libraries were in general slow, timid, and sometimes even hostile. In 1973, the Science Council, which is an advisory committee in the Ministry of Education, made public its third proposal, which contained several recommendations concerning the science information problem. In this proposal, a name "the second library network system" appeared. In my interpretation, the Science Council thought it hopeless to build a network of existing libraries and had to put forward the idea of creating a new library network.

Science Information System Now

Seven years later, in 1980, the Science Council submitted a new proposal to the Minister of Education. The proposal was entitled "A New Plan for a Science Information System in Japan." In this report, the Science Council abandoned the idea of the second library system and advised the construction of a nationwide network which would connect existing libraries and computer centers. As a center of such a network, the establishment of a National Center for Science Information System (NACSIS) was recommended. Its proposed functions were fivefold: (1) liaison and coordination, (2) planning, (3) database service (which involves providing information of a union catalog database of library materials to be constructed in collaboration with participating university libraries), (4) research and development, and (5) education and training of personnel.

Having gone through a few stages, NACSIS was formally established in 1986. In spite of the government finance deficit and tight national budgets, NACSIS is developing steadily. Let me briefly review its present state of affairs with respect to the library network. By the end of March 1988, 61 university libraries have participated in the network and are collaborating in building up a union catalog. Of these 61 libraries, 49 are national university libraries and the rest are private. The number of participating national university libraries will increase to 60 by the end of March 1989 and this number corresponds to more than 60 percent of the total number of national universities, that is, 95. On the other hand, there is no participating library from 52 municipal universities and only 12 from 334 private universities. This means that we have a long way to go before we can boast of a real national network of university libraries.

The main reason for this rather slow increase of participating libraries is that a university has to bear the cost of buying adequate terminals as an initial investment and of communication charge as a running cost. More importantly, university libraries will not gain much because the union catalog database is still small. In short, it is simply not cost effective at the present time.

As for the communication charge, a marked improvement started in 1986. The NACSIS has rented a high-speed digital line and connected NACSIS with the Universities of Tokyo, Nagoya, Kyoto, and Osaka. The users at these universities can use this dedicated line free of charge. This system is called Science Information Network. In 1987, the Network was extended to the Hokkaido University in the north and to Kyushu University in the south, connecting several other universities on the way. This network will be developed farther in 1989, and its effects are expected to be far-reaching.

Jun Adachi and Eiichi Kurahashi have reported the current state and future plans for developing NACSIS databases in detail. I would like to add just one remark to their reports concerning the problem of retrospective input of bibliographic data of books held in the university libraries. The problem I would like to consider is, How much time do we need to complete the retrospective input? The number of books held at universities is 150 million. As of April 1988, the number of records in NACSIS bibliographic and holding files is 450,000. These records were accumulated by participating university libraries over a period of about one year. If we go on at this rate, we will never finish, especially since the holdings of university libraries are increasing by 6.5 million a year. Fortunately, however, the NACSIS online cataloging system is designed in such a way that once bibliographic and holding data are put into a file, it is much easier to add the holding information of the same book to the file. The time needed for the latter is roughly one tenth or less than the time needed for the former operation. Therefore, the problem of practical importance is how much time we need to complete the retrospective input of catalog data of independent monographs (titles). Here I am using the word "complete" in a very loose way: if 90 percent is achieved I will call it complete simply because some of our holdings are very old, sometimes written in strange characters, and it is impossible to make the data machine readable.

If I make several very bold assumptions (see Appendix), the number of titles would be only 4.3 million. On the same set of assumptions, the number of titles would increase about 100,000 a year. The performance of input operations within the last six months at NACSIS indicates that the number of titles we could input is at least 300,000 a year. Using these numbers, we can conclude that we can finish retrospective input of titles in 23 years. The assumptions I have made in this estimate are so crude that the number 23 may change by a factor of two. This estimate is also based on the assumption that we use only the online cataloging system currently used. Now NACSIS is planning to construct a batch retrospective system that uses catalog cards—often handwritten—as a sole source of information. This plan is being tested and is proving to be efficient, although the problem of identifying a book from several similar records seems to be a difficult one and this has to be solved in an efficient manner. Anyway, if this batch retrospective input system is used in parallel, the time for completion will undoubtedly be shortened.

The Japanese university libraries, which had been operating individually until several years ago, are now on their way to taking part in a network. The purchase of books and periodicals and ILL are being computerized. In some libraries, catalog cards for new books are not made and thus the cardless age for libraries is now beginning. The great reduction of human power thus envisaged will make a more thorough and active reference service possible. This is the time of hope for university libraries whose aim is to provide necessary and useful scientific information to all researchers and students in universities.

Problems and Expectations of Future Science Information Systems

One of the biggest drawbacks of the present library network is that only a small number of terminals in a university are connected with the library computer. In order to obtain access to a database at a library, one has to go to the faculty library room. One can access a database at NACSIS through a terminal connected with a computer at a large-scale computing center but one cannot use this terminal to access a database at a library. Nowadays there are many minicomputers on a campus. For example, in our university, about 2,200 personal computers could be used as terminals, but only 64 are connected with a library computer. In order to solve this problem, two conditions must be met. One is to build a high-speed communication intracampus network—a campus local area network (LAN). The other is to power up library host computers to meet the increase in the number of terminals. Campus LANs are being built at the universities of Tokyo, Tohoku, and Kyoto. Several other universities are trying to follow. The library computer at our university can deal with 70 terminals simultaneously, and the host computer at NACSIS can deal with about 200. When access from a personal computer in a laboratory becomes possible, host computers of both types will have to deal with ten times more active terminals.

The next problem is the problem of speedy acquisition of primary information resources. Knowing a location of the literature of interest is only the first step and is meaningless if one cannot obtain it. High-speed facsimile will be a great help particularly suitable for an article in a journal. Ideally, all primary information resources would be stored in optical discs or compact disks and those wanted would be sent online to users who would make a hard copy whenever necessary. I am not a specialist in the field but my understanding is that this is now technically feasible. Whenever a new technology is born, it is usually very expensive. However, when more and more people want to use it and the number reaches a certain threshold, prices go down quickly and this of course accelerates the speed of the use of this technology. I, for one, do hope that this will happen and then we can really speak of an online or electronic library.

The third and perhaps quite fundamental problem is the inadequacy of the present bibliographic data. Don't we need deeper and more detailed information about literature or a book? We have been so used to a card system that presently the items in bibliographic data are essentially restricted to the same as those written or printed on a card. Let me first consider the case of an article in a journal. What we normally do is find pertinent articles in *Current Contents* and note where they appeared; that is, journal name, volume, page, year, etc. Then we use a cataloging system for serials to find their location. It would be more efficient if we used key words in the title, made up a suitable search formula and used a computer for these processes. However, if key words or a title are not sufficient for finding pertinent literature, then one has to make a literature database for specialists in a particular field. As I told you before, I am a quantum chemist. A group of Japanese quantum chemists, with a collaboration of a number of graduate students and a few foreign researchers, is making such a database. At present, 11,000 articles, which contain results of so-called *ab initio* quantum chemical calculation, have been collected from the journals published from 1978 to 1986. The database has been published in a printed form yearly. In addition, all the data and a simple but efficient database management system (DBMS) are stored in a small magnetic tape (MT) and these MTs are available. Any computer that has more than 500KB main memory and a FORTRAN (level 4) compiler can load the data and the DBMS and can offer online searching of this database. I anticipate that more and more of these kinds of literature bases will be made and used.

As for monographs, this problem of the inadequacy of bibliographic data is more serious. For example, it is not easy to know the content of the book *The Chrysanthemum and the Sword* from its title. This is not uncommon, especially for books in the field of humanities and social sciences. It would be very convenient if one could see on a terminal screen the titles of chapters and/or a preface. The realization of this service is going to be an enormous task but should be easier when the task of storing all primary information resources on optical discs or compact disks is accomplished. Perhaps this service could be accomplished before sending the original literature online to users.

These are the future problems of the science information system which come to my mind. It goes without saying that international cooperation is necessary to solve these problems. Leading nations in computer and communication technologies are the United States, West European countries, and Japan. It seems to me most appropriate to begin with cooperation between U.S. and Japanese university libraries in order to meet many problems, which are common in nature although different in many minor ways. For this purpose, I believe that this fourth International Conference of U.S. and Japanese University Libraries is an important step forward.

Epilogue

The purpose of research is to add *new* knowledge to human society. Thus, it is absolutely essential to know which knowledge is new before one starts doing research.

This is difficult if one wants certain knowledge for some practical purpose. Suppose we want to know a certain property of material. It is conceivable that to know the property by experiment or by calculation is more economical in time and money than to search the literature. However, the knowledge thus obtained is not new for human society and the total amount of human knowledge does not increase a bit.

This is the essential difference between research and simple knowledge acquisition. To obtain easy access to human knowledge is very desirable for the latter but is an absolute must for the former. The university libraries are the most powerful organizations we have developed for this purpose.

Appendix

Approximations of the Number of Independent Titles Held by Japanese University Libraries

Among 466 universities, the seven universities called Imperial Universities before the Second World War are by far the largest. In fact, these seven university libraries hold one-sixth of the 150 million books owned by all universities. Thus we make the following approximations:

Approximation A: Independent titles are held by the seven university libraries. In any university, the same book can be held by various faculties, departments, and laboratories. Let me call this number "multiplicity." First, we have to estimate average multiplicity in a university. This is about 1.3 in the case of Hokkaido University.

Approximation B: The average multiplicity is 1.3 in the seven universities. It is more difficult to make even a rough estimate of the average multiplicity between the seven universities. The number of books held by the largest university, that is, University of Tokyo, is a little more than two times that of the smallest. I assume that the multiplicity of the holdings of the smallest university is seven, that of the second smallest university is six, and so on. If we calculate the overall average multiplicity of the seven universities, it turns out to be four.

Approximation C: The average multiplicity of seven university libraries is four. The number of independent titles quoted in the text, namely 4.3 million for all universities (the total holding being 150 million) and an increase of 100,000 each year (the total increase being 6.7 million), is estimated by using the above two assumptions.

Science and Technology Information and Cooperation with Special Libraries

by Takayasu Miyakawa

Special libraries as well as academic libraries have been playing an important role in the strengthening of cooperative relations between U.S. and Japanese libraries in the global flow of information, which is the very subject of this conference. Flow information covers many topics; for example, the flow of scientific and technological information between the United States and Japan; the particular role and function of academic and special libraries in this information flow; and the current situation of cooperative relations between these two types of libraries in both countries. In this paper, I would prefer to concentrate on the topics that relate directly to the discussions in the working groups of the conference, rather than to deal with the entire subject.

Definition of Special Libraries

Japan and the United States are countries where special libraries have developed for many years. The activities of special libraries began in the United States early this century, whereas in Japan they began in part after World War I and on a full scale during the 1950s.

Special libraries are defined in the two countries as follows:

In Japan: "Special libraries mean those organizations, including libraries, established either as an independent organization or a special departmental branch of both central and local governments, of public cooperations, of private enterprises, of universities, of learned societies, of trade associations and international organizations, where they collect, process, store information materials in a specialized field and make them available to their users." (Special Libraries Association of Japan, Research and Statistics Committee.)[1] Therefore, special libraries include a variety of facilities, covering documentation departments, or sections in central and local government organizations, information service sections in the private enterprises as well as academic libraries in a specific subject field and libraries in the research institutions attached to universities.

In the United States: "A special library is defined as: (a) A library or information center maintained by an individual, corporation, association, government agency, or any other group; or (b) A specialized or departmental collection within a library; for the organization and dissemination of information, and primarily offering service to a specialized clientele through the use of varied media and methods."[2]

The expressions between the two definitions differ a little, but the meanings themselves are similar. Then what are the actual situations of special libraries in both countries? Although there exist no comparable data, based on the same criteria, I will try to sketch the membership structure of special libraries associations in both countries.

In Japan, Special Libraries Association (Senmon Toshokan Kyogikai) was established in 1952 and has 670 member organizations as of March 1988. Its basis is on an organization membership principle, and it accepts only a small number of individual members. It publishes, every three years, the results of a survey on special libraries in Japan, including member libraries and nonmember organizations as well. According to its latest survey, conducted in December 1987, there are altogether 2,116 organizations, which can be regarded as special libraries. Table 1 shows a distribution of mother organizations. One can find that libraries and documentation sections within government organizations, central and local, make the largest group; that is, 36 percent of the total number,

Table 1. Distribution of Special Libraries among Various Parent Organizations in Japan (1987)

Parent Organizations	Number	%
1. Legislative, administrative and judicial organizations	38	1.8
2. National institutions	161	7.6
3. Public and governmental organizations	48	2.2
4. Local government organizations	511	24.1
5. Research institutions attached to universities	454	21.5
6. Learned societies and independent organizations	276	13.0
7. Private enterprises	599	28.4
8. Foreign government organizations	29	1.3
Total	2,116	99.9

Source: (Special Libraries Association of Japan), *Directory of Special Information Organizations (1988)*.

followed by the information service section of private enterprise, and then, libraries in the research institutions attached to universities.

As for the membership structure of U.S. Special Libraries Association, which was established in 1909, nearly a half of its members belong to private enterprises, 20 percent of the members come from academic libraries and a quarter work in government and public organizations (table 2). The American organization is based on an individual membership principle. Therefore it is not appropriate to compare directly those figures with the Japanese figures, but it might still safely be said that there exists no significant difference between member structure and activities of special libraries of both countries.

Cooperation between Special and Academic Libraries

Cooperative relationships among various types of libraries have not yet been well developed in Japan. This is due to the differences between the primary functions of libraries and the administrative and legislative barriers among them. Therefore, a substantial library network, linking different types of libraries, has not yet been formed. Actually, cooperative relationships between academic and special libraries are maintained in particular subject fields among specialized organizations. Seen from the special libraries' point of view based on a recent Special Libraries Survey, the most frequently listed outside organizations for interlibrary loan and reference work are governmental information service organizations such as Japan Information Center for Science and Technology (JICST), Japan Patent Information Organization (JAPIO), Japan External Trade Organization (JETRO) and others. National Diet Library follows them by;

Table 2. Membership Distribution of SLA among Parent Organizations

Parent Organizations	%
1. Private enterprises	49.0
2. Universities and research institutions	18.0
3. Public organizations	15.0
4. Government organizations	10.0
5. Self-employed	5.0
6. Others	1.0
Total	98.0

Source: David Bender (Special Libraries Association of U.S.).

academic libraries are listed as outside cooperative organizations by both. library sections in the government organizations and libraries within private enterprises. It is natural that three-fourths of university-attached institutional libraries are clients of academic libraries. It is not possible to sketch out definitely the future of these relationships, because any data on the details of mutual cooperation have not yet been made available. The American scene of cooperative relations between special and academic libraries would show a different and interesting situation, but it is another topic for us to follow in the near future.

Flow of Scientific and Technological Information between the United States and Japan

The subject of this conference is "Strengthening the United States–Japan Library Partnership in the Global Information Flow." Comparing the flow of information from the United States and Japan, one can understand that whereas the United States has been playing an important role as supplier of scientific and technological information to foreign countries, Japan has been recognized very recently as an important producer of such information. The availability and accessibility of Japanese scientific and technological information are drawing an increasing amount of international attention. Efforts to collect and to use Japanese scientific and technological information in foreign countries began early in the 1980s. Information organizations of the federal agencies such as the United States Department of Commerce, National Technical Information Service (NTIS), and the Department of Energy Technical Information Center have made contacts several times with Japanese public information service organizations such as the Ministry of International Trade and Industry (MITI), Japan Information Centre of Science and Technology (JICST), and National Diet Library (NDL), sounding out the possibility of establishing cooperative arrangements to support U.S. efforts to collect Japanese scientific and technological information since early in the 1980s. In 1981 NTIS assigned a full-time specialist in Tokyo to collect Japanese scientific and technological information. In the library and information science field, the first formal workshop on Japanese scientific and technological information was organized by Massachusetts Institute of Technology in January 1983, and since then workshops, seminars, and conferences with similar purpose have been repeatedly organized by various institutions.

On the other hand, the U.S. Congress began to investigate and discuss the policy to recover economic and technological competitiveness of U.S. industries *vis-à-vis* Japanese competition, faced with a huge trade deficit with Japan. In March 1984, the U.S. House Committee on

Science and Technology had a two-day public hearing on the availability of Japanese scientific and technological information in the United States, which was the first of a series of similar hearings before the Congress.[3] Furthermore, in June 1986, the Japanese Technical Literature Act was approved by the Congress, so that federal government agencies can monitor, collect, evaluate, and translate particular Japanese scientific and technological information and provide data to industries and academic institutions. Thus, an issue on the flow of scientific and technological information between the United States and Japan, is amplified to be a subject in the trade and diplomatic negotiations of two powerful governments.

The problem raised by the United States is, to my understanding, that scientific, technological and industrial information produced in Japan is difficult to access by users in the United States. However, it is not clear what types of information and which subject fields are difficult to access, and by what kinds of users. These questions have to be made clear before we take any measure to deal with these situations. The problems are discussed currently only in general terms and there exist no detailed and specific discussions on subjects, types of information, and users' needs. We suppose that a part of Japanese scientific and technological information is not so difficult to access for U.S. users, but some parts are doubtlessly difficult. We need more detailed and concrete data on the actual situation before we consider this topic further. However, I would like to present here an interpretation from a special librarians' point of view.

The first reason for difficult accessibility of Japanese scientific and technological information for foreign users is a language barrier. The most important and fundamental measure to solve the problem is to improve an imbalance of language proficiency in the United States, but it will require a lot of time. Translation is an effective measure but only as a second-best means. The second reason is a lack of systems, partly in Japan, that collect, organize, and disseminate certain types of information; for example, doctoral dissertations, and the so-called gray literature for which abstracting and indexing work has just begun in recent years in Japan. This work is still in too early a stage to expect a comprehensive and retrospective search. The third reason is the lack of accessibility of some databases of Japanese scientific and technological information through the internationally available bibliographic networks.

Being aware of these situations, Japanese information centers and special libraries have continued their efforts to improve the accessibility of Japanese scientific and technological information in recent years. The total number of commercially available databases produced originally in Japan is 425 as of October 1987. They are almost all compiled in the Japanese language and distributed through domestic online network services.[4] Of these Japanese databases, an increased number of English versions have now become accessible to overseas users, either online or offline (table 3).[5] However, if one compares the number of imports and exports of databases to and from Japan, it is evident that there is a large gap (table 4).

These statistics cover commercially available bibliographical databases as well as factual data in all major fields of science, technology, economics, and business, but do not include the flow based on intergovernmental exchange arrangements and interacademic institutions' exchange activities. Therefore the figures show only a part of the international flow of Japanese scientific and technological information. Anyhow, they reflect a large gap in the accessibility of various Japanese domestic databases *vis-à-vis* accessibility of foreign databases.

These situations will be improved further in the near future, because the efforts to step up overseas supply activities of Japanese-produced databases are strengthened both by government information service organizations and private enterprises. However we have not sufficient supporting data yet on the usage of Japanese databases in overseas countries. Therefore, it is a pressing task for us to recognize, in more concrete terms, the foreign needs and to develop appropriate means to meet them. It is important for the Special Libraries Associations in both countries to promote further their current efforts to exchange ideas and personnel.

Table 3. Japanese-Produced Databases Accessible Overseas

Year	1987			1988		
Type of service Language	Online	Offline	Total	Online	Offline	Total
Japanese	5	2	7	22	6	28
English	10	6	16	17	3	20
Japanese and English	13	2	5	28	7	35
Total	18	10	28	67	16	83

Notes: Offline service includes those through magnetic tape, floppy disk and CD-ROM.
Date of survey, March 1, 1987, and July 31, 1988.
The number of databases relates only to those available commercially.

Source: Database Promotion Center, *The Outline of Database White Paper*, 1987 and 1988.

Table 4. Import and Export of Databases in Japan

	1982	1983	1984	1985	1986	1987
Foreign-produced databases commercially accessible in Japan	334	552	725	1,008	1,187	1,370
Japanese-produced databases commercially accessible overseas	n.a.	n.a.	n.a.	n.a.	28	83

Source: Database Promotion Center (DPC) and Database Industry Association of Japan (DINA).

NOTES

1. *Directory of Special Information Organizations* (Special Libraries Association of Japan, May 1988).
2. Special Libraries Association, Bylaws, revised as of August 14, 1974, Article II, Membership.
3. "The Availability of Japanese Scientific and Technical Information in the United States," Hearings before the Subcommittee on Science, Research and Technology of the Committee on Science and Technology, House of Representatives, 98th Congress, 2nd Session, March 6, 7, 1984 (GPO, 1984).
4. *Directory of Databases* (Ministry of International Trade and Industries, 1987).
5. "Database Services in Japan: the Outline of Database White Paper" (Database Promotion Center, 1988).

DISCOVERING THE BASIS FOR FUTURE COLLABORATION

by Haruo Kuroda

We have finished all the scheduled programs of the fourth U.S.-Japan Conference on Library and Information Science in Higher Education, which has been held for these four days from October 3, 1988; and now, we close this conference. On behalf of the Japanese delegates to this conference, I would like to express our sincere thanks to the members of the U.S. organizing committee, in particular, to Theodore F. Welch, the chairman of the committee, for their efforts in organizing this wonderful conference. I wish to express our thanks to the Johnson Foundation which has co-organized this conference and provided this beautiful and architecturally memorable building as the conference site. I also wish to express our thanks to the American Library Association and the Japan-U.S. Friendship Commission for their sponsorship of this conference. As a member of the Japanese delegation, I should also acknowledge the financial support received from the Ministry of Education, Science, and Culture and many other Japanese organizations such as Japan Electronic Industry Development Association and Japan Book Importers Association, for support given to us for attending this conference.

As pointed out by both Dr. Welch and Hiro Yamazaki in their progress reports, thirteen years have passed since the previous conference was held in Kyoto in 1975. During this long blank period, there have been considerable changes surrounding university libraries both in the United States and in Japan. The computerization of university libraries has progressed recently with considerable speed in Japan, and the cooperative online cataloging system through a computer network connecting university libraries and the National Center for Science Information System (NACSIS) is now in progress. In this way, university libraries in Japan are proceeding step-by-step in the formation of a library network that should have a great significance in resource sharing. I would like to point out also that a considerable change has taken place in Japan in these ten years regarding the general situation concerned with the formation and flow of databases of scholarly information. In this conference, we have exchanged information on the present status of university libraries and bibliographic databases in both countries, and discussed a variety of issues of common interest. I believe that the information exchange and discussions held during this conference will provide a very important basis for future collaboration between the university libraries of the two countries.

We have focused on several substantial issues and the preprints of the papers to be presented in the conference were distributed in advance to all the delegates of the conference. These arrangements made this conference very successful. I became the chairman of the Japanese committee of this conference last April succeeding Hiro Yamazaki both as chairman and as university librarian of the University of Tokyo library system. Professor Yamazaki and Dr. Welch had spent much time discussing the scope and arrangements of this conference before I was involved. I should mention that the success of this conference is largely owing to their efforts.

I think that various important issues concerned with university libraries have been frankly discussed between U.S. and Japanese delegates to this conference. There are a variety of issues on which a consensus has been established between the delegates of the two countries, and at the same time, there are some issues on which differences in viewpoints have been made clear. Through discussion we have also come to recognize in what aspects a difference does exist between the two countries regarding the present situation of university libraries. I sincerely believe that the mutual understanding of the librarians of the two countries has very much progressed through the frank discussion at this conference.

After this conference, necessary actions will be undertaken by the U.S. and Japanese committees for the realization of those feasible resolutions proposed by each working group. I think that it is also of great significance for future collaboration and personal exchange between the libraries of the two countries that we were able to meet our old friends and make new friendships during this conference.

REFLECTIONS ON THE FOURTH U.S.-JAPAN CONFERENCE ON LIBRARIES IN HIGHER EDUCATION

by Theodore F. Welch

As co-chair of this conference, I am extremely pleased to see the progress, in terms of improved dialog, compared to the past conferences. With specific reference to delegate participation, level of mutual understanding, open and specific dialog, and determination to identify and resolve issues, this conference has been a milestone of achievement. Somewhere, somehow, during these twenty years since we first met, the relationship has matured. There are, no doubt, many reasons for this maturation. Japan's emergence as a clear-cut leader in the world economy; the need for all countries, including the United States, to know more about Japan; Japan's commitment to providing access to its growing scholarly and technical databases—these are some of the reasons why delegates from university and specialized research libraries in both countries seriously met this week to strengthen a very real partnership. Both countries have experienced, over the past two decades, a growing awareness of the relationship between access to good information sources and productive research and social and economic development. It was time again to share progress reports and concerns after more than a decade since the third conference in 1975, held in Kyoto.

I am grateful for the good offices of the Johnson Foundation, the Japanese University Libraries International Relations Committee, fellow members of the American Library Association's Committee on Liaison with Japanese Libraries, and the Japan-U.S. Friendship Commission, for their support and efforts in mounting this conference, the second such binational bibliographic summit held at Wingspread. The 1972 meeting, the second of the four in this conference series, was also hosted by the Johnson Foundation at this impressive Wingspread conference site, famous for its Frank Lloyd Wright Prairie Home architectural setting. I am grateful to the chairman of the Japanese committee, Haruo Kuroda, and his predecessor Hiro Yamazaki, for tireless effort in planning and implementing this conference. To Hisao Matsumoto and Warren Tsuneishi, on behalf of all us, let me extend appreciation for the papers translated into English. Also, we are grateful for the translation into Japanese of our papers expedited by our Japanese colleagues.

Over the past three days, intense deliberation has involved nearly eighty delegates from over forty different U.S. and Japanese public and private academic institutions, plus many specialized organizations, such as the Library of Congress, the National Diet Library, the Mitsubishi Research Institute, the U.S. Special Libraries Association, the National Center for Science Information System (NACSIS), the Research Libraries Group (RLG), and the Online Computer Library Center (OCLC).

The conference format has differed only slightly from previous conferences. Fewer general session papers allowed more time for small group discussions. This provided time for much interaction and identification of problems needing considerable discussion. Therefore, thirteen preprinted and translated technical papers presented during two general sessions have been interspersed with eight working groups meeting over two and a half days. Issues were discussed both directly—many delegates from both countries are bilingual—and through simultaneous interpretation.

It has been my impression since 1954, when I first visited Japan, that in Japan, personal networking relationships are the foundation of much of the professional and industrial achievement which has characterized that country during the past two decades. Library-to-library relationships have only begun to change to reflect the interdependence they must maintain to function efficiently in a global information environment.

In the United States electronic networking involving the Library of Congress and the two major U.S. bibliographic utilities, OCLC and RLIN (RLG's Research Libraries Information Network), has been a cornerstone for unparalleled growth of computer-based library services. Library relationships in the United States have changed radically in recent years as well.

A primary accomplishment of this conference has been to forge personal links between Japanese and U.S. academic library leaders and bibliographic system experts. It is expected that the people-to-people understandings catalyzed at this conference will result in continuing discussions and negotiations leading to technical exchanges. The participants have strongly endorsed the importance of planning a fifth conference, to be held in Japan; and of convening interim meetings on specialized topics. In the past, these conferences were held every three years. I welcome this resolve to meet regularly.

Many of the delegates to this conference represent the major Japanese-language collections found in the United States. Because of the drastic decrease in the value of the U.S. dollar in Japan, the continuation and growth of these scholarly collections have been reduced from thousands of volumes a year in most collections to a few hundred. Over 3,000 publications of value to research in the United States are published in Japan each year. Only one U.S. academic institution reached the goal of purchasing that many last year. In view of the growing difficulty in recent years of systematic acquisitions, I am encouraged that libraries in Japan and the United States will endeavor to help each other in their respective collection development activities, for both Japanese and American publications, insofar as possible. There is a shortage of librarians qualified to select (for acquisition) and process Japanese materials in American libraries. It is hoped that librarians in Japan could cooperate with American libraries, when requested, in recruitment of subject librarians. This includes the dissemination of information of such need among Japanese librarians and sending staff members, perhaps on a short term basis, to American libraries where needed. (In sending librarians in response to American libraries, consideration should be given so that the absence would not adversely affect the librarians' career development.) The call this week for increased exchanges is a welcome one.

Discussion this week of the topic of database development was somewhat slowed by the need to distinguish databases covering book records (national publishing catalogs or library catalog data) and databases covering scientific, technical, and other scholarly periodical articles, patents, reports, business and economic data, etc.

A highly important future topic is the issue of how Japan and the United States can consider a variety of matters relating to the production of databases and the resulting need for resource sharing in the special libraries' context. Future conferences should incorporate the activities of this area of librarianship into the ongoing dialog between academic librarians in both countries.

I recall that Japanese and U.S. delegates to the second conference (1972) planted a tree here on the grounds of the Wingspread conference center. Unfortunately, we have not been able to locate the planting; no map was kept. Yet, somewhere out there on the spacious grounds, a tree still grows straight and tall, having been placed in the soil over sixteen years ago. I know it's there; I helped plant it. The ideas we shared then, and again this week, have also taken root, and I firmly believe will flower into full programs of library cooperation between our two countries. Some will not be clearly identifiable as coming from this conference; however, others, I know, will be connected to our cooperative efforts.

APPENDIX
Final Communique

Delegates to the Fourth U.S.-Japan Conference on Libraries and Information Science in Higher Education, recognizing the role that they must perform in facilitating the flow of scholarly information within the global community, exchanged views on the changes in libraries in the two countries, following on the Third Conference held in 1975. Delegates discussed a variety of current issues and succeeded in deepening mutual understanding between the representatives of the libraries of the two countries. The delegates arrived at a consensus on the following measures in order to strengthen cooperative relationships between university libraries in the two countries.

1. In order to further promote cooperation between libraries in the two countries, the delegates recommended that a fifth conference be convened in Japan at an appropriate time in the future. The date, theme, and topics of the conference will be determined by representatives of the countries. With reference to the number of participants, it was decided that the scale of the conference should be at a level similar in size to the fourth conference.
2. In order to increase the effectiveness of the fifth conference, the delegates felt it was desirable, in the interim, to convene small-scale meetings on specialized topics as needed. Such meetings need not necessarily be held under the sponsorship of the two organizing committees of the binational conference, but may well be held under the aegis of other organizations. It would be useful, moreover, if representatives of the two countries could take advantage of appropriate opportunities to contact each other and exchange views on the next conference.
3. The delegates recommended that the promotion of the interna-

tional flow of CJK bibliographic data reflect a respect for the development of language processing capabilities most appropriate to the countries of East Asia. Each country should be free to develop its own national character code standards. Further, in planning for the international flow of data compiled according to these standards, it is desirable that points of liaison be established in each country and that the national standards, once established, be maintained and all changes that are made in those standards be promptly communicated to these liaison points.

4. The establishment of measures to counteract the deterioration of library materials because of acid book paper was considered an urgent matter. The delegates stated that libraries in Japan and the United States should endeavor to raise the consciousness of society in general on this problem, request publishers use alkaline paper, develop deacidification technologies, and promote the creation of microform masters, optical discs and other new technologies for preservation purposes. Further, it is desirable to promote the exchange of information on the status of technological development on preservation and the creation of master copies in the two countries.

5. It was also resolved, in view of the growing difficulty in recent years of systematic acquisitions, that libraries in Japan and the United States will endeavor to help each other in their respective collection development activities, for both Japanese and American publications, insofar as possible.

6. The mutual use of bibliographic databases of the two countries should be further promoted, and at the same time, the exchange of information and collaboration in developmental activities should be promoted to improve the quality of the databases.

7. In view of the fact that linkages are progressing between scholarly information networks in the two countries, delegates felt there should be an ongoing examination in both countries of the need, scope of service, and linkage modalities of library networks.

8. It was recommended that current relevant clauses in the copyright laws of the two countries governing copy services be provided to support ILL and that copyright continue to be protected.

9. The issue of how Japan and the United States can consider a variety of matters relating to the production of databases and resource sharing in the special libraries' context, thereby incorporating the activities of this area of librarianship into the ongoing dialog between academic libraries in both countries, is considered highly desirable.

EDITORS AND CONTRIBUTORS

Editors

MARY FRANCES GROSCH is a senior Business librarian at Northern Illinois University where she is a Business/Economics subject specialist. Grosch's primary interests lie in library management and business and economics reference services. Her professional affiliations are with the American Library Association in the LAMA, ALCTS, and ACRL divisions. She received a BA in Art History from St. Norbert College and an MBA and an MSLS from the University of Illinois, Champaign.

WARREN M. TSUNEISHI is currently Chief of the Asian Division at the Library of Congress. He is president of the International Association of Orientalist Librarians and the Library of Congress representative to the Research Libraries Group East Asian Program Committee. His primary interests lie in foreign-language collections, international library relationships, and libraries in foreign countries. A longstanding member of the ALA Advisory Committee on Liaison with Japanese Libraries, Tsuneishi has attended all of the U.S.-Japan conferences. He was co-editor (with Thomas R. Buckman and Yukihisa Suzuki) of the proceedings of the first conference, *University and Research Libraries in Japan and the United States* (ALA, 1972), and he gave a paper at the second conference. Tsuneishi received an MA and an MLS from Columbia University; has a PhD in Political Science from Yale University.

THEODORE F. WELCH is currently Professor in the department of Foreign Languages and Literature at Northern Illinois University. Before that Welch held the positions of Director of Libraries at Northern Illinois University, Assistant University Librarian for Development at the Northwestern University Library, and Executive Director for the Center for the Study of U.S.-Japan Relations at Northwestern University. Welch is chair for the ALA Advisory Committee on Liaison with Japanese Libraries, the ALA International Relations Round Table (1987–88), and chair-elect for the OCLC Advisory Committee on College and University Libraries. His publications include *Toshokan: Libraries in Japanese Society*, *Proceedings of the Japan-U.S. Seminar on Library Technology in Higher Education*, and twenty-seven articles on Japanese librarianship and libraries in *Encyclopedia of Japan*. Welch received his Ph.D. in Library and Information Science from the University of Tokyo and has worked extensively in Japan-U.S. library relations.

EIICHI KURAHASHI is the Associate University Librarian for the University of Tokyo Library System and is also a member of the Japan Library Association, Secretary-General of both the Association of National University Libraries and of the International Liaison Committee of University Libraries of Japan. He has written "The Development of Library Technologies and Services in Japan" in *Proceedings of the Japan-U.S. Seminar on Library Technology in Higher Education*, "Library Catalogues in the Science Information System: An Explanation" in *Journal of College and University Libraries*, and *Tokoshan Johogaku Handobukku (A Handbook for Library and Information Science)*.

HARUO KURODA is the University Librarian at the University of Tokyo Library System and a professor in the Department of Chemistry. Kuroda is also a member of the Chemical Society of Japan and the Physical Society of Japan and is chair of the Association of National University Libraries and the International Liaison Committee of University Libraries of Japan. Kuroda, author of over 280 research papers in the field of physical chemistry, is concerned with administration and library networking and has visited the United States a dozen times for international conferences and collaborative research projects.

Contributors

JUN ADACHI, currently an Associate Professor at the National Center for Science Information System (NACSIS), designed and implemented the NACSIS online cataloging system and network. Adachi is also Senior Specialist for Scientific Research, Ministry of Education, Science and Culture and has professional affiliations with the Information Processing Society of Japan, the Institute of Electronics, and Information and Communication Engineers. Adachi specializes in automated information systems.

HENRIETTE D. AVRAM currently is Associate Librarian for Collections Services, Library of Congress, and is a member of the American Library Association, American National Standards Institute Information Systems Standards Board/International Standards Coordination Committee (ISSB/ISSC), International Federation of Library Associations and Institutions (IFLA), and Council on Library Resources Linked Systems Project (LSP) Policy Committee. She is also chair for the International Relations

Committee of the National Information Standards Organization and Library of Congress Network Advisory Committee (NAC). Avram has written or published approximately one hundred papers, books, and articles on library automation, networking, standards, and bibliographic control.

PATRICIA BATTIN, President of the Commission on Preservation and Access, is also a member of the American Library Association, the Council on Library Resources Board of Directors, and a Trustee for EDUCOM. Battin has written many articles on preservation and management, and her work in libraries is in the areas of library management, professional library education, and preservation.

ROWLAND C. W. BROWN has been President and Chief Executive Officer of OCLC, Online Computer Library Center, Inc., since 1980. He is also a member of the American Library Association, Ohio Library Association, Special Library Association, the American Society for Information Science, and the American Association for Higher Education. Brown, who attended Harvard Law School, was a practicing attorney in Washington, D.C., for a number of years, and also completed the Senior Executive course at the Sloan School of Management, Massachusetts Institute of Technology. Brown has been actively involved in many aspects of business and education, and has received a variety of awards for his efforts. Among these are the Phi Delta Kappa Education Award for leadership and awards from the Anti-Defamation League and M.I.T.

JOHN W. HAEGER is the Vice-President for Programs and Planning with the Research Libraries Group. Before that Haeger was Director, Corporate and Foundation Relations, the Asia Foundation, San Francisco, and Chairman, the Department of Chinese at Pomona College in Claremont, California. Hager has edited *Crisis and Prosperity in Sung China* and written articles in *Journal of Asian History, Journal of Asian Studies*, and *Journal of American Oriental Society*. Haeger's library work is in the field of automation.

TAKAYASU MIYAKAWA is the Director, Information Management Division at the Mitsubishi Research Institute, Inc., and is also Director of the Japan Special Libraries Association and President of the Japan Database Industry Association. Miyakawa was editor of *Mitsubishi Shashi* (Mitsubishi Company documents), 1979–82. His main area of concern in librarianship is networking among special libraries.

KIMIO OHNO is Director of the Hokkaido University Library, as well as a Professor in the Hokkaido University Department of Chemistry, and is also a member of the Chemical Society of Japan and the Physical Society of Japan. Ohno received degrees from the Department of Physics at the University of Tokyo, and has been a visiting research Associate Professor at the University of Florida and a visiting Professor at Texas Technological University.

MASATOSHI SHIBUKAWA is the Executive Director at the Keio University Libraries and Information Centers, is a member of the Japan Library Association Mita Society for Library and Information Science, and is also chairman for the Project Committee of the Mita Society, the Committee on Training Academic Librarians, Japan Association of Private Colleges and Universities and the Committee on Library Automation, Japan Association of Private University Libraries. His publications include *Toshokan joho gaku gairon* (An introduction to library and information science) (Tokyo: Keiso-shobo, 1983), *Shin toshokangaku handobukku* (A new handbook of library science) (Tokyo: Yuhzankaku, 1984), and *Toshokan joho gaku handobukku* (A handbook for library and information science) (Tokyo: Maruzen, 1988).

TOHRU SUGAWARA is the Head of the Department of Scientific Information Systems at the Waseda University Library. Sugawara is a member of the Japan Library Association, Japan School Library Association, Nippon Association for Librarianship, and Japan Society for Library Science and is interested in the organization of materials. Sugawara has written such works as "Dai 4 sho tosho no bunrai" (*Gakko toshokangaku, dai 2 kan*) and "Classification of Books" (Chapter 4) in *An Introduction to School Libraries*, volume 2.

KAZUO TAKAHASHI is the Director in the Preservation Planning Office of the National Diet Library and is a member of the Japan Library Association. Takahashi's main concern lies with preservation and conservation of library materials, and he lectures frequently on these subjects. He has written "Mass Deacidification Facilities in the Library of Congress and the National Library of Canada" in *The National Diet Library Monthly Bulletin*.

HISAFUMI TANAKA is Director of the National Center for Science Information System and is a member of the Japan Library Association and Mita Society for Library and Information Science. Tanaka has written *State of Arts of Automation in University Libraries, A Planned Science Information System and After* and was co-editor for *Proceedings of the Japan-U.S. Seminar on Library Technology*. He is currently concerned with new trends in information service in the academic community.

HIRO YAMASAKI is a Professor in the Department of Mathematical Engineering and Information Physics, Faculty of Engineering, at the University of Tokyo. He is a Senior Member of the Society of Instrument and Control Engineers and of the Institute of Electrical Engineers of Japan. Yamasaki's publications include *Nichibei daigaku toshokan semina* (Proceedings of Japan-U.S. seminar in library technology in higher education), *Sensa kogaku no kiso* (Fundamentals of sensor technology), and *Sensa kogaku* (Sensor technology). Yamasaki's current work in librarianship is in the development of retrospective conversion of catalog cards.

まえがき

　1988年10月3日から6日までの4日間にわたって、米国 Wisconsin 州の Racine にある Wingspread Conference Center で「第4回日米大学図書館会議」が開催された。第1回の日米大学図書館会議は1969年に東京で開催され、第2回が1972年に今回と同じく米国の Racine で、第3回は1975年に京都で開催されており、今回の会議はそれらに続く第4回目の会議であるが、第3回と第4回の会議の間には実に13年もの空白期間が存在する。このように長い期間にわたって第4回会議を開催しようとする動きが出なかった原因は種々あると思われるが、その最も大きな理由は、10数年以前には日米の大学図書館の差があまりにも大きくて実質的な討議を行う基盤が整っておらず、会議に具体的な成果を期待することが困難であったことにあるのではないかと思われる。

　1986年に東京で IFLA 総会が開催されて米国の図書館関係者が多数来日したが、その機会に東京で「大学における図書館技術」と題する1日セミナーが開かれ、両国における図書館関連技術の最近の発展について情報が交換された。これが契機になって、第4回日米大学図書館会議を開催しようという相談が進展し、米国図書館協会日米図書館連絡委員会委員長であるノーザンイリノイ大学図書館長の Welch 博士を中心とする米国側実行委員会の手で会議開催の準備が進められた。日本側では大学図書館国際連絡委員会の下に日米大学図書館会議実行委員会を設け、米国側実行委員会との連絡、日本側からの参加者派遣の準備等を開始した。このような経緯を経て第4回日米大学図書館会議が開催されたのである。会議開催に至る経緯のさらに詳細については、本会議録に収録されている Welch 博士ならびに山崎弘郎教授の報告を参照されたい。

　今回の会議では、参加者全員が出席する全体会議を午前中に行い、午後は2会場に分かれて主題別の部会討議を行う形を取った。全体会議では、会議の各主題に関連して日米双方からの論文を発表し、それらの講演内容を踏まえて午後の部会討議で各課題についての討議が行われ、当面する問題の解決策等が議論された。そして、部会討議の結果をもとにして、両国の実行委員会責任者達が会議の「最終コミュニケ（案）」を起草し、会議の最終日の全体会議で討議にかけて採択された。それが本会議録に収録されている「最終コミュニケ」である。

　今回の日米大学図書館会議では、日米両国の大学図書館の現状や

直面している諸問題について、両国の参加者の間で率直かつ活発な討議が行われ、大変実り多い会議であった。今回の会議は、日米両国の大学図書館の相互協力の新しい展開に向かってその第一歩を刻んだものとも言えよう。そこで、この会議の内容を広い範囲の方々に知って頂くことを願って、会議で行われた講演の内容を日米二か国語で収録した会議録を出版することにした。

　本書は、第4回日米大学図書館会議の全体会議で日米双方から発表された論文を集めたものである。部会で行われた報告の中で会議録に収録しておくのが適切と編集委員会が考えたものについては会議後報告者に論文の形にまとめて頂いて本書に収録した。今回の会議の特徴は部会で実り多い議論が日米双方の参加者の間で活発に交わされたことにあるが、その部会討議の詳細を収録するのは困難であるので、残念ながら部会討議の内容を本書に載せることは断念した。『大学図書館研究』第34号に掲載されている「第4回日米大学図書館会議」の報告には部会討議の概要が記されているので、関心のある方はそれを参照して下さることを希望する次第である。

　　1989年12月

　　　　　　　　　　　　　　　　　　　日本側編集責任者　黒田晴雄

目　次

まえがき……………………………………黒　田　晴　雄………… i

この20年を振り返って－日米大学図書館会議（1969－1988）
　　　　　　　　　　　Theodore F. Welch…………　1
第4回日米大学図書館会議への歩み－Progress report－
　　　　　　　　　　　　　　　　山　崎　弘　郎………… 11
終わり無き戦い－コンピュータ、図書館と東洋研究－
　　　　　　　　　　　John W. Haeger………… 16
和図書ファイルの持ち方………………菅　原　　　通………… 24
日本における古資料そのものの原形保存方策とその取り組みの現状
　　─国立国会図書館における資料保存の対策と現状─
　　　　　　　　　　　　　　　　高　橋　和　雄………… 59
光ディスクファイルシステムと資料保存
　　　　　　　　　　　　　　　　渋　川　雅　俊………… 71
知識の保存：社会全体のための方策
　　　　　　　　　　　Patricia Battin………… 91
日本における学術情報データベースの形成と提供活動
　　　　　　　　　　　　　　　　安　達　　　淳………… 100
日本における総合目録データベース形成の現状と問題点
　　　　　　　　　　　　　　　　倉　橋　英　逸………… 114
米国におけるデータベース形成にまつわる諸問題
　　　　　　　　　　　Henriette D. Avram ………… 128
米国におけるネットワークの発展をとりまく問題
　　　　　　　　　　　Rowland C. W. Brown ………… 139
日本における情報資源のためのネットワーク
　　　　　　　　　　　　　　　　田　中　久　文………… 144
"学術情報システム"と大学図書館　─期待と問題点─
　　　　　　　　　　　　　　　　大　野　公　男………… 157
科学技術情報と専門図書館の協力………宮　川　隆　泰………… 163

閉会の辞……………………………黒　田　晴　雄………… 170

閉会の辞……………………………Theodore　F. Welch………… 172

最終コミュニケ……………………………………………………… 176

著者紹介……………………………………………………………… 178

この20年を振り返って
―日米大学図書館会議（1969－1988）―

Theodore F. Welch

　第4回日米大学図書館会議は、そのテーマを「グローバルな情報流通に向けての日米大学図書館協力の強化」としております。この会議はまずは、学術情報の流通・交換に関する二つの国のシステムが当面する問題を理解し合うための対話を目的としています。そしてまたこの会議においては、情報の共有を可能ならしめる最近の活動、中でもとくに図書館に関する動きを確認し、お互いに共通の認識に立って、両国及び両国間で共有できるデータベースの開発をめぐる重要な問題点に対する解決策を探索することになりましょう。例えば、中国語、日本語、朝鮮語（CJK）のファイルを作成する機関が直面している独特な問題、言語あるいは技術環境の違いにかかわらずデータベースをネットワーク化する問題、そしておそらくは最も基本的なことですが、どのような形式のものであれ情報（資料）を将来における有効な利用のために保存・保護することへの挑戦といった問題があります。

日米間の情報流通を左右する会議の構成
　1977年の暮れに読売新聞に載った記事は、10年前と同じく今も正しいでしょう。アラン・ミラーは、次のように記事を書いたのです。「日米両国を知悉している人々は、よく両国間の＜情報格差＞について話題にすることがある。日本の新聞や週刊誌は、カーター大統領のワードローブから婦人開放まで米国の話に溢れているし、『大統領の陰謀』（"President's Men"）から『ルーツ』（"Roots"）にいたるまでの米国のベストセラーは、すぐさま日本語に訳され国中でむさぼるように読まれる。東京では米国映画の方が日本映画より人気があり、学校においては生徒が米国民主主義をきちんと学び、どの高校生も米国大統領の名前をいうことができる。」　一方、東京が日本の首都であることを知っており、そして三木が首相（その当時、今は竹下だが）だということを知っているのは、学生を含めて一握りの米国人だけだと、彼はこれに続けて言っています。

　しかし知識の差はこのような点にとどまりません。不釣り合いなほどに日本が米国で知られていないのは、多分米国の外部の世界に対する一般的な無関心や、アジアでの戦争の終結以降とくに拡がり

つつある孤立主義のせいでしょう。だが、世界は日々、より複雑化しており、そしてこの事実を無視できる国は存在しません。最近の中東での出来事によって、われわれはある程度無関心の衣を脱がされました。われわれがとった無関心と無視という態度に対して、償わねばならない成り行きになったのです。このような世界情勢の認識に立って、私は、米国の最大の貿易相手国であり、最も重要なアジアの同盟国に焦点を合わせたいと考えます。それに、このところ両国間の緊張が高まったり緩んだり、また高まったりしていることも気になります。われわれが直面しているこの問題は、米国内の伸びない生産性、インフレーション不景気の悪夢、ドルの減価に、そして、われわれが見舞われているこの危機がすべてとは言わないまでも多くの点で日本に責任があるといった感情に動かされた見方に、その原因があります。

　日本の経済成長の達成は、1970年代初期の石油価格上昇期のことを勘案しても、公平ではない点があるようにみえます。半世紀前には予想だにしなかったことですが、日本のハイテクノロジーによって、われわれは逆の役割につかされそうになっています。米国は民主主義や近代化という分野では日本の「家庭教師」であると思ってきました。そして日本は、われわれや他の国から多く学ばなくてはならないという考えを強く持ち続けてきました。そのとおりかも知れません。西欧側の情報の扉はずっと広く開かれていたのです。現地を訪問することによっても、米国、英国そしてその他の西欧諸国が構築した書誌ネットワークを通じても、情報にアクセスすることは容易でした。もし知識が「力」であり、情報が技術研究、技術革新を刺激し推し進めるいわば「電気」であるならば、情報は当然、国際経済競争における貴重な商品と考えざるを得ません。米国は世界で最も高度の完備した情報システムを持つ、科学技術分野においては最も情報化が進んだ国です。しかしながら、近年日本がわれわれに教示できる何かを持っているという声を聞きます。日本が「ナンバーワン」という虚名を得ようとしていようがいまいが、「西欧側は日本の科学技術情報について何を知っているのか」という問題が提起されているのです。その答えは最近の調査や米議会での質問で明らかなように、「極めてわずかしか知らない」ということです。政府が出資している日米文化教育交換会議（CULCON）の報告によれば、米国においてはわずか12の大学図書館が、日本研究の分野における「最低限の研究機能」を持っているだけです。

　日本は、その有力な同盟諸国から、情報の送り手というより情報を収集する国と見なされてきています。先進諸国から日本への科学

情報のこの一方通行は、「情報の赤字」に注意をむけようとする米議会に激しい検討と行動を引き起こしました。日本は、1986年に制定となった上院法案1073号（日本技術文献法、下院法案ＨＲ.3831）の通過と、それによって米国が継続的に情報格差の是正要求を持ち出してくることを予想し、その答えとして、日本科学技術情報センター（JICST）が、日本の科学技術及び医学文献の英語版のファイルをつくりました。JICSTは東京やその他の場所で行われた国際集会において、JOIS（JICST Online Information System）と呼ぶオンラインシステムを展示しました。1985年分の約25万件（そのうち15％に抄録がついている）を収録したJOISの英語版は、1986年の夏初めて披露されました。収録項目の大部分は、化学、生化学、生命科学及び医学の雑誌記事、技術レポート、及び論文であります。

　日本は、科学技術研究に対する日本の投資額などいくつかの基本的な問題点について、西欧や他の国々の研究者の疑問の解決に手を貸し始めています。1983年に日本が研究開発に投資した額は、273億8400万ドルで、これは国民所得の2.95％です。その22％が公費によるものです。比較すると、1983年に米国は研究開発のために876億7800万ドル使っており、これは国民所得の2.99％で、その46％が公費で支出されています。私が把握している英国の数字は1981年のものですが、それによると総額122億1900万ドル、国民所得の2.76％で、49.8％が公費支出です。（ドル換算は、IMFの国際金融統計の1983年の年間平均レートによる、1ドル237.5円）　総額はかなり異なっていますが、三つの国の国民所得比はそれぞれ3％弱で非常に似かよっています。（データは、Japan 1985 : an international comparison. Tokyo : Keizai Koho Center, 1983. 3による）さらに、われわれは研究労働力の構成や質を知る必要があります。このような研究事業について報告しているものとして、どのような文献が存在するのでしょうか。日本で行われている研究について、本当にわれわれはどの程度知っているのでしょうか。西欧の、というより日本以外の研究者にとって、どのようにすれば文献が入手できるのでしょうか。日本の技術情報を日本国内並びに国外で入手する可能性についての質の高いそして時宜をえた分析として、現在拠ることのできる著作は、ロバート・W・ギブスンとバーバラ・K・クンケルの"Japanese scientific and technical literature : a subject guide."（Westport, Conn. : Greenwood Press, 1981）です。私の知るところでは、この本は日本の科学技術情報の入手方法について、最も質が高くそして全般にわたる考察を行っているものであります。その結びの章でギブスンとクンケルは、西欧の研究者に日本の科学

技術情報をもっと役立つようにするための方策を掲げています。一つの提案は次のようです（下線は筆者）
　　　「雑誌論文や報告書の索引・抄録作成についての日本の一層の努力と、書誌情報管理に対する重点的な施策の必要性をとくに力説しつつ、<u>日米大学図書館会議の会議録にみられるような、西欧と日本の図書館人の対話を増やすこと</u>」
　ギブスンとクンケルの研究は、前3回の日米大学図書館会議の後に実施されましたから、この会議により生じた好意と個人的な交流のおかげで、生きたデータを集めるにはよい環境だったはずです。生きたデータにアクセスしにくいことが、日本の科学情報にアクセスする場合の問題点でした。（日本と米国及び西欧諸国との間の科学情報の流通に関するもう一つのよい情報源は、英国図書館日本情報サービスとウォーリック大学との共催で1987年9月にウォーリックで行われた、日本の科学技術並びに産業についての情報に関する第1回国際会議の会議録です。このプログレス・レポートの一部はその会議に報告したものです。）
　前3回の会議の頃やその後の期間に、多くの重要な交流がありました。その中には会議の成果に直接に関連するものもあり、また会議とは無関係なものもあります。しかし、この二国間会議が、日米の図書館人が本日ここで享受している積極的な関係を形づくるよう支えてきたということを、この私の報告は大前提としているのであります。また米国図書館人が日本とのつきあいで得た人格的つながりの最高の証左はおそらく、ライブラリアンシップの分野で両国の関係に貢献のあった人々に対する日本政府の六つの勲章の授与でしょう。その人々とは、故ヴァーナー・クラップ、ダニエル・ブースティン、アンドルウ・クロダ、ロバート・ギトラー、ロバート・ダウンズそれにフォスター・モーハートです。（T. Welch : Japan Honors America.　Dublin, Ohio : OCLC, 1988を参照）

最近の交流（1986年の東京1日セミナー）

　前3回の日米大学図書館会議は、両国学術図書館の関係の歴史に大いに寄与するものでありました。第1回は1969年に東京で、第2回は1972年にウィスコンシン州ラシーンにおいて、第3回は1975年に京都において開催されました。第3回会議以来、3年ごとの定期的な開催は見合されており、第3回会議の招集以来13年もの年月がたってしまいました。これまでの各会議は、十分に議論をつくすためにそれぞれ数日間の会期を用意しました。したがって、1975年以来初めて両国の大学図書館及び研究図書館の人々が公式に参集し、

両国において研究者への図書館サービスが当面している共通の問題を話し合ったのは、意義深い催しでありました。その1日セミナーのテーマは「日米の大学における図書館技術」でありました。このセミナーは、1986年8月24日東京の学士会館において22人の米国の代表が参加して行われました。米国からの参加者は、主に大学図書館の人々でしたが、議会図書館、研究図書館、研究図書館協会（ARL）、研究図書館グループ（RLG）、OCLCの幹部も参加しました。日本側代表団は、国公私立大学の代表それに文部省の担当官などから調和よく構成されていました。米国側の議長で、セミナーの共同議長は、米国図書館協会日米図書館連絡委員会委員長である私が務めました。また日本の国公私立大学で構成している大学図書館国際連絡委員会委員長は、山崎弘郎東京大学図書館長であり、セミナーの開催国側の代表を務めました。

東京での1日セミナーは、公式の接触が途絶えていたせいで生じた10年間の空白をうめる一助になると考えて、1986年8月に東京で予定されていた国際図書館連盟年次総会にあわせて設定されたのです。そしてセミナーのテーマには、図書館機能やサービスにおける技術の発展についての相互の問題や関心事がとりあげられました。セミナーの計画当初は、30名から40名の米国の代表が参加するものと予想していましたが、急激な円高のために、参加者数は日本側2対米国側1となりました。

セミナーでは、両国の図書館管理者及び実務者にとって重要な事柄について、二国間でこれまでどのように扱ってきたか、現在はどのようであるか、あるいは将来の見通しなどについて議論されました。具体的には、米国でJapan MARCが使われていない問題、著作権について二国間協議とするか多国間協議とするかの問題、米国におけるデータベースの所有権とその価格政策及び実状、日本のデータベースの構成、学術情報センターの約50のデータベースの確認及びその利用の方法などでした。結局、多くの議論は、情報資源の共有についての効果的な政策を展開するように国内的及び国際的に問題を設定する必要があるという点に収斂しました。大学の枠を超えた解決がなされなければならないわけです。両国の国公立並びに私立の機関の協力が必要です。多くの情報アクセスに関連する問題に取り組むときに生じてくる先取権の考え方についても、議論がありました。両国の代表は、この話し合いにおいてわずかな時間ではありましたが、10年以上放置されたいくつかの基本的な問題を急いで取り上げることができました。70年代の後半以来、図書館にもたらされた技術革新には驚くべき変化がありました。それは同時に、

図書館活動の本質にドラマティックな衝撃をもたらしたのです。提出された六つの報告（相互に三つずつ）による腹蔵のない意見交換に加えて、そこで行われた率直な議論のレベルは、将来も続けられる対話の性質を決めるものでした。また、この会議が媒介となって、公式の接触以外に、両国の図書館人による見学などかなり多くの非公式の友好的な交流がありました。

　1日セミナーは、財政面で日米友好基金（ワシントンD.C.と東京）と島津科学技術振興財団の支援を得ました。日本側代表団の国内旅費や両国代表団の宿泊費、それに同時通訳や食事、コーヒー・ブレイクの費用などを含む会議経費がそれでまかなわれました。友好基金の決定は米国議会の管理下にあります。われわれの会議への政府の支援は、日米文化教育交流会議がその公式の議事の項目として図書館情報学を挙げなくなってから、ほとんどゼロにまで減りました。（今回の第4回の会議は、再度ジョンソン財団と日米友好基金の支援によっています。）　国際理解に高い立場で関わっているこの二つの機関からこの会議に寄せられた激励、関心、支援に対して特別の感謝の意を、ここで申し述べたいと存じます。この種の会議の将来の財源は極めて不確実でありますが、うまくいけば民間の財団や法人寄付によって実現できるのではないかと思います。

1日セミナーの勧告

　次の勧告文は正式には1986年の夏東京で採択されました。

　本日の日米大学図書館セミナーにおける両国の参加者は、本セミナーの成果を高く評価し、今後の両国の大学図書館の緊密な協力関係の維持、発展を願い、次のとおり勧告する。
1．過去3回にわたり開催された日米大学図書館会議（1969、1972、1975）の意義と成果を思い起こし、その後の両国の大学図書館の急速な変貌と発展を考え、両国の大学図書館の抱える問題を広範かつ総合的に討議し、情報交換するため、第4回会議が近い将来に開催されることが望ましい。
2．両国における書誌ユーティリティ（Bibliographic Utility）の発展を考慮し、すべての、あるいは特定の主題もしくは領域の機械可読の目録・所在データの交換を実施し、それぞれの書誌ユーティリティにおいて大学図書館の利用に供すること。また、両国間の図書館のネットワーク化を推進すること。
3．光ディスクその他の、いわゆるニューメディアの進展を考慮し、それらの図書館サービスへの利用のための標準化について

の適切な方策について検討すること。
4．これまでの両国間における専門職員の交流が、図書館専門職能の発展のみならず、両国文化の理解に貢献していることを考慮し、今後も引続き円滑な人的交流と両国の教育機会の拡大を推進する。
5．大学における研究は、すでに民間機関との間で多くの協力が進められている。大学図書館活動は、今後それらの専門図書館と共通の課題をもつことが考えられ、必要な連携を推進するための方策について両国においてそれぞれ検討すること。

　最後の勧告には、これまでのものと際立った違いがあります。これまでも双方の国立図書館は最初から一連の会議に参加してきましたし、大きな公共図書館や、ニューベリイ図書館のような特定分野の規模の小さい私立図書館も代表を参加させることがありましたが、専門図書館を入れることについてはとりたてて何かをすることはありませんでした。この勧告は、両国双方にとってすばらしい試みだと思います。国公私立の大学図書館の代表による実行委員会という包括的な組織を構成したことは、日本における重要な成果であります。ところで日本の専門図書館協議会の事務局は国立国会図書館にあり、また学術的な世界とは人的に密接な関係を持っていますが（いくつかの専門図書館は実際どちらの国においても大学に所属する機関です）、専門図書館と学術図書館がそれぞれの問題を持ち寄って議題を考えるほどに、両者の連携を十分密接にすることには、なお努力を要するでしょう。自然な触れ合い以上の関係をつくろうとする主たる動機の一つは、双方にとって将来への基金の実質的な拠りどころ、すなわち法人に対して専門図書館が持つ関わりであります。このことは両国にあてはまることです。
　正式な勧告文にはありませんが、1日セミナー計画の段階で取り入れられたもう一つの新機軸は、会議出席者の年齢構成を考慮することと、引き継いでいく世代を決めておく必要性であります。現在の米国側委員会は、1969年の第1回会議以来の古参のメンバーで構成されています。また日本においては、実行委員会の重鎮はこれまた年長の管理者です。どちらの側も継承性を確保するために、今や若い専門家たちを将来の会議に含めなければならないことに気づいていました。第4回会議は、新しい血が計画段階においても討議の場においても、任務を持つべきだとの考えに立って計画されたのです。

情報流通に関する不均衡是正の努力

　今日及び今後の会議において対等な協力関係が作られる基盤があることを保証する一つの因子は、情報の不均衡という提起されている問題に日本が対応し始めていることであります。日本では文部省による全国的なデータベースの整備が学術情報システムという設定で行われつつあります。全米技術情報サービス（NTIS）の出版や索引作成計画のようなものはなお存在しませんが、「ネットワークのネットワーク」づくりが広く議論されています。JOIS の英語版抄録は一つの出発点です。しかし、索引作業が基本的なものの90％台をカバーするのにはまだ間がありましょう。この仕事は長く遅れていたものです。そして本当に、この分野に日本が着手し始めたことは本当に大きな意義を持っていると思います。

　結論として私は、情報の流れにおける現在の不均衡を正すために、双方ができるいくつかの道を示したいと思います。第一には、外国人は日本語を学ぶべきです。それは不可能な言葉ではありません。米国ではスペイン語が外国語として最も多く学ばれる言葉で、フランス語、ドイツ語、イタリー語、ロシア語、ラテン語がそれに続きます。最近の調査によれば日本語は、9番目から上がって7番目、ヘブライ語、ギリシャ語の前です。高校では、外国語への要求が急速にたかまっており、またそれが大学入学のためのいくつかの選択科目の一つとなっています。外国語がしばしば大学入学のための必須科目としての位置を美術や音楽と競い合っています。しかし、それはわれわれの市民の基礎的な教育にとって必須のものとみなされるまでには至っていません。国家の安全、経済的福利、そして文化的な誇りにとって極めて重要な外国語学習と口先だけのお世辞をいっているのです。われわれは、言語能力の不均衡を是正しなくてはなりません。幼少のころから、書き言葉であれ話し言葉であれ、外国語に親しみ、そして学生や専門家はその専門領域に関係する言語を知っていることが求めらるべきです。日本人の手で英語にされているものが、日本における研究の「最善」のものか「最悪」のものかはわかりません。日本人がかれらの研究成果を「選別」していると考える根拠は全くありません。日本の科学者が英語を使う世界のために発見内容を発表する場合、両極端のどちらかを注意深く選り出す明らかな傾向が認められるわけでもありません。しかし、われわれの言葉でわれわれに伝達せよと日本人に要求し続けることがどうしてできましょうか。そして質あるいは量についてこぼすことは、米国人や英語を使う研究者が深く反省すべき別の問題です。

　日本に対しては、日本人の科学研究の結果を国際的に利用可能な

ネットワークに展開する努力をしていただきたいと申上げましょう。他の国々とのコミュニケーションを確保するために日本が費やす経費はある程度割が合うものです。英語への翻訳に要する費用が減れば、抄録や索引サービスのための財源に回せましょう。RLIN や OCLC の中国語、日本語、朝鮮語（CJK）の原語ファイルを作成する高度の技術は、西欧の企業家的精神による外国の文字のコンピュータ化への挑戦を示すものです。Japan MARC か US MARCかの問題を解決するのは、技術的問題というよりは、政策あるいは政治的問題であります。日本語で書かれた研究しか収録されていないとしても問題はありません。われわれの科学者たちの多くが非英語の論文に臆病であることは確かですが、もし重要かもしれない情報が含まれているとすれば、利用者はその資料を翻訳してもらう方法もみつけだすものです。体系的な索引がなければ、情報にアクセスする僅かな機会すらないのです。日本は国内で行われている研究をカバーする書誌情報を供給することによって、国際的な平衡を保っていくことができるでしょう。

　われわれは、自然資源が減少しつつある時代に生きています。情報は自然に入手できるものと同じく大切で保存価値のある資源でありますが、地球上の他の自然の宝とは違っています。それは時とともに増えます。われわれは、われわれの愛する、そしてわれわれがよろこんで話題にする、確かな情報の得られる賢明で世界的に拡がったコミュニティが永らえるとするならば、不必要な情報の重複を省き、情報を保存し、われわれの共通の福祉のために情報を共有しなければならないのです。

公刊された会議録（日本側の対応するものを付け加えた―訳者）
* Thomas R. Buckman, et al.　University and research libraries in Japan and the United States : proceedings of the First Japan-United States Conference on Libraries and Information Science in Higher Education, Tokyo, 15-19 May, 1969. Chicago : American Library Association, 1972. 299p.
　（『第１回日米大学図書館会議議事録　昭和44年５月15日～19日』第１回日米大学図書館会議議事録編集委員会編、東京、大学図書館国際連絡委員会、1970．314p.）
* Warren M. Tsuneishi, et al.　Issues in library administration : papers presented at the Second United States-Japan Conference on Libraries and Information Science in Higher Education, Racine, Wisconsin, October 17-20, 1972. New York ;

London : Colombia University Press, 1974. 181p.
（『第2回日米大学図書館会議報告書：70年代の大学図書館（昭和47年10月17日－20日）』 第2回日米大学図書館会議議事録編集委員会編、東京、大学図書館国際連絡委員会、1974．159p.）

＊Robert D. Stevens, et al. Japanese and U.S. research libraries at turning point : proceedings of the Third Japan-U.S. Conference on Libraries and Information Science in Higher Education, Kyoto, Japan, October 28-31, 1975. Metuchen, N. J. : The Scarecrow Press, 1977. 240p.
（『第3回日米大学図書館会議議事録：昭和50年10月28日～31日』第3回日米大学図書館会議議事録編集委員会編、東京、大学図書館国際連絡委員会、1977．247p.）

『日米大学図書館セミナー会議録＝Proceedings of the Japan-U. S. Seminar on Libray Techonology in Higher Education：昭和61年8月24日　於東京』山崎弘郎［ほか］編、東京、丸善、1987．211p.

第4回日米大学図書館会議への歩み
― Progress Report ―

山 崎 弘 郎

　これまでの経過とその背景とを主として日本側の視点から記述する。

過去3回の日米会議

　この会議の第1回会議は1969年に東京で開催され、テーマは「日米大学図書館間の効果的協力関係の推進」であった。第2回は1972年で、この Racine で開催され、「70年代における大学図書館における大学図書館と研究図書館」がテーマであった。第3回は1975年に京都で開催され、テーマは「大学図書館の相互協力システムとその課題」であった。これらの会議については記録が詳細な報告書や論文集として残されている。3回の会議を通じて、戦後急速に高度化した米国の図書館活動に接して、日本側出席者は非常に啓発され、参加の成果をその後の大学図書館の発展に役立てることができた。

　また、第1回会議開催準備過程において日本側に大学図書館国際連絡委員会（国立7大学、公立5大学、私立7大学の図書館から構成される）が組織され、以後本会議の日本側対応窓口になった。

　会議の定期的開催は、第3回会議の後中断され、13年の歳月が過ぎた。その間かなり多数の図書館人、特に若い世代の人達が米国図書館に派遣され、研修の実をあげたし、米国からも図書館関係者の訪問があったが、代表者達が協議する会議は開催されなかった。

　日本の大学図書館の中には定期的な日米会議の開催を望む意見も少なくなかったし、また、国際連絡委員会の組織もそれを前提とする形をとっていたが、それを実現するきっかけがなかった。

　わが国には十年一昔と言う表現がある。世代の交替が進み、周囲の状況が変化して様相が一変することを意味している。one decade はアメリカにとっても、いろいろな事情が大幅に変化するだけの歳月である。

　この13年間、日本の大学図書館界では特に大きな変化が生じた。それはコンピュータと通信技術による機械化とネットワーク化という言葉に集約される。この変化はアメリカが先行し、日本がそれを追う形で進行した。

日本の大学図書館の電子化とネットワーク化およびその背景

　ここで、一大学研究者の立場で、進行しつつある研究環境の変化を述べつつ図書館の変化の背景に簡単にふれてみたい。

　図書館の機能は収集、保存、利用の三機能に集約できる。収集とは情報の空間的移動であり、保存とは情報の時間的移動とみることができる。利用はサービスシステムとして利用者とのインターフェイスの役割とみなせる。ところが基本的機能である収集、保存、利用の各面で、多くの図書館が次の難問をかかえている。

　論文爆発とでも呼ばれるほどの勢いで増加する学術情報の中で、大学図書館といえども必要文献をすべて収集するのは経済的に不可能になった。また増大する資料を保存する空間が不足している。このほか、利用サービスのための高度な要員の不足、急増する情報の管理などが問題である。それは予算と空間と人という資源の制約に他ならない。

　電子技術は前述の資源の制約の克服に大きく貢献できる。空間次元及び時間次元の両方において電子的信号処理技術による高密度、高速度の情報電送手段が確立されている。すなわち、情報の空間的移動には通信技術を、情報の時間的移動にはコンピュータの記憶能力と高速処理機能を活用して高速化、省力化、省空間が可能である。また、検索や貸出返却など利用サービスではコンピュータ利用による高速化、省力化の効果は大きい。したがって、コンピュータの情報処理能力と通信システムを結合したコンピュータ・ネットワークシステムが図書館に不可欠になった。

　図書館ネットワークシステムの基本的性格は資源共有で、予算や空間や人の様な有限な資源を有効に活用するための方策である。個々の大学図書館や研究所に所蔵される情報資源を共有資産として活用するため、デジタル通信回線を介して文献情報データベースを構築するのが学術情報システムである。学術研究のインフラストラクチャーを構築する文部省の施策としてそれが実現した。そのナショナルセンターの役割を果す学術情報センター（NACSIS）が1986年4月東京に設置された。そのネットワークには現在約68大学の図書館と7大学の大型計算機センターが接続されている。接続図書館はセンターの総合目録データベースにより所在情報サービスを受ける一方、自館の書誌情報を入力してセンターのデータベース形成を分担する。センターのデータベースのなかには各種の二次データベースも入っている。NACSIS がもつ通信能力を利用して電子メールサービスも開始された。

　大学研究者は身近な端末から直接あるいは大学図書館経由でこの

システムにアクセスできる。

　我々の大学図書館人と研究者とは世界共通の問題にコンピュータと通信技術を活用して対処したのである。システムはまだ発展中であり、結論を下すのはやや時期尚早といえよう。しかし、将来に対して我々は進むべき道について展望を持てるようになった。

　幸いなことに近年における日本のコンピュータ技術と通信技術の進歩には驚くべきものがあり、それらに強く支援された形で大学図書館の機械化とネットワーク化が急進展し、めまぐるしいほどの変化が生じた。

第4回会議の胎動

　第3回会議のあとの空白を埋めたのは1986年8月に開催された日米大学図書館セミナーであった。同時期に開催される IFLA 東京大会のために、多くの図書館関係者が東京に集まる機会を利用して、日米セミナーを持つことが Dr. Welch から提案された。日本側は大学図書館国際連絡委員会がそれに同意して、それがホストとなって一日セミナーが開催された。

　セミナーの主題は限定され、「library technology in higher education」であった。セミナーでは、Dr. Welch と私、山崎とが Co-chairman を勤め、アメリカ側24人日本側57人の参加を得て、6編の論文発表を中心に活発な討論がなされた。セミナーは両国の参加者にとり有益であったが、特にアメリカの参加者にとって、前述の日本の図書館の変化は目新しいものであったのではないだろうか。

　また、データベースのダウンロードが話題となった。コンピュータ関連技術の開発速度が分野により大きく異なるためにネットワークコストに対してメモリのコストが著しく低下した。光ディスクや CD-ROM など急速に進歩した高密度情報蓄積手段を利用すると図書館は従来よりはるかに多量の情報を分散貯蔵できる。ネットワークシステムに依存したオンラインアクセスに対して、専有資源によるオフライン分散処理のメリットが急激に増大してきたことが理由であろう。技術進歩のアンバランス、それは技術開発の宿命でもあるのだが、それが図書館にも影響を与えることの一例で、ネットワーク化を進めるに当たって今後避けることの出来ない問題となると感じた。

　セミナーを総括するにあたって勧告が議決された。その中で最も重要なのは第4回日米大学図書館会議の早期開催を要請したことであった。

　この要請にしたがって、アメリカ側関係者が準備を進められた結

果、1987年4月にはJohnson財団と日米友好基金との援助によりこのWingspread Conference Centerにおいて開催することが提案された。

　日本側の組織者である大学図書館国際連絡委員会は、第3回会議後の空白期間には組織を簡素化し、活動規模を縮小していたが、日米セミナーの際には準備委員会を組織して対応した。また、第4回会議開催に備えて組織を改め積極的に対応できる体制とした。さらに、第4回日米大学図書館会議実行委員会を1987年4月に組織し、会議の性格、主題の選定、予算などについて活動を開始した。

　また、1987年7月、前年の日米セミナーのProceedingsが、原文と訳文とが前半和文、後半英文の形で編集され、丸善から『日米大学図書館セミナー』として出版された。

　1987年9月に、英国CoventryのWarwick大学で、同大学と英国図書館主催で日本の科学技術および産業の情報に関する国際会議が開催された。Dr. Welchと山崎が二人とも参加した機会を利用して第4回会議の内容を協議しつつ原案を作った。

　3回の日米会議の結果を反省し、実質的な成果が期待できる会議とするべく討議を重視し、具体的な結論を指向するように、主たる問題点、考えられる解決策、その中で最適と思われる提案、の形をとることとした。また、そのような討議が実現できるような主題を選定した。さらに第5回以降の会議の性格についても議論する場を設けた。

　この原案は双方の委員会で検討され、一部修正の上決定された。メインテーマとして、「グローバルな情報流通に向けての日米大学図書館協力の強化—Strengthening the U.S.-Japan Library Partnership in the Global Information Flow」とした。

　参加者数をそれぞれ30人とし、さらに、6人ずつの若い世代の図書館人を加えた。後者は、空白期間に生じた世代の交代による人的関係における不連属性を回避し、将来の会議における中核的人材の育成を意図したものであった。

　1987年後半からspeakerやmoderatorの決定、代表団の編成などの準備が大学図書館国際連絡委員会において進められた。

　代表団の旅費の捻出は我々にとって困難な問題であった。一部を企業からの寄付をあおぐために一橋大学附属図書館の森田館長を主査として募金小委員会が大学図書館国際連絡委員会の下に設置され、この会議の意義を説明して協力を求めた。また、会議参加と並行して、北米大学の図書館における目録所在情報形成システムの調査を実施することとした。

この結果、公立大学、私立大学関係からも支援が得られ、出版業や電子工業の企業からも支持を受けることができた。さらに、文部省からも特別の配慮を得ることができた。
　このほか、講演者として、また専門家として国会図書館、NACSIS、専門図書館協議会などから代表メンバーに加わっていただくことができた。このような広く各方面からのご支援に対して、この機会をかりて厚くお礼を申し上げたい。
　1988年4月、任期満了で東大附属図書館長が山崎から黒田教授に交代した。その結果、大学図書館国際連絡委員会や日米会議実行委員会の委員長も黒田館長が引き継がれた。また、事務局長も田中久文氏から倉橋英逸氏（東大附属図書館事務部長）に交代した。
　黒田委員長のもとで代表団が正式に決定され、それぞれの役割を分担した。
　北米の大学図書館や議会図書館など海外調査の訪問先のご好意により調査スケジュールが作成された。我々は2班に分れてそれぞれ約2週間の調査を行い、所期の目的を果たすことができた。ここに訪問させていただいた機関や訪問に際して調整していただいたWelch氏、米国議会図書館のTsuneishi氏、カリフォルニア大学デービス校のDaily氏らに謝意を表したい。
　1988年9月、Dr. Welchが来日され、黒田委員長以下の関係者と最終の打ち合わせを行って、細部を決定した。
　以上が会議開催に至る経過である。あらためて会議を実現した関係者のご努力と内外から寄せられた暖かいご支援に深く感謝するとともに、会議の成功を心から祈りたい。
　また、さらに日米会議の将来の開催が両国の大学図書館にとって有益であり、相互協力の成果が、それによってもたらされることを確信していることを付け加えて私の報告を終える。

終り無き戦い―コンピュータ、図書館と東洋研究

John W. Haeger

　東洋図書館（East Asian Library）の自動化についての会議が、たまたま、あるいは世話人の巧妙な仕掛によってかどうかは別にして、北アメリカで記念すべき10回を数えることとなった。1978年10月に、ユージン・ウ、カネコ　ヒデオ、パット・バッテンと私は、プリンストン大学のモート教授とスタンフォード大学のウォード教授と共に米国学会協議会（American Council of Learned Societies）のニューヨーク事務所に集まりました。それは、ACLSと社会科学研究協議会（Social Science Research Council）と米国研究図書館協会（Association of Research Libraries）の東洋図書館研究プログラム（East Asian Library Program）をスタートさせるためのものでした。図書館の自動化を最初の目標にする気持ちはなかったのです。それよりはむしろ、わが国では外国の地域研究のための学外からの援助に翳りがみられるなかでの、東洋の言葉で書かれた資料を入手し整理するために要する経費は増加していること、また、紙の保存という面での問題、さらには、東洋図書館の専門家を新たに養成することの困難の方に関心があったと言えます。しかし、図書館の自動化はいろいろな意味で大学・研究図書館の業務に影響を及ぼしていたことは気になっていたので、共同事業のための諮問委員会は、自動化ということにかなり素早く関心を示しました。しかし、自動化そのものとして終始してしまうのでなく、相変らず関心の的であった経済性、専門性と構造的な問題を処理する手段として強調していたのです。

　1979年6月に諮問委員会（advisory committee）は、漢字処理システムについて調査するための特別委員会を組織して日本に派遣しました。その年の暮に、委員会は東洋の書物とその書誌的統一（bibliographic systems）に関する国際会議を企画、開催したのです。1980年には研究図書館グループ（RLG）は、メロン財団、フォード財団、米国人文科学基金（National Endowment for the Humanities）の援助をうけて、世界ではじめて図書館オンライン・ネットワークでの業務処理と東洋の言葉で書かれた資料の情報検索システムへの途を拓きました。1983年9月には、研究図書館情報ネットワーク（RLIN）で東洋のものが十分に処理できるようになりました。数年後にはOCLCも同様の機能をもつようになったのです。さらに、

台北にある国立中央図書館（National Central Library）のローカル・システムができましたし、日本では学術情報センターの共同目録システムがスタートしましたし、Utlas ではジャパン・マークを利用した目録システムについて発表を行っています。中国国立図書館（National Library of China）は、CJK の自動的処理機構（an automated CJK capability）を開発する契約を WLN と結びました。また、国立国会図書館と国文学研究資料館（National Institute of Japanese Literature）のシステムも利用可能となりました。

　RLG（研究図書館グループ）のCJK レコードは、ほぼ400,000に達しました。それらのレコードは、ＬＣと RLG 参加館によってオンラインで入力されたものです。これ以外のものとしてはフーヴァー研究所とカリフォルニア大学バークレー校が所蔵している日本の政府刊行物、台北にある国立中央図書館所蔵の中国古典籍、学術雑誌総合目録、北京にある中国科学院（Chinese Academy of Sciences）作成の論文抄録などのデータが中国中央図書館、中国国立図書館、国立国会図書館のマークと同じように今年の暮から来年（1989）にかけてロードされる予定です。RLIN の目録・受入れモジュールにおける CJK 処理機能（CJK capability）と一体となっているこれらのデータベースが、ハードウェアの値段が高いにもかかわらず、多くの機関が CJK を処理するために要する経費の上昇を食い止め、ないしは削減するための手助けとなっていることは疑う余地がありません。このことは、ACLS（米国学会協会）の委員会がまさしく意図したことだったのです。

　RLIN のこれからの方向の中には、東洋図書館が抱えている諸々の問題に共同で取り組むことも含まれています。米国人文科学基金とルーチェ財団からの援助を得て、RLG の６つの機関とＬＣ（議会図書館）は、1880年から1949年の間に出版され崩壊の危機に直面している中国の資料をフィルム化するという２年間にわたるプロジェクトを1986年に発足させました。同様に、こわれかけている日本と韓国の資料の保存プロジェクトも計画に引き継がれることになっています。フィルム化することが決定されたもの（順番待ちリスト）とマイクロ化された資料の書誌データは共に RLIN のデータ・ベースに収められています。26の RLG 傘下の東洋図書館の代表で構成されている東洋委員会（EAPC：East Asian Program Committee）は、オリジナル目録作業と高額資料の購入に伴う負担を分けあうことを検討する共同プロジェクトとして活動しています。EAPC は、たとえば、オリジナル目録作業をＬＣの主題区分ないしは言語によって分担することができるか、また、例えば全集などの多巻もの

（multi-title sets）を含めて買集めたもの（backlogs）が共同目録作業によって処理しなければならない程沢山あるのかについて検討（摸索）しているところです。日本語の資料についてふれてみますと、円がかつてなかったほど強くなりました。その影響を少しでも少なくするため、東洋委員会では、予算が足りなくて過去2年にわたって継続購入を中止しているもの及び値がはる日本語の雑誌およびセットもののリストを作成し、こうした資料が RLG の参加館のどこかで購入または整備されることを担保するようにしています。これらの資料に対するグールプ内での付託（institutional commitments）を RLIN の書誌レコードのローカル注記に記入し公示できるようになっています。次に、合同で遡及変換（retrospective conversion project）が提案されたのですが、結果として仏教、中国経済を含めて東洋関係の特定の主題に関する CJK レコードが30,000ほど RLIN に加わりました。

　1978年以降、利用者のアクセスおよびデータ処理に関して、私共が期待していた以上の変革がありました。1978年には私共の世界は確かに紙中心（bibliocentric）になりました。

　私共は、図書館の問題、すなわち、購入・受入れ、整理、保存ということに関心がありました。私共は、カード目録に取り囲まれる形で影の薄かった端末をみて、カード目録を端末に置き換えてしまおうということについて朧気な展望を抱いていました。しかし、かなりの数の端末を整備できるのか、中央演算処理装置（CPU）にそれをサポートできるだけの容量があるのかについての不安もありました。1980年はじめのパソコン革命はそうした状況をすっかり変えてしまいました。ほぼ一夜のうちに端末専用機（terminals）は過去のものとなったのです。個々の研究者向に、図式的で窓に似た形をしている処理容量の大きいワークステーションが出現したのです。このワークステーションは、文字処理（word processing）機能をもち、データベース機能をもち、他のことへの発展性もあり、デスクトップ・パブリシング（＊卓上できれいな印刷物を作成する。このためには、PCS とプリンターの双方にソフトが必要）ができるものでした。そして、大学のローカル・エリア・ネットワーク（LAN）への接続および他の数多くの書誌ユーティリティへの道をつける（gatewayed＊コンピュータ同志の接続）こともできますし、また、相互利用の要求および電子メールをするため、および、ワークステションの操作によってデータを取込む（download）ことを目的として、実用的なデータベースにアクセスすることも可能です。さらに、引用したデータとテキスト環境の情報源からの書誌データ以外の情報

（全文、統計、イメージ情報）とを統合することも可能なのです。
　この新たな展開は目ざましい程の割合で確実なものとなりました。第一世代のパーソナル・ワークステーションは確かにすばらしいものでした。例えばA／UX（＊ソフトウェアの名称）で作動するマークⅡは機能的なものとなりました。多くの大学では広がりをもったネットワーク（broad band network）が構築されました。BITNET（＊IBMの遠隔スプーリング通信サブシステム－RSCS－のプロトコロルを用いて構築された大学間の情報交換用ネットワーク、30か国950大学が接続）をはじめ、CSNET, ARPANET, NSFNETのように端末サポート機関によって提供されているネットワークは、国内外に拠点（nodes）があり計算機本体と相互接続しています。このように進んだ、そして機能的なワークステーションのためのソフトウェア市場規模は、数億ドルの産業となっています。
　当然のことながら、パーソナル・コンピュータ（ワークステーションより機能が少ないもの）を持った研究者はなお少数います。つまり、ネットワーク型のパーソナル・コンピュータは、文字処理機能だけの単独型（stand-alone）の4倍にもなっています。また、一部の大学だけがキャンパス内のネットワークを利用して所蔵目録をオンラインで検索できるようにしました。利用者が書誌ユーティリティにアクセスするには、OCLCのキャンパス間接続（CompuServe gateway）とRLGのTELENETを利用したパイロット・プロジェクトに限定されています。しかし、めざましい速度で変革が進んでいます。研究的なものに利用するワークステーション（scholar workstations）で必要とされる機能はすべて満たされています。技術的に誤っているものはありません。すくなくともローマ字や数字の世界でこれからやらなければならないものがあるとすれば、それは個々の要素を統合すること位でしょう。しかしながら、東洋の文字で表現されている我々の書誌データないしその他のデータに関しては、なお重要な問題に直面しています。東洋の諸国が作成した書誌データを簡単に移動し異なるシステム（disparate system）間でデータを交換することに関しては、ソフトウェアの世界でその展開が始まったばかりです。この夏にRLGは第三世代のCJKハードウェア、つまり多言語ワークステーション（multiscript workstation -MSW-）を導入します。この多言語ワークステーション（MSW）は、中国語、日本語、韓国語の文字だけでなくヘブライ語、キリル文字で書かれた書誌情報を処理できるようになっています。多言語ワークステーションとは、IBM-PC/ATクラスのパソコン（＊海外で販売されている一般的なパソコン）にワイズ700高解像度モニター

と東洋の文字を入力できるようにデザインされた利用者用のキーボードを装備したものです。また、MSW は、RLIN の端末としても利用できるようにソフトウェアを組み込んでいます。さらに大切なこととして、アンハイム（California）の JHL 研究所で開発・製品化され、国内特許となっている CJK の２バイトコードに、RLIN のデータベースと OCLC でも使われている３バイト・コード表をそのソフトとしていることです。（＊RLIN の DB では JHL の２バイトコードを基本にして３バイトコード表を作り、それを MSW のソフトとした。）チャイナ・スター（China Star＊ソフト名）は、JHL 特有の文字生成と画面制御（JHL translator＊コード変換プログラムとも言う）システムを基本にしています。MSW には、市販の文字処理（コマーシャル・ソフト名：Write^{tm}）、データ・ベース（ソフト名：dBaseIII）作表（ソフト名：Lotus 1-2-3）といったソフトも使用でき、これらのプログラムで作成された表などのフィールドに CJK 文字を挿入することが可能です。JHL コード（市販のソフトウェアの影響を受けている）RLIN コード（EACC：書誌記述用東洋文字コード－NISO　規格草稿－）との間の変換表（map）は、RLIN, OCLC のような書誌情報源（bibliographic resources）と大量の市販ソフト間でデータの置き換えを行うために欠かせないもの（key）であるといえます。

　現在の状況からみると良いニュースだけがあることになります。しかし、ワークステーション同志の接続（workstation-network-gateway）によってファイル転送とかデータ通信がくまなく行われるようになるには、なお時間がかかるでしょう。こうしたことを可能にするのには、特殊な機構（device）とか固有のコードとか、また、規格外のものとか、それだけにしか使えないとかがあるという点で、多くの事柄を解決しなければなりません。ここで例をあげて説明します。

第１点、JHL コード変換プログラムは、ごくごく一般的にパソコンのディスプレイに表示する内容を入れたメモリー（＊日本では video rom といっている）管理することのできる市販のソフトエア・パッケージでしか作動せず、JHL とは異なったやりかたで文字を制御（コントロール）しようとする場合には使えません。また、作動するパッケージの中には Word Perfect（ソフト名）のようなポピュラーなプログラムは含まれていないのです。

第２点、多言語ワークステーション（MSW）は表示制御装置をもった特殊なハードウェアです。したがって、JHL コード変換プログラムは個々の表示制御装置それぞれに組み込んでいかなければなりま

せん。
　第3点、RLGが選択した東洋の文字を入力するための装置は、独特な語句解析（component-sequence-analysis）と一般的なキーボードが一緒になったようなもので、スイッチによって入力システムを切り換えるようになっています。すなわち、入力方法を一通りではなく、どのような文字を入力するとしても、区切記号、スラッシュなどの入力上の問題が残るので、ローマ字入力のためのキーボード（QWETRY keybord）のような一般的な入力システムとの切り換えができるようにしておく必要があります。したがって、入力システム内でのコード切り換えのためには対応表が必要ですし、それは誰かが常に管理しなくてはならないでしょう。
　第4点、個々の文字（体系）によって作成されたデータをソートする（ローマ字の世界でデータをアルファベット順にする）場合、東洋の文字を一様にならべるための体系―EACCも含めて―、つまり辞書を編纂する場合にとる意味のある配列法がないので、システムではソートされたデータを16進コードに置き換えて行っています。
　第5点、作成された記録（データ）は、ワークステーションが同じハードウェアとソフトウェアで構成されている場合にのみ、読まれたり処理されます。アメリカのベンダーが扱っている市販の東洋の文字処理用ワークステーションは内部コードを独自のものにしているので互換性はありません。文字セットの国際交換のためのISO規格は、東洋の文字を含んだデータを異なったシステム（disparate systems）間でも処理・出力できるようにすることを考慮に入れて、現在検討されています。もし提案されているフォントの登録が、多様な東洋のフォント（字形）をEACC（書誌的利用のための東洋文字コード）の体系に写像（map）するものであるならば、学術情報の交流をさらに助長することになるでしょう。したがって、規格が採択されたならば、まずそれを広め、取入れるべきでしょう。しかし、どのレベルでの登録が提案された場合に書誌的なニーズに合致するのかははっきりしていません。また、それぞれのシステムで生成されたデータを統合しようというのであれば、コンピュータの世界と図書館の世界の間に生じた、ISOのテクニカル委員会でもみられた両者の対立の溝を埋めるようにしなければならないでしょう。
　最後に、データ通信の領域ではかなり深刻な問題があります。文字コードとして最低位7ビットのアスキー（ASKII）の基準とちがって、JHLのようなところの文字コードはすべて8ビットになっています。多くの通信機器は、通常、最低位7ビットで認識するようになっているので、JHLのようなコードを用いた精度の高い電送装

置はサポートされません。アメリカの立場からすると、他に最も好ましいものはと言えば、それはかって NISO および ISO に登録されていた EACC（書誌的利用のための東洋文字コード・セット）であると言えます。EACC はあらゆる通信のためのプロトコルとして ISO にしたがって開発されたという点で有利であると言えますが、不幸なことに、それは一般的なワークステーションのソフトとして普及していない3バイト文字のためのものであるという不利な側面をも兼ね備えています。データ通信のためには、EACC コードへの変換、EACCコードからの変換は避けられないことのように思えます。さらに、EACC はアジアでは採用されないでしょうから、データ・ファイルが太平洋を渡ってきた時には、EACC と日本語、中国語、韓国語の文字との間のコード変換がさらに必要となり、いくつかの文字コードが現実の体系とは関係なくコード変換の過程で浮かび上ってくるでしょう。

あらゆるコード変換は、概念的には単純ですが、実際は複雑であり、少なくとも高いものになる可能性があります。言語史および正字法の発達という視点でみると、お互に国の統一的な文字コードを描くことはインテレクチュアルであると同時に重要な仕事です。コード化の仕事は大変なものになるでしょう。というのは、JIS 以外の統一コードは最近になって実現したものであり、また、東洋の文字（セット）はもともと動的で一定した形がないので、国の標準コード自体が不安定なものとなり絶えず調整する必要がありましょう。また、調整のプロセスは東洋の標準化機構とか利用者団体にはよく理解されないでしょうし、責任をもって合意されることもないでしょう。さらに、日本には日本工業規格があり、それはコンピュータ・メーカーによって面目を与えられ実施されているものなので、日本を除外して考えると、機械のコードは、入・出力のためにデータを国の標準コードから、また、国の標準コードへの変換のための要請から、固有ないし排他的なものとなってしまうのです。

ローカルな図書館システムの場合は、東洋の文字について他の厳しい状況があります。アメリカのローカル図書館システムでは、蔵書管理、雑誌管理、目録の維持、受入れ、オンライン目録検索が早く実現されました。100万レコードがユーティリティからローカル・システムへロードされました。しかし、CJK のデータを含んだレコードが特殊な問題を提起しています。一般的なローカル・システムで CJK データを扱うことができるようになっているものはありません。現在、RLG（研究図書館グループ）は、ローカル・システムの端末に RLG-JHL の文字生成のためのキーボードをつけて CJK

の文字をディスプレイで表示できるのか、また、アプリケーション・レベルでの変更も必要となるのか、その結果、ベンダーおよび利用者が負うべき負担がどの程度大きくなるのかについて調査しているところです。

　ここ10年の間に東洋文字を書誌情報の処理の分野で扱うことについてはすばらしく進歩しました。ユニマーク基準に準拠したナショナル・マーク・フォーマットが日本、中国、台湾で定められました。ＵＳマークの場合も、非ローマ字のデータを並行したフィールドで扱えるようにフォーマットを拡張しました。情報交換のために、漢字コードを多平面的（multi-planar）なものとして開発したこと（CCCII）、すなわち3バイトコードは異形文字（＊同じ漢字でありながら字体が異なったり意味が異なったりするもの）をリンクするための技術として確立されました。RLIN による CJK システムの完成、OCLC による CJK ワークステーションの開発、さらに日本における学術情報ネットワーク・システムの出現によって、CJK の書誌データが多くの機関によって作成されるという状況が生まれました。RLG の CJK シソーラスは国の標準的な文字コード間の変換表の決定版といったものとなりました。しかし、東洋の多くの地域ではコンピュータ革命がゆきわたっていないこと、またコードとかフォントに関して産業界全体への広がりをもった標準的な規格がないという点では、まだハンディを背負わされていると言えましょう。システム間相互のデータ通信やファイル転送はまったくやっかいです。東洋の文字を使っている人々は、さまざまな障害が取り除かれる時が来るまでは多くを期待できないでしょう。

和図書ファイルの持ち方

菅 原　　通

はじめに

　命題は、日本語、中国語、韓国語のファイルをどう持つかということであった。ことに、日本において、データ・ベース上において中国語、韓国語の文献の書誌データを日本語の文献の書誌データと混在させられるか、ということである。ところが、これには、コトバの問題と漢字へのアクセスの仕方、換言すれば、日本語、中国語、韓国・朝鮮語における漢字とその形の問題を解決しないかぎり困難であると言わざるを得ない。

　コトバ、文字の問題は特に日本語と中国語の間に存在する。それは、両国語とも同じように漢字を用いる言葉だからである。漢字は表意文字であるから、〝読み〟と漢字形が一致して始めて情報が誤解なく伝達できるという側面をもっている。たとえば、「現代中国之出版自由」という文献があるとする。中国語では、アルファベットを用いた四声（pinn）でこれを表記するから、
　　　　xiandai zhongguo zhi chuban ziyou
となる。ところが、日本人はこれを漢文を読むのと同じ要領で、
　　　　ゲンダイ　チュウゴク　ノ　シュッパン　ノ　ジユウ
　　　　　　　　　　　　　　　　　　　　　　（カナ表記）
　　　　Genndai chuugoku no shuppann no jiyuu（ローマ字表記）
と表記して読み下してしまうことができる。中国語を上記のように日本語形で表記するのは誤りであるが、仮に読み下してしまった場合（この可能性は十分ある）これの持つ意味は変わらないから、これは、表記されているのを見る限り、日本語の文献なのか、中国語の文献なのか理解できない。さらに、索引画面に
　　　　中国之　　出版　　自由
　　　　中国の　　出版の　　自由
と表示された場合、上に表示されているのが中国語の文献で、下に表示されているのが日本語の文献だととっさに判断できる利用者はどの位いるであろうか。

　ところが、英語、ドイツ語等々欧米諸国語の場合は、それぞれの言語によって同じ単語であっても多少の変化があり、また発音（読み）も異なるから、

1　…Anne…

2　…anne'…

となっていても、その識別は可能であるが、索引画面で〝出版〟という文字を見ただけでは、これは、日本語なのか中国語なのかの区別は困難である。もっとも中国では簡体字がかなり増えているので、この場合は容易に識別可能であるが、日本人はその字体を導入して日本語の中で用いてしまうこともある（著作物の中で用いられることは稀である）ので、完全に識別できるとは言いがたい。このように、同じファイルの中での日本語と中国語における漢字の識別は、表記（読み）によってのみ可能と思われる。しかし、システムの中で一つの漢字に日本語の「読み形」（標音）、中国語の「読み形」（併音ないしはアルファベット表記）、韓国・朝鮮語の読み形を与えることは可能であろうか。換言すれば、漢字をコード化する場合は、一つの言語におけるコード化（たとえば、JIS＝Japan Industrial Standards）であって、この中に字形が同じであるという理由で中国語の漢字に日本の漢字コードを与えてしまって何等支障をきたさないかということである。

　ここで、漢字のコードについて若干ふれてみたい。コンピュータで情報を処理する時の単位にはビット(bit)よりも上位の単位としてバイト(byte)があることは周知のことである。通常、8ビットで1バイトである。8ビットというのは、2の8乗、10進でいえば256の大きさである。換言すれば、1バイトの数値を使えば、256の異なったものを表現できる。英字は大文字、小文字をあわせても52字、数字は10文字、また、カナは濁点や半濁点を独立した1字と考えれば約50字というように、これらは文字の種類が少ないから、1バイトの大きさのなかで十分表現できる。ところが、日本語の漢字・かなまじり文を処理するため、文字コード化しようとすると、漢字の場合は、その種類が多く、1バイトでは対応できず、コードに2バイトの容量を持たせることになる。2バイトは16ビット、2の16乗、10進で65,536という大きさになる。JISの漢字コードは、この領域の一部を漢字やその他の文字、記号に割当てた体系である。[1]このように、日本では漢字のみならず日本語の文章に現れる英数字などにもコードを与えてしまっているのである。ところが、中国語の文章にでてくる漢字は、日本語の文章のそれと字形は同じでも、「読み」と「意味」は全く異なるから、JISの体系の中に入れると漢字を重複して持つことになり、混乱を来たしかねないのである。

　次に、視点を変えて日本語と英語について考えてみたい。日本におけるシステムでは、日本語のかな、漢字は2バイト、アルファベットで書き表わす欧米諸国の言語は1バイトで持つことにしている。

ところが、日本人は、日本語の文字列のなかに外国語を混ぜて文章を書くことがある。たとえば、「VAN の理解を求める本」などはその例であるが、VAN は英語の value added network の略語である。本来は英語の略語であっても日本語の文字列に用いられる場合にはその言葉が日本語のなかに定着しているかぎり、日本語と同じように2バイトで表記する必要がある。そのため、入力に際し、"V" は日本語の "V"（2バイト）と注意しなければならない。しかし、日本語の文字列の中にあっても、VAN は英語なのだから、1バイトで表示せよ、という人があるかも知れない。この場合、1バイトで表示されていようが、2バイトで表示されていようが、その識別は可能であるが、1バイト、2バイトが混在しているためにロジックを間違えやすい。

さて、私のいる早稲田大学図書館は、日本語の書誌データと外国語の書誌データを同一のファイルにもっている。つまり、現代中国語（中文）、ハングル（韓国語）、キリル文字などシステム化が困難な言語を除いて、ファイル上における言語の区別をなくした。言語の区別は個々の書誌データの固定長フィールドで言語コードを与えているだけである。日本語と外国語（キリル文字などを除く）の図書の書誌データを同一のファイルに持たせることはできたが、中国語、韓国・朝鮮語については当面除外をせざるを得なかった。また、現時点では、いつになったら、中国語、韓国・朝鮮語を扱えるかの見通しもない。その主な理由は、(1)中国語の漢字のコード化ができないこと、つまり、JIS 漢字コードと重複させないように中国語の漢字をコード化するためには、2バイトのどの領域を使うのか、3バイトにするのかについて日本における方向を見定めることができないためである。さらに、システムへの入力方法の問題もコード化の後にひかえているのである。(2)中国および韓国・朝鮮の図書を「漢文で書かれたもの」と中国語文図書ないしハングルに分けて扱いたいとの意向が図書館の現場には強い。このことは、漢字のコード化とも密接に関連すると思われる。「漢文」と「日本語の漢字・かなまじり文」のファイルを同じにするのであれば、JIS でコード化されている以上の漢字をシステムに持たせなければならないからである。

このように、一口に CJK といっても、日本では、日本語と漢文は同一ファイルが可能であるのに対し、漢字を用いる日本、中国、韓国・朝鮮の図書を同一のファイルでくくろうとするアメリカとでは、その認識の仕方に違いがあるように見受けられる。この違いはさておき、中国語, 韓国・朝鮮語における漢字のコード化、および

ハングルのコード化について、日本ではこれから検討されることになろう。
　私は、今回、以下の2点について報告したい。
　第一は、日本におけるマークの現状と、私の所属する早稲田大学図書館で開発した和図書と洋図書を同一のデータベースで持つ方法。とくに、その場合のデータ項目の変換の問題を中心に考えてみたいと思う。
　第二は、日本において CJK という考え方があるのかについて歴史的に検討してみたい。また、私の専門ではないが、漢字のコード化の問題と中国語図書のデータベース化の問題についての私見を述べたいと考える。

日本語（和図書）マーク（MARC）の現状

　本来マークとは、国の全国書誌作成機関が作成した機械可読目録（Machine Readable Catalog）を指したものである。ところが、日本では全国書誌作成機関である国立国会図書館によって作成されているジャパン・マーク（JAPAN/MARC）の他に民間（大手取次会社）によって作られている市販マーク（民間マーク）がある。ジャパン・マークの場合、図書が国立国会図書館に納本されてから、その書誌データが機械可読化されるまでに平均90日を要するが、納本の遅れなどの原因によって、それ以上経過したのちに書誌データがマークに掲載されるといったケースも少なくない。これに対し当初は自社の商品取引のための管理用データとして開発された市販マークの場合は、流通の問題とも深くかかわっているので図書が出版されてから出来るかぎり早くその書誌データを収録する必要があった。そのため、図書が出版されてから2ないし3週間後にはその書誌データが市販マークに収録されている。したがって、市販マークはジャパン・マークよりタイム・ラグ（time lag）が少ない点を買われ、また、日本には目録情報の提供（Cataloguing in Publication＝CIP）といったシステムがなく、市販マークがその役割を果たしていることもあり、公共図書館、学校図書館、大学図書館などで目録作業、図書の選択・発注に利用されている。

1．市販マークの現状

　市販マークは、公共図書館がコンピュータを導入したのにともなって図書館界に根をおろしはじめたと言ってよい。日本図書館協会が1983年に実施した調査によると、131の公共図書館中33館が何らかの形でマークを利用し、その目的として、(1)整理業務の軽減　(2)資

料検索　(3)総合目録の作成をあげている。

　このように、公共図書館が図書館の機械化に合わせてマークを使いはじめたら、公共図書館における利用を目標におくかたちで、市販マークは急速に広がったと言えよう。その理由として次のことが考えられる。

(1)　今日、公共図書館のコンピュータ化の目的が貸出管理から図書情報の管理へと進んできていること。浦安、杉並などでサービス・ポイント間のネットワーク化が公共図書館でかなり見受けられるようになった。従来は、図書を借り出した場所に行かなければ返却などができなかったが、どこのサービス・ポイントで図書を借りても、借りた場所にその図書を返却に行かないでも最寄りの場所で図書の返却ができるという利用者サービスを考えてのネットワーク化であったと言える。しかし、最近では、情報の一元化にネットワーク化の目的を置いているところが多い。

(2)　情報管理、情報の一元化のためには、検索に耐え得る目録情報の入力が必要である。しかし、規模の小さい公共図書館では、情報管理のために十分な専門的職員を抱えることは不可能であろう。そのために、マークの活用は有効な手段である。現在も、公共図書館では購入した図書の整理・装備を図書整備会社に外注することが多く、かつ、その図書整備会社は大手取次の系列にあることが多い。そこでは、かなりの量の図書の整理・装備を短期間に完了させることを要請されていたため、そこでは系列会社の作成したマークを利用することでその要求に応えてきた。したがって、図書の発注・納入・整理・マークの提供がセットとなっている感がある。

(3)　公共図書館で購入する図書の大部分は新刊の読み物資料ないし実用書である。また、最近では利用者からのリクエストによって図書を購入することも多い。利用者が地域の図書館に求めるものは、新聞などの広告でみた読み物的資料であり、それらを利用者に迅速に提供するためには、図書の受入・整理を急がねばならない。したがって図書を整理するためにジャパン・マークを利用することはタイム・ラグの点から殆ど考えられないであろう。

　現在、日本で市販されている民間マークは、(1)日販マーク（日本出版販売図書センター編集、大日本印刷入力、ジャパン・コンピュータ・テクノロジー販売）(2)TRCマーク（日本図書館協会編集。凸版印刷入力、図書館流通センター＜TRC＞発売）(3)大阪屋マーク（大阪屋、フィルム・ルックス編集、東洋情報サービス入力、大阪屋発売）の3種類である。名称および体制から推察できるように、

市販マークは図書の取次会社によって系列化されている。すなわち、日販マーク → 日本出版販売㈱＜日販＞、TRCマーク → 東京出版販売㈱＜東販＞、大阪屋マーク → 大阪屋という組合せである。このように、図書の販売取次会社自らの商品取引データの管理のための市販マークは、同時に、図書販売市場としての図書館攻略を武器として開発・販売されてきた、と言うべきであろう。

　以上、考察してきたように、市販マークが取次の系列によって作成されていることによって、市販マークはいくつかの制約を負わされていると言うことができる。

　その第一はデータの内容に関することである。市販マークは、新刊図書の市場への流通というタイミングに合わせる関係から、データの作成・提供の迅速性が問われることにより、データの詳細さ、正確度にはある程度目をつぶらざるを得ないということがある。たとえば、書名の扱いもその一つである。『日本古代文化の探求　馬』（社会思想社）の場合は、「日本古代文化の探求」をシリーズ名ととるか、総合書名ととるかによってデータの内容に差がでるとともに、検索にも影響を及ぼす。この書名を、ある市販マークでは、「日本古代文化の探求」が総合書名、「馬」を部編名と扱い、マークでは、

　　　Tag 251 $a 日本古代文化の探求 $d 馬　　とした。

　これをシステムに出力した場合、システムにおける索引画面の表示は

　　　　　　　日本古代文化の探求　馬　　　　　　　　　1

となる。

　また、「日本古代文化の探求」をシリーズ名、「馬」を本タイトルとすると、システムにおける出力は

　　　　　　　　　　　馬　　　　　　　　　　　　　　1
　　　　　　　日本古代文化の探求　　　　　　　　　　9

のようになる。こうした相違が市販マーク間に見られるであろう。また、主題分析の結果としての分類番号、件名は、それぞれが異なったものを与えていることが多い。[2]

　充分な資料情報の作成には、それなりの時間をかけざるを得ないという、スピードと精度の間の矛盾は、取次会社の業務においても新刊配送管理からの要請と、出版情報管理からの矛盾として現れてくる。この解決方法として、日販、東販においては、いわゆる市販マーク（日販マーク、TRCマーク）とはべつに「書籍銘柄データ」（日販）、「東販ゼロ・マーク」といった新刊マークを作成し、新

刊配送の際の物品管理用データとして用いている。この新刊マークは、データとして、書名、著者名、出版社、配送年月日、ISBN、書籍コード等（各社により記入内容は若干異なる）について、簡略な記入をしているにすぎず、英・米における CIP データに相当するものとはなり得ていない。市販マーク各社とも、この新刊マークを先に出し、一定の時間をかけて出版情報管理データを作成しているが、このようにマークを2本立にするからといって、出版情報管理のためのマーク作成の時期を、新刊書の最も取引量の多い時期からはずすことはできないであろう。というのは、まだコンピュータを導入していない公共図書館、学校図書館では、整理業務軽減のために、注文した図書を納入する際に図書カードを添付してくれることを期待する向きがあり、また、市場開拓のため、取次会社の間でも競合して印刷カード添付サービスを始めたという実情があるからである。図書に添付される印刷カードは、現在では、すべてマークから出力されたものとなっている。

　第2にカバー率の点にふれておきたい。市販マークには、それぞれの取次会社の取引ルートにのった図書の書誌データが入力されている。収録される図書の範囲は、いずれも系列取次扱いの図書および地方小出版物流通センター扱いの新刊図書である。実際に新規にマークに入力される点数は、コミックなど図書館が購入しそうもない図書は除かれ、また官公庁の出版物は商業ルートからはずれるので、ジャパン・マークの年間5万点強に比較して6割程度しかカバーしていない。(3)

2．各市販マークの概要
2．1．日販マーク
(1) 沿革

　市販マークの先駆けとしての日販は、1976年より出版物のデータの蓄積をはじめ、1978年東京・王子の流通センターでオンライン出版情報検索システム（Nippan Information Processing System=NIPS）を稼働させ、1984年より、注文・取引を含めたオンライン・システム NOCS（Nippon Online Communication System）を稼働させている。

(2) データ量

　1976年以降のもの35万点（1986年1月現在）である。これ以外に各種出版賞の受賞出版物等の不完全な書誌データが20万点程度ある。

(3) タイム・ラグ

新刊図書の出版後2週間で提供可能の状態になる。図書館への提供は注文後2週間とのことである。
(4) 新刊マーク

新刊図書の発売前日までに「書籍銘柄データ」と呼ばれる一種のマークを作成している。ただし、これは図書館等には提供されていない。新刊マークに記入されている内容は、書名、著者名、出版社、送品年月日、日販書籍コードなどである。また、データはすべて「かな」または英数字によって記述されており、検索を対象としたものではなく、新刊配送の際の物品管理のためのものである。

書籍銘柄データと日販マークとは「日販書籍コード」でリンクされており、両者の自動置き換えは可能である。ただし、「日販書籍コード」は3カ月周期で同一ナンバーを使用しているので、置き換えの際は「書籍コード」と発売年月日の両方をキーにする必要がある。また、日販マークには地方小出版物流通センター扱いのものが追加され、コミックなど図書館で購入しないものは削除されているので、100%の一致、置き換えはできない。

(4) 提供方法

当該年に発行されるものは、週単位の磁気テープ（600フィート）で提供される（年間50本）。

提供されるマークの仕様は、(a)4096バイトの可変長フォーマット（ジャパン・マーク仕様）と (b)1024バイトの固定長フォーマットの2通りである。書誌データの内容は、『日本目録規則　新版予備版』に準拠している。また、漢字コードは、JIS C 6226 第2水準、英数字のコードは、EBCDIC である。[4]

2．2．TRC マーク

(1) 沿革

TRC マークは、1981年に図書館流通センターにより発表された。出版情報の提供という面で日販より遅れていた東販は、1982年、日本図書館協会事業部を引き継いで設立された「図書館流通センター＝TRC」（1979年設立）と業務提携を行った。1983年より東販は、TRC の出版情報データを活用して東販 PICS（Publishing Information Catalog Retrieval System）を開発、さらに、1984年から TONETS（Tohan Total Online Network System）を稼働させている。

(2) データ量

1975年よりのデータ34万件（1985年8月現在）、これ以外にカ

ナのみのデータが15万件程度累積されている。新規に入力されるものは、東販と地方小出版物流通センター扱いの新刊図書であるが、新刊図書以外でも図書館から注文があり、図書館流通センターを通過した出版物で未入力のものは収録されることになっている。データの増加量は年間3万5千件程度である。

(3) 新刊マーク

　新刊図書の配送管理用に、発売前日までに「東販ゼロ・マーク」を作成している。これも図書館への提供は可能であるが、週単位にフロッピー・ディスクに落として発送しているため、図書館への到着は多少遅くなる。ゼロ・マークの項目は、書名（漢字20文字、かな20文字）、著者名（漢字10文字）、出版社（漢字7文字）、送品年月日、ISBN、Gコード、大きさ、である。ゼロ・マークとTRCマークはGコードでリンクされており、自動的に置き換えられるが、収録範囲が異なるので、全ての置き換えができるわけではない。

　なお、市販のTRCマークには、Gコードが入っていないため、図書館が新刊マークとTRCマークの両方を購入して置き換えをする場合には、TRCマークの方にGコードを注文、加工入力してもらう必要がある。

(4) 提供されるデータのタイプ

　TRCマークの場合は、提供するレコード・フォーマットを次の3通りとしている。

(a) Ⅲタイプ：固定長で300バイトである。検索の対象となるのは、書名1つ、著者名1つ、というように簡易なものであり、主に貸出管理用のデータである。

(b) Ⅵタイプ：固定長で1024バイトであり、検索用として利用可能である。

(c) Ⅴタイプ：256バイトを1ブロックとして、それを任意の数だけ連結することにより、必要なレコード長を確保しようとしている。

　現在、上記のいずれかの仕様によりTRCのデータ・サービスを受けている図書館は160館を超えるといわれる。[5]

2．3．大阪屋マーク

(1) 沿革

　このマークは現在市販されているマークの中では最も後発のものである。従来より提携関係にあった大阪屋と図書整理会社「フィルム・ルックス」が共同で開発したもので、1983年4月より販

売を開始した。
　このマークの特色として、次の点が指摘できる。
(a) 図書とマークを完全に切り離して、図書、マークのそれぞれを販売する方法をとっている。大阪屋がこうした販売方法をとるまでは、TRC、日販は、マークと図書とをセットにして販売してきた。その意味でマークの販売方法にひとつの先鞭をつけたと言えよう。
(b) 新刊図書マークの全点一括販売を開始したことである。従来、TRC、日販は、必要な書誌データを JLA 番号なり、NPL 番号によって切売りするという販売方法をとってきた。
(c) 新刊マークと市販マークの2つに出版情報データを分離せず、新刊マークのタイミングで市販マークを作成・販売した。このため、情報としてのデータ内容は粗く、情報検索には不向きと言われていた。こうした方法を採用したのは、次にあげる特色と密接に関連している。
(d) このマークは単独で利用されることを想定したものではなく、ジャパン・マークとの併用を考慮して作成したものであること。
(2) データ量
　1972年以降のもの約13万点を機械可読化したが、1982年以前の分は、日本図書館協会の『選定図書総目録』に掲載されたものだけを収録した。新規入力は、大阪屋扱いの図書で年間2万7千点である。
(3) 提供方法
　マークのみの販売、図書とのセット販売、全点一括販売、1点ごとの販売、のいずれも利用者の希望により選択可能である。[6]

2．4．書籍データ・センターについて

　日本出版取次協会の書籍統一コード委員会が中心となり、出版業各界と図書館界が協力する形で検討を進めてきた「標準 MARC」作成・提供の機構である㈱書籍データセンターが設立されることが報じられた。
　それによると、データセンターの事業目的は、(1)新刊書籍の標準的書誌記述を日本図書館協会（Japan Library Association=JLA）の監修により作製し、プロデューサーたる東販、日販、TRC の3社から、取次協会員社を経て業界各方面に提供する。(2)「標準マーク」から書籍単品項目データを「書籍流通情報 MARC」（流通マーク）として作成し、業界各方面の利用に供する。(3)業界の情報ネットワークのため、ISBN コードを管理する、となっている。[7]

この報道を読んだ限りでは、現在の市販マークとの関係が不明確である。「標準マーク」についてプロデューサーとして名前のあがっている1社に確認したところ、マーク・データの記載内容40項目について記述の統一を図った後、それぞれの市販マークに変換されるとのことであった。「標準MARC」（注、となると実体不明）が図書館に提供されるのではなく、必要があれば図書館は従来どおり市販マークを購入することになり、日本における市販マークの販売競争は今後も継続されることになりそうである。

和図書マーク（日本語マーク）の分析とシステムへの出力について

　日本の多くの大学図書館において、外国図書の蔵書全体に占める割合は、40～50％程度であろう。こうした状況を考慮し、早稲田大学図書館では、図書館システム・パッケージDOBIS/LIBISを導入した際、和図書と外国図書のファイルを分離せず、すべての書誌データを一つのファイルに持つこととし、そのための開発を行った。開発の概要については、同図書館副館長の成田誠之助、および開発担当係員の斎藤明が第6回DOBIS/LIBISユーザー・グループ会議（1987年9月於：ニース、フランス）で報告をしているので、私は和図書マークのデータの変換の問題に絞って説明させていただくこととする。

　和図書のマークと当面ＬＣマークを一つのファイルに持つためには、それぞれのマークの項目とそこに記述されている内容を分析し、フォーマットを一つにするための変換プログラムを作成しなければならない。幸いDOBISマークとＬＣマークのフォーマットは、ほぼ同じなので、われわれは、ジャパン・マークからＬＣマークへのフォーマットの変換を行った。この場合、ＬＣにあって、ジャパン・マークにないコントロール・フィールド（タグ0）については、ジャパン・マークを出力した場合、ない項目はブランクにした。

　次に、目録規則の違いから生じる記述方法の相違は、項目間を関係づけることによって、その解決を図った。項目間を関係づけるだけでは解決できない問題もあるので、それぞれのマークは、書誌プール（マーク・データだけを蓄積するファイル）にアップ・ロードし、マーク・データと同じ図書が所蔵され、書誌データを書誌プールからシステム目録上にコピーしてきた際に修正を加えることとした。

　現在、目録記述法で日本と国際書誌記述基準（ISBD）とで大きく異なっているのは、多巻、多冊出版物の扱いかたについてであろう。『日本目録規則　新版予備版』では、記述の単位を1物理単位（ブ

ック単位）としたために、分割記入方法を原則とした。ところが、AACR2およびISBDでは、多巻・多冊出版物については著作単位の記入とし、多段階記述法を採用している。この記入の単位の扱い方の違いがそれぞれのマークにも反映されている。日本でも昨年目録規則が改正され、『日本目録規則　1987年版』が公表され、そこでは、ISBDとの整合性が再検討され、ISBDの区切記号と多段階記述法が採用されている。しかし、「記入の記載方法においては、"MARCレコードから出力する場合は、各種の目録記入の記載方式に柔軟に対応することが可能なため」[8]多段階記述方式を含め、複数の記載方式をあげ、目的に応じて選択するかたちをとっているのである。また、従来の慣行が変更できない場合を考慮し、別法が作られている。このように、1987年版は、従来の手作業による目録記述に加え、ISBDに準拠したマーク・レコードの作成も考慮したため、規則が複雑なものとなっている。[9]

　こうした中で、ジャパン・マークをはじめ市販マークがISBDに準拠する形で、多段階記述ができるようにそのフォーマットを変更するかどうかについては全く予測できない。

　ところで、日本語で書かれた文献を検索する方法は、「読み」をとおして行われる。漢字検索は、まだ一部で行われているにすぎない。また、漢字検索においても、検索キーとなる漢字は「読み」から導かれる。したがって、和図書のマークには、アクセス・ポイントととして記述の「読み」のフィールドが存在する。これは、表音文字でできている外国のマークでは考慮されない項目である。この2点の違いをどう調整するかが、ファイルを一つにするかのカギになると考える。ここでは、ジャパン・マークの概要説明、項目の分析、それら項目の変換などについて説明する。

1．ジャパン・マーク

　国立国会図書館では、1971年にコンピュータを導入して以来、各種システムの開発を行いながら、コンピュータによる漢字データの処理について研究を行ってきた。そして、1977年1月より和図書データの入力を開始しているが、入力したデータをジャパン・マークとして外部に頒布を開始したのは、1981年4月第1週の『日本全国書誌　週刊版　1981年13号』に該当する書誌データからであり、それまでは『納本週報』の編集に利用してきた。

　既入力データについても、遡及分として1981年1〜12号分については同年8月に、また、1979年〜1980年分についても1982年4月に頒布し、1977〜1978年分についても一部データの手直しを行い、1984

年4月に頒布を完了している。

　また、国立国会図書館は、新規のデータ入力と並行する形で国立国会図書館蔵書目録の入力を行っている。蔵書目録第3期（1969～1976年）分の約22万件のデータ入力作業を分野別に行っており、作業が完了した分野から順次頒布を行っている。この蔵書目録第3期分全10編の完成予定は1990年2月である。さらに、1988年から蔵書目録第1－2期（1943～1968年）分のデータ入力を開始する。この分は1992年3月に完了する予定である。また、国内で刊行されている逐次刊行物（中国語、ハングル、その他アジアの諸言語を除く）の書誌データをジャパン・マーク（シリアル）として刊行することとしている。

　ジャパン・マークに収録されている資料は、1983年を例にとると、官公庁納入資料が13,357点、民間納入資料が40,196点の計53,553点である。

2．ジャパン・マーク・フォーマットの特徴
　ジャパン・マークの仕様は次の通りである。
A．原則
　(1)　磁気テープのレコード・フォーマットはISO　2709に準拠している。
　(2)　書誌レコード内における収録書誌データ要素の排列、構成などはUNIMARCを参考とした。
　(3)　論理レコード。フォーマットの構成は、レコード・ラベル、ディレクトリー、書誌データからなっている。
　(4)　文字表現形式
　　(a)　EBCDIC またはJIS C6220
　　(b)　漢字符号系（JIS C6226）＊国立国会図書館内部の和図書データでは独自の漢字コードで入力されているが、ジャパン・マークとして刊行する際に漢字コードの変換を行っている。
　　(c)　漢字符号系制御文字（JIS C6225）
　　(d)　JIS C6226以外の文字コードは予備エリアに配置している。
B．特徴
　第1に文字表現形式の標準化について若干コメントしておきたい。ジャパン・マークでは漢字を取り扱うための標準化を行った。それは、日本人が文献を検索する場合「読み」からアクセスすることが多いので、漢字に対して「読み」を与え、その表記法として、カタカナおよびローマ字（訓令式）による分ち書きを採用したことである。

第2にジャパン・マークは、日本語の文章を処理するため、日本語の特色としてあげられている次の事柄に配慮の跡が見られる。
(1)　日本語では文字の種類が多く、かつ字形が複雑であることへの対応として、新字体を優先し、旧字体は新字体に直して使うこととした。
(2)　日本語には同音異義語が多い。漢字が表意文字であるから、漢字を用いている限りこれを避けることは出来ない。たとえば、「デンキ」という読みに対して、電気（electronics）、伝記（biography）などが対応する漢字形である。したがって、「読み」を与えただけでは同音異義語の区別がつかないから、漢字と読みを対でもちいて区別をして処理できるようにした。
(3)　日本語には「分ち書き」の習慣がない。たとえば、英語では、university△library というように語と語の間にスペース（ここでは△で示す）が入る。ところが、日本語では「大学図書館」というように書きあらわす。このように日本語では「語」単位の区別がないので、検索用のキーワードを抽出することができない。この対策として、日本語の「かな混じり文」の中から、キーワードを切り出せるように、「読み」の部分で「分ち書き」をした。この方法では「読み」形からしかKWIC索引は作成できないので、検索上の不便を解決できないし、又、KWIC索引画面における検索上で、同音異義語を区別することができない。
　したがって、ジャパン・マークでは、「漢字・かなまじり文」を記述するフィールドとは別に2つの「読み」のフィールドを用意して、それぞれに「カタカナ」形の読み、「ローマ字」形の読みを記述している。したがって、ある部分は、記述形、カタカナ形、ローマ字形の三重の構造になっている。そのため、書名、著者、件名のフィールドはこの構造になっており、フィールドのタグ（tag）で関連づけを行っている。この関係を示すと次のようになる。

＜記述ブロック＞	＜アクセス・ポイント・ブロック＞[10]
タグ251　書名と著者に関する事項	タグ551$aカナの読み$Xローマ字読み タグ771$a著者カナ読み$X著者ローマ字読み
タグ291　多巻ものの各巻の書名と著者名に関する事項	タグ591$a巻書名のカナ読み$Xローマ字読み タグ791$a著者カナ読み$X著者ローマ字よみ
タグ280叢書名に関する事項	タグ580$aカナの読み$Xローマ字読み
タグ650　人名件名 タグ658　一般件名	タグ650$a人名のカナ読み$Xローマ字読み タグ658$aカナ読み$Xローマ字$B漢字形

3．三重構造部分の変換・出力について

　ジャパン・マークでは、ＬＣマークのタグ245に対応するものが2つある。これは、すでに述べたように目録記入単位の相違からくるものである。日本では目録を物理単位で記述することにしたため、多巻ものの場合、『日本目録規則　新版予備版』では、「巻書名」という独特の概念を生み出した。AACR2では、多巻ものの場合は、多段階記述をとっているので、日本で巻書名の位置に記述されたタイトルが固有の標題となる場合、ジャパン・マークのタグ251は、ＬＣマークでは全体レベルの記述のタグ245に該当し、また、ジャパン・マークのタグ291は、各巻レベルの記述のタグ245に該当する。早稲田大学図書館では、ジャパン・マークとＬＣマークとを日本語の特徴を生かしながら極力近づけることとしているので、いくつかの変換を行った。

　その第1は、漢字形とその「読み」を同じフィールドに持つことである。第2は、「読み」の部分だけが「分ち書き」されていて、記述部分（漢字形）で分ち書されていないのでは、漢字形のキーワドを作成できないから、それを作成するため、読み形、漢字形の双方を「分ち書き」した。この「分ち書き」の作業を人手によるのでは、その労力と時間的にも大変なので、まず機械的な処理をし、処理しきれなかった部分を人手によることとした。機械的処理の方法として採用したのは、日本語キーワード自動抽出プログラム（Automatic Japanese Keyword Extraction Program=AJAX)および KMATCH(Keyword Match＝早稲田で開発＝分ち書きされたキーワードについて、漢字形と読み形の語数を一致させる)である。第3は、書誌構造を AACR2 のそれに近づけることなどである。これらについては、ジャパン・マークの分析と対応させながら説明をしていきたい。まず、漢字形とその読みを同じフィールドに置くことを、書名（タグ251）を例にとって説明する。

ジャパン・マークでは、3重構造の部分の部分は、次のようになっている。
　　タグ251$A 限りなき前進 $B 日本アメリカンフットボール五十年史 $F タッチダウン株式会社//編　　　　　（記述部分）
　　タグ551$A カギリ△ナキ△ゼンシン $XKagiri△naki△zennsinn$b#251　　　　　（書名の読みの部分）
　　タグ751$A タッチ△ダウン△カブシキ△カイシャ//ヘン $XTatti△daunn△kabusiki△kaisha//henn$B タッチダウン株式会社編#　　　　　　　　　　　　　（責任表示の読みの部分）

上記のマーク・データを次のように出力することとした。
　a．タグ251は、DOBIS の tag245 にロードする。
　　　$A と $B（書名と副書名）の間に△:△を機械的に付与する。
　b．タグ551(書名の読み形)$A(カナ読み)の部分だけを DOBIS の tag245 に@△を挿入のうえ置く。
この結果、DOBIS tag245 の表示は、
　　　本タイトル△：△タイトル関連情報△'@'△本タイトルのカタカナ形（読み）△：△タイトル関連情報のカタカナ形（読み）
　　　　　　　　　　　　　　　　（△はスペースを表わす）
となる。このロードの際に事前処理として、AJAX により「読み形」をベースに記述部分が「分ち書き」され、さらに、ジャパン・マークの「分ち書き」は音節によっているので、このままにしておくと「なき」がキーワードととして切り出されてしまうので、こうした修正のため KMATCH 処理を行う。また、ジャパン・マークでは、副書名の「読み形」がタグ551に与えられていないので、AJAX により副書名の読みの付与と「分ち書き」を行うこととしている。
　c．タグ251$F(責任表示)は、DOBIS の Tag245$C: Remainder

of title page（note）にロードするとともに、Tag100（アクセス・ポイント）にロードされる。

「日本目録規則　新版予備版」では基本記入の標目という考え方をとっていない。この点は、USマークとのもう一つの異なるところであろう。

この結果、システム上では、以下のようになっている。タイトルおよび索引画面のコピーを図1－3に示す。

```
┌─────────────────────────────────────────────────┐
│  目録                                             │
│                                                   │
│  Entry summary       共同目録                     │
│                                                   │
│   1 First code       表示                         │
│   2 Second code      not applicable               │
│   3 Entry            限りなき 前進 ： 日本 アメリカン フットボール 五十
│ 年史 ＠ カギリナキ ゼンシン ： ニホン アメリカン フットボール ゴジュウ
│ ネンシ                                            │
│                                                   │
│     Diacriticals                                  │
│                                                   │
│                                                   │
│     Sort form     fg■og■■■■ :pt■ax■f■■lnt ─ ■■■cr■■ ＠ 限 ■og 前進 ： 日本 a
│ x■f■■lnt ─ ■ 五十年史                             │
│                                                   │
│                                                   │
│     数字またはコードを入力して下さい。            │
│                                                   │
│                                           y yes   │
│                                           e 終    │
└─────────────────────────────────────────────────┘
```

（図1）

```
検索
タイトル

1                    安田        善次郎伝
2                    限りなき      前進 ：日本アメリカンフットボール五十年史
3                    日本の       前進
4         /    体育の限りなき     前進をめざして2
5         / -  体育の限りなき     前進をめざして1  --------------------------
6                                先輩官職資料                                        1
7                    ドラマと     全人教育
8                                全人教育の手がかり                                  1
9                                先進工業国の雇用と失業                                2
10        ----------------       先進国への道程  -----------------------------       1
11        /    モデルニオウベイ    センシンコクオセンリツサセルアジアノニュージャパ
12        /    への準備：真の    「先進国革命」をめざして
13                   農業・      先進国型産業論：日本の農業革命を展望する
14        /    のソフト化に伴う   先進国間・南北間の諸問題

数字またはコードを入力して下さい。

t 別検索語   f 次頁                        p 新書誌作成
i 別項目     b 前頁
                        d 詳細      e 終
```

```
検索
タイトル

1                                日本 "合法ファシズム"の忠君愛国主義的構造            1
2                                日本．1－先縄文・縄文時代－                         1
3         /    集コミンテルンと   日本．2
4                                日本．2；目覚めゆく女性の哀歓                       1
5         -----------------      日本．3－古墳時代－  ----------------------------  1
6                                日本．4－歴史時代－                                1
7              ソ連の現状と       日本．続
8                                日本・アジア・アフリカ編                            1
9                                日本アマチュアスポーツ年鑑                           15
10        ----------------       日本アマチュアスポーツ年鑑．1987  ---------        1
11             南北貿易：         日本・アメリカ・EECの視角
12        /    文化文学論考：     日本アメリカメキシコ比較生活文化事典                 1
13        /    文化文学論考：     日本・アメリカ・ヨーロッパ
14             限りなき前進：     日本アメリカンフットボール五十年史

数字またはコードを入力して下さい。

t 別検索語   f 次頁                        p 新書誌作成
i 別項目     b 前頁
                        d 詳細      e 終
```

(図2)

```
┌─────────────────────────────────────────────────────────────────┐
│ 検索                                                             │
│ タイトル                                                         │
│                                                                 │
│  1           絵で見る      アメリカン・フットボール               │
│  2                         アメリカン・フットボール             2 │
│  3                         アメリカンフットボール               1 │
│  4           ラグビー・    アメリカンフットボール                 │
│  5  / - レーヤーのための   アメリカン・フットボール技術百科 ----- │
│  6                         アメリカンフットボール公式規則解説書 1 │
│  7  /    なき前進： 日本   アメリカンフットボール五十年史         │
│  8                         アメリカン・フットボール入門         1 │
│  9  /                      アメリカン・フットボール百科 ：勝利への戦略と技 1 │
│ 10  / ------------------   アメリカン・ボディ ：多民族社会を維持するための 1 │
│ 11                         アメリカン・マガジンの世紀           1 │
│ 12                         アメリカン・マラソン ：米大統領への道 1 │
│ 13                         アメリカン・ラビリンス               1 │
│ 14  /                      アメリカン・リアリティーズ ：アメリカ現代史を彩 1 │
│                                                                 │
│ 数字またはコードを入力して下さい。                              │
│                                                                 │
│ t 別検索語    f 次頁                         p 新書誌作成       │
│ i 別項目      b 前頁                                            │
│                        d 詳細       e 終                        │
└─────────────────────────────────────────────────────────────────┘

┌─────────────────────────────────────────────────────────────────┐
│ 検索                                                             │
│ タイトル                                                         │
│                                                                 │
│  1           ラグビー・    フットボール                          │
│  2  /    めのアメリカン・  フットボール技術百科                   │
│  3  /                      フットボールクレイジー ：心理学者のスポーツ・コ 1 │
│  4           アメリカン    フットボール公式規則解説書             │
│  5  / - 日本アメリカン     フットボール五十年史 ---------------   │
│  6           新            フットボール専科                       │
│  7           アメリカン・  フットボール入門                       │
│  8                         フットボールの社会史                 2 │
│  9  /   ス人： ラグビー    フットボール発達の社会学的研究         │
│ 10  / ----- アメリカン・   フットボール百科 ：勝利への戦略と技 -- │
│ 11           読書の        フットルース                          │
│ 12  /                      Ｆｏｏｔ ｗｏｒｋ足の生態学 ：すべての演劇的な 1 │
│ 13                         フットワークがすべての基本だ         1 │
│ 14                         物納小作料等に関する調査結果昭和６１年度 1 │
│                                                                 │
│ 数字またはコードを入力して下さい。                              │
│                                                                 │
│ t 別検索語    f 次頁                         p 新書誌作成       │
│ i 別項目      b 前頁                                            │
│                        d 詳細       e 終                        │
└─────────────────────────────────────────────────────────────────┘
```

(図3)

4．書誌データ・フィールドの出力

　前節において、ジャパン・マークの記述部（漢字形）とアクセス・ポイント部（漢字形の読み）の扱いについての基本的な考え方を示したので、ここでは書誌データ・フィールド各部のシステムへの出力について説明をしたい。

4．1．タイトル・フィールド（タグ251およびタグ751）の出力について

　ジャパン・マークでは、タイトルの記述部としてタグ251が、アクセス・ポイント部としてタグ751が用意され、また、巻書名の記述部としてタグ291、アクセス・ポイント部としてタグ791がある。ダンプリストを出力して点検をしたところ、巻書名として入力されているデータの約70％は、タイトルと見て差し支えないものであった。したがって、ここでは、タイトルのフィールドが2つ用意されていると説明したい。

　さて、タイトルのフィールドが2つあるということは、出力にあたって、いくつかのケースを考え、パターン化しなければならないのである。

　なお、タイトル・フィールドは次のサブ・フィールドで構成されているので補記しておきたい。

　　　　サブ・フィールド　　＄A　　書名（本タイトル）
　　　　　　　　　　　　　　＄B　　副書名（タイトル関連情報＊タグ551にこのフィールドはない）
　　　　　　　　　　　　　　＄D　　巻次等
　　　　　　　　　　　　　　＄F　　著者表示（読み形は、タグ751に分離されている）
　　　　　　　　　　　　　　＄W　　資料種別表示（＊タグ551にこのフィールドはない）

(1)　ケース　1．　単行書

　　ジャパン・マークでは、タグ251＄A（：＄B）＄Fおよびタグ551＄A（カナ形の読み）＄X（ローマ字形の読み）＄B（対応する漢字データのあるフィールド識別子番号）とタグ751（責任表示）＄A（カタカナ形）＄X（ローマ字形）＄B（漢字形）にデータが入力されている。

　　したがって、原則により、

　　　　タイトルは、タグ251＄A（'：'＄B）'@'タグ551＄A（'：'＄B＝AJAXにより付与された読み形）の形でタイトル・フィールド（Tag245に該当）へ

責任表示は、「標題紙上のタイトル以外のデータ／責任表示」部（Tag245＄C＝システムではnoteの先頭に位置づけられている）へ出力している。

なお、ジャパン・マークにはタグ251＄B（副書名）に対応する「読み形」がない（TRCでは「読み形」を独自に作成している）ので、AJAXにより機械的に付与している。

(2) ケース 2. 多冊出版物ないしは継続刊行図書

1部2冊以上からなる図書で各巻が固有のタイトルを有しない場合である。これらは、次にあげるものと同じように多段階記述で対応すべきものであろう。しかし、ジャパン・マークでは、記述部としてタグ251＄A（＄B），＄D，＄F、アクセス・ポイントとして、タグ551＄A，＄X，＄D，＄Bおよびタグ751＄A，＄Xにデータが入力されているだけで、多段階記述とはなっていない。ところが、DOBISでは、「レコードタイプとしてのボリューム・レコード」の存在を許容しているので、出力の際に、サブ・フィールドDを切り離すかどうかが検討の対象となったが、＄D（巻次など）だけのデータを存在させると、機械的に書誌データと巻次をリンクできないことから、＄Dが18バイト以下の場合

　　タグ251＄A（'：'＄B）．△'＠'タグ551＄A（'：'
　　AJAX読み）．△＄D

の形で書誌プールのタイトル・フィールド（Tag245）に出力することとし、所蔵した時点での修正に委ねることとした。

ところで、ジャパン・マークのタグ251、サブ・フィールドDには、単に巻次だけではなく、年月次、回次など18バイトを超えるデータが入力されている場合がある。たとえば、

　　　　＄D昭和51年版△婦人と社会保障　　　　　である。[11]

この場合、「婦人と社会保障」は、昭和51年版だけに与えられた個別のタイトルである。したがって、「部分タイトル」としてタグ252＄Aにリピートするか、タグ291に入力すべきでなかろうか。さらに、＄D昭和49〜50年△水産編のようなものもあり、定義が不明瞭な部分も見受けられるので、検討を望みたいところである。

(3) ケース 3. 多巻ものの場合

ジャパン・マークでは、タグ251の他に、タグ291にもデータをもっている場合である。ジャパン・マークでは、タグ251は、

　　＄A新英文法選書＄D第5巻＄F太田朗、△梶田優//責任編集

タグ291には、

　　　　＄Ａ句動詞＄Ｆ嶋田裕司//著
のように記述されているであろう。
　この記述方法では、タイトルと責任表示が分離されてしまう。つまり、「新英文法選書」の責任表示は、「太田朗、梶田優」であるが、「第５巻」が間に挿入されたために、「第５巻」の著者が「太田朗、梶田優」であるかの印象をあたえてしまうのである。(12)
　ジャパン・マークの場合は、タグ251＄Ｄに入力しようとしたデータが長すぎた場合、その残りがタグ291＄Ａに入力されているケースも見受けられるので、タグ291に記述された「巻書名」が必ずしも「固有の標題」であるとは限らない。そこで、タグ291が「各巻レベルのタイトル」となり得るかどうかの機械的な判断（タグ291＄Ａに対応する「読み形」があるか、タグ291＄Ｆがあるかなど）をして、
　ａ．巻書名をタイトルと見做した場合は、
　　　タグ251＄Ａ　　→　　タイトル・シリーズ（Tag440）
　　　タグ251＄Ｄ　　→　　Tag440の Volume　へ
　　　〝タグ251＄Ａ'＠'タグ551＄Ａ';'＄Ｄ〞の形にして
　　　タグ291＄Ａ　　→　　タイトル・フィールド（Tag245）へ
　　　〝タグ291＄Ａ'＠'タグ791＄Ａ〞　　　の形にして
　　出力することとした。なお、タグ291＄Ｆ（各巻の責任表示は、Tag245＄Ｃに出力するとともに、Tag100＝個人標目にもおく）こととした。また、タグ251＄Ｆは、その巻の責任表示を明確にする意味から、一般注記に出力してある。
　ｂ．巻書名がタイトルとなり得ない場合は、
　　　タグ251＄Ａ　　→　　タイトル・フィールド（Tag245）に
　　　〝タグ251＄Ａ．△＄Ｄ'＠'タグ551＄Ａ．△＄Ｄ
　　の形で出力し、前項の場合と同じ扱いとする。なお、タグ291＄Ａは内容注記に出力しておくこととした。
(3)　叢書名に関する事項の出力
　ジャパン・マークの「叢書名に関する事項」（タグ280）のサブ・フィールドは、次のようになっている。
　　　　　＄Ａ　　叢書名
　　　　　＄Ｂ　　叢書番号
　　　　　＄Ｄ　　副叢書名
　　　　　＄Ｆ　　副叢書番号
　これを出力するための原則は、次の通りである。
　ａ．叢書名は次の形にして、タイトル・シリーズ・フィールド

(Tag440)に第1順位で出力する。出力の形は、
"タグ280＄A'＠'タグ580＄A';'タグ280＄B"である。

ただし、ジャパン・マークでは、叢書が出版社シリーズ（publisher's series）でその下がいくつかの叢書に分割されて出版されているような場合、記述形（タグ280）と読み形（タグ580）は1対1で対応していない場合がある。たとえば、タグ280＄A教育社新書＄D産業界シリーズ＃
タグ580＄Aサンギョウ　カイ　シリーズ＄X Sanngyou kai siriizu＄B産業界シリーズ
のようなデータが存在する。[13]

多段階記述をする場合、このデータから3レベルの記述を作成するかどうか判断がいるところではあるが、ジャパン・マークでは、「教育社新書」をアクセス・ポイントとはしない方針から、アクセス・ポイントとするものだけを「読み形」として記述したと思われる。しかし、この判断は、各図書館に委ねられるべきものであろうが、早稲田大学図書館では、出力する際に「読み形」のないものには、機械的に「読み形」を付与して出力形を統一しているので、これらについても、
"タグ280＄A'＠'タグ580＄A（AJAXによる読み形付与）"
"タグ280＄D'＠'タグ580＄D"
の形にして、タイトル・シリーズ・フィールド（Tag440）に繰り返して出力している。

 b．タグ251がタイトル・シリーズ・フィールド（Tag440）に出力される場合でもタグ280はタグ251に優先して出力することとした。これは、タグ280からさらに上位レベルの書誌レコードを作成し、3レベルとできることを指示したものである。

4．3．責任表示関係の出力について

ジャパン・マークでは、タグ251＄F（著者表示）はタグ751とリンクしている。また、各巻レベルの著者表示（タグ291＄F）はタグ791とリンクしているので、漢字形と読み形を合成して、次の要領で出力している。

 a．タグ251＄Fは、「標題紙上のタイトル以外のデータ/責任表示」フィールド（remainder of title pape＝Tag440＝注記の先頭に位置付け）に出力している。

 b．個人標目（name field＝tag100）へは、ジャパン・マークの

タグ751＄F～759＄F，タグ791＄F～799＄Fの順に出力する。その形は、タグ751＄B（漢字形）'＠'751＄A（カナ読み形）とする。
　　　ただし、外国人の場合、ジャパン・マークでは751＄Aにカタカナ形が＄Bに原綴が2重松葉括弧（《》）で入力されているので、この括弧を削除し原綴形（＄B）のみを出力することとした。
　c．LCマーク Tag100（個人標目）にはインディケータ1で人名の種類が指示されているが、ジャパン・マークにはこれがない。当システムのネーム・フィールドにおいても1．名のみ　2．単一姓（ひとつの通常の姓名）3．複合姓　4．姓のみ（家族名）を指示することとしているので、ジャパン・マークのタグ751＄Bのデータを機械的に判断して出力した個人名に1．名のみ、2．複合姓、の指示子を与えている。一般的には、日本人の場合は単一姓を与える場合が多いが、これだと名からの切り出しができない。ところが、名の方で有名な人が多いので、あえて複合姓を利用して名からの検索ができるようにした。
　d．ジャパン・マークでは、姓と名の間に2重スラッシュ（//）を挿入しているが、これはスペースとして扱うこととした。
　e．現在、AACR2では、標目とした個人名に対して、その人の役割（＄C）を補記していないが、ジャパン・マークでは著者表示で役割を示している。この役割表示をネーム・リレーター・コード（name relator code）として、そのための表（table）を用意した。したがって、ジャパン・マークの役割表示と「表」とを照合して、個人名にセットすることとした。

4．4．出版事項の出力について

　ジャパン・マークのタグ270（出版事項）には、サブフィールド＄A（出版地）、＄B（出版者）、＄D（出版年月）があるが、記述に対応する「読み形」はない。
　システムでは、出版者もアクセス・ポイントとして典拠コントロールの対象としているので、次の形に変換して出力することとした。
　　変換形：タグ270＄B（出版者＝漢字形）'：'＄A（出版地＝漢字形）'＠'＄A（AJAXによる読み）'：'＄A（AJAXの読み）
　なお、2番目以降の出版社があるときの発売者が別にあるとき、ジャパン・マークでは、タグ350＄A（一般注記）に入力しているが、これを取り出して出版事項を繰り返す形で出力している。

4．5．件名の出力

　ジャパン・マークでは、アクセス・ポイントとして、個人件名（タグ650）と一般件名（タグ658）の2つのフィールドに件名を分けて記述している。システムでは、フィールドは1つとし、与えられた件名に、個人名（種類別）、団体名（種類別）、地名、一般件名などとその種別（属性）を与えるとともに、基づいた件名表（件名のソース）を与え識別している。したがって、ジャパン・マークから件名を出力する際、件名のタイプとしては、1．個人件名、2．団体名、3．一般件名、の属性を自動的に付与し、件名のソースとして「国立国会図書館件名標目表」を使用している。これは、典拠管理の必要から出たものであるが、件名のソースが異なれば、表示は別々にされるので、検索に際しては、複合検索を行わなければならない。

　　a．個人件名の出力形はタグ650から漢字形とカナ読み形を合成したものとする。

　　　　タグ650＄Ｂ（漢字形）'＠'＄Ａ（カナ読み形）

　　　なお、漢字形がない場合は、タグ650＄Ａのみを出力する。また、データ中の「//」はブランクとして扱う。

　　b．一般件名は、タグ658から次の形で出力する。

　　　　タグ658＄Ｂ（漢字形）'＠'＄Ａ（カナ読み形）

　　　なお、データ中にカンマ（,）が用いられている場合は、カンマ以下を別件名として出力した。また、データ中の「//」は件名の細目を表す記号ダッシュ（－）に変換してある。

市販マークの利用

　前項においてジャパン・マークとＬＣマークがファイル上で共存できるようにするために、ＬＣマーク・フォーマットに合わせる形でジャパン・マークを変換・出力する方法の概要を紹介した。早稲田大学図書館では、ジャパン・マークのほかに市販マークの1つであるＴＲＣマークを購入し、出力している。この点について若干コメントしておきたい。

(1)　2つのマークを出力するとなると、それぞれの書誌データをファイル上で並列に持つのか、置き換えられるものは、ＴＲＣの書誌データをジャパン・マークの書誌データに置き換えてしまうのかの問題に行きつく。この解決法が現在のところ見出すことができなかったためと、所蔵している資料の検索と情報検索（マーク・データの検索）とを分離したいとの考えから、購入しているマークはすべて書誌プールに出力することとした。

(2) 書誌データ・ファイルに2つ以上の書誌が存在する場合、同一の書誌データであることを識別する何等かのキーが必要である。ジャパン・マークは、ＪＰ番号というユニーク・キーを持っているが、TRCマークのそれはJLA番号である。これらは、図書館が必要とするデータだけを切売りしてもらうための番号にすぎないのである。となると、存在する重複データを機械的に識別するために有効なキーはISBNということになろうが、ISBNは1冊の図書に2つ与えられていたり、全3冊ものの図書にセット番号しかなかったりで、ユニークなキーとはなっていない。存在する両者を識別する確実な方法は手作業によるしかない、ということになるであろう。現物がない限りその方法も厳密な意味で問題を含んでいると言えよう。そこで、2つのデータを統合することはせずに、それぞれのデータにどのマークから出力したものかが識別できるように、典拠（マーク・ソース）を明示することとした。
(3) TRCマークは、内容識別子（タグ）およびサブ・フィールド（＄）は、ジャパン・マークと同じにしているから、出力のための基本的な仕様は、ジャパン・マークの場合と同じでよい。しかし、TRCが独自に追加した項目があるので、それらをどこに出力するか、また、出力しない項目を指定するなどの検討が必要である。以下にTRCが独自に追加した項目またはサブ・フィールドを示す。

ブロック	タグ	フィールド名称	＄	サブ・フィールド名称
0	080	JLA番号		
2	251	書名と著者表示	＄T	副書名の版
	265	版に関する事項	＄F	版の著者名
	270	出版に関する事項	＄T	発売地
			＄R	発売者
3	350	注記1	＄R	一般注記の版
	360	注記3	＄J	特価
			＄L	セット価
			＄T	価格注記
	365	注記（独自）	＄A	利用対象
			＄B	流通コード
			＄D	配本回数
5	551	書名の読み形	＄T	単一記入制のための標目指示
			＄R	＄Tのカナ読み形

			$H	$Rのローマ字形
5	560	副書名の読み形（独自）	$A	カタカナ形
			$X	ローマ字形
			$R	カタカナ形
	561	巻次の読み（独自）	$A	カタカナ形
			$X	ローマ字形
			$B	漢字形
			$D	巻次
	562	副書名の版のよみ（独自）		現在データナシ
	565	版のよみ（独自）		現在データナシ
	580	叢書名の読み	$R	カタカナ形
			$N	叢書コード
	581	副叢書名の読み（独自）	$A	カタカナ形
			$X	ローマ字形
			$B	漢字形
			$R	カタカナ形
			$D	叢書番号
			$N	叢書コード
	591〜	多巻ものの各巻の書名の読み	$R	カタカナ形
			$H	$Rのローマ字形
	567	注記の版の読み		現在データなし
	570	内容注記の書名の読み		現在データなし
6	665	書名件名（独自）		現在データなし
7	751	著者の読み	$T	単一記入制目録のための標目指示
			$R	カタカナ形

<TRC提供の「要素の分析手稿」データによる>

この他にもタグ780に「出版社の読み形」があるなど、サブ・フィールドの数にして19の目がある。

CJKファイルについて：結論にかえて。

早稲田大学図書館では、書誌データは和・洋の区別なく一つのフ

ァイルに持つことができるとの考えに基づいて、和図書マーク・データの変換・出力を行った。このことは、実質、和図書のデータ記述を AACR2 によって行っているようなものである。しかし、日本には独自の日本目録規則があり、和・洋の目録記述が同一の次元でなされるところまでには至っていない。

　和・洋のデータを同一のファイルに持てるという考え方は、わが国唯一の書誌ユーティリティである学術情報センターでも示唆されていた。しかし、学術情報センターの共同目録システムでは、目録規則が異なるなどの現状とシステム管理の効率上の問題から、和・洋別にファイルを構築した。[14]

　和・洋図書の書誌データを同一のファイルに持つための基本的な仕様は、すでに述べたように、記述部（漢字・かな形）とアクセス・ポイント部（カタカナ形またはローマ字形の読み）を同一のフィールドに出力することであり（マーク上では、別のフィールドに入力し、リンケージのための番号をもたせ、両方を同一のフィールドに出力する方法も可能であるが）、これは学術情報センターの目録記述および OCLC の CJK ファイルにも見られるところであり、この方法によって、オンライン目録記述の一つの方向が出されたと言って差し支えないであろう。[15][16]

　しかしながら、目録データの記述法についての方向は出されても、中国語、韓国・朝鮮語の書誌データを現在あるファイルに入力できる段階にまでは至っていないと言わなければならない。その原因は漢字コードの設定の仕方などにある。学術情報センターが出した現在の指針では、次のように述べられている。

(1) 中国語、韓国・朝鮮語図書を漢字で、あるいは日本語に翻訳して和図書書誌ファイルに登録することができる。

(2) 中国語、韓国・朝鮮語図書を漢字で洋図書書誌ファイルに登録することができる。

(3) 中国語、韓国・朝鮮語図書を翻字して洋図書書誌ファイルに登録することができる。当面翻字法は問わない。

　どの方法によるかは各参加館が定める。

　以上の全てにおいて、中国語の簡化字は使用せず、対応する目録システム用文字セットで代える。[17]

　このように、中国語、韓国・朝鮮語図書を和図書として扱うのか、洋図書として考えるのかについての方向が日本の図書館では定まっていないと言える。以下でその理由について若干検討してみたい。

1．日本は漢字文化圏の中にあり、大陸の強い影響をその文化形成の過程で受けている。漢字は中国のはるか古代から、ある時代、

ある地域においてさまざまな思いつきによって創作され、時とともに統一され、その字体も変化してきたと言われている。宋代になって木版印刷の技術が発達したが字体の統一までに至らず、明の康熙帝（1661-1722在位）の時代に編纂された『康熙字典』によって字体が確立されたと言われる。漢字の日本伝来は3世紀頃と言われ、また、漢字とともにその発音が日本に移入され、それが日本に漢字の「音」（音読み）として定着した。しかし、「音」は必ずしも中国での発音と一致するものではなく、日本人にとって発音しやすいものへと転化したものと言われている。さらに、訳語として用いられたものが固定してできた和訓を生んだともいわれる。[18]

　中国から日本に伝えられたのは、漢字だけでなく、書物もその一つである。中国人が漢文で書いた書物を総称して漢籍（Chinese classics）と言っている。[19] この漢籍は日本人にとって必読の書であったので、日本人は中国の発音に似せた「漢字の音」または和訓（漢字、漢語をそれに相当する日本固有のことばをあてて読み取ること）によってそれを読んできた。[20] それ以来、漢文は日本人にとって切っても切り離せないものになっている。こうした伝統が日本の図書館に和図書と漢籍を一緒にした「和漢書」という一つの概念を形成させることになったと思われる。日本で長い歴史をもつ図書館では、漢籍も和図書と同じように配架され、同じ箇所が図書の整理をするので、漢籍のデータを和図書書誌データと同じファイルに持つこととなったにしても違和感はないであろう。

2．一方、中国における文字改革は中国の文化にとって基本的な課題として、長い漢字の歴史を通じてしばしば取り上げられてきた。外国人が中国語をローマ字で書き表わすようになったのは17世紀の始め、明末以降のことと言われるが[21]、それはさておき、中国自身が漢字を問題にして文字改革を考え出したのが1915年以降の啓蒙期、文学改革以降のことであった。中華民国政府時代の1928年、中国政府の手によって「国語ローマ字」が公表されたのである。この「国語ローマ字」とは別に1912年に「訓音統一会」という委員会ができてルビを作ることと標準音を定めることをその任務とした。「訓音統一会」で作成されたのが「注音字母」（漢字の読み方を示すための表音文字で、日本語のカナにヒントを得たと言われる）であった。その後、中国語の発音表示の近代化はいろいろな経緯をへて進められたが、その決定版と言われるのが「併

音字母」（p-inn-tung）である。

　ところで、文学革命以降の中国人の文章は漢文とは異なるとされ、また、標音を付すようになってから（1912年以降）書かれた図書を中国文図書として漢文とは区別している図書館が日本には多いのである。中国における文字改革は図書を区別する上での一つの目安であると言える。というのは、漢文には読みがなかった。つまり、英語のような表音文字であれば、ルビをつけなくても読むことができる。

　日本にはカナという便利なものがある。表意文字である漢字を使っている日本では、表音文字であるカナの力を借りてルビづけ（漢字の読み）の問題は解決されるのである。ところが、中国には漢字の他に文字がなかったので、漢字の読み方は口伝えに聞いて覚えていった。この口頭伝承が漢字の読み方の始まりであり、その後、反切（ハンセツ：2つの漢字を用いて1つの漢字の読み方を示す中国独特の方法で漢206～220B.C.の末に考案されたといわれる）という標音の方法が暫く続いていた。この反切にしても、いたってやっかいなもので、一般の人が手軽に使用できるものでもなく、標音符号としては大衆のものとは言えなかったのである。[22]　換言すれば、漢文の時代の中国には「読み」がなかったと言えよう。日本人は反切法を用いないで、独自の方法で漢文を読み下してきたのであるから、中国の書物を1912年を境にその前後に区分することもひとつの合理性があると言える。

　それ故に、日本においては中国の図書（Chinese books）という西欧諸国が考えているような概念は存在せず、1912年以降の著作（Chinese books）は洋図書（Foreign books）として扱いたい、という考えが生まれてくるのである。

3．次に韓国・朝鮮の書物について考えてみたい。朝鮮も日本と同じように中国の漢字文化圏にあったのである。その中で、15世紀中頃李朝の四代目の王であった世宗大王（セジョンデワン）によって創案されたのがハングル文字であった。当時、李朝の文字としては、ごく限られた上流階級の者が使用していた漢字、漢文があったのみで、一般民衆は書くための文字をもたなかったと言われる。したがって、ハングル文字は、一応通用していた漢字による表記手段に代わって「民に教える正しい文字」、すなわち「訓民正音」（フンミンジョンウム）と名付けられた。しかし、19世紀後半までは、漢字の占めていた地位をゆるがすことはできなかったし、公文書も漢字で書かれていたのである。その後、20世紀

初めに言文一致の運動が始まり、次第に漢文くさい文から口語的なハングル漢字まじり文へと変化した。今日に至っては、完全にハングル上位が定着しているが、漢字が全く使用されなくなった訳ではない。[23]

このように韓国・朝鮮の書物には、漢文で書かれたもの、とハングル漢字まじり文で書かれた書物の両方が存在する。日本では、前者を便宜的に韓本（Korean classics）として韓籍と同じに扱い、後者を朝鮮文図書（Korean books or Hankul alphabet books）として、洋図書として扱いたいとする考えが強いのである。

1. 次にコードの設定とその見通しについて述べたい。
(1) 日本では漢字コードとして JIS-X0208（情報交換用漢字符号系、以前はC6226）を設定している。JIS-X0208 は、通常の国語文の表記に用いる図形文字の集合とその符号について規定している。図形文字には、数字・ローマ字・平仮名などがあり、そのうち漢字は、第一水準漢字集合2,965字、第二水準漢字集合3,384字の計6,349字である。第一水準には内閣告示（常用漢字表など）や都道府県コード（JIS-C6220）などの漢字を入れ、それ以外のものを第二水準としている。[24] なお、この規格は5年毎に見直される。

ところで、日本語および漢文の中ではどの程度の漢字が必要なのであろうか。漢字の字形を確立したと言われる『康熙字典』には47,034字、日本で最大の漢和辞典である『大漢和辞典　修訂版』（諸橋轍次編　全13冊）には、日本で生まれた漢字（国字）を含めた親字49,964が収録されている。[25] これをもとに編纂された『広漢和辞典』（諸橋轍次等編　1981〜1982. 4冊）でも親字20,000が収められている。日本における現代の漢字かなまじり文、日本の古典、漢籍の書誌データのファイルを構築するためには、現在 JIS でコード化されている以上の漢字が必要である。

(2) 中国語文図書で用いられている漢字は、日本の漢字とは統一できない。たとえば、中国の簡体字は8種類の方法によって作られ、日本の新字体が主として筆画の簡略化によっているのに対し簡略化の方法が基本的に食い違っているからである。[26] また、表記の方法も異なるので現代中国で用いられている漢字と日本語の漢字は、別にコード化すべきである。別にコード化する場合、対象となる漢字は約10,000字になると考える。たとえば、中国で1956年に出版された『同音字典』（商務印書館出版）には、中等文化人（？）程度の人のためにつくったものとして10,503字が収録さ

れており(27)、また、日本で編纂された『中日大辞典』（愛知大学中日大辞典編纂処　1968）には、7,876字（簡体字2,238を含む）が収録されているのである。
(3) ハングルのコード化は可能であろうか。ハングルの場合は、表音文字化しているので日本語のカナと同じようにすればよいであろう。ハングルの基本母音は10、基本子音は14である。その基本をもとにして母音は11加わり、子音は5加わるので計40となる(28)が、ハングルの反切表（パンジョルピョ：日本語の五十音表に相当）によると、日本語の五十音の約三倍弱の140語になっている。(29)　ところで、ハングル漢字まじり文で用いられている漢字は、日本語・中国語の漢字とは別のコードを設定すべきであろうが、その数は1,800字程度であろう。(30)

2．結論

　日本には、和図書と漢文（漢籍、韓本＝ＣＪ）という考え方はあっても、CJKという概念はない。こうした考え方の背景と中国語文図書、ハングル漢字まじり文図書の書誌データのシステムへの入力の可能性、見通しについてここでは考えてみた。すでに述べたように障害は、さまざま言語の中で使われている漢字のコード化と、新たなるソフト開発につきるように思える。コード化、ソフト開発の問題となると、図書館員としての私の力量をはるかに超えたことなので、具体的な提案はできない。しかし、次のことを漠然と考えることはできる。
(1) 各国が責任をもって作成したマークをそのまま利用して別システムを構築することである。この場合、各国が設定した漢字コードをそのまま利用することになる。
(2) 次に考えられることは、日本でコード化された漢字と中国の漢字コード（ＧＢ2312）を比較して、すべての条件を満たした同じものは、共用基本文字としてコード化することである。また、それぞれの国で固有の漢字は、別個にコード化することになる。これら、漢字のコード化は、2バイトの領域の中で行いたい。
　しかし、日本で目録業務のシステム化にとって必要なことは、中国・韓国の漢字をコード化することだけではない。この場でのテーマはCJKに限定されているが、私共にとっては、他の東洋の文字、およびキリル文字などについても、同じように考えなければならない。アメリカではキリル文字をアルファベットに翻字しているが、日本では翻字をせずに使いたいとの希望が強い。したがって、JISではキリル文字にもコードを与えている。このよう

に、2バイトの中でコード化すべきものは多いので、簡単に事を運べないのである。

　漢字のコード化は、膨大な作業をともなうけれども、やってできないことはないと思うのである。CJKファイルを考えるにあたって、私は文字のコード化以上に大きな問題があると思う。それは、入力をどうするかである。日本では、読みから漢字への変換入力、すなわち、カナ・漢字変換、ローマ字・漢字変換が実現し、さらに文節変換も可能である。漢字コードを使っての入力は特殊な文字に限られているのである。ところが、中国における漢字、韓国、朝鮮のハングル文字の場合、入力方法として確立されたものがない。たとえば、"読み"から漢字に変換するにしても、現在のp-innは大衆化されてないし、ウェード式といったローマ字表記法は外国人のためのものであった。したがって、現在台湾等における漢字の入力は、漢字をいくつかの部分に分け、それらを合成して一つの漢字を作りだす方法などがあるが、いずれにしても単漢字変換である。

　日本における目録のシステム化は、データベースの構築ということ以外に、目録作業の合理化という側面をもって進められているので、現在RLINなどで行われている部分を合成・変換する単漢字入力、ないし、個々の漢字コードを調べて行うコード変換などの入力方法は、図書館の現場からの抵抗にあうであろう。それ故、日本においてCJKファイルを構築することは、CJKという概念の問題以上に、漢字の入力方法の問題が解決されない限り困難であると言わざるを得ない。

　最後に、漢字のコード化について一言ふれておきたいと思う。現在まで、漢字のコード化は、各国の責任で行ってきた。日本にはJISコードがあり、中国も漢字コードをもっている。また、マークに関しても同様に各国の書誌作成機関が責任をもって作成してきた。さらに、各国が作成したマークを利用してデータベースを構築することは、マークを利用する側の責任であると考えられてきた。したがって、マークを利用するにあたって、文字のコード化が必要であるならば、マーク作成国の漢字コードを導入するなり、構築するデータベースの内容によって共通文字セットを作成するなりの作業も、基本的には、マークを利用する者が行うことであると考える。今後の課題として、異なる漢字コードをもつそれぞれのマークを同じ条件で利用できるようにするために、書誌情報交換のための共通文字セットが必要であるという考えは理解できる。だからといって、こうした問題を情報先進国、たとえばアメリカなり日本が主導する形

で、東洋の諸国に広めようとすることには、別の面で問題を生じさせかねないであろう。CJKファイルをもつかどうかの問題も含めて、この問題の解決のためには、IFLA東京大会プレ・カンファレンスでわが国の田辺広氏が提案したように、東アジアの書誌情報に関する常置委員会をなんらかの形で設けることが必要であろう。[31]また、その委員会において、情報処理の先進国は、東洋諸国の意見を十分聞く必要があると考える。

参考文献

1. 『漢字を科学する』　海保博之編　有斐閣　p.p.76-77.（有斐閣選書）
2. 長島俊樹　「JAPAN MARCとTRC MARC：比較検討と問題点の整理」（『大学図書館研究』No.26．1985．5．p.p.21-28．）も参照のこと。
3. 戸田あきら「日本で市販されているマーク」（『マークをうまく使うには：機械可読目録入門／黒沢正彦、西村徹編』　三洋出版貿易　1985．p.p.93-104．）
4. 『NIPPAN図書館管理システム』日本出版販売株式会社　[1986] p.p.17-39.
5. 『TRC営業の御案内』㈱図書流通センター　[1986] 13p.
6. 戸田あきら　『前掲書』　p.p.103-105.
7. 『図書館雑誌』　vol.82．No.1．1988．1．p.4.
8. 『日本目録規則』本版第3次案　日本図書館協会　1986．150p.
9. 真弓育子「書誌情報および図書館目録の標準化」（『図書館目録の現状と将来』日本図書館学会研究委員会編、p.81.　日外アソシエーツ　1987．）（論集・図書館学研究の歩み　第7集）
10. 『JAPAN/MARC マニュアル』第2版　国立国会図書館（日本図書館協会発売）1987．p.p.4-5.
11. 『前掲書』p.20.
12. 『新・目録法と書誌情報』　丸山昭二郎編　雄山閣出版　1987．p.p.111-2.
13. 『JAPAN/MARC マニュアル』　『前掲書』p.7.
14. 学術情報センター　『目録システム利用マニュアル：データベース編』　学術情報センター　1986．p.7.
15. 『前掲書』p.10., p.57.
16. User guide for creating/editing OCLC CJK bibliographic records. OCLC 1987 March. 19p.

17. 学術情報センター　『前掲書』p.24.
18. 遠藤哲夫『漢字の知恵』　講談社　1988. p.p.34-48.（講談社現代新書）
19. 草野正名編著　『最新図書館学事典』　学芸図書　1974. p.41.
20. 鈴木修次　『漢字：その特質と漢字文明の将来』　講談社　1984〔c1978〕p.159-161.（講談社現代新書）
21. 鐘ヶ江信光　『中国語のすゝめ』　講談社　1986〔c1964〕p.p.63-64.（講談社現代新書）
22. 鐘ヶ江信光　『前掲書』p.p.59-62.
23. 海保　博之　『前掲書』p.p.165-169.
24. 草野　正名　『前掲書』p.41.
25. 海保　博之　『前掲書』p.2.
26. 鐘ヶ江信光　『前掲書』p.p.54-55.
27. 鐘ヶ江信光　『前掲書』p.p.48-49.
28. 金容権　『ハングル初歩の初歩』　南雲堂　1986. p.15.
29. 渡辺吉鎔、鈴木孝夫　『朝鮮語のすすめ：日本語からの視点』　講談社　1988〔c1981〕p.p.135-6.（講談社現代新書）
30. 海保博之　『前掲書』p.168.
31. 田辺　広　「東アジアにおける書誌情報の交換」（『多言語・多文字資料利用のための図書館自動化システム　－－　問題と解決』　雄松堂出版　1988. p.264. *IFLA publications 38.* Edited for the Section on Library Services to Multicultural Polutions and the Section on Information Technology by Christine Bossmeyer and Stephen W. Massil. Papers from the Pre-Conferene: 1986年8月21-22日　東京　日本大学会館）

日本における古資料そのものの原形保存方策とその取組みの現状
—国立国会図書館における資料保存の対策と現状—

高 橋 和 雄

はじめに

　一国の刊行物は、その国の文化のバロメーターであると言われている。又、紙は文化の象徴であるとも言われている。紙によって知識を得たり、記録し、伝達し、保存したりしていく。紙は、知的文化的生活には全く欠かすことのできない存在であり、その源流である。国立国会図書館は、わが国唯一の納本図書館として、国内刊行物を網羅的に収集し、蓄積し、利用に供すると共に、文化遺産として恒久的に保存し、可能な限り原形の形態で後世に伝えていくことを使命としている。自国の出版物は自国の文化遺産であり、これらを原形を保ちながら後世に残していくということは、ひとりわが国のみならず、各国立図書館の共通した認識となっている。

　近年複写機の性能の向上や普及によって閲覧者や郵送による当館資料の複写申込みは年々増加して、電子式複写だけでも年間450万枚を超えるに至った。図書館が利用されることは、大いに歓迎すべきことであるが、一方において利用に伴う資料の物理的破損も見逃すことができなくなっている。又、酸性紙に起因する資料の劣化問題は、われわれ図書館人にとってまことにショッキングなことであり、図書館の危機さえ感じさせる大きな問題となっている。

　日本では、一部の研究者が酸性紙問題を認識し研究していた程度で、1980年代の初め頃までは、一般の図書館人には、まだそれほど認識はなく関心は高くなかった。ここ数年の間に一挙に吹き出したように関心が高まり、対策と同時に保存問題が強く言われるようになった。酸性紙問題や保存問題が議論され、原形保存が強く言われるようになったきっかけは、米国におけるBarrow研究所をはじめ議会図書館、各大学図書館及び図書館振興財団（CLR）等の資料保存についての研究や諸活動を知ってからである。そして今では図書館ばかりではなく公文書館等も含めて資料保存に力を入れ始めている。昨年12月日本に公文書館法の制定を見たのもその現れの一つである。

　資料保存問題は単に書誌学的問題だけでなく物理学、化学は勿論のこと各種の分野を取り込んでのダイナミックな研究領域となっており、世界的問題としても認識されつつある。

　IFLAの国立図書館長会議でも、コア・プログラムの一つである

PACでも、資料保存問題を世界的規模で捉え、出版物をこの地球上から守ろうと活発な活動を進めている。当館もこれらの活動を期待するとともに世界の一員として、各国と一体となって、国際協力を進めていくつもりである。

国立国会図書館における資料と劣化状況

当館の1988年3月末現在の図書の所蔵数は約480万冊である。このうち酸性紙本は、和紙を使用している和古書等を除いた約400万冊強と推計される。

1　日本の和古書及び当館の和古書

日本に初めて洋紙の製紙会社ができたのが西暦1874年（明治7年）、木材パルプによる洋紙が本格的に生産され始めたのが1895年（明治28年）、日本における洋紙の生産量が和紙の生産量を追い越したのが1912年（明治45年）頃であった。従ってそれまで日本では古い伝統により生産された優雅で強靱な和紙が日本の需要を満たしていたのである。日本の和紙は1000年以上も日本で生き続け、日本の文化を支えてきたものである。

紙資料で日本に現存している最古のものに、西暦606年頃書かれた『法華経義疏』があり、また奥書きにより作製年代が特定できる最古のものとしては、西暦685年の『金剛場陀羅尼経』がある。その他西暦600年代から700年代にかけての資料は数多く奈良の正倉院に保存されている。これらは1200年後の現在に受け継がれ、われわれの前にその姿を見せてくれることができる貴重な資料であり、遺産である。この外和紙による書籍は、虫や火による被害を除いて保存管理が適切であれば、数百年はおろか千年以上も永く保存できることが日本で数多く実証されている。

当館では西暦765年の『百万塔陀羅尼』や同740年の『集一切福徳三昧経』を所蔵している。又、平安・鎌倉時代（およそ600年～1200年経過している）の資料は少数であるが、室町・江戸時代（およそ300年～600年経過している）にかけての資料は多数所蔵している。これらはいずれも紙の劣化は極めて少なく、紙にも強靱さがあり、適切な保存環境のもとで管理すれば今後相当長期間の保存は可能であると期待できる。

当館では、これら和古書は帙という一種の保護箱に入れ、貴重書については、さらに桐の箱に入れて、キャビネットに格納し、キャビネットは空気調和設備の整った書庫に並べている。また書庫内は保安灯のみを残し消灯して、その保全に万全を期している。

2 国立国会図書館における劣化資料の実態調査とシンポジウム

① 実態調査

複写による資料の物理的損傷が無視できなくなり、また、酸性紙に起因する紙の劣化の記事が新聞等に紹介され始めた頃、1983年7月、当館では図書非図書を問わず、所蔵資料の全般について保管状態ならびに保存のための問題点と今後の対策を検討するため、資料別または破損や劣化の原因別に分け、次の7つ (a)貴重書 (b)マイクロ資料 (c)音盤 (d)磁気テープ (e)虫害 (f)複写による破損本 (g)酸性紙 の対策班を設け調査を行うこととなった。これらの班はおよそ6か月間の調査期間を経て、その結果を各班長から館長に報告した。この報告には各資料の保存について、貴重な提言が数多く含まれていた。

そのうち酸性紙対策班は、対策をたてるにあたって、米国やIFLAでのこれまでの紙の研究や保存のための諸活動についての文献及び情報の収集から始め、次いで当館蔵書の劣化状況の実態の把握が第一と考え、和紙による和古書等を除く当館の図書全般にわたって、劣化度の実態調査を行った。このような調査は、これまでわが国には前例も経験がなかった。

そこで米国ミシガン大学図書館及びノースカロライナ大学図書館における調査方法を参考として、当館独自の紙の劣化度の基準を決め、資料を損傷しないように用紙の劣化、変色と製本の状態を眼で見て、手で触って調べる官能試験の方法によって実施した。その時の調査対象、紙の劣化度の基準及び年代別の劣化状況等の結果は後出の「国立国会図書館における資料の劣化状況」のとおりであった。

② 実態調査の結果

ⅰ) 日本の国内刊行物

日本の国内刊行物は、外国刊行物と比較して劣化の被害は少なかった。Very Brittle という崩れかかっているようなものは外国刊行物のほうがずっと多かった。これは和紙の普及の影響もあって、日本においては木材パルプによる紙が本格的に生産されたのは、欧米よりも30年～40年ぐらい普及が遅かった為ではないかと思われる。ただ、1944年頃から1960年頃までの十数年間に刊行された出版物は、戦争の影響を受け物資がなく、劣悪な紙が使用されていたため、劣化がひどく、これらは今後長期的保存は難しいと考えられ、早急にマイクロ化する等他のメディアへの変換が必要である。（後出の図1と図3参照）

ⅱ) 外国刊行物

図書も雑誌も非常に類似の傾向を示している。（後出の図2と図

4参照）1860年代以前と比較して、それ以後1899年頃までは徐々に悪くなっており、欧米の図書館で紙が100年から120年乃至130年でボロボロになるという報告と同じような結果が得られている。

ミシガン大学図書館やノースカロライナ大学図書館における調査結果と比較して、よく類似している結果となった。（後出図2と図9参照）

③　シンポジウム

同年11月9日に「紙の劣化と図書館資料の保存」と題して、図書館関係、公文書・博物館関係、出版関係、製紙・印刷・製本関係、図書館情報学関係、製紙科学者、その他合計40名を招きシンポジウムを開いた。

午前中は、講演会と実態調査の報告を半公開で行い、午後は講演者、招待者及び当館職員による74名の小規模なパネルディスカッションを行い、実りあるシンポジウムとなった。このことがあってから、酸性紙問題が一段と多く新聞等に取り上げられ、図書館界を始め一般にまで認識を深めていった。翌1984年開催の日本全国図書館大会では、はじめて保存分科会が開かれ、関心の深さを示した。当館からは基調講演や写真・パネルの展示コーナーを設け、協力した。

④　資料保存対策委員会

1984年1月から2月にかけて、前記7対策班長が館長に報告したことにより、その任務は終わった。その後引き続き保存対策の検討、保存についての内外の情報の収集及び調査研究のため、同年6月資料保存対策委員会が設置された。委員には7対策班の班長を中心とした8名と酸性紙対策班として5名が命ぜられ、委員長他14名で発足した。

国立国会図書館における資料保存対策の基本とその取組み
1　新館完成後における資料保存のあり方

1986年9月の完成をめざして、本館の隣に新館の建設を1981年から始めていた。（新館が完成すると、本館・新館をあわせて、建物の延面積は約145,000m^2となり、図書の収納能力は、1,200万冊となる。）

この新館完成を期に今後の当館における資料保存のあり方はどうあるべきかについて、将来計画調査会は、資料保存対策委員会の意見を参考として慎重に審議した結果、〝新館完成後における資料保存のあり方〟として1985年3月館長に報告している。これは当館の資料保存についての指針であり、対策の基本を示すものであり、当館の資料保存対策はこの線に沿って進められている。

この報告書は、当館の資料保存対策の基本方針として、まず、
a) 当館は納本図書館として、国内資料を収集・蓄積し、後世に残す義務を持つこと。
b) 国内資料は利用との調整を図りながら、原形保存に最大の努力を払うこと。

を決めている。そしてそのため複本を整備すること、原形での長期保存が不可能な資料、劣化の進んだ資料、貴重書等利用制限の必要がある資料は、積極的にマイクロ化を進めること、及び保全のための幾つかの措置などがうたわれている。

又、組織としては資料保存対策を担当する部門として、資料保存対策室及び資料保存課を設けることも記されている。

2 資料保存対策の現状

① 組織

前述の新館完成後における資料保存のあり方に基づいて1986年6月の機構改革に際し、新しく資料保存対策室が設置され、同時に従来の製本課を資料保存課に改めた。これによって当館に資料保存を担当する組織ができ、資料保存を中心とする業務体系が生まれた。資料保存対策室の企画・調査・研究面に対して資料保存課は技術・実施面を担当し、資料保存対策室と資料保存課とが連携して全館的観点で対応していくこととなった。

② 原形保存への対応

当館の資料保存対策の基本方針は、国内資料の収集・蓄積と、原形保存に最大の努力を払うことである。原形を保ちながら永く保存するための有効な1つの方法は脱酸処理であり、又原形に忠実な修復作業である。さらに有力な他の方法としては、複数納本制又は複本の整備である。

ⅰ) 脱酸処理

酸性紙に対する保存対策は、脱酸処理を施すことが最も効果的でありかつ、原形保存が可能な対応である。従って、大量脱酸処理設備に期待するところが大である。当館が所蔵する大量の酸性紙本を半永久的に残すためには、脱酸設備を保有することは必要不可欠であると考える。さらにわが国の中性紙普及状況を勘案すると、今後なお当分の間、当館には年間数万冊の酸性紙本が増加すると予測される。

従って今後既存又は開発中の各国の大量脱酸設備についての情報収集や成果を見守ると共に当館として基礎的研究を重ね、当館にとって最もふさわしい設備の建設、取得に結びつけたいと考えている。

当館の脱酸処理については、欧米各国より立ち遅れており、ようやく Single 法やスプレー法による脱酸がはじめられたところである。今後幾多の制約や試練がわれわれを待っていることと思うが、これらを乗り越えて資料保存の責務を果たさなければならない。

ⅱ）修復

当館の資料修復は、可能な限り原形に忠実な作業を行うと同時に長期的使用に耐えうる製本への創意工夫及び保存性の高い材料を吟味しながら作業を実施している。当館の製本作業は1898年（明治31年）に国立国会図書館支部上野図書館の前身である帝国図書館以来続いている。以後90年間館内にあって、数多くの書籍の修復や製本を行い、その間に培われた技術は、当館の資料保存を支えるのに十分なものである。ただ、従前の修復や製本についての考え方は永く使用に耐え得る堅牢な製本に中心主眼をおいた作業を行い、原形に忠実な修復・製本ということを第二義的に考えていたきらいがある。現状では可能な限り原形に忠実な製本を目標にしている。

ⅲ）二部納本制または複本の整備

当館は開館と同時に一部納本制を実施している。1986年及び1987年に二部納本制実施のため経費を要求したが、厳しい財政状況のもとで認められなかった。二部納本制は、経費の問題の他に法律改正の問題もあり、現在は実施されていない。

複本の整備については、1987年から国内刊行図書保存のための経費が若干認められたので、経費の範囲内で保存用図書の充実を図っている。

③　他の媒体への変換

劣化等のため原形保存や長期保存が不可能な資料については他のメディアへ変換し、知的内容を保存することとしている。又、その外に貴重書や重要な資料、利用頻度の高い資料等についても他の媒体へ変換し、原資料は保存し、変換したものを利用に供する等の措置をとっている。

ⅰ）資料のマイクロ化

資料のマイクロ化に際しては、必ずオリジナル・フィルムと活用フィルムの二種類を作成し、原資料とオリジナル・フィルムは保存し、活用フィルムを閲覧や複写等の利用に供している。

当館では、現在、新聞、雑誌、図書等のマイクロ化を実施している。

図書として特に、貴重書等重要な資料、憲政関係の各家文書類、劣化図書及び国際交換用の官庁資料に重点をおいている。

ⅱ）その他のニューメディア

保存のための光ディスク化は当館ではまだ実施していない。ただ、CD-ROM は、当館で作成した書誌情報の提供に利用し、〝Japan Marc on Disk″として本年4月から発売を始めている。これは一枚のディスクに約10年分、50万件の書誌データの記憶が可能であり、その活用が期待されている。

④　環境条件の整備

資料の保管条件はメディアにより若干異なるが、資料にとっては、温度、湿度、光（照明）塵埃等の諸条件が保全に欠かすことのできない重要な要件となっている。環境条件が資料の劣化に与える影響は無視することはできない。資料の劣化は環境条件の複合作用により促進されたり倍加されていくのである。当館では次の措置をとっている。

ⅰ）書庫内温湿度

当館の書庫内温湿度については、温度は22℃に、相対湿度は55％（±5％）に設定し、空気調和設備により、設定条件の維持管理に努めている。新館には本館を含む電気・空気調和等のエネルギー・センターを設け、コンピュータにより24時間管理を実施しており、順調に稼働している。しかし、本館書庫は建設されて20年～28年を経過しており、設備の一部に劣化も認められる。新館設備と比較して機械等の形式も古くなっおり現状は必ずしも設定条件が得られていない。本館書庫の改修に向けて、その改善点を検討しているところである。

ⅱ）照明

本館書庫は無窓式（17層）、新館書庫は完全地下式（8階）を採用しており、書庫として理想的構造となっている。光の直射を避け、照明にも工夫している。新館書庫は熱センサーの利用により書架間照明を自動点滅方式とし、保存と省エネルギー化を図っている。ただ、資料保存のために書庫内照明には紫外線防止用の蛍光灯の使用が望ましいが、予算的制約もあって、現在まだ一般の蛍光灯を使用している状態である。本館書庫は、自動点滅装置はないので、不必要なところは努めて消灯している。

ⅲ）塵埃

空気調和設備に付随して、吸塵装置も取り付けて、塵埃の除去を行っているが、本館書庫は長年の使用により吸塵装置の劣化もあって、必ずしもその役目を果たしていない。従って、これも本館改修時に改善する計画である。

ⅳ）その他

本館・新館書庫の消火設備は、ガスによる方法とし、本館書庫は

炭酸ガスによる消火方法を、新館書庫はハロゲン消火物による消火方法を採用している。ハロゲン消火物の方が炭酸ガスよりもやや安全性が高いと言われている。

⑤　中性紙の普及度調査

資料保存対策室が発足してから、酸性紙対策の一環として、毎年8月に新しく受け入れた新刊図書一週間分のうちから、標本として500冊〜600冊を抽出し、携帯用ガラス電極pH計によりpH値を測定している。国内刊行物の中性紙使用状況を知る手がかりとしている。本年8月測定した結果が、ｐＨ値別百分率で示すと、

　　　pH　6.5以上　　　　46.7%
　　　pH　5.0〜6.4　　　　37.8%
　　　pH　4.9以下　　　　15.5%

であった。pH 4.9以下の強酸性あるいは中酸性の用紙は、1986年と比較して約12%減少していた。又、pH5.0〜6.4の弱酸性の用紙は、1986年と比較して約10%増加していた。4年〜5年前はほとんどの書籍用紙はpH 4.0前後であったと考えられ、徐々にではあるが、中性紙化へ進みつつあると思われる。なお、民間出版物と官庁出版との比較では、民間出版物の方が中性紙の使用率は高かった。ちなみに当館の出版物は1985年4月から全部中性紙へ切り換えている。

おわりに

当館所蔵の酸性紙本は、刊行されてやがて100年〜120年の時期を迎える。酸性紙本の劣化は現在も徐々に、間違いなく進行している。我々はこれに対応していかなければならない。

当館に資料保存のため、臨時の対策班が設けられ活動したのが、1983年7月で約5年前、資料保存対策室及び資料保存課が組織されたのが、1986年6月であり、当館の本格的資料保存対策は始まったところである。従って、これからやらなければならないことは、多種多様で盛り沢山である。欧米の文献や情報を集め研究すると共に、米国をはじめ保存問題の先輩のご意見を聞き、当館に最もふさわしい保存対策を進めていかなければならない。

大量脱酸設備建設に伴う検討、資料のマイクロ化の促進、環境条件の整備や維持管理、各種ガイドラインの作成、保存対策の国内的対応（その推進とリーダーシップとしての役割）その他中性紙の普及、複写機の改良等いろいろある。国際的にはIFLAのPACの地域センターとなることも期待されている。アジアを始め世界各国と連携・協力し、資料保存のため活躍したいと考えている。

日本では資料保存の問題は、古いようで新しい。われわれは世界

的連携の環を強く結び、資料保存という大命題に勇気をもって立ち向かわなければならない。

国立国会図書館における資料の劣化状況
(1983年9月～10月　実施)

1　調査の対象

対象資料	対象年	調査分析冊数	
国内図書（和装本を除く）	1870～1969		2,067冊
外国図書	1810～1969		1,078冊
国内雑誌	1870～1980	56種	1,026冊
外国雑誌	1660～1980	42種	1,029冊
法令・議会資料	1820～1980	10種	248冊
計			5,448冊

（注）国内図書、外国図書のうち、以下は調査の対象から除外した。
　1）国立国会図書館分類表（NDLC）により分類排架したもの
　2）大型本として別置したもの

2　紙の劣化度の基準

		紙の劣化状況	点数
劣化の度合	Excellent	非常に良好な状態	4
	Good	しなやかで、折り曲げても簡単に折り目のつかない状態	3
	Fair	折り曲げると折り目はつくが、切れてしまうことはない状態	2
	Brittle	折り曲げると切れてしまう状態	1
	Very brittle	くずれかかっている状態	0
変色の度合	中程度までの変色		0
	はなはだしい変色		－1

（注）この基準はミシガン大学図書館の方法を参考にした。

国立国会図書館における資料の劣化状況

年代別紙の劣化状況（平均点数による比較）

図1．国内図書　　　　　図2．外国図書

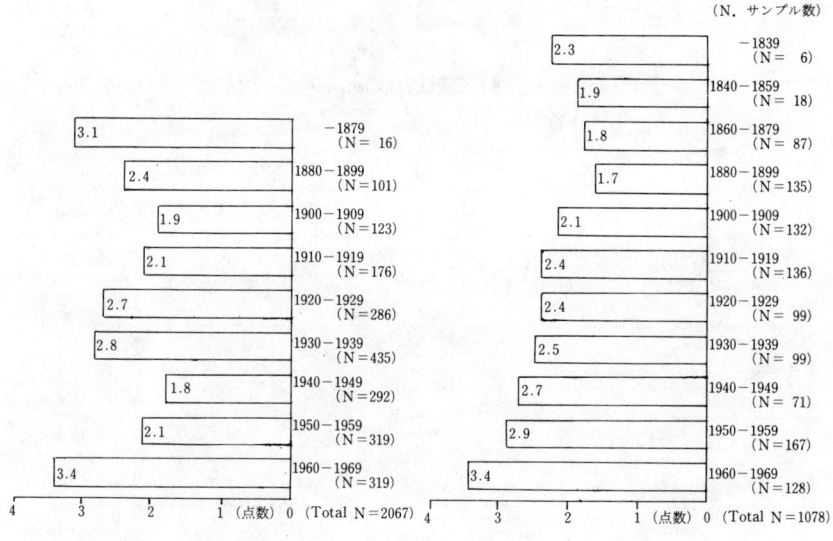

図3．国内雑誌　　　　　図4．外国雑誌

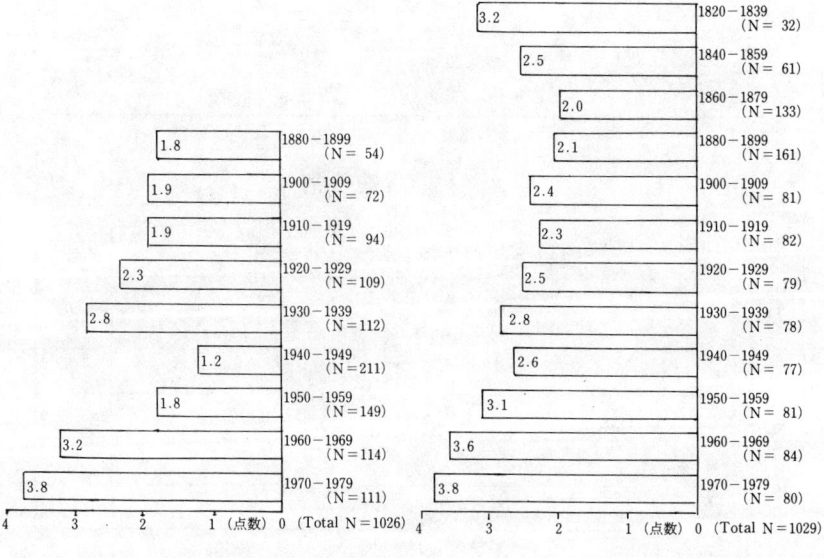

国立国会図書館における資料の劣化状況

年代別紙の劣化状況（劣化度別の比較）

図5．国内図書　　　　図6．外国図書

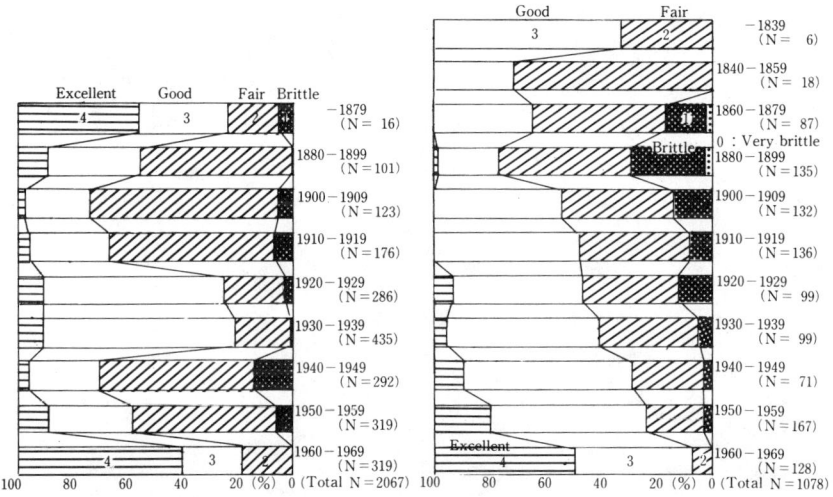

図7．国内雑誌　　　　図8．外国雑誌

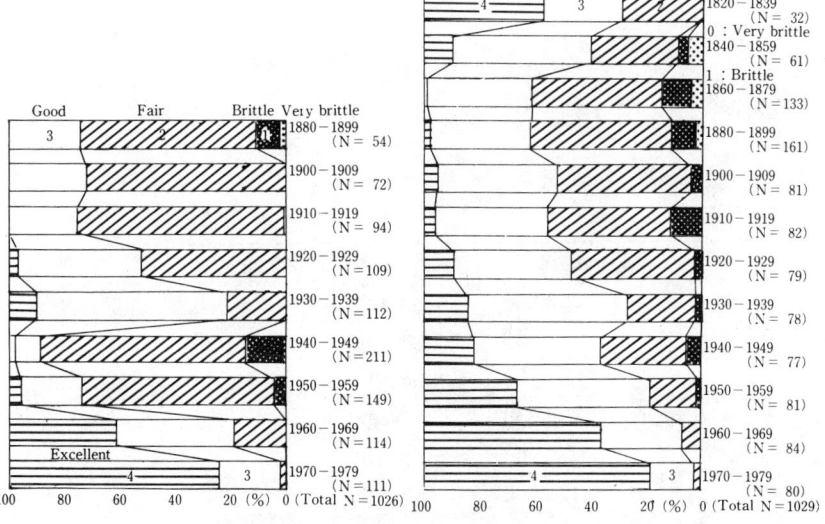

図9．ミシガン大学図書館調査

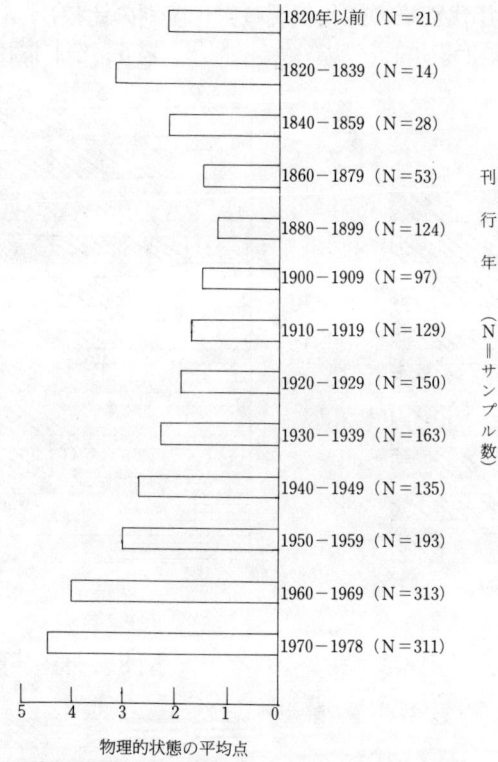

出典：Rose Mary Magrill et al〔2.p.53〕

国立国会図書館における資料の劣化状況

3　調査の結果

　　紙の劣化資料概数

（単位：冊）

紙の劣化度	Fair	Brittle	Very brittle	小　計
国 内 図 書	286,500	33,600	0	320,100
外 国 図 書	90,600	24,500	1,200	116,300
小　　　計	377,100	58,100	1,200	436,400
国 内 雑 誌	66,000	2,800	300	69,100
外 国 雑 誌	40,000	3,100	300	43,400
小　　　計	106,000	5,900	600	112,500
合　　　計	483,100	64,000	1,800	548,900

光ディスクファイルシステムと資料保存

澁 川 雅 俊

はじめに

 つい先だってまで、資料保存の問題に対して私は冷淡であった。酸性紙の使用のためであれ、過度の利用のゆえであれ、また自然の老朽化であれ、その理由のいかんによらず図書館資料がいずれは消滅してしまうことはいたしかたないことだと考えていた。

 それを惜しむ気持ちはもちろんあった。しかし、『平家物語』の冒頭のあの文句、「祇園精舎の鐘の音、諸行無常の響あり、沙羅双樹の花の色、盛者必衰の理をあらわす」が、心の奥底でいつも強く支配していた。すべてのものが生じ、とどまり、変化し、そしてやがては消滅するという四つの相は、人間や動物にかぎられることではない。生住異滅は、時間の差こそあれ、いずれも経なければならない自然の理である。

 医師が衛生思想の普及と医療技術の発達に努力し、その結果、人間の寿命が延びたように、図書館員が図書館資料の寿命を永らえようと努力することの重要性を認識するものではある。しかし、大学図書館の現場で運営実務にたずさわる者としては、そのことを重視し、その努力に対して敬意を払うものではあっても、いまその専門職集団の英知と労力、そして財源の多くをそれに投入することに逡巡せざるを得ない。大学図書館は、いまその転換を迫る多くの課題を抱えている中で、そうすることの決定に対して学内同意を得ることはむずかしい。

 運営実務の立場を離れて考えてみると、事情は少し違ってくる。もともと "living with books" を基本理念として専門教育を受け、その理想の下で四半世紀の間図書館で仕事を続けてきた者としての使命感が湧いてくる。関心領域の違いや基礎知識の欠如などの理由から、資料保存の問題に専心打ち込むことが私にできるかどうかわからない。しかし、わが国にも、そうしたいと思っている一握りの図書館員がいるに違いない。

 わが国の図書館の発展は、どの側面においても、そういう人たちの個人的な努力に端を発している。大掛かりなR&Dプロジェクトを組むことがなかなかできないわが国図書館界にあって、何か問題があれば、小さな力を結集していろいろな問題を解決してきた。

 一人か、二人の図書館員が別々にあることがらに対して問題意識

を醸成させる。彼らは、どの問題についてもまず諸外国の事例をよく調べ、そこで得た方法を彼らの図書館で応用してみる。一つの図書館というミクロな範囲であるとはいえ、そこに至るまではいつも容易ではない。そして、もしそれが成功すれば、それは他の幾つかの図書館にインパクトを与える。やがてどの図書館でもそれを応用して問題が解決されるようになると、最初の方法は標準的な方法として確立する。資料保存の問題に対して、わが国ではいま、そういう個別的な努力がなされている。

最近わが国でもことによっては共同のリサーチプロジェクトとして形成されるような機運が現われ始めているのは喜ばしい。それは、わが国大学図書館に図書館協力の基盤がようやく形成されたからである。学術情報センターの設立のように国が政策的に推進しようとするテーマが現れたこともその背景となっている。すでに米国では、図書館界だけでなく、郷土史協会、公文書館などと協力し、資料保存の運動を開始しているという[1]。わが国でも、まずは、これを図書館協力のひとつのテーマとして掲げ、やがてはそれが社会的課題として一般の人々の意識の中に固定するような展開を考えなければならない。そしてこの問題の解決のために関連する諸団体はもとより、産業界の技術協力を得る必要があろう。

資料保存の新しい媒体

資料保存を媒体の代替えによる保存に限定するならば、すでに私たちは、マイクロフォトグラフィ（マイクロ化）という技術をもっている。それは、いわば、確立された技術である。マイクロ化は、情報処理技術の観点からみれば、写真撮影により書写・印刷資料の一葉、または一頁、場合によっては二つの葉頁を一画面の画像処理として、光学的に連続してフィルムベースに置き換えるものである。しかし、これはこの会議に期待されている新技術ではない。近年森羅万象何でも情報化しようという考えが発達した。それを促進したのが電子工学であるが、その先端的な技術の中でマイクロ資料と同様に代替え媒体による資料保存を可能にし、しかもマイクロ資料にはない、新しい機能を備えているものはあるだろうか。

しばらく前のことであるが、慶応義塾図書館のカード目録の行く末を考えたことがある。その理由は、ひとつには、先行きカードボックスを配置展開するスペースがなくなるという問題があったこと、いまひとつには、機械可読型目録への移行の期待があったことである。かつて米国図書館で盛んに議論されたカード目録凍結の必要が、私の図書館でも生じたわけである。この問題について、ひとつには、

G．K．ホール社方式、つまり、目録カードのマイクロ化、ゼロックスコピーフローによる印刷、そして製本というプロセスでカード目録を冊子形目録へ変換するという解決法がある。事実この方法は、他の理由で一度採用したことがあった。しかし、いまの時代である。今度は電子工学的な方策を調べてみた。
　目録データのディジタルコード化によるデータベース構築がその後の計画との関連で論理的には正しい選択である。しかし、その当時、コンピュータ目録への転換の環境は、技術的にも、財政的にも整っていないと判断せざるを得なかった。他に何があるかを調べていた時、ひとりのセールスマンが、光ディスクによる文書ファイルシステムを売り込みにきた。この時の状況は、一般に先端技術商品についてのメーカー側の販売促進目標と消費者の生活感覚のずれを象徴するようで興味深い。このずれは、情報処理機器と図書館用品の間でとくに著しいように思われる。
　若いセールスマンの狙いは、図書館の中で業務上発生する事務文書の整理・保管にこのシステムを採用してはどうかということであった。しかし、このシステムの使用・用途の説明を聞きながら、私はまったく別のことを考えていた。この種のものが図書館サービスに利用できるかもしれないことを、最初彼は思いつかなかったらしい。このことは、とりもなおさず、メーカー側が図書館を情報処理機器や技術のマーケットとして十分に知りつくしていないことを示している。
　いずれにしても、このシステムの特性を利用してカード目録を光ディスクの目録へ変換することを私は思いついた。この方法は、電子工学的な情報処理技術によるが、いわゆる機械可読目録とは異なり、代替目録の作成の際にデータのコード化を必要とせず、目録カードイメージをそのまま（実際には、文書単位容量に合せてマウンティングし、Ａ４判１文書画面当りカード４枚それをひとつの画像として）を光ディスクに入力するというものである。これは、米国議会図書館において試されているものとは違う方法である[2]。この新しい媒体に目録情報を記録し、スペースの節減を図ろうとする考えは、新奇なものではあったが、うまくいくかもしれないと私は思った。
　しかし、光ディスク目録の変換は慶応義塾図書館ではいまだ単なるアイディアに留まっている。その最大な理由は、コストの問題である。必要と思われる最低の諸装置を備えた光ディスクファイルシステム一式が、2,100万円（５年リースで年間450万円）、そして年間95万円の保守料が必要となるという見積であった。もちろん、これ

以外にも、この光ディスク目録作成にかかる初期コスト、とくに情報入力にかかわる人件費を忘れてはならない。やはりコストのことが最初に気にかかった問題であった。[3]

この金額が高いか、そうでないかを判断するには、問題解決の緊急度と成果の効率を考えなければならない。また、それ以外にも技術的な側面で解決されなければならない問題もある。とくに検索システムの問題は重要である。

カード目録を光ディスク目録に変換する場合、基本的には、カード目録と同様利用者にとって簡便な手順で目録情報が得られるように検索できなければならない。そのためには、まず、カード目録の検索手順を新しいシステムに置き換える必要がある。その手順は人々が自然に身につけた技法である。それは、著者名からであれ、書名からであれ、また分類コードからであれ、きわめて単純な方法として認識されている。それゆえにそれをどう置き換えるかが大事になる。最終的にどう置き換えられようとも、最初はそこから出発しなければならない。問題は、この単純な検索方式をメーカーに理解させることに非常に困難を感じたことである。それが理解されないかぎり、本当はかなり複雑な仕組みになるはずのものをうまく設計することは期待できない。それゆえ私は、もしかしたらメーカーはこれに対応しきれないのではないかと考えた。

それからしばらく年月が経過した。これらの点がどのように改善されたか、いまは私は知らない。この間、慶応義塾図書館においては、コンピュータ目録作成について徐々に条件が整ってきた。したがって光ディスク目録製作の可能性はわからない。しかし、このいきさつから、このたびのテーマに関して、書写・印刷資料媒体から光ディスクへの変換の可能性を私は思いついた。以下で光ディスクへの代替えによる資料保存の可能性について若干調べてみたことを報告する[4]。

光ディスクファイルシステム[5]
1　光ディスク

光ディスクについては、技術的な解説とは別に、一般的には、このように説明されている[6]

まず、その形態は、音楽レコード音盤などのような円盤状のものである。その材質は、まず基盤がアクリルやガラスなどの材料で作られ、その表面に酸化テルルなどの気体金属や有機物、あるいはアモルファス金属の皮膜が張られている。この皮膜がメモリーコアになる。

情報は原情報をスキャニングして得た画像情報をレーザー光によって円盤皮膜を熱分解させることによって入力される。画像の固定化は、原理的には、原画像をレーザー光の操作によって点（ピット）に分解し、その点の集団をデジタル化して数値的に記録することによってなされる。そして画像を読むときは、その数値を読み画像に再生する、という方法による。なお、記録方式によって再生専用光ディスク、追記可能な光ディスク、書き替え可能な光ディスクがある。記録容量はディスクのサイズ（直径13、20、30cmの三種）によって違うが一枚の光ディスクで、Ａ4判文書が、ほぼ1万6千枚から10万枚の記録が可能であり、アクセス速度はきわめて迅速である。

こうした性能を持つ光ディスクは、光ディスク・ファイルシステムの記録媒体として活用されることにより、大量の画像情報をコンパクトに記録できること、システム内部での二次情報管理により入力情報の検索が容易なこと、また、画像編集操作により情報の再編成ができること、などの特性を発揮する。また、現在スタンドアロンで使用する前提になっているこのシステムにより、光ディスクに入力された情報はファクシミリ、ホストコンピュータ、ローカルエリアネットワークなどとの接続ができ、情報の遠隔地への配送、検索性能の高度化などの拡張性能をもつ。

この簡単な説明から、さきに私が提起した課題を解く糸口が見出せる。すなわち、先端技術が発達しているさなか、その新しい技術の中でマイクロ資料と同様に資料の代替え保存を可能にし、さらにマイクロ資料にはない付加価値をもつものは、もしかしたらこの光ディスクかもしれない、という考えである。[7]

以上にも述べられているように、光ディスクには再生専用型と追記型と書き替え型の三つのタイプのものがある。再生専用型は、ビデオディスクやコンパクトディスクとして音楽や映画メディアとして市販されており、すでに図書館資料のひとつのタイプとして確立している。また、音声情報や画像情報だけでなく、最近では、文字情報をディジタルレコード化して書き込んだ CD-ROM が現れ、電子出版として商品化されるようになった。このようなことは、商品化されたマイクロ資料が、新聞や雑誌や古書などの分野での資料の代替えを促進したように、光ディスクによる資料代替えを可能にする兆しでもあると言ってよいであろう。

追記型光ディスクは、簡単に言えば、光ディスクファイルシステムの利用者がその必要に応じて一回だけだが書き込みができ、また必要なときにはいつでも再生できるというものである。ただしこのタイプの光ディスクにはマイクロ資料と同様に静止画像しか記録で

きないという限定があるが、必要な装置さえあれば、ひとつの図書館の中で新聞や雑誌や古書を光ディスクに変換できることを示している。また、書き替え型光ディスクは、通常のカセットテープ、ビデオカセット、フロッピーディスクと同様に情報の記録・消去可能なものである。しかしこのタイプのものはまだ実用の段階に至っていない、と報告されている[8]。

このように情報処理関連の新技術を調べてくると、光ディスクがマイクロ資料と同様に資料の代替え保存を可能にする新しい媒体の可能性がより一層高まってくるように思える。とくに、追記型光ディスクは代替え資料をフルテキストで、ディジタルコード化の手順作業を踏まずに、自家生産する場合の媒体として注目される。

2　電子ファイルシステム

電子ファイルシステムは、外見上はパーソナルコンピュータのように、ディスクトップ型でコンパクトにまとめられたワークステーションである。このシステムの適用範囲はオフィスの文書管理から本格的な電子情報処理システムまで広範囲である。その一番の特性は、文書上の文字、図形、画像をそのままの姿、つまり「イメージ」のままで読み取り、記録できることである。またこのシステムの操作は、非常に簡単で、まるで複写機を使い原稿をコピーする感覚で行うことができる。それはいわば、イメージコピーをしてイメージファイリングができる便利な事務用機といえる。しかも、光ディスクをイメージファイルの媒体に使用することによって、数万頁の文書を蓄積することができ、また、必要に応じて素早くイメージを検索できるという便利さも備えている。

TOSFile の電子ファイルシステムについてはこのように説明されている[9]。

システム販売促進の説明の中で述べられていることであるので、本当に簡便なものかどうかわからないが、基本的には、この通りのものであると言ってよい。システムの基本構成は図のようになる。いまわが国では主要な電子機器メーカー、あるいはOA機器メーカーがそれぞれ光ディスク・ファイルシステムを発売している[10]。各社のシステムも、それを構成する各装置の呼称が違っていても、基本的には同じである。

まず、画像イメージを読み取り、自動的にディジタルデータに変換し、光ディスクに入力する装置がある。TOSFile では、階層スキャナーといい、原資料を読み込むのにブックモード入力と自動給紙入力の二つの方式をとることができる。Ａ３、Ａ４、Ｂ４、Ｂ５判

の原稿をそのまま、あるいは縮小して入力できる。入力の際、原稿の印字に濃淡があれば、5段階の濃度指定、および解像度指定もできる。

　出力装置は、光ディスクに入力されている画像を印刷する装置であるが、高い解像力で印刷できるようにレーザービームプリンタが使われる。出力の用紙はＡ３とＡ４が標準であるが、それ以上のサイズのコピーの出力が必要な場合には、オプションハードの中から適宜装置をつけ替えることができる。コンソールは、画像表示と操作ガイドに使用されるディスプレイとキーボードによって構成されている。ディスプレイは、縦型判文書に適合するように縦型のものが付けられている。TOSFile の場合には17インチ縦型のものが付けられており、画面が見易いような機構、モノクローム輝度調節およびチルトスウィプル機構が付いている。キーボードは JIS 標準になっている。

　制御装置にはマイクロプロセッサシステム、画像処理システム、8インチフロッピーディスク装置、磁気ディスク装置などが内蔵されている。この装置には、マイクロコンピュータが内蔵されているので、必要となれば、ホストコンピュータやファクシミリなど外部システムとのインターフェースへの拡張が可能となる。

　光ディスク装置は、このシステムの中核となっている装置で、画像を光ディスクに書き込み、そして、検索指示によって再生する働きをしている。イメージを電気信号に変換して記録しているのでファクシミリ通信が可能であり、また遠隔操作もできる。TOSFile では、光ディスク・ドライブユニットと言うが、このドライブユニットには光ディスクを内蔵している光ディスクカセットを使用する。これをドライブユニットの挿入口に入れると自動的にセットされる。

電子ファイルシステム（TOSFile）の構成

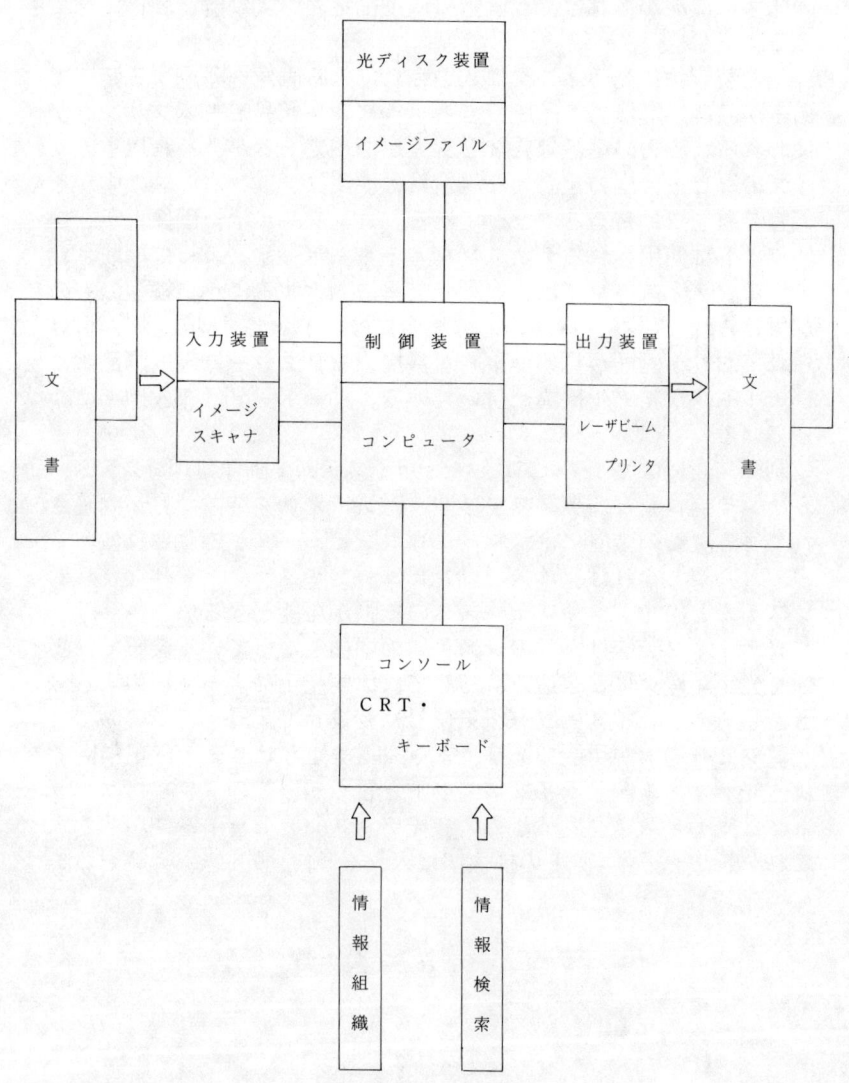

3　電子ファイルのオペレーション

　電子ファイルシステムで印刷資料を光ディスクに変換する作業を調べてみると、それは、あたかも複写機でコピーをとるように非常に簡単である。また、光ディスクに記録された情報をとり出すのも、操作に慣れれば、マイクロ資料リーダープリンターを使ってマイクロ化された情報を読むのと同じくらい簡便である。その基本操作は次のような手順で行われる。

(1)　画像情報の入力

　まず始めに、光ディスクを光ディスク装置に挿入する。これはＣＤをＣＤプレーヤーにセットするのとまったく同じ要領である。次に画像情報の入力モードを設定する。たとえば、図書や雑誌論文など一括して大量に画像を入力する場合には、連続入力方式を指定する。

　入力の際最も大切なことは次の操作である。光ディスクの中に記録されるいろいろな情報を電子ファイルとして体系化するために、あらかじめ設定されているメニューの中から個々の画像の入れものを選択する。TOSFileの場合には「キャビネット」・「バインダ」・「書類」・「頁」の四種類の入れ物がある。この段階で所定のファイル編成方式に従い必要なデータ（たとえば資料を入力する場合には、書誌データや分類コードや件名標目など）をキーワードとして入力する。

　電子ファイルシステムの操作とマイクロ化の操作とを比較するならば、画像を電子ファイルシステムによって光ディスクに変換する方法の特色は、このステップに集約されており、資料のマイクロ化とこの点できわだって異なっている。

　検索キーの入力がすめば、後の操作は簡単である。入力情報となる画像、すなわち、印刷資料を画像読み取り装置にかけ、光ディスクに入力する。そして、最後に所定の手続ですべての画像を登録すれば、入力作業はすべて完了する。

(2)　画像情報の検索と出力

　まず始めに、すでに画像情報が入力された光ディスクを光ディスク装置にセットする。これは、マイクロ資料をマイクロリーダーやリーダープリンターにセットするのと同じようなものである。

　次に必要な画像をとり出すためにメニューの中から検索モードを選択する。TOSFileでは、ダイレクト検索、注釈一覧、多項目検索などの検索方式が、あらかじめ設定されている。このステップと次のステップは、マイクロ資料の画像検索にはない光ディスクによる電子ファイル固有の手順が必要となる。マイクロ資料の

場合と違って少しやっかいだが、検索キーが的確に入力されていて、検索手順を適正に行えば、求める情報の確実な出力が保障される。TOSFile では「キャビネット」など独特の名前がつけられているファイルを選択しながら、対話型で必要な画像を含んだイメージコードの検索を行う。

　必要なイメージコードが見つかったら、必要な画像を探すためにディスプレイ画面に表示させる。そして、画像をモニターしながら、求めている画像を選択し、求めている画像を確認したら、プリンターでハードコピーを打ち出す。

4　可能性と問題

　資料の代替え保存の媒体として光ディスクがマイクロフィルム、あるいはマイクロフィッシュにとって代わることができるかどうかについては、光ディスク・ファイルシステムの特性をマイクロ資料と比較しながら検討することによって明らかになる。

(1) 簡便な入出力操作

　光ディスクに原資料を置き換える操作の簡便さは、これまで説明してきた作業手順から容易に見当がつく。写真撮影の場合のように露出、焦点、そしてまた現像の段階でのこまごまとした手順は、原則的には、一切不要である。もっとも入力された中身を読むために入力の際に所定の登録手続が必要になる。そしてそれがマイクロ資料とは異なる簡便な出力を可能にしている。また、何よりも魅力があるのは、入力の際にディジタルコード化が自動的になされ、そのための人手を一切必要としないことである。

　実際に画像を呼び出す場合、マイクロ資料も何の造作もないようにみえる。しかし、フィルムやフィッシュを装填し、画像を正確に読み易い形で画面に呼び出すまでの間に幾度となくイライラすることを思いだす。光ディスク・ファイルシステムの場合には、まずディスクをディスクドライバーに挿入する。その後ファイルシステム固有の立ち上げの手順、画像検索の操作が多少必要になるが、そうした操作は、いまの人々の日常生活の一般的技法の中に入りこんできつつあり、それほど不自由を感じない。画像検索にしても、いわゆるアナグロのよさがあるかもしれないが、求める画像を映し出す際にフィルムを捲き過ぎたり、フィッシュの画面を右往左往するようなことは少なくともない。

(2) 画像検索

　求める画像を検索する手順がどのように簡便かを理解するためには、光ディスク・ファイルシステム固有のファイル構造をみて

みる必要がある。TOSFile 3200のファイルの構成を調べてみると次のように説明されている。

　大量のしかも多岐にわたるビジネス書類に適したファイルとして、トスファイルでは階層化文書管理体系を採用しています。分類の体系には、「キャビネット」、「バインダ」、「書類」、「頁」という一般的紙ファイルの名称をそのまま使っていますから、親しみやすく、どなたにも理解できるファイルが構築できます。
　また…（中略）…トスファイルでは登録書類1件ごとに、キーワード（タイトル）が6項目までつけられます。そのキーワードの名称、種類などはバインダごとにユーザーサイドで自由に設定（タイトル設計）できます[11]。

　ファイル構造にこうした仕組が考えられているならば、これらの四つのタグの定義を変え、そしてその運用・操作を多少手直しすれば、稀覯本や雑誌のバックナンバーの中身を光ディスクに置き換え、それをこのシステムで再生して読むことは容易にできるはずである。
　どのように容易か、ここで例を挙げて考えてみよう。最近早稲田大学では、劣化が懸念されているわが国明治期の刊行物をマイクロ化し、それをマイクロ資料として出版するプロジェクトが始まった[12]。同大学図書館では、このコレクションにおよそ10万冊の資料が収録されるものと推定している。この分量は明治期に刊行された出版物の約20％ぐらいになろうが、これらの資料を、主題別にグルーピングし、10〜15年でマイクロ出版するのがこの計画である。
　これを仮りに電子ファイルシステムで光ディスクで製作するものとして考えてみる。
　それらの資料の各頁を光ディスクに入力する場合、何がどのように入っているかを同定できるように電子ファイルにおけるファイル構成をきちっと設定しておかなければならない。先のファイル構成についての説明をそのままあてはめるならば、ある一つの主題でまとめられる資料群の「キャビネット」のキーワードはその主題である。「バインダ」のキーワードはひとつひとつの資料の書名または誌名となり、「書類」には目次、または論文名が入力され、「頁」には、文字通り、各章あるいは論文所蔵の頁が表示される。

ビジネス文書と違って図書館資料の場合には、実際には、これほど簡単にはいかないものと推察できるが、基本的にはこうなるだろう。こうしたキーワードをキーボードから入力すれば、求める文献が画面に現れ、必要に応じてプリントできる。

かくして福沢諭吉の『豊前豊後道普請の説』のフルテキストは、光ディスクの中に『新聞報道・論説』という「キャビネット」の、『交通』という「バインダ」の、『郵便報知』という「書類」の、『明治7年11月17日』の「頁」から得られることになる。

(3) 画像編集

TOSFile 3200に画面編集端末を接続することによって、さらに便利な情報入出力も可能である。この装置は、オプショナルなものであるが、光ディスクに入力されたいろいろな文書テキストを、新聞のクリッピングや雑誌論文の抜刷を集めてまったく新しい文書を作るように、画像を編集加工できる機能を備えている。これを使えば、次のようなこともできるはずである。

福沢諭吉の『豊前豊後道普請の説』は明治初期の論述だが、彼はこの小論文の中で今日的な意味での「情報」の概念を示唆している。わが国で情報の意義を正確に理解し、近代国家形成のために情報流通の諸々の方法・手段整備の急務を提唱した最初の人物である。

福沢は、「インフォルメーション」という言葉と「情報」という言葉を示し、その意義を多くの論文の中でいろいろな形で説明している。上記の検索システムを使って、さらに綿密なファイル構成を設計することができるならば、そのすべての論文の中の情報についての論述を一括検索し、そして探し出したテキストをひとつの画面に表示し、プリントアウトしたり、その新しい文書を情報として入力することも可能である。かくして、先の文献の他に、彼の『明治七年六月七日集会の演説』、『学問のすゝめ 初篇』、『学問のすゝめ 二篇』、『民情一新』などの諸論文の中から、「情報」というものの彼の考えを示す数々のテキストが得られる。

先の検索機能といい、この画面編集機能といい、こういうことが可能になるのはコンピュータを内蔵している光ディスク・ファイルシステムの特性であり、これがマイクロ資料にはない新しい便宜を提供することになる。

(4) 資料の収容能力

1枚の光ディスクにどれくらいの資料が収められるか。通常35ミリマイクロフィルム100フィート（1リール）には800コマが収

められる。資料を見開きで撮影するとしておよそ1,600頁である。これに対して光ディスクの場合12インチのものでＡ４判文書が8万枚記録できる。これを単純に8万頁とすれば、マイクロフィルムの50倍の収容能力である。

先の明治期刊行物マイクロ出版の場合をもう一度引合にだしてみよう。10万冊の資料が含まれるとする。1冊あたり、仮りに、200頁として2,000万頁、これを35ミリのマイクロフィルムに撮影するとして、おおよそ12,500リールとなる。12インチの光ディスクでは、250枚である。両方の書庫占有スペースを計算し、比較するまでもなく、スペースセービングの観点からみれば、これは非常に有効な手立てとなる。

ファイルシステム自体の収容能力は、TOSFile の最近のブロッシュアでは、基本システムにドライブユニットを2台まで連結できるというが、250枚のディスクにもなるとそれではもちろん足りない。また、最近25枚のディスクを収納できる「光ディスク高速オートチェンジャー」が開発されたという。単純に考えれば、この装置を10台連結し、ホストコンピュータで制御するような拡張システムにすれば、10万冊の明治期刊行物コレクションの電子図書館を作ることができるはずである。もちろんそれなりのコストがかかるわけだが、このことは資料の保存だけでなく、資料の蓄積、保管、供与の新しい方向を示すものと考えられる。

(5) コスト

本文の随分前に記したことだが、慶応義塾図書館の光ディスク目録の可能性を検討している段階で、ある業者がそれに必要なシステム一式（ファイルコントローラー、シングルディスクデッキ2台、80ＭＢ拡張検索装置2台、17インチ検索ターミナル2台、フラッペットスキャナー、レザービームプリンタの構成）の価格を見積らせたところ、2,100万円（5年リース価格で年間450万円）で、さらに年間95万円のシステム保守料が必要ということであった。

現在わが国の13のメーカーが光ディスク・ファイルシステムを売りに出しているが、その価格は、小規模なものは400万円ぐらいから、中規模のもので1,500万円程度である[13]。外国では、たとえば、最近英国 Philips から売りに出された69,000ポンドのものや Tandem の142,600ポンドのものがある[14]。システムの価格は、大規模なものはともかくとして、いま売りに出されているものはこの程度のもので、国際的に同じような水準にあり、少し安くなってきている。なお、生の光ディスクの値段は、サイズにもよる

が、1枚25,000円から35,000円程度である。
　では、250枚（文書で2,000万頁）の光ディスクに収められる明治期刊行物コレクションの光ディスクファイルを可能にするシステムは、もしそれが可能だとして、どれくらいの価格になるだろうか。メーカーはこの仮想のシステムに概算であれ、見積価格を出せないという。手許にある TOSFile3400H シリーズの標準価格表で概算してみると、本体価格と光ディスク高速オートチェンジャー10台、それに必要となると思われる若干のオプションハードを加えると、約2億円になる。それに主要装置の保守料が年額およそ800万円程度である。

(6)　光ディスクの標準化、耐久性、画像の鮮明度
　光ディスクを媒体に資料保存の可能性を考える場合、新しい媒体の資料特性、すなわち、標準仕様、耐久性などの特性や光ディスク・ファイルシステムを構成する各装置、とくにスキャナー、コンソール、プリンタなどの使い勝手なども検討してみなければならない。
　まず標準化の問題であるが、光ディスク明治期刊行物コレクションが TOSFile によるものであれ、他のメーカーのシステムによるものであれ、そのどれかによって一括入力され、頒布されるのであれば、光ディスクの標準化の問題はさほど重大ではないのかもしれない。そのコレクションを購入する図書館は同じシステムを購入すればよいからである。しかし、別のコレクションが Panafile で作られ、そしてその方式の光ディスクが発売されるようになると標準化の問題がにわかに重要性を帯びてくる。どの図書館でもそのためにもうひとつ別のシステムを導入する愚挙は犯すことはあるまい。また、資料保存のためにこの新しい媒体を採用すると仮定して、ある図書館は TOSFile を、またある図書館では Panafile を使って、光ディスク資料を自家生産するとなると、資料保存のための図書館協力は何の力にもなり得ない。
　光ディスクの標準化については、少し前から国際標準化機構において検討されており、サイズや機械的特性など光ディスクの物理的要素について合意をみたといわれているが、肝心の光ディスクドライブについてはいまだ各メーカーの裁量に任されている状況で[15]、メーカー側はそれ以上の答えをもっていない。このことについては、しかし、VTR の「ベータと VHS」問題の再現になるかもしれないが、標準化が進展しないばあいには、有力な方式間のコンバータなどが現れるかもしれない。
　もうひとつの問題は、光ディスクの耐久性である。これは資料

保存という観点からきわめて重要である。いろいろな特性は別にして、保存ということだけを考えるならば、これが最大の要件となる。

マイクロフィルム（銀塩）では半永久的に保存できるということが定説になっている。光ディスクはそんなにもたないというのが支配的であるが、TOSFileのブロッシュアは、「10年以上の媒体寿命」を標榜している。聞くところによると、メーカーはその耐用年数を、大きな負荷を掛けて算定していると言っており、実験データでは、40〜50年はもつだろうとも言われている。また、原光ディスクから子光ディスク、子光ディスクから孫光ディスクと中身の寿命を繋いでいけば、資料保存の目的を達成できるとも言う。仮りにそうするとして、画像の精度が落ちることはないだろうか、という心配もでてくるが、文書から文書の複写とは違って画像の鮮明度が低下することは、技術的には考えられないとメーカー側は答えている。

画像の鮮明度については、スキャナー、ディスプレイ、プリンタに一応の配慮がなされている。しかし、幾度かのデモンストレーションを見るかぎり、若干の不安がある。たとえば、スキャナーの性能がよすぎるのか、それとも光ディスク記録原理の関係でそうなるのかわからないが、おそらく光学的な処理技術が原因であろうが、原稿の汚れ、折りじわなどまで写ってしまうことがある。また、ディスプレイ上の画像の鮮明度も少し気になる。大判の現文書を縮小して入力したものなど、老眼の人には苦痛である。この問題は、とりあえずはディスプレイの上で画面を拡大することによってある程度解決されているが、いずれはスキャナーの改良や大画面ディスプレイ[16]などによる展開がみられるかもしれない。

まとめ：展望と課題

光ディスク・ファイルシステムは、もともと事務文書管理の効率化（スペースセービングと迅速・効果的な検索による省力化）を図ることを目的として考えられ、そして商品化されたものである。したがって、図書館資料媒体の代替えにこれを採用する場合、事務文書管理システムの根底にある発想を私達の発想に、つまり資料保存の代替え媒体として光ディスクをベースとしたファイルシステムの可能性ということに変換してみなければならない。

ちょっとした思いつきから発展したこの考えを、本当は、その妥当性を精密に検討する必要がある。しかしそれは別の機会に譲ると

して、ここではいましばらく、曖昧な比類による私の発想が正しいものと信じて、それが可能かどうか私の考えを述べたいと思う。

1 技術的問題の解決

光ディスクによるファイルシステムは、いま揺籃期にあり、まず、技術的改良の動向を測りながら資料保存への利用の可能性に答えをださなければならない。

① 耐久性と標準化の問題

まず光ディスクそのものの、そして当然のことながら、それに連動して光ディスクファイルの改良が必要であろう。とりわけ耐久性と標準化については私たちの目的に対しては最も重要な要件になる。これらのことについてメーカー側の考えを調べてみたが、いまのところ確実な展望は得られなかった。

この新しい技術を採用するかどうかを判断するとき、たしかに私たちはまず経費を考える。しかし、本当は、耐久性と同様に光ディスクの標準仕様も大事な要件になる。各図書館がどのメーカーのシステムを導入しようと、それぞれが資料の代替え保存用に光ディスク資料を作り、それがどの図書館でも使えるようにならなければ、私たちは、また別な原価計算をすることができる。それが国際的な広がりの中で可能になればなおさらである。もともと私達が保存しなければならない資料は無数であり、それゆえにどうしても各図書館が分担して保存版光ディスクを作成せざるを得ないからである。

これらの要件が技術的に可能ならば、私達はおそらく少し高めのコストでも、光ディスクによる資料の代替え保存を真剣に考えることになろう。先ほどの私の試算が正しいとして、初期経費に仮りに2億円、メインテナンスに800万円掛かるとする。そのとき私たちは、いま、10万冊の資料を保管することができる図書館を新たに建築し、それを運営していく経費がどれほどのものか算定し、比較してみることになるだろう。

② 検索システムの問題

光ディスクによる資料の代替え保存を考える場合、耐久性と標準化が、同時に第一の要件になる。それはまた、対費用効果上の判断の条件にもなるが、運用上の可能性を判断する第一の要件は検索システムであろう。求める資料が的確に、迅速に、しかも簡便に検索できなければ、私たちのユーザーは承知しない。

マイクロ資料に収められた画像の検索は、それに添付される収録文献目録、あるいは索引によっているが、それらは補助的

に作られているに過ぎず、その検索性は無いにひとしい。一方光ディスク・ファイルシステムでは、セールストークを信ずるならば、検索性が高まるかもしれないという期待がもてる。しかし、たとえば、福沢諭吉の膨大な著作のなかから「情報」に関する啓蒙的な論述を検索し、またさらに同時代の他の論述をも合せて検索できるようなきわめて高度な検索システムを想定するとすれば、先に述べたような「キャビネット」、「バインダ」、「書類」、そして「頁」といったファイル構造では不十分であろう。もっと精巧な仕組が必要となる。

　この側面での技術開発については、半分は私たちの責任でもある。カッター以来、いやそれ以前から図書館員は効率的な資料組織の方法を開発すべく努力してきた[17]。そしていまもコンピュータを利用してその方法を探している。このことに関するノウハウを私たちは十分にもっているはずである。あとはその蓄積されたノウハウをもって光ディスクファイルシステムのメーカーと技術的協力で効率的な検索システムを開発するだけである。

2　メーカー＝図書館間協力

　媒体の耐久性、標準化、そしていま言った意味での検索システムは、印刷資料の代替え保存の目的からすれば、現在のファイルシステムでは不十分である。いずれも、今後解決されなければならない技術的な問題である。

　技術的な問題の解決に図書館は無力である。それはまったくメーカー側に任せざるを得ない。その場合メーカーが気にするのは、ひたらく言えば、それがお金になるかどうかということであろう。つまり、私たちの目的と彼らの目的とが合致するかどうかが問題になる。これで儲かるかどうか、私たちのサイドからは、いま、何も言えない。ただ、もしそのことを尋ねられたら、いまあまりお金にならない、と答えておいたほうが賢明である。むしろ、私たちがしなければならないのは、メーカー側に資料保存の意義と代替え媒体の図書館での運用法を正しく伝え、協力を請願することであろう。私たちに技術と企業の力の援助を請願することではなく、一緒に文化を担っていくことを説き、パートナーとして協力するよう要請すべきである。

　メーカーと図書館との間に、こうした基本的なレベルで、資料保存の協力体制ができ上れば、一方は先端技術をもって、もう一方は資料活用のノウハウをもって、新しい方法のための協同開発は可能

であると考える。

3　何をどう保存すべきか

　とはいえ資料保存の問題はやはり私たちの問題であると認識すべきであろう。たしかに、同様の課題をもつプロフェッションもあるが、書物のことは図書館員の問題である。それゆえ、技術的な面やそれ以外の側面で他に協力を要請することも必要となろうが、それ以前に私たちの間で解決しなければならないことである。

　その問題のひとつは、何をどのように保存するかである。何をというのは、冒頭の生住異滅の自然の原理に逆らって、どうしてもその命を長らえる必要がある書物を特定する、という意味である。私たちがその保存に心掛けなければならないものはたくさんあるが、捨ててしまってもよいものも、また、たくさんあるように私には思える。したがって、しなければならないことは、私たちの誰もが数え上げることのできないほど膨大な図書館資料の量を、ひとまず、限定することではないだろうか。

　どのようにというのは、資料保存の技術だけではなく、ひとりではできないこのことを図書館界全体が共同して行う方法のことである。

　それにもましてしなければならないことは、資料保存の意義を社会全体に浸透させる努力であろう。その根底は文化を担うことであり、そのことが図書館の、とくに学術図書館の任務であることは、おそらく、誰もが理解するだろう。しかし、その重要性が理念的に理解されるだけでは、ことが少しも進展しない。何によらず図書館の仕事は金の掛ることばかりだが、そういった現実的な条件を伴った理解を求める努力を、今後私たちはつづけなければならない。

　さて、こう考えてきて、最後に、では光ディスクによる資料保存の可能性について私の答えを出さなければならない。慶応義塾図書館が所蔵する学術雑誌をこの媒体に変換し、光ディスクファイルシステムで利用することを、いま同僚の図書館員や大学の財政当局に提案すべきだろうか。

　その答えを出すには、本文中で疑問を呈した諸点についてメーカーからの的確なコメントが欲しいところである。しかし、マイクロ資料から光ディスクへの変換は時期尚早であるとして、いまこの考えを捨て、他の可能性を考えることは私にはできない。現にわが国でもごく最近、図書館資料や類縁の資料の光ディスク変換の事例をみることができる[18]。

注

(1) J. Bery : Preservation, priorities, and politics. *Library Journal*, 112(20)1987, p.6.

(2) B. Sulpor : An optical disk system that will allow the Library of Congress to print 5.5 million catalog cards "on demand". *International Journal of Micrographics and Video Technology*, 2(4)1982, p.p.281-285.

(3) W. O. Van Arsdale : The rush to optical discs. *Library Journal*, 111(16)1986, p.p.53-55.

(4) 調べてみておどろいたことだが、この問題についての米国の文献は非常に多い。多くの関連文献が最近のLISAからみつけられる。これに対してわが国では、当該技術についての文献はあっても、図書館資料の媒体として光ディスクをとらえたものは少ない（注18参照）。

(5) 斉藤　孝『電子情報管理システム入門 ― 光ディスク電子ファイルシステムの活用』HBJ出版局　1987　202p.
　　光ディスクファイルシステムの現状　日経データプロOA　第1巻 part 1-186　日経マグロウヒル社　1987

(6) 『現代用語の基礎知識』'87 自由国民社　1987　p. 905, 939.

(7) A. Bender : Optical disc technology for records management: a user perspective. *Electronic Library*, 5(5)1987, p.p. 276-281
　　C. Chen : Libraries in the information age: where are the microcomputer and laser optical disc technologies taking us? *Microcomputers for Information Management*, 3(4)1986, p.p.253-265.

(8) 『現代用語の基礎知識』'87〔前掲〕
　　A. Scott : Memories of the future: new library technolgies in information transfer, processing and storage－the Library Association Information Technology Group's Third Annual Conference, 12-14 June1987. *Program*, 22(1)1988, p.p. 81-83.

(9) 特設記事「低価格化で新展開を迎えた光ディスク・ファイル・システム」（『コンピュータ＆ネットワークLAN』5(4)1987, p.104-111.）

(10) 斉藤　孝〔前掲〕p. 24-29, 76-77.

(11) 『TOSFile 3200Hシリーズ』東芝電算機・OAシステム事業

部　1986, p. 9.
(12)　「明治期資料マイクロ化事業計画の意義とその計画について」早稲田大学図書館明治期資料マイクロ化事業室（『早稲田学報』41(10)1987, 12, p.p.42-45. ）
(13)　特設記事「低価格化で新展開を迎えた光ディスク・ファイル・システム」〔前掲〕
　　　「光ディスクファイルシステムの現状」（『日経データプロОА』第1巻 part 1-186〔前掲〕p. 003）
(14)　Pilips upgrades document storage system. *Communication Technology Impact*, 9(11)1988, p.11
　　　Tandem announces optical storage system. *Communication Technology Impact,* 9(4)1988, p.p.4-5.
(15)　吉田富夫「光ディスクメモリ」（『情報処理』27(6)1986, p. 636. ）
　　　「光ディスク　規格作りに着手」（『日本工業新聞』昭和62年10月27日）
　　　「13センチ追記型光ディスクISO規格決定」（『電波新聞』昭和63年1月4日）
　　　「光ディスク　互換性確保重要」（『電波新聞』昭和63年1月11日）
(16)　倉橋浩一郎「大画面ディスプレイ」（『情報処理』27(7)1986, p.p.711-717. ）
(17)　澁川雅俊『目録の歴史』草書房　1985年　212p.
(18)　「世界で初めての試み　古文書を光ディスクで保存へ　船橋市西図書館」（『東芝 TOSFile の活用シリーズ』昭和62年7月）
　　　「世界で初めて、コンピュータによる美術研究と美術品のデータバンクを構築」（『東芝 TOSFile の活用シリーズ』昭和61年9月）
　　　The paperless plan of the Japanese Patent Office. *World Patent Information,* 8(3)1986, p.p.210-217.
　　　伊藤　陽ほか「特許制度と特許管理・特許情報　その歴史的考察」（『情報管理』28(1)1985, p.p.73-74. ）
　　　小原博生ほか「機械検索」（『情報管理』28(11)1986, p.p. 991-1012. ）
　　　杉田繁治「国立民族学博物館におけるマルチメディアデータベース」（『情報管理』30(12)1988, p.p.1131-1141）

知識の保存：社会全体のための方策

Patricia Battin

　記録物管理者の責務となっている知識の保存に対する責任は、図書館業務の中でも最も高く評価される伝統であろう。そして、長い間世の中では疑問の余地のないものとされてきたこの伝統的業務は、今や酸性紙による劣化によって危機的な状況にある。我々がわかち合っている文化の知識の内部を徐々に焼き尽くす炎への懸念は、他の国々と同様に両国にとっても等しくまた、はかり知れないほど重要になっている。

　石を捨て去って以来、我々が創り出したものを記録するために用いてきた全てのメディアは、劣化にさらされている。実際、高度化した我々の技術は劣化しやすく、蓄積に用いているメディアはもろいものである。急速に使い捨て社会に向かいつつある現在では、これまでの経験は価値がなくなり、新しい知識が急速に増えるとともに、昨日の知識は明日に役立たないほどである、というような落とし穴に陥りがちである。

　米国人文科学基金（政府が資金援助している米国の人文科学への助成を行う機関）の委員長であるLynne Cheney博士は最近、社会に対する我々の文化的遺産の重要性について述べている。我々の社会のまとまりに対して、ホワイトヘッドの「シンボル・コード」、すなわち分担された共通知識の概念が重要である。博士によれば、「知識は各世代の経験を反映しなければならず、一方では社会を一体化する伝統と結びつけなければならない。……過去へのこの連帯がなければ、我々はどこにいて、誰であり、一体となった米国民としてなすべきことを決めるのには何が重要であるのか、を知ることができない状態に陥ってしまう。ホワイトヘッドの言うように『修正の自由のあるシンボルへの敬意に合体できない社会は、衰えざるを得ないのである。』」

　これまで150年にわたり、ほとんどの「シンボル・コード」が印刷されてきた酸性紙が劣化するということは、歴史的、国際的な規模での危機に陥っていることを示している。我々は一つの大きな共同体の中に住んでいるので、こうした危機は、大きな関心を呼び起こしている。

　酸性紙のもろさは、記念物に対して災厄とともに好機もつくり出している。

知識の基盤のかなりの部分を急速に失いつつあるというのが、災厄という側面である。こうした危機はおそらく、ウォールストリートの大暴落で5,000億ドルを失うのと同様に理解を絶するものである。1850年以後、抄紙工程にアラム・サイズ剤を導入したため、米国の研究図書館が所蔵する3億500万点のうち、控え目に見積もってもその25%、7,800万点はもろくなっており、塵となりつつある。アラムは空気中の水分に反応して、紙の結合力を強めているセルローズを破壊する。

好機というのは、新しい技術の可能性という側面である。これには、機械可読のテキストから要求に応じてたやすく冊子体の出版物を作り出し、これまでは一様に利用できなかった知識に対して、より広い利用ができるようになるばかりでなく、新しい研究方向を示し、強力にそれを押し進めることができるように新しい形態を利用することも含まれる。資料の保存の危機は、近代社会の記録された知識に対する広範なアクセスの重要性をもう一度確認し、最新の蓄積媒体の保存性を調べ、まとまりのある社会にとって不可欠なシンボル・コードを守るため、我々の持つこれまでの知識を未来の研究者のニーズと結びつけるような実験の場となることができる。我々は、資料保存への挑戦により、研究図書館の意義を根本的に考え直さざるを得なくなる。

もし我々が、資料保存の問題を研究と出版に起こる根本的な変化に関わらない単なる「再記録化」操作上の狭い問題であると見るなら、自らの責務を放棄した事になるであろう。我々が朽ちるのを放置するなら、将来に対して過去は失われる。次第に情報技術に支配されつつある社会における図書館の再検討に注意を喚起するような広範な課題に対し、資料保存問題は一つのパラダイムを示している。これらの課題には、効果のある協力活動、各分野の研究方法の知識、形態の選択、選択の規準、書誌調整のしくみ、新しい技術の利用、著作権関連問題、ネットワークの標準化・互換性・利用、分散利用のシステムの運用、民間部門の役割、予算についての新しい戦略が含まれる。

現在、資料保存の第一の課題は、新しい技術の可能性ではなく、こうした技術を、これまでの知識に対する強力な利用手段を経済的に提供するような方法で豊かに使用するための戦略を立てて、実行することが決定的に必要である点にある。

ここ30年の間に、米国の図書館では、図書館資料の保護と保存に関する問題について様々な活動を行ってきた。こうした努力には、紙の化学と資料保存についての調査、資料保存の専門家やコンサベ

ーターの教育・訓練計画の設置、新聞や劣化した本のフィルム化共同計画、National Register of Microfilm Masters の機械可読化、フィルムにかかわるものとマスター・ネガの存在の両方をオンラインで記録する方法の開発、個々の蔵書の保存必要性についての自館内調査が含まれている。米国社会の多元性を反映して、これらの活動は多数の独立機関や研究図書館によってなされてきた。ここで全てを挙げるには多すぎるが、その大多数は *Library Literature* で調べることができる。広い範囲の努力がなされ、資金援助がなされていることを示すためにいくつかの例を挙げておく。

米国議会図書館は、研究図書館界に対して、National Preservation Programs Office を通じ、また(1)10〜12年間をめどとした75万点のマイクロフィルム化、(2)酸性ではあるが、まだ劣化していない資料の大量脱酸化の広範な研究、(3)光ディスクを利用した雑誌論文の蓄積・検索の実験計画を通じて指導的な地位を果たしている。

米国国立医学図書館は、全国の医学図書館のネットワークと協力して、医学研究と診療に重要性の高い歴史的資料の蔵書とともに、*Index Medicus* の収録誌の劣化した資料をマイクロ化する計画を進めている。

米国農学図書館は、養殖関係資料の保存のために画像処理技術の利用可能性を調査している。

コロンビア大学図書館学科では、メロン財団と米国人文科学基金からの助成によって、先駆的な資料保存管理者・技術者教育課程を創設した。現在まで33名がこの課程を終えており、33名以上が終えつつあり、また19名が新たに入学している。この計画が成功したことは、資料保存活動を行っている研究図書館が、1978年の5館から1988年の54館へ増加したことに現れている。

米国人文科学基金は、米国の新聞の分散マイクロ化計画を助成している。

36の研究機関からなる RLG（Research Libraries Group）は、民間団体と親機関の助成を通して、参加館所蔵貴重書の一連のマイクロ化計画を援助している。

米国神学図書館協会は、参加館の会費をもとに、40万点の劣化した手稿本と図書をマイクロ化する長期計画を支援している。

これまでの15年間に、ARL（Association of Research Libraries）は、この問題を周知させるとともに、調査活動の支援を通じて参加館の資料保存活動を促進し、教育訓練計画の必要性を強調してきており、さらに、分散化されたマイクロ化計画が重複のないようになされるように、マイクフィルムのマスター・ネガの書誌データを機

械可読化する必要性を認めている。

　資料保存活動への国内、国外のかかわり合いが強まっているおり、広範囲にわたる既存の活動を調整する必要があることを認識したARLの会員館は、1984年に、図書館振興財団(CLR)に対して、資料保存の全国的政策を策定するように求める決議を行った。図書館振興財団は過去30年間に、バロー研究所の紙の化学研究への援助に始まる広い範囲の資料保存活動を支援してきた。ARLの期待に応えて、1986年に「資料保存・利用委員会」（Commission on Preservation and Access）が設置された。これは、図書館振興財団の援助を受けた18ヵ月におよぶCommitee on Preservation and Accessの勧告に従ったものである。多数の大学や民間団体によって支援されたこの委員会の管理組織は、大学職員や図書館員を含んでいる。この委員会の目標は、あらゆる形態の記録の保存を確実にし、学術情報へのアクセスを強化するために、全ての図書館や関連団体の間の体系的で目的の明確な協力活動を促進し、発展させ、支援することにある。

　図書館や文書館の永続的な活動の中の活発な部分として、資料保存の制度化を促進するために、できる限り少数のスタッフで既存の組織を通して活動することがこの委員会の意図である。運営面の支援に加え、委員会の計画は、様々な助成先から5年間で約500万ドルから600万ドルの助成を得ることになろう。こうした助成は、広範な関心を集め、社会的な援助のもとで大がかりな資料保存活動を進めるのに必要な研究・広報計画、コンサルタント、技術的助言、研究者を支援するためのものである。委員会は、重度な劣化状態にある300万点の内容をマイクロ化やその他の技術によって保存するのに必要とされる大規模な協力活動を支援するためには、連邦、州、自治体から約2億ドルを集めるための努力を払うことになろう。

　我々は、この「資料保存・利用委員会」の考え方、すなわち自立組織の広範な既存の活動を基に成り立つ全国計画の策定と調整を小規模な機関で行うという考え方は、多元的な社会では適切な方策であると信じている。さらに我々は、将来のための方策は、一連の新しい認識、つまり研究図書館のサービスに重点をおいたこれまでの仮定に挑戦する、以下のような認識に基礎を置かなければならないと信じている。

- 図書は利用者にとっては優れた伝達形態であるが、永続性という面からはもろい蓄積形態である
- 今後のために両者の機能をみたすようにする必要がある
- 離れた場所にある知識に対するアクセスの強化により、公私立

大学や研究図書館によって維持されている蔵書の保存を連邦政府が支援する根拠が与えられる
- 従来の助成原則は、図書館やそのサービスを支援するには不自然で、不適切である
- 資料保存活動は、我々の社会への情報サービスの提供方法を変える転機をあらわしている
- 情報サービスを見直すことは、個々の機関で戦略的計画策定を行う得がたい機会を与える。つまり、もはやこのようにするべきであるというような「大学図書館」の枠は存在しない

莫大な費用や我々が対処しなければならない増大する一方の出版物、研究者の要求の変化、絶え間なく変化する技術力により、自立した機関による協力活動が必要とされている。累積された知識を蓄積し、アクセスを強化するための費用がかからず効果的な手段を提供するような全国的、国際的な基盤を作り出すために技術が存在している。我々は、こうした技術を利用するための国際的な方針と協力組織を作らなければならない。

実行方法の多様性の原則、すなわち多数の選択肢を認めるような全国的な調整活動を行うという原則を強調しておきたい。必要度が多様であり、現在の社会では技術の変化が速く、そして知識の最前線を広げ続ける研究者の情報要求は絶え間なく変化するために、全国計画を考える最上の方策では、次のような点を考慮すべきである。
- 人類の記録に長期間の広範囲なアクセスを保証する基本原則
- 資料の形態、書誌調整、資料保存活動のための基準
- それぞれの機関の学術的使命、財源に基づいている蔵書の特色が明らかになっている個々の機関に対する一連の選択肢

資料保存・利用委員会は、次のような二重の目的を持っている。
1）一般的には記録物の保存、特に最初に取り組むべき劣化した本の問題のために極めて広範囲で調整された協力活動に対する国際的環境を作り上げる。
そして
2）以下のような活動を確立し、それぞれの機関での資料保存の処理過程を確立する。
- 災害対策
- 気候に対する対応
- 職員や利用者の訓練
- 修復、製本、資料保護の技術
- 蔵書を調査し蔵書の知識を持つこと、継続的な維持管理の手順
- さまざまな形態をもつマスター・コピーを共有する「全国的蔵

書」という環境で技術社会における蔵書を実現するための方策の策定

　この委員会は全国的な協力体制のもとで、劣化した図書の内容を残すために新しいマスターコピーで大規模なマイクロ化を推進し、配布センターを作ってこの新しい「全国的な蔵書」にアクセスできるようにすることを第一の目的としている。現在までに、マイクロ化技術は、耐久性と利用のための基準が国際的に受け入れられており、唯一の安定した技術となっている。重要な点は、マイクロフィルムを好まない人々がいても、蓄積した形態で利用する必要はないという点である。数年以内にマイクロフィルムのディジタル化ができるようになり、標準化されると期待できる。しかし、将来にわたって長期保存形態として、電子技術よりも写真技術が選ばれ続けても不思議はない。電子的情報を広範に利用するのに必要なハードやソフト、ネットワーク技術は、費用がかかり、変化の速度が速く、また、標準化が行われておらず、数十年は安定しないと考えられる。

　劣化図書対策計画（Brittle Books Program）は三つの部分からなっている。
- 出版社の中性紙（アルカリ紙）使用を促す
- 脱酸化の可能性を追求する
- 劣化図書の知的内容を長期保存のできるマスターコピー形態にする

　究極的には、個々の機関や各々の研究者が自らの目的や用途のため、さまざまな形態で入手できる、ディジタル化された知識ベースの存在を考えることができる。当初は、この「全国的な蔵書」は、オンラインサービスと24時間配送サービスを通じて利用できるマイクロフィルムの集中コレクションの形態をとり、この蓄積、検索、提供方法の強化は、研究者の技術の利用増大と研究者集団に提供されるネットワークの拡充をもたらすであろう。

　知識の保存は、図書館の問題と限定されず、社会問題とみなされるため、この委員会は、以下のような活動も行うことになろう。
- 問題自体と行動の必要性の理解を得るために学識経験者を動員する
- 出版社に中性紙の使用を促す
- 新しい技術の経済的な応用方法の開発にメーカーを巻き込む
- マスター・マイクロフィルムの共用データベースの作成やマイクロ化の分担作業のために国際的な連絡体制を作る
- 新しい技術の開発、自動化によるマイクロ化費用の削減、現在の家内工業的な処理から大規模マイクロ化施設による大量処理

への転換のための研究計画を助成する
- 資料保存という語を広めさせるとともに、我々の遺産を守り、情報の自由な利用への信頼を取り戻すための国家的な努力に広範な草の根の支持を得る

単純に考えれば、年間に1,000点以上の資料保存処理を行っているのはわずか数機関であるという現状の中で、数百万点のマイクロ化の全国計画を策定するのは、不可能に挑戦しているように見えるであろう。しかしながら、米国の図書館には、7,800万点の劣化資料があり、そのうち6,800万点は重複しているとみなすなら、問題とするのは、1,000万点に減らすことができる。さらに、この1,000万点のうちの約300万点が保存を要する中心的な蔵書と考えられ、問題は、解決可能な規模になってくる。今後20年間に300万点を保存するための努力と資金を結びつけるには、公私立大学、連邦、地方行政機関、協会、企業、個人の間の新たな協力が必要とされている。

全国的方策には以下のような基本的な活動方針が含まれている。
1）包括的な蔵書を持つ研究図書館が属する20の大規模な機関は、1年に7,500点をマイクロ化する。これにより、20年間で300万点となる。
2）連邦政府は、米国人文科学基金を通じて、準備とマイクロ化の費用として1点当り60ドルが支出されよう。
3）参加館は、各大学の支出や行政機関、基金、企業、市民からの寄付を通じてその他に必要な資金をまかなうことになろう。この300万点のマイクロフィルムの全国的蔵書によって恩恵を受ける非参加館からの寄付も求められよう。
4）参加館は、連邦政府の助成に対して以下の活動を行う必要がある。
    - マイクロ化が計画されているものを、たやすくオンラインで探せるようにする
    - マスター・コピーがあるものを、たやすくオンラインで探せるようにする
    - マイクロ化の規定について合意を得る
    - 書誌調整用の最小規準について合意を得る
    - 配布センターにおけるマスター・ネガの集中保存
5）委員会は、購入したり、貸出したりするために様々な形態（冊子体、フィルム、マイクロフィッシュ、CD-ROM、磁気テープなど）での迅速な検索手段を提供する配布センターの設立を監督する。このセンターは固定費と利用料を通じ、利用を必要とする人々によって助成される。

6）対象資料の選択規準や形態上の選択事項を見直すため、研究者や図書館からなる分野別の諮問委員会を設置する。

　過去5年間にわたって全国的に劣化図書の所蔵箇所調査や重複率の標本調査をもとに費用を見積もる調査が何回も行われてきたが、まだ、こうした問題について正確なデータはない。しかし、次の5年間の方向を明らかにするためには、この計画の最初の5年間に学んだことは多い。マイクロ化には、これまで個々の図書館が行ってきた経験からみて、1点当り40ドルから100ドルの費用がかかっているが、低い価格で提供する地域マイクロ施設の設立、準備作業からのこれまでのような生産性の低い手順の排除、それに重複したマイクロ化を避けるためのオンライン情報源の作成により、1点当り60ドルまで減らすことができると考えている。ただ、小規模な専門的蔵書によって埋めることが可能な大規模な総合的な蔵書の中の欠陥状況や蔵書の重複についての正確なデータを集めたい。

RLG（Leserach Libraries Group）によって始められ、ARL（Association of Research Libraries）が引き継いでいる「全国的蔵書調査計画」（National Collection Inventory Program）があり、これは、初期の対象資料選択のための基盤として優れたものである。専門分野の研究者を支援できるように拡大するには、こうした選択をさらに検討していくことになる。劣化図書対策計画は知的な内容の保存を第一の目的としているが、分野によって要請があれば、芸術作品としての本についても検討を迫られよう。現在のマイクロ化計画は、(1)主題と年代　(2)書名　(3)利用頻度　(4)貴重書　(5)様式を示したり代表例となるもの、などの様々な選択方法を考案中である。この計画は完成までに20年かかるので、選択した形態が21世紀の研究者の情報ニーズを満たすものであるという点が重要である。

　美術史、生物学、医学のような分野では、文章と画像の両方に知識が含まれており、特別な問題が存在する。現在のところでは適当な解決策はなく、その本が書庫で崩壊する前に、地味な選択を行っていくしかない。こうした問題や同じ様なジレンマが研究・広報計画委員会につきまとっている。

　こうした結果、誰でもが利用できる保存された資料の全国的蔵書によって、個々の図書館は、自館で行う業務を明確にした方策をたてることができるようになる。全国的蔵書の共有によって、出版物が増え続け、利用できる建物の空間が減っていくに伴い、次第に厳しくなっているスペースの問題が緩和されるであろう。知識の「全国化」は、我々が偉大な社会の本質と見なしている情報の広範で自

由な利用を必然的にもたらすことになる。これまで、知的な情報源はわずかな限られた図書館でのみ利用できたにすぎなかったが、大学が学生と教員のための広域ネットワークへと向かうにつれて、全国どこでも利用できるようになっている。急速に増加するが、頻繁に利用されない蔵書の蓄積費用は、全国的蔵書への協力、電子的情報源助成への予算配分、独自の利用頻度の多い蔵書の強化、そして資料保存の努力の拡大を通じて、減らすことができる。

　この偉大な社会のための前例のない全国計画の成功には、我々が自身のこれまでの習慣と知恵を新たな現実に合致するように変えようとするにつれて、図書館員の高度のリーダーシップと調整能力が必要になっている。我々は不確実さと共存することを学ばなければならない。なぜなら、絶え間なく変わっていく環境の中で特定の目標を設定することを強要するのは、我々の進歩に制約を与えるからである。これまで、図書館員は、学問の世界を支援する立派な、そして生産性の高いシステムを作り上げてきた。しかし、我々は誇りを高くもちすぎて、将来のための計画を抑えるようなことがないように気をつけなければならない。

日本における学術情報データベース の形成と提供活動

安 達　　淳

はじめに

　本稿は、わが国のデータベース形成及び提供活動について、大学における学術情報を中心として、できるだけ全体像が把握できるように紹介しようとするものである。まず、わが国の最近のデータベース関連の動きについて概観し、次に学術情報に焦点をあわせて活動状況を紹介する。そして今後、国際的な情報流通を拡大する際の課題について、最後にまとめている。

　従来から、わが国は情報に関しては一貫して輸入過多であった。近年、電気通信やコンピュータを駆使した情報流通の仕組みが整うとともに、社会全体の急激な国際化に伴って情報流通の問題も国際的に注目を集めるようになった。

　一般に、国際問題というものは、別の見方をすれば、個々の国にとっての国内問題と読みかえることもできる。すなわち、国際間の情報流通の問題に即して言えば、わが国内での情報形成・流通等の仕組みが未熟であること、まちまちであることなどのために、外からは理解しにくいという結果になっていると思われる。従って、まずなによりも国内の体制を明確にすることが必要であるという考え方も出てくるわけである。

　そこで、本稿では日本におけるさまざまな動向を概説し、その理解をベースにして、今後データベースについての国際的な協力、流通の体制を整備して行くための問題を整理したい。

日本におけるデータベース・サービスの概観
1　全体的な状況

　電子機器のハードウェア製造技術では世界の中で先端的な位置を占めるに至った日本も、情報提供や流通に関わる活動やサービスにおいては、先進国の米国に比して、約10年の遅れをとっていると言われている。

　まず、データベース振興センターの報告[1]に基づいて、1987年のわが国の情報サービスを概観しよう。1987年における日本の情報サービス業全体の売上は、1兆9,159億円であるが、その中で、データベースなどに関わる情報提供サービスの売上げは、約6％の1,143億円となっている。これは1975年と比較して約8倍の規模であり、年間

平均約20％で増大していることになる。ちなみに、1987年の米国のデータベース市場規模は、約44億8千万ドルである。（日本の約5倍）

1987年においてわが国で利用可能なデータベースの種類は、1,483種となっているが、この中の約80％は海外からのもので、国産データベースの占める20％という割合はこの数年ほぼ一定である。この中で、従来は「自然科学・技術」と「ビジネス」分野が均衡していたのに、徐々に「ビジネス分野」が増大し、50％（そのうち、日本製23％）近くを占めるに至った。一方、「自然科学・技術」分野の割合は漸減し、約30％（そのうち、日本製14％）である。「社会科学・人文科学」分野は、わずか4％（日本製は1件）を占めるに過ぎない。

また、データベースの内容については、従来は抄録を収めた文献データベースの割合が多かったが、1987年にはこの割合が50％以下になり、ファクト・データベースや全文データベースの割合の方が上回った。

利用可能なデータベースの本数の約80％を海外製が占めるのに対し、利用料金の割合では日本製が66％、海外製が34％と逆転している。この中で利用頻度の高いデータベースとしては「JICST科学技術文献ファイル」、「日本特許情報ファイル」、「日経」が上位を占めており、一方、システムとして人気があるのは、上位から、JOIS、DIALOG、PATOLIS、日経であり、次いで STN、ORBIT、BRS などが続き、日本のサービス機関が健闘している。

わが国のデータベース・サービス機関としては、JICSTが1976年から科学技術文献抄録データベースや MEDLARS を JOIS というシステムの上で商用サービスを行っている。その後、日本特許情報機構（JAPIO）が1978年から特許情報のオンライン・サービスを PATOLIS というシステムで行っており、これは英訳されて ORBIT の上でも公開されている。ビジネス関係は、データベース・サービスの最も盛んな分野であり、日本経済新聞社をはじめ証券関係など多くのオンライン・サービス会社がある。

2 わが国のデータベース・サービスの傾向

わが国データベース・サービスの特質として、海外製のデータベースの依存度の高さを指摘することができる。米国では、データベースの黎明期の1960年代に政府の援助を得て大規模な投資が開始されたのに比べて、遅れて出発したわが国では、既に米国では商用化されているデータベースの利用から始まった。データベースの構築

には一般に多大な初期投資及び継続的な作業経費と組織を必要とするが、わが国ではこのような先行投資が見られず、その結果、海外への依存度が高いまま経過してきたと言える。

　この傾向は、例えば、人文・社会科学分野でのデータベース形成活動が極めて弱体であることに顕著である。一方、先端技術分野での研究開発の進展に伴い、科学技術分野・特許などではそれなりにデータベース形成が進められてきたが、近年の特徴は、経済、証券分野における市場の拡大であろう。これは急激なビジネス国際化に伴う必然的な結果とも言えよう。また、新聞記事をそのままデータベース化した全文データベース・サービスも、パソコン通信の展開にあわせて拡大してきている。このような事情が、ビジネス分野のデータベースの増大、ファクト・データベースや全文データベースの増加として反映していると推察される。

　データベース形成に対し、大規模かつ継続的な投資があまり行われてこなかったことにもよって、現在、わが国のデータベースのオンライン・サービスは少数のデータベースを保有する多くの中小サービス会社の並存という形になっている。これを利用者側から見れば、網羅的にデータベースを備えた大きなサービス機関が無く、個々の分野のデータベース毎にサービス・システムを選んで利用せざるを得ないという状況になっている。

　このようなデータベース・サービスを支える基盤となるのは、パーソナル・コンピュータの普及と電気通信の使い易さであろう。パーソナル・コンピュータは急激に普及しているが、わが国ではそれ以上に日本語ワードプロセッサの普及の方が優勢である。パーソナル・コンピュータについては、米国の業界標準と異なるアーキテクチャの機種が普及していることと、日本語処理の必要性のために米国製応用ソフトウェアがそのままでは流通が難しいことを指摘しておきたい。

　一方、電気通信については、1985年の法改正により、国内においては通信事業の独占が崩れ複数業者間の競争が始まったが、NTTの民営化が米国における自由化ほど徹底したものではなかったため、通信料金体系は依然として米国よりも高い水準にある。これはオンライン・データベースを始め、それ以外の付加価値通信サービスの拡大を抑える結果となっていると言えよう。また、ISDNについては、サービスが始まったものの契約回線の伸びは鈍くその拡大についてはまだ予測できる段階ではない。国際通信についても自由化が進められており、国際VANサービスが本格化されれば、国際間のデータベース利用の隆盛に寄与するものと期待される。

以上のような状況とも相俟って、わが国ではまだオンライン・データベースのゲートウェイ・サービスは本格的に始まっておらず、今後に期待される課題の一つになっている。しかしながら、パーソナル・コンピュータをサービス対象としたパソコン通信は急激に拡大している。各種ネットワークの会員の総数が1987年には10万人を超えた段階である。

CD-ROM については、日本でも辞書類のデータベースを中心に試作や商品化が進んでいる。米国では、将来オンライン・データベースのかなりの部分が CD-ROM へ向かうという予測（1991年にデータベース市場の7.4%を占める）がある。日本では米国製のデータベースの利用が多いので、CD-ROM の利用についても米国と同じ流れを追従することになると思われるが、パーソナル・コンピュータのアーキテクチャが米国のものと異なるので、まだ動向はつかめない段階である。

3　わが国の大学におけるデータベースの利用

　大学では、社会全般におけるデータベースの利用態様とはかなり異なった利用がされている。大学での状況を、1986年に学術情報センターが行ったデータベースの利用動向調査[2]に基づいて紹介しよう。

　大学の研究者のうち平均約20%が何らかの形でデータベースを利用している。利用者の割合は医学が一番多く約30%で、それに続き工学、理学での利用が多い。データベースの種類としては、書誌・抄録に関するデータベースの利用が多く（利用者の約50%が使用）、数値データベースやファクト・データベースの利用は思ったほど多くない。利用の多いデータベースは、順に CAS、MEDLINE、INSPEC となる。利用の多いシステムは、DIALOG、JOIS の他、大学の計算センターでのデータベースを利用している場合が多い。

　本人が自ら検索する割合は44%であり、他の38%が図書館での代行検索を利用している。端末については、49%が図書館所有のものを利用し、38%が研究室から利用している。（パソコンの利用は約半数である。）

　利用者の意識としては、現在利用していない人が挙げる「利用しない理由」には、「端末がないこと」、「使用法が不明」、「必要なし」、「予算不足」などがあり、現在利用している人にとって不満な点としては、経費不足を挙げる人が圧倒的に多く、ついでデータベースの内容についての不満が聞かれる。

　以上のことから大学の研究者が、自らの研究費を使ってデータベースを利用する場合のボトルネックは利用料金にあることは明らか

であり、一方、潜在的利用者やコンピュータになじみの薄い研究者に対する普及啓蒙活動が不足しているという点を指摘することができよう。データベースの利用については、依然として文献調査のためのツールとしての利用が主体であることを示唆している。

学術情報データベースに関わる活動

第2節で紹介したデータベースの概要は、全般にわたるものであり、大学等におけるデータベース形成活動は含まれていない。ここでは、大学の研究者および大学図書館、学協会等に関わるデータベース関係の動きについてまとめる。

1　学術情報データベースの形成

以前から研究者サイドにより、学術や教育に必要となるわが国独自のデータベースの形成の促進と充実の必要性が指摘されている。文部省でもこれを積極的に支援してきており、予算増額への努力を払ってきている。

データベース形成についての文部省の施策は2つの層に分けて実施されている。まず第一段階として、データベース形成を試みようとする研究者グループに対し、科学研究費補助金（科研費）による補助を行っている。1988年度には、表1に示すように45件のグループに総計2億6千万円の援助が行われる。申請の採択率は約70％である。

科研費によるデータベース形成は、
(i)　データベースの必要性は高いが欠落している分野
(ii)　わが国で発展を遂げた分野
(iii)　わが国が研究や情報の世界的なセンターになっている分野
などを主に対象として取り上げている。この中には漢籍の全文データベース、高分子物性のデータベース、音声波形のデータベースなどが含まれている。このように科研費によるデータベース形成は、研究者の研究活動と密接に結びついており、それはファクト・データベースの占める割合から推察される。これらのデータベースは、一定期間の作業で完成するものであるが、やはり継続的な作業を必要とするものも多い。さらに言えば、広い分野にわたる文献抄録データベースの構築のように、継続的かつ組織的な活動が必要になるデータベース形成は、科研費補助だけでは行いにくいきらいがある。

データベース形成における網羅性、継続性の必要性は、文部省でも十分認識されていて、第二段階の施策として、経常的な予算を大学、研究所等に措置している。このようなデータベースは現在20件

に達して、年間予算総額は3億2千万円程である。(表2) この経費は、研究機関における継続的なデータベース形成事業にあてられ、安定的な活動ができるようにしているわけである。その成果はオンライン・サービスなどで広く研究者に公開されることが前提になっている。大学や研究所では、それぞれの分野に応じて専門的・特殊な学術情報データベースの形成を行っている。例えば国立遺伝学研究所はDNAデータベースを作成しており、米国のGenBank、ヨーロッパのEMBLとの国際協力のもとにわが国のDNAデータベース形成の拠点として位置づけられている。

学術情報センターにおけるデータベース形成もこのような施策の一環として行われている。学術情報センターには、特定の大学や研究所などでは作成することが難しい一般的、普遍的な大型データベースの形成が期待されており、1988年現在、表3のようなデータベースを作成している。

表1 科研費によるデータベース作成件数 (1988年)

分 野	総数	英文	ファクト
人文系	12	4	4
理工系	11	5	10
医学系	8	5	2
学際的	14	7	6
計	45	21	22

表2 事業によるデータベース作成件数 (1988年)

分 野	総数	英文	ファクト
人文系	6	1	2
理工系	9	8	7
医学系	2	1	
学際的	3	3	
計	20	13	9

表3 学術情報センター作成のデータベース (1988年)

名 称	件 数
目録所在情報データベース (洋雑誌)	9万誌/62万所蔵
目録所在情報データベース (和雑誌)	4万誌/100万所蔵
学位論文索引データベース	21,350件 (1984年から)
データベースディレクトリ	約500件
科研成果概要データベース	13,340件
学会発表データベース	約2,000件
化学全文データベース	
医学症例データベース	

2 データベース形成と流通のための環境

　全国の国公私立大学において、データベースの利用等を促進し学術研究を支援するための総合的な情報政策を文部省では「学術情報システム」と呼んでいる。このシステムに参画するものは、各大学（約500、内国立95大学）および附属図書館、共同利用研究所、大学の計算センターなどで、1986年に発足した学術情報センターが全体システムの計画・調整にあたる。

　学術情報システムの中で、図書館のシステム化とネットワーク化も行われている。また、主要7大学には強力なスーパーコンピュータを持つ共同利用の大型計算機センターが設置されている他、46国立大学に計算センターが設置されている。学術情報センターは、これらの機関を相互接続する全国的な学術情報ネットワークの建設を進めている。これは高速ディジタル回線を利用したパケット通信による自営のネットワークであり、大学等の間で情報資源の共有を図ることを主目的としている。

　このネットワーク上には、
- (i) 計算センター間のリモート・ログインサービスの利用
- (ii) オンライン・データベースの利用
- (iii) 図書館ネットワーク
- (iv) 電子メール

などの応用が載っており、今後大学病院の医療情報ネットワークなどもこの学術情報ネットワークの上に形成される予定である。

　この学術情報システムは、大学や研究所がデータベース作成活動やサービスを行うための枠組みとなる。データベース作成に携わる研究者は、作業のために計算センターや学術情報センターを使用する。完成したデータベースは、研究者の属する大学の計算センター、大型計算機センター、あるいは学術情報センターなどで運用・サービスされる。サービスするセンターは、個々のデータベース毎に運用のし易さや性格によって最適の場所が選ばれる。図1に7つの大型計算機センターでサービスされている主要なデータベースを示す。これらの一部は海外から磁気テープで購入したデータベースであり、他はわが国の大学で開発されたものである。

　さらに広域網の建設と並行して、現在いくつかの大学ではキャンパス情報ネットワークの敷設が進んでいる。これはいわゆる LAN (Local Area Network)と呼ばれるもので、大学内のホストコンピュータ、パーソナル・コンピュータあるいはワークステーションを相互に接続しようとするものである。この結果、研究室の端末から全国の学術情報データベースを、より効果的かつ高度に利用するこ

東北大学大型計算機センター

METADEX	金属関係の文献データ (米国、英国)
C-13NMR	炭素核磁気共鳴に関するデータ
SEDATA	溶媒抽出平衡に関するデータ
QCLDB	量子化学文献データ

その他MEALS (同)日本食品標準成分表に基づくデータ)等3種類

北海道大学大型計算機センター

FRM	誘導体に関する文献
HGEN	遺伝情報のデータ
NRDF	核反応の実験データ
SESS	ソ連経済統計データ

その他ALTS(東心眼測系のデータ)等9種類

京都大学大型計算機センター

CHINA(I)	中国現代・科学者合情報
ERIC	教育学関連文献情報 (米国)
IDEAS	DNA・蛋白質の配列データ等
INSPEC(A)	物理学関連文献情報 (英国)

その他SAO(東心眼測系のデータ)等34種類

大阪大学大型計算機センター

PROTEIN-DB	蛋白質のデータ (米国)
GEODAS	地球学のデータ
JSR	科学技術の2次情報
BIOSIS	生物学の文献 (米国)

その他CHEM(化学の文献)等8種類

九州大学大型計算機センター

日本語単語辞書	自立語・付属語
トーマス・マン ファイル	全文
GENEDB	核酸のデータ
RAMBIOS	分子生物科学文献

その他KONTYU(昆虫学の文献)等7種類

東京大学大型計算機センター

CASearch	化学文献 (米国)
MOL	化学物質辞書
XDC	結晶構造の文献・数値 (英国)
IEE	計算機・制御工学のデータベース (洋雑誌)第12種類

その他PSDB (蛋白質の一次構造)第18種類

名古屋大学大型計算機センター

SVDBANK	振動に関する文献
PLATE	板の理論に関する文献
FEMBANK	有限要素法の文献
SECND	材料力学・構造力学の文献

その他ETL#(文字認識のデータ)等18種類

学術情報センター

Life Science Collection	生命科学の文献 (米国)
MathSci	数学の文献 (米国)
COMPENDEX	工学の文献 (米国)
El Engineering Meetings	工学の会議論文献 (米国)
Harvard Business Review	雑誌の全文
ISTP & B	科学技術の会議論文献 (米国)
EMBASE	医学・薬学の文献 (オランダ)
SciSearch	自然科学の文献と引用文献 (米国)
Social SciSearch	社会科学の文献と引用文献 (米国)
A&H Search	人文科学の文献と引用文献 (米国)
JPMARC	日本の本の書誌
LCMARC-Books	米国の本の書誌
LCMARC-Serials	米国の雑誌の書誌
目録所在情報データベース (和雑誌)	大学図書館所蔵雑誌の書誌・所在
目録所在情報データベース (洋雑誌)	〃
科学研究費研究成果概要データベース	科学研究費研究成果報告書の概要
学術論文索引データベース第1系	国内博士論文の索引
学会発表データベース第1系	電気・情報・制御関連学会での研究発表概要 (日本)
データベース・ディレクトリ	大学等で作成・運用しているデータベースの案内情報

図1. 大学環境で運用されているデータベース

とができる。

　大学で作られたデータベースは基本的に学術的なものであるから、研究活動に資するために全研究者に公開されることを前提としている。但し、一部医療情報など個人のプライバシーに関わるような情報を含むデータベースについては、限定的な利用が行われている。

3　大学等におけるデータベース作成の動向

　1987年の学術情報センターの調査[3]によれば、750件以上のデータベース作成が大学等で行われている。資金の面からは、公的な補助として、74％が大学等の予算、33％ほどが科研費に依っている他、各種の研究資金が投入されている。（重複回答を許している）分野では、理、工、農、医が63％を占めている。データベースの形態としては、数値データベースが多く、約52％を占める。使用言語としては、67％が英語あるいは英語併用となっている。データベースの公開については、約51％が公開されているが、その対象は学内や研究者グループに限っているものが多い。使用しているコンピュータについては、パーソナルコンピュータが43％、大型コンピュータが42％となっている。

4　学術情報システムにおけるデータベース関連の活動の特徴

　以上に述べた学術情報システム下の大学における活動の特徴をまとめると次のようになる。
　(1)　大学における最先端の研究活動と直結している。計算センター、図書館のコンピュータなどの情報施設が、研究者のデータベース形成活動を効果的に支援するように配慮されている。
　(2)　総合的な情報サービスを目指している。個別的にデータベース・サービスのためのシステムを組むのではなく、統合的な情報システムとして、データベース、図書館情報、電子メールなどの各種の情報サービスを統合する学術情報ネットワークを形成しようとしている。
　(3)　情報資源の共有を目指している。単に科学技術分野にとどまらず、人文社会科学を含むすべての学問分野をカバーし、研究者の共有の資産として情報を利用することを目的としている。従って、海外から購入するデータベースも、研究者間の共有ユーティリティとしてできるだけ低廉なコストでサービスできるように意図されている。

　学術情報システムは、学術情報や資料の共有と円滑な流通を通じて、多様な学問分野における研究活動を援助しようとするものであ

り、ネットワーキングはこの目的を達成するための重要なメカニズムとして位置づけられている。

5 学術情報センターにおける事業動向

学術情報センターは、わが国における学術情報形成・流通の中心的役割を果たす機関として1986年に発足した。学術情報センターで行っているデータベース関連の活動動向を列挙すると次のようにまとめられる。

データベース・ディレクトリ等のデータベース形成

学術情報センターでは、多くの学問分野で共通して利用する価値のあるデータベースや大型のデータベースについて特に集中的な形成努力を払っている。そのひとつの例が、データベース・ディレクトリである。これは、大学等で作成あるいは提供されているデータベースに関するプロファイル情報を与えるもので、学術情報システム下のさまざまな活動状況を把握するのに役立つ。

また、科研費研究成果データベースは、文部省の補助する研究プロジェクトの成果、生み出された研究論文、研究者グループ等についての最新の情報を与えるものである。科学研究費補助金はわが国の研究者に対する公的な研究助成の最大の柱であり、すべての研究分野での最新の活動を網羅する。しかも、継続中のプロジェクトの途中経過の報告も含まれ、また英文でも報告することが義務づけられている。

学位論文索引データベースは、わが国の大学で授与される学位の索引をデータベース化したものである。

以上のように、学術情報センターの形成・サービスするデータベースは、わが国の大学における研究活動を把握するのに役立つものである。

学術雑誌総合目録等の書誌所蔵データベース

学術情報システムの特徴は、大学図書館の活動と結びついた形で、総合的なデータベース形成および提供サービスを行おうとしていることである。図書館ネットワークによって形成される総合目録データベースは、オンラインで一般研究者にサービスされている。これは、研究に必須の原報を入手するための基本的な情報源であり、各種文献データベースと連携して用いることにより、強力なツールとして機能している。

学協会との協力

　学術情報センターの活動に見られるもう一つの特徴は、学協会と連携したデータベース形成である。わが国では、米国のように巨大で幅広い分野をカバーする学協会が成長しておらず、狭い分野で中小の学会が数多く並存するという状況になっている。学術情報センターでは、分野別に学協会と協力し、分野での需要に応じた形でデータベースの形成協力を開始している。例えば、化学分野では、英文学術雑誌の電算写植データベースを流用することにより、全文のデータベース化を図っている。情報、電気・電子、制御工学分野では、年次大会やシンポジウムの予稿の文献抄録データベースを作成することにより、一番ホットな情報の提供を行っている。また医学分野では、ファクト・データベースとして症例データベースの形成を開始しようとしている。

　文部省では、学術研究のため、従来からさまざまな形で学協会活動を支援しているのであるが、学術情報センターにおける上述のデータベース形成活動は、広い意味での学協会支援としてとらえることができる。

データベース・サービスの国際接続

　学術情報センターは、1989年1月より米国との間の国際回線を開設し、情報ネットワークの相互接続を行う。米国側の窓口はNSFであり、ここにアクセスポイントを設けることにより、電子メール・ネットワークの接続とわが国の学術情報データベースの米国への提供を行おうとしている。サービスの詳細についてはまだ未定であるが、情報システム相互接続に向けての突破口は開かれたわけであり、今後はこのリンクを効果的に活用していくことが望まれる。

　学術情報センターを窓口とした国際ネットワークの形成は、今後欧州やアジアに対して拡大していく計画である。

国際的な観点からみたわが国の情報提供サービスの課題

　近年、日本についての情報に対する関心が高まり、1987年には英国において日本情報に関する国際会議も開催されるに至った[1]。この会議では、主に科学技術情報を中心に日本における研究開発動向を知るための問題について幅広く議論されたが、この会議の際に行われたアンケート調査結果等を見ると、背景にある最大の問題が日本語であるという点には、参加者の中に異論はなかったと思われた。先の会議は政治的な色彩はなかったため、感情的に流れず、現実的な分析や提言が出されて成果があったが、筆者にとっても改めて、

言語が最大の障壁として根源的な問題であることが再認識された。

　図書館における目録作業が和書と洋書の二本立てで行われていることで分かるように、わが国では外国語がいろいろな面で情報活動に影響を与えている。研究活動においても外国語の習得は必須であり、外国、特に米国からの情報入手については、研究者個々人がなんらかの方法を身につけていると言えよう。学術研究とは本来言語を超えた普遍性を持つものであり、データベース形成に携わる研究者も、自らのデータベースが国際性を具備することの重要性を十分に認識していると言える。例えば、大学等で形成されるデータベースのうち、バイリンガルな形で作られているものの比率が高いこともそれを示していると言えよう。

　現在の学術情報システムでは、特に外国のための配慮、例えば翻訳などを行ってデータベースを提供するという一般的な方向性はまだない。それよりも、日本語のままでよいからなるべく幅広くわが国のデータベースを国外からアクセスできるような環境にもって行くことが急務であると認識されている。1989年に予定してる学術情報センターの国際接続もこの考え方に沿ったものである。

　言語は文化的な相互理解のレベルの問題にとどまらず、現実的には、データベースの記述の際の文字コード、それを表示するための端末機器にまで影響がおよんでいるので、この問題の解決は容易でなく、その解消には長い期間を要すると思われる。

　第二の問題は、わが国の情報に対するアクセスの仕方についての適切な情報が不足している点である。これは、例えば米国のDIALOGのように包括的に情報をサービスしているような機関がわが国にはなく、分野別に各種の中小システムや企業が並存している状況にあることにも起因し、予備知識のない外国の初心者が容易に情報アクセスできる体制が確立されていない。その結果、情報に対してわが国がオープンでないような印象を与えていることは、たいへん残念である。しかし「オープンでない」というのはまったくの誤解である。少なくとも学術情報に関しては、学術情報センターを中心にアクセスのためのパスを明確にしようとする努力がなされていることに注目されたい。例えば、情報ネットワークの形成・運用という環境作り・またデータベース・ディレクトリ、科研費成果データベースあるいは書誌所蔵データベースなどの作成はすべて、わが国の持つ情報資源にアクセスするための包括的な手段を提供するプロセスとして位置づけられる。

　但し、ここでさらに問題となるのは、国内においては学術情報システムは、第一義的に学術コミュニティーをサービス対象としてお

り、商業ベースでのサービスを行っていないという点である。その結果、国際的なサービスを展開するに当たっては、利用資格や経費負担の面で、制度の違いによる制約を加えざるを得ないことが発生する可能性もあろう。この場合、学術コミュニティーの国際的な相互協力関係を維持発展して行くために現実的な解決策がとられることが期待される。

　第三の問題は、個々の学術情報データベースの形成が特定専門領域のものになりがちで、米国にみられるような大規模・網羅的なデータベース形成が行われにくいという点である。これは、学術情報システムにおけるデータベース形成の施策の在り方から、形成活動が研究者のごく近くで行われている場合が多いということにも起因する。一方これは、対応する国外の研究者グループにとっては、研究活動に直結したデータベースとして魅力あるものが形成され易いということを意味するとも言える。このようなデータベースは、数値やファクト・データベースであることが多く、言語を超えた普遍的な価値を持つことが多いことに留意したい。この問題は、ネットワークの国際接続により研究者間の直接的なコミュニケーション経路が確立すれば、徐々に解消していくと考えられる。

　大規模データベースの形成においては、すでに先行している米国の活動と相補的な協力関係を確立することが重要であり、決して競合的な形成活動にならないように配慮する必要がある。例えば、わが国から発生する情報のデータベース化については、わが国が担当し、それを他国のデータベースと統合するといった役割分担を行うことが一つの方法である。データベース・プロジェクトによっては、すでにこのような協力活動が開始されている。

　最後の問題は、料金の設定であり、特に国際的な通信料金が割高であることが情報アクセスの障害となる可能性がある。わが国の学術情報システムでは、学術情報の提供サービスについては非営利的に行うことの方針が確立しており、極小の経費しか利用者に負担させていない。従って、全体のコストを下げるには、通信における規制の排除を待ち、自由競争により料金低減を期待するしか手がないようである。1989年に予定されている国際リンクの開設もこのような思想に沿ったものである。

おわりに

　わが国のデータベース関連の活動において、「学術情報システム」は原資料の収集・提供、学術情報データベースの形成から流通に至るすべてのプロセスを包含する総合的な計画として極めてユニーク

なものである。大学図書館はこの中の情報収集・提供機関として、また書誌所蔵データベースの形成の担い手として、重要な位置づけにある。また、学術情報システムは図書館が新しい情報サービスを展開して行くための新たなネットワーク環境でもある。このような計画に沿って、まず国内での情報提供のメカニズムを整備して行くことが急務である。しかもこれを常に国際的な視野から、より効果的な方向に向かうようチェックしつつ、並行して国際協力の具体的な方策を捜して行くことによって、学術情報システムの有効性が発揮されて行くことを期待している。

参考文献
(1) データベース振興センター『1988年データベース白書』1988。
(2) 学術情報センター『データベース利用動向調査報告書』7月（1987）。
(3) 学術情報センター『学術情報データベース基本調査報告書』7月（1987）。

日本における総合目録データベース形成の現状と問題点

倉 橋 英 逸

学術情報センターの目録システム

1 学術情報センターの機能

1980年代に入り、データ通信のための DDX (Digital Data Exchange) が開通すると、大学の計算機センター間の異機種電算機接続が可能となり、遠く離れた他の大学の計算機とのデータ通信ができるようになった。

このような時代を背景に、日本における今後の学術情報システムの在り方が検討され、全国の国・公・私立大学の図書館や計算機センター等を通信網で結ぶ学術情報システムが計画された。

この学術情報システムは、資源共有の理念の下に、(1)一次情報の収集・提供機能の充実、(2)情報検索システムの確立、(3)データベースの形成、という三つの事業を遂行することとなった。

これらの事業を円滑に行い、それらの諸活動を効果的に実施するために、全国的な学術情報システムの中で、連絡・調整、計画、データベース・サービス、研究・開発、及び教育・訓練の五つの機能を果たす学術情報センターが、学術情報システムの中枢機関として、1986年に設置された。

学術情報センターの五つの機能のうち、データベース・サービスについては、(1)情報検索サービス、(2)目録支援サービスがある。前者については、NACSIS-IR という名称で国内外の専門的データベースにより、大学等の研究者に対して情報検索サービスを行っている。後者については、大学図書館に対する目録支援サービスとともに、全国的な総合目録の作成を目的としてサービスを開始した。

2 学術情報センター目録システムの目的

大学図書館は、大学における研究・教育に必要な学術情報を収集・蓄積し、それを研究者に提供することがその任務であるが、近年学術情報の生産が飛躍的に増大し、研究者が必要とする全ての学術情報を収集することが困難になった。

学術情報センターの目録システムは、全国の大学等に収集される図書や雑誌の目録支援サービスとともに大学図書館の共同分担目録により、全国的な総合目録データベースを形成し、この総合目録データベースを仲介して全国の大学図書館の一次情報の相互利用を促

進しようとするものである。

　学術情報センターは、この任務を効果的に達成するために、LC MARC や Japan MARC 等各国の MARC をできるだけ多く導入し、これらの MARC の目録レコードを利用することにより、参加館のオリジナル目録の量を少なくし、参加館の目録業務を軽減しようとしている。また、各国の MARC を利用できないオリジナル目録についても、一旦最初の大学図書館が入力すれば、その他の大学図書館もこれを利用することにより、各大学図書館の目録作業の大幅な省力化を実現しようとするものである。

　さらに、各大学図書館は学術情報センターの総合目録データベース形成に協力するだけではなく、このようにして作成された当該大学の目録レコードについては、複製して個々の大学図書館システムに取り込み、それを OPAC(On-line Public Access Catalog)として学内の研究者や学生に利用させることができる。このように、学術情報センターの目録システムは、資源共有のための総合目録データベースの形成と個々の大学図書館の目録作業の負担軽減という二つの目的を同時に実現しようとするものである。

3　総合目録データベース形成の基盤

　従来、日本の総合目録としては、学術情報センターが編集してきた『学術雑誌総合目録』と国立国会図書館が編集してきた『新収洋書総合目録』が代表的なものである。

　『学術雑誌総合目録』は、その編集の作業の大きいことから、従来「和文編」、「人文科学欧文編」、「自然科学欧文編」に分けて編集してきたが、現在、機械編集により後者二者を一本化して「欧文編」として1988年には編集を完了する予定である。「和文編」については既にデータベース化されているので、雑誌については総合目録データベースが完了したことになる。

　しかし、この『学術雑誌総合目録』のデータベースは一定期間毎に更新しなければならず、その改訂をするためには、その都度、雑誌名とその所蔵の変更について大規模な全国的な調査を行わなければならない。この調査を実施することは非常に大きな仕事であるので、今後は、この作業を学術情報センターとの接続を完了した大学図書館から徐々に、オンラインによる共同分担目録に切り換えることになっている。

　一方、『新収洋書総合目録』も全国の主要図書館の収集する洋書の目録カードを集めて、1954年以降その編集・刊行を続けて日本の主要図書館間における洋書の相互貸借の道具として、非常に重要な

役割を果してきた。

　しかし、この編集作業の負担が大きいことから、国立国会図書館は1987年版をもってこの『新収洋書総合目録』の編集を打ち切ることを決定しており、今後は学術情報センターの総合目録データベースが、この役割を引き継ぐことになる。

　このように学術情報センターの総合目録データベース形成事業は、日本の大学図書館間の相互貸借のために非常に重要な役割を果たすことが期待されており、これをネットワーク時代にふさわしいオンラインによる共同分担目録によって実現しようとするものである。

　この事業が円滑に行われるためには、まず、学術情報センターの目録システムが、それを使用する大学図書館員にとって使い易いものでなければならないし、また、大学図書館側にとっても、その共同分担目録によって得られる当該大学分の目録レコードを有効に利用できる図書館システムを持つ必要がある。

　全国的な総合目録データベースを形成する中で、学術情報センターの目録システムの利用性と効率的な大学図書館システム開発は非常に重要であり、両者は言わば車の両輪の関係にあり、そのどちらが欠けても、総合目録データベースの健全な発展は望めないであろう。

学術情報センター目録システムの改善
1　目録システムの特徴

　学術情報センターの目録システムは1984年12月にサービスを開始したものであり、OCLC、RLG、WLN、Utlas と比べると最も新しく出発したのであり、先発機関よりも新しい技術や新しいシステムを開発しようと目指したことは当然である。そこで学術情報センターは、先発機関の経験を参考にし、書誌的な厳密性を確保するために書誌階層の概念と典拠コントロールの概念を導入した。

　書誌階層とは、目録の対象となる図書にシリーズ名がある場合、それを上位書誌とし、書名を下位書誌とし、各々独立した目録レコードを作成し、それらを相互にリンクする考え方である。したがって、一冊の図書は、そこに記載されているシリーズ名の階層数に合わせて、理論的には無限に階層化されることになる。

　従来、日本の大学図書館は、一著作物の目録作成のために複数の目録レコードを作成したことがなかったので、新しい経験をすることになった。

　また、典拠コントロールについては、著者名の統一と同一著者の著作物の一括検索を可能にするため、著者典拠レコードの作成及び

それと目録レコードとのリンク作業が全参加館に義務付けられた。
　従来、日本の大学図書館では、殆んどの図書館が典拠コントロール作業の経験がなく、これも新しい経験となった。

2　目録システム利用の実際

　以上のように学術情報センターの目録システムは、先発機関の経験を踏まえ、書誌的な厳密性に重点を置いた目録システムを開発し、それによってサービスを開始したのであるが、参加館からは著作物一件あたり目録作業の時間が長すぎるという意見がでてきた。
　一方、この目録システムにより、実際に目録業務を行っている大学図書館の中には、作業時間を短縮するために、いろいろと便法を考え、書誌階層については階層を少なくするように工夫し、典拠コントロールについても詳しく調査された「著者名典拠レコード」ではなく、単なる「著者名レコード」を入力する図書館が現れた。
　しかし、何にも増して大きな問題は、学術情報センターの目録システムのサービスを開始して参加館も徐々に増加しているにもかかわらず、目録レコードの入力件数の伸びが低かったことである。この原因としては、(1)まだ、目録システムのサービスが開始されたばかりで、参加館の目録担当者がこの目録システムに慣れていなかった。(2)初期の段階では、目録レコードの入力件数が少ないので、共同分担目録の効果を十分に挙げることができなかった、ということが考えられるが、基本的にはこの目録システムによる目録担当者の作業負担が大きかったことによるものと思われる。
　従来、日本の大学図書館は、書誌の階層化の経験は全くなく、典拠コントロールについても殆んど経験がなかったので、書誌の階層化と典拠コントロールは、目録担当者の作業負担を増大させる結果となった。

3　目録システムの改善

　このような事態を改善するために、参加館の代表が学術情報センターと協議し、参加館の目録作業の機能を向上させるために、1987年から(1)書誌階層については2階層以下にし、(2)典拠コントロールについては参加館の選択性とすることになった。
　書誌の階層については、世界で初めての試みであり、その成り行きが注目されたが、現実の参加館の作業量の負担の大きさから2階層以下に止めざるを得なかった。
　また、典拠コントロールについても、実際にその作業が可能な大学図書館とそうでない大学図書館に分け、より現実的に対応するこ

ととなった。

　この改善により、一著作物あたりの目録作業時間が大幅に短縮され、その他の条件の向上とも相俟って、学術情報センターへの目録レコードの入力件数も大幅に上昇した。

　現在、学術情報センターの参加館は60館を超え、その目録システムも安定してきており、名実共に書誌ユーティリティとしての体裁を整えてきた。

　学術情報センターは、そのサービスの開始にあたって、目録システムの一部変更という経験をしたが、今後も参加館にとって利用し易い目録システムにするために、書誌的な厳密性の保持と参加館の作業負担との均衡を保ちながら、改善の努力が続けられると思われる。

大学図書館システム
1　大学図書館電算化の問題

　学術情報センター目録システムにより、全国的な総合目録データベースを形成するためには、その共同分担目録により作成される当該大学分の目録レコードを有効に利用できる効率的な大学図書館システムの開発が重要である。

　日本の大学図書館の機械化は1970年代に始まったが、この時代の電算機はアルファベットの大文字とカタカナのみしか使用できなかったので、図書館の業務の中で最も基本的な目録業務の電算化は不可能であり、図書貸出、図書受入、雑誌管理の業務が電算化の対象とされた。

　1980年代になると、データ通信が可能となり、いわゆるネットワークの時代となって、書誌ユーティリティとしての学術情報センターが設置され、Utlas や OCLC も日本に進出した。

　1970年代と1980年代の大学図書館の機械化とを比較すると、最も大きな違いは、目録の電算化が可能になったことと、その作業を他の図書館と共同して行い、いわゆるネットワーク化することが可能になったことである。

　したがって、新しい時代の大学図書館の電算化は目録業務を中心に置き、学術情報センター目録システムへの接続とOPACの開発が優先すべきであるが、1970年代に培われた図書館の電算化の考え方が大学図書館に根強く定着しており、図書貸出、図書受入、雑誌管理等の業務が優先して、目録業務の電算化が最後になるという傾向が強い。この考え方を新しいネットワーク時代にふさわしい考え方に変えることが目下の急務となっている。

また、日本の大学図書館の電算化の特徴は、その大学図書館独自のシステムを開発する要求が強いことである。
　この理由は、これまで大学図書館はその歴史や規模により、各々独自の業務方式を採用してきたので、電算化する際にもその業務方式をそのまま電算機にあてはめようとするからである。
　したがって、電算化に際しては先発館の開発した大学図書館システムの大幅な改造や新規開発の要求をしてきたが、最近では電算機販売会社もそのような要求に応じなくなっており、小幅な手直しに応ずるのみとなった。
　本来、電算機システムは、社会や技術の発達により、変わっていくものであると思われるが、現在のように個々の図書館が独自の改良要求を出していては、小幅な手直しにより多種多様な大学図書館システムがつくられることになり、基本的な改良はなされなくなる恐れがある。
　今後、大学図書館職員のシステム開発の負担を軽減し、開発された大学図書館システムの改良が容易に行われる環境を作るためには、少なくとも電算機メーカー毎のユーザー会のようなものを結成し、共通の改良要求を行い、共通のシステム、つまりパッケージ・システムを育てることが必要であろう。

2　カード目録から OPAC へ

　カード目録は、最新性と通覧性に優れ、カード目録出現以前の冊子目録の欠点を克服した画期的な発明であったと思われる。
　しかし、出版物が飛躍的に増加した現代になると、大規模図書館ではカード目録が急成長し、通覧性が悪くなり、目録カードの排列の作業負担が増大し、その排列の遅れにより最新性も保てなくなった。
　このカード目録の欠点を克服しようとして最初に導入されたのがCOM (Computer Output Microfilm) 目録であった。COM 目録は補遺版の作成と一定期間毎の更新の問題があったが、電算機の発達により図書館に OPAC が導入され、COM 目録の欠点も克服された。OPAC は、カード目録や COM 目録と比べると、排列や更新に手間がかからないだけでなく、利用者にとっても、これまでのカード目録と異なって、多角的な検索が可能となり、まさに夢の目録が実現したと言うことができる。
　しかし、目録業務を電算化した大学図書館の中には、入力された目録レコードから目録カードを出力している例が多い。勿論この中には OPAC を導入している大学図書館も多いが、従来、大学図書館

は目録カードを利用者目録だけでなく、他の用途にも使ってきたので、OPAC を導入しても目録カードと縁が切れず、カード目録を出力して利用している例が多い。

また、極端な例では、OPAC を導入せず、従来どおり利用者目録のためにカード目録を出力して、電算機を単に印刷機の代わりに利用している例もある。

この結果、カード目録出力のために電算機資源の負担を増大させ、出力作業のための労力の負担を避けることができず、OPAC のもつ長所を完全に生かすことができない。

OPAC の最大の長所は、目録カードの排列の負担をなくすことにあるので、カード目録にいつまでもしがみついていては大学図書館の電算化の効果を十分に発揮できないので、カード目録を作成しない工夫が必要である。

3　大学図書館の電算化の在り方

学術情報センターを中心とする大学図書館ネットワークの基本的な考え方は、目録業務のように電算機資源と入力の負担の大きい業務は共同分担目録とし、その他の OPAC、図書貸出、図書受入、雑誌管理の業務は個々の大学図書館システムにより電算化し、集中システム（目録システム）と分散システム（大学図書館システム）の統合により、効率的な大学図書館の電算化を実現しようとするものである。

学術情報センター目録システムによる総合目録データベース形成事業が成功するためには、それに最も適した大学図書館の電算化を達成しなければならないが、現在の大学図書館の電算化は、これまでに述べたように、(1)図書貸出、図書受入、雑誌管理業務の優先開発、(2)独自システムへの願望、(3)カード目録への愛着という特徴が見られる。

これらに共通していることは、過去の電算化の考え方であることである。学術情報センターの目録システムを中心とするネットワークを前提とする大学図書館の電算化は日本においてはまだ始まったばかりであり、大学図書館はこの新しい考え方になじめず、1970年代の図書館の電算化の考え方にまだ強く影響されていると考えられる。

現在の大学図書館は過去の蓄積によって存在するのであるが、電算機と通信技術の利用という図書館史上画期的な変革の時代にあっては、過去をそのまま引き継ぐのではなく、それを現在の新しい考え方に合せて引き継がなければならないであろう。

現在の大学図書館の電算化に最も強く求められるのは、このような大学図書館の電算化の考え方の改革であると思われる。

総合目録データベース形成の諸問題
1　収録範囲

　総合目録は、その参加館が多ければ多いほど、価値を増すのであるが、現在学術情報センターの参加館は、学術情報センターの歴史が短いこともあって、まだ少なく、国立国会図書館の『新収洋書総合目録』の有力大学図書館の中にはまだ参加していないところもあり、今後、参加館を如何に増やすかが大きな課題であろう。

　また、参加している大学図書館においても必ずしも全学的に参加しているのではなく、本館と一部の部局図書館が参加する例もある。この傾向は特に大規模大学ほど強い。今後は大学の全ての図書館が総合目録データベースの参加館となるよう努力しなければならないであろう。

　次に収録範囲に関しては言語の問題がある。現在の学術情報センターの目録システムは、中国語や韓国語を扱うことができず、また、ロシア語についても原綴で入力するのか翻訳で入力するのかが不明であるので、大学図書館によってこれらの言語の図書の扱い方が異なっており、それらの中には学術情報センターの目録システムに登録されないものもある。今後は総合目録データベースに収録する言語の範囲とその入力方法（翻字）を明確にする必要がある。

　しかし、これらの言語以外の図書であっても、大学図書館によってはその目録レコードが学術情報センターに登録されていない場合がある。

　目録業務の電算化は、学術情報センターの目録システムにより目録作業を行い、それによって作成される当該大学の目録レコードを自館のOPACに取り込んで利用できるのが基本であるが、多くの大学図書館システムでは、オリジナル目録を直接自館のOPACに入力することも可能である。

　したがって、もし総合目録データベース作成事業に参加しているという環境が希薄で、学術情報センターの目録システムを単なる自館の目録レコード作成のための道具であると考えると、簡単に複製できる目録レコードは学術情報センターの目録システムを利用し、作業負担のかかるオリジナル目録レコードは直接自館OPACに入力することになる。

　日本の大学図書館は、これまで自館のためにのみカード目録を作成してきたので、共同分担目録の考え方に完全に移行するには多少

の時間が必要であると思われる。

　本来、総合目録データベースは、それに参加する図書館の収集する全資料の目録レコードが入力されてはじめて価値の出るものであるので、大学図書館は、その収集するすべての資料の目録レコードを入力するために、従来の個別目録の考え方から共同分担目録の考え方に切り換えなければならないであろう。

2　遡及入力

　データベースは対象とするデータが網羅的に収録されることによってその価値を増すのであるが、学術情報センターの目録システムに参加する大学図書館は、まず、参加時点からの新規受入図書の目録レコードから入力を開始するので、この作業が軌道にのると、次に問題になるのは過去に収集した資料の目録のレコードの遡及入力である。

　目録レコードの遡及入力は、個々の図書館が各々独自に行うとすると、その負担が非常に大きいので、通常は一つの大規模図書館の蔵書の目録レコードをすべて入力するか、あるいは REMARC のように冊子体の総合目録の目録レコードをすべて入力して、他の図書館がそれらを利用するのが最も経済的である。

　日本の図書については、国立国会図書館がその Japan MARC を1948年にまで遡って入力することになっており、それが間もなく完成する予定である。第二次世界大戦以前の日本の出版物はあまり多くないので、これが完成すれば、これを利用して、各大学図書館は比較的容易に日本語の図書の目録レコードの遡及入力を行うことができるものと考えられる。

　日本の大学図書館は、その蔵書の半分位は洋書で占められており、これらの図書の目録レコードを遡及入力することは大変大きな事業である。

　現在、国立大学の大規模大学図書館が協力して、目録レコードの遡及入力の効果的な方法を研究し始め、カード目録の自動読み取りや音声入力を研究しているが、この技術の完成までにはしばらく時間がかかるものと思われる。

　一方、一部の大規模大学図書館はその蔵書の目録レコードの遡及入力を開始したが、短期間に全蔵書の目録レコードを入力することは困難であり、今後この問題の解決が大きな課題である。

3　重複書誌

　学術情報センターの目録システムによる総合目録データベースの

作成事業も3年を経過してある程度軌道に乗ってくると、当然のことながら重複書誌の問題がでてきた。

学術情報センターの目録システムの基本的な考え方は、一旦入力された目録レコードは他の図書館もこれを使い、同一目録レコードの重複を許さないことであるが、実際には同じ目録レコードが重複して入力される事例が出てきた。

現在、約1％の重複書誌があると推定されており、この率が多いのか少ないのかは評価の仕方によるのであるが、重複書誌の原因としては、(1)目録担当者の不注意によるもの、(2)目録担当者の故意によるもの、(3)目録システム自体に原因があるもの等があるが、(1)によるものが最も多い。

重複書誌については、必要悪と見なし、これを是認する考え方もあるが、現在、重複書誌防止の努力が続けられ、自動重複書誌発見プログラムの開発、発見された重複書誌を修正するための関係大学図書館への連絡方法、重複書誌の入力館間の調整方法等について検討されている。今後あまり重複書誌が多くなると、修正のための負担が大きくなるので、基本的には重複書誌が発生しないような方策を講ずるべきであろう。

重複書誌の発生原因は不注意によるものが最も多いので、重複書誌を作成しないための目録担当者に対する教育・訓練を徹底する以外には、重複書誌を防止する手段はないであろう。

CD-ROMと総合目録データベース
1　目録業務とCD-ROM

米国では早くからLC MARCをCD-ROM化したBibliofileが普及しており、日本においても最近になり、語学辞典、人名辞典、新聞・雑誌等のCD-ROM化が行われ、実際に利用されるようになった。

このような傾向を背景に、Japan MARCのCD-ROM化が検討され、Japan BISCという名称で1983年春から販売されることになった。

Japan BISCは、Japan MARCの10年分、約50万件の書誌情報を一枚の光ディスクに収め、豊富な索引によるブーレアン検索、目録レコードの複製・修正・追加、オリジナル目録の作成、及びそれらの目録レコードのダウンローディング、目録カードの出力が可能である。CD-ROMの更新は年4回となっており、3月毎に新しいCD-ROMと交換することになっている。

また時を同じくして、米国のThe Library Corporation社の

Bibliofile も日本で販売されることになり、一枚の光ディスクに約200万件の書誌情報を収め、Japan BISC に劣らない機能を備えている。

　日本の図書館界では、学術情報センター、Utlas、OCLC といわゆる書誌ユーティリティが目録支援サービスを行い、互いに競争しているが、その活動の歴史は浅く、まだ、出発点の域を出ていないというのが実情であるが、その書誌ユーティリティの活動がまだ完全に定着していない前に CD-ROM の洗礼を受けることになり、新たな局面を迎えることになった。

　日本の電算化の歴史は、1970年代の分散処理の時代から、1980年代の集中処理（目録）と分散処理（目録以外）の併用の時代を経て、ここに目録自体も集中処理（書誌ユーティリティ）と分散処理（CD-ROM）の併用の時代を迎えたと言うことができる。

2　CD-ROM と書誌ユーティリティ

　Japan BISC や Bibliofile の特徴は、廉価であること、個々の図書館独自の利用ができること等であるが、他方、同時接続端末台数に制限があること、CD-ROM の更新が遅いこと、オリジナル目録の率が高くなること、総合目録データベース作成に適していないこと等の短所をもっていると考えられる。

　したがって、予算の少ない小図書館、他の図書館に対する資料依存度の少ない小図書館、総合目録より自館目録作成に関心の強い小図書館に対しては、この CD-ROM が普及する可能性は十分にある。

　日本には約490の大学が存在するが、その図書館の中には、総合目録よりは自館の目録作成、OPAC よりはカード目録作成により強い関心をもっているところがあり、このような観点から、CD-ROM を見ると、CD-ROM は非常に便利な道具と受け取られるものと考えられる。

　したがって、日本の大学図書館界では、資源の共有を前提としない大学図書館は CD-ROM に向い、相互貸借への依存度が高い大学図書館は学術情報センターの目録システムによる総合目録データベース形成事業に参加するというように二分化する可能性がある。

　CD-ROM の挑戦を受ける書誌ユーティリティは、今後目録システムの操作性や利用価値等の改善を行い、相互貸借等 CD-ROM にない付加価値を付けて、CD-ROM に対抗していくことになるであろう。

3　CD-ROM と共同分担目録

　書誌ユティリティと CD-ROM は、集中処理と分散処理、共同分担目録と個別目録というように相互に対局する関係にあるというこ

とができる。したがって、CD-ROM は基本的には個別図書館の目録作成に適していて総合目録データベースの作成には適していないと思われる。

非常に形式的に考えれば、目録レコードのフォーマットと目録規則が標準化されていれば、CD-ROM によって作成された個別書誌目録レコードを集め、総合目録データベースを作成することも不可能ではないとも考えられる。ただし、CD-ROM はその更新が遅いことと、他館のオリジナル目録を利用できないことから、重複書誌が発生するので、これを除去する仕組みが必要となる。

この仕組みとして考えられるのは、自動重複書誌発見プログラムの開発であるが、実際には個々に作成された目録レコードを検索し、重複書誌を発見・除去するプログラムの開発は不可能であろう。

特に共同分担目録の思想がまだ定着していない現在、多数の個性ある目録レコードを機械的に判定することは至難の業であり、CD-ROM による総合目録データベースの作成は多数の重複書誌を発生させるものと思われる。

総合目録データベース形成事業は、書誌ユーティリティによる共同分担目録以外では不可能であろう。

今後の課題
1 相互貸借システム

総合目録データベースは、単にそれを作成するのが目的ではなく、それを道具として図書館間における図書や雑誌の相互貸借をすることが目的である。

図書館における図書や雑誌の相互貸借が図書館の利用者にとって真に便利なものになるためには、その手続きが迅速に行われ、相互貸借の申込みから資料の入手までの時間が可能な限り短縮される必要がある。

従来、図書館における相互貸借は、申込みから資料の送付まで郵便によって行われており、特に相手館から謝絶されるような場合に利用者の求める資料が到着するのが非常に遅くなることが多かった。

このような利用者の不満を解消しようとするのが学術情報センターの相互貸借システムである。この相互貸借システムを使えば、参加館は端末を通して相手館に相互貸借の申込をすることができ、また相手館も即座に端末を通してその申込みに対する諾否を回答することが可能となる。

現在、この相互貸借システムのサービス開始に関連して、国立大学図書館では従来国の会計法規により国の機関以外に対する文献複

写の料金が前納制になっていたので、利用者に迅速に複写物を提供するために、複写料金を後納制に変えることも検討されている。

現在、学術情報センターへの参加館はまだ少なく、この相互貸借システムは稼働していないが、プロトタイプシステムは完成しており、そのサービス開始が待たれている。この相互貸借システムが実際に運用されるようになれば、大学図書館間における相互貸借の手続きが著しく迅速化されることになるであろう。

2　ファクシミリによる複写物の伝送

学術情報センターの相互貸借システムにより、相互貸借申込みやそれに対する返答の通信が迅速になっても、図書や雑誌論文の複写物の送付に時間がかかるようでは相互貸借システムの効果も半減するであろう。

図書自体の相互貸借については、これまでのように郵便や自動車による配達に頼らざるを得ないと思われるが、雑誌論文の複写については、ファクシミリを利用するのが最も効果的であろう。

現在、主要国立大学をノード大学として、日本列島を縦断する形で専用通信回線を持つ計画が年次計画により実施に移されており、いくつかの大学では学内キャンパスLANの相互接続が計画されいる。

これに伴い、この通信回線を使って大学図書館間の文献複写物をファクシミリを使って伝送する計画も実施に移された。1988年までに30の国立大学図書館にファクシミリが設置され、本年から実際にこのファクシミリを使って文献複写物の伝送を行うことになった。

まだファクシミリを設置する大学図書館の数が少ないことや大学間の専用通信回線が全国に延びていないこと等により、大学図書館間の文献複写サービスを全面的にファクシミリによる伝送に切り換えられることにはならないが、大学図書館間の文献複写物の伝送の迅速化のために大きな進展をしたと言うことができる。

今後は大学間の専用回線の延長に伴いファクシミリ設置大学図書館の数も増大し、大学図書館におけるファクシミリによる文献複写物の伝送がますます増えるものと思われる。

3　相互貸借の国際協力

総合目録データベースの作成の目的は、これを仲介として図書館間における図書や雑誌論文等の相互貸借を行うことにあるが、これを国内に限るのではなく、国外からもこの総合目録データベースを検索し、オンラインで相互貸借の申込みを行い、さらには文献複写

物をファクシミリで送ることが可能になれば、図書館の情報提供能力を飛躍的に増大させることが可能と思われる。

　勿論、現在でも世界的規模において図書館間の相互貸借が郵便で行われているが、これを電子的通信手段を使って実現すれば、国際的な相互貸借が飛躍的に迅速化されるであろう。

　これを実現するために、国際的な通信プロトコルの整合性の問題があるが、現在日本の学術情報センターと米国のNSF(National Science Foundation)との通信接続が具体的に進められているようであるので、この問題については一歩進展したと思われる。

　また、これを実現するにあたっては、そのほかにも解決しなければならない様々な制度的な問題があると思われるので、これらの問題に対する十分な検討が必要であろう。

　通信技術は日進月歩で発達しており、国際間の通信もますます発展しているので、国際的な相互貸借も案外近い将来に実現するかも知れない。その前に重要なことは総合目録データベースを真に利用に値するように内容的に充実することであろう。

米国におけるデータベース形成にまつわる諸問題(1)

Henriette D. Avram

　私が初めて日本を訪問したのは1976年のことでしたが、その目的は国立国会図書館の人達に会って、その頃から明らかになり始めていたユニマーク・フォーマットに基づく情報交換のフォーマットの開発について協議することにありました。その頃、既にローマ字について、ＡＬＡの文字セットは事実上国際基準になっており、国内及び国外の基準活動にたずさわる人達は非ローマ字の文字セットについて考え始めておりました。私が日本を訪問したその頃は、漢字の入力、表示、操作それに出力といったことにもっぱら関心があって、その交換の問題についてはまだそれ程ではありませんでした。

　しかしそれから時が流れて、世界各国で考案されたものと同様、日本製の機械可読書誌レコードを利用する方法について考える時、フォーマットと文字セットは米国にとって今でも重要な問題であると私には思えるのであります。米国だけでなく世界各国のデータベース開発者が今日かゝえる問題の中でとりわけこの二つは、より効果的な資源共有という観点から関心をよんでおります。

　私は書誌データベースを二つの点にしぼって取り上げてみようと思います。一つは蔵書の中の個々の資料を表示する図書館目録の機械可読変換であり、他は書誌ユーティリティで管理されるデータベースであります。後者は多くの参加館の協力で作成される書誌レコードのリソース・データベースで、図書館が自館に合うように選択し、取り込んでいくものであります。書誌ユーティリティのこの機能は分担目録作業又は資源共有として理解されているものであります。

不変性（一慣性）(2)

　米国の多くの図書館では今日、機械可読に基づく書誌データ交換用に開発された基準に従っております。事実、よく言われるように、そのような基準を成功裏に確立し、採用しているのはこの情報社会の中にあって、図書館が唯一の主要な機関であります。このように米国のネットワークが進み各方面の技術進歩に伴って、目録規則とその慣行、フォーマット、それに文字セットのような標準を遵守することによって、データ交換の新しい手段を実用化することが促進されてきました。しかしこのことの意義は大きいのにもかかわらず、

自館の目録の一貫性を保持するために書誌レコードのうちアクセスポイント（著者名、件名）を書誌ユーティリティから取り込む時に依然として修正をほどこしている図書館は多いのであります。一貫性のために行うこの修正はオリジナル目録を作成するよりははるかに安くつきますが、それでもコストのかかることであることには変わりありません。

　図書館の果たす主な機能には、受入、分類、索引作成、保存、それに情報検索があります。これらの機能は収書方針、分類体系、目録基準、それに保存・検索システムの影響を強く受けます。取り込まれた書誌レコードは図書館の目録となりますが、そこでは、不変性が決定的な意味をもちます。

図書館の目録がどのような形、即ち冊子、カード、あるいは機械可読で編纂されるにしろ、目録の機能に違いはなく、それは多様なアクセスポイント、例えば、著者、書名、件名、配架場所などによって探し出すツールであります。それは又、同一著者及びある特定の主題のすべての著作をまとめることに役立ちます。一貫性あるデータベースを持つことはデータベース管理の成功を保証するものであります。そのことは結局、費用効果を促進し、収書における高価な重複を防ぐことによってデータの有益性を高め、さらに利用者により早く、より容易に情報にアクセスできるようにします。

　重要なアクセスポイントである、著者名、件名は既に目録化されているものに一致するよう充分な配慮が必要であります。そのような末端の管理は一貫性あるファイルを作成する効果があり、典拠レコードはファイル中のアクセスポイントについてこの望ましい一致をもたらす慣行と体系を具体化します。もし一貫性が保持できなければ、目録の利用者は検索の結果、実際は図書館に所蔵されているのに見つけ出せないことが発生します。これは目録に一貫性がないことに起因します。

　目録の一貫性を保持することは高くつくという理由で、その経済性に疑問を持つ図書館は多いのです。レコードは書誌ユーティリティのリソースファイルから選択されて、自館で既にとられた目録と一致するかどうか必要な確認をしないまま自館の目録に加えられております。機械可読目録にはカードや冊子体では得られない機能があると言うだけで、目録の一貫性の属性に目をつぶっているのであります。

　私の知る限り、今日迄、この点を解き明かす確定的な研究がなされておりません。しかしながら、個々の図書館が手間のかかる修正をせず、より容易に一貫性を保つには、書誌ユーティリティ（書誌

生産物とそのサービスを提供する他の組織を含めて）のレコードについて今迄単一のデータベース向きでなく目録化して来た項目を表示すべきであります。言うまでもなく米国のような広い国ではそれは難しいことではありますが。

　一貫性の促進を目的とする二つの計画は目下進行中で、それは目録の重複を減らすと同時に有用な目録レコードを必要な時に取り出せるようにし、分担目録作業に役立つ標準的なレコードの増加をはかることが目的であります。

　これらの計画を詳しく見る前に、ＬＣ、ＲＬＧ、それにＯＣＬＣを互いにコンピュータで結ぶ共同事業について簡単にふれたいと思います。それはＬＳＰ（Linked Systems Project）と呼ばれるもので、それにより各システムが所有する書誌データの膨大なファイルを直接にかつ迅速に共有しあうことができるのであります。

　1960年代後半から1970年代の初期に出現した書誌ユーティリティのデータベースの成長に伴い、はっきりしてきたことはＬＣのデータベースの他にマーク配給サービス（ＭＡＲＣ　Distribution Service）経由で、ＬＣのデータベース配布とは無関係の異種のシステムに蓄えられた膨大なファイルが存在することであります。ＩＳＯの異機種間相互通信システム（Open Systems Interconnection：ＯＳＩ）Reference Modelに基づくプロトコルを利用して、ＬＳＰのメンバーは標準ネットワーク相互通信（the Standard Network Interconnection）という、ある通信手段を開発し、全米の書誌ネットワークを構築しました。ＬＳＰ環境によって、例えばＲＬＩＮのメンバーはそのユーティリティ又は自館の検索コマンドを使って、他のユーティリティ例えばＬＣのデータベースの検索が可能なのであります。ＬＳＰプロトコルはレコードを他のシステムに転送することを可能にすると共にデータ交換のためのテープ・ローディングを不必要にします。ＬＳＰ結合を利用することにより、間に介在することのない直接のアクセスが得られ、重複の減少がもたらされました。

　1977年以来、典拠データのための機械可読レコードがＬＣとその参加館により作られて来ました。全国目録調整作業（National Coordinated Cataloging Operations：NACO）計画に基づきＬＣに保持される全国のデータベースを作る目的からであります。このレコードはマーク配布サービスやＬＳＰ経由で図書館に提供されております。今迄、ＬＣの典拠ファイルに加えられた著者名典拠レコードの約25％の5万レコードは43加盟館により作成されました。参加館の数は現在も増え続けております。それは全国規模のものなので、

このデータベースの維持は一貫して LC が行ってまいりました。

全国目録調整計画（National Coordinated Cataloging Program：NCCP）と呼ばれる第2の計画は典拠レコードだけでなく全国レベルの目録の使いやすさを増すのが目的であります。この計画は現在、試験的段階で参加大学は、シカゴ、カリフォルニア・バークレー、ハーバード、イリノイ、インディアナ、ミシガン、テキサス、それにエールであります。

NACO 及び NCCP の計画の双方においては、協力館がレコードを作る際に LC の目録慣行に従っております。レコードは LC が保持する一つのデータベースに統合され、LC データのすべての利用者に使えるようになっていなければなりません。それ故、そのデータベースはもはや単なる LC の目録ではなく、LC の壁をはるかに越えた一貫性のある書誌レコードの源となっているのであります。これらの他の機関も同様に、より大きな図書館グループのリソースレコードになることによって所属するユーティリティや登録機関のメンバーにのみ役立つだけでなく、広くデータベースを公開しております。

NACO の典拠レコード、それに NCCP の書誌レコードが書誌ユーティリティを通じて利用でき、しかも分担目録だけでなくオリジナル目録にも使用されるようになれば、今後全米規模の一貫性の増大には期待がもてるでしょう。

著作権問題

技術進歩の激しい今日の社会における知的所有権は、図書館及び情報を取り扱う機関が直面する最も重要な問題になっております。それはやっかいな問題なので、データの製作者やデータベースの構築者に、著作権法上の適当な保護を確保するためには、その複雑さをときほぐすのに充分な時間とエネルギーが注がれねばならないでしょう。過去数年、米国では、非常な関心が向けられて来ましたが、満足すべき結論に至るにはこれからもっと議論が必要でありましょう。私はこの著作権問題の議論を進めるために、米国の関連機関が行った活動をふり返ってみようと思います。

連邦政府はこの問題の重要性を認めて、1986年、技術評価局（Office of Technology Assessment：OTA）を通じて『電子と情報時代における知的所有権』を刊行しました。これは議会の要請に応えて、データベースを含めた知的所有権に対する情報技術の影響を国際的視野から検証したものであります。

1987年4月[3]、及び1988年の3月[4]、LC のネットワーク諮問委

員会（Network Advisory Committee：NAC）[5]はこの問題について二つのプログラムからなる会合を持ちました。1987年の議題の中心は、(1)ＯＴＡ報告の全般、特に法的概観、(2)1976年著作権法の成果の評価、(3)知的所有権に関する米国議会小委員会の見解、(4)知的所有権についての図書館側の意見、(5)私企業における営業活動上の所有権の状況の呈示。この会議はこれらの不透明な状態をさらに掘りさげる必要を裏がきするにとどまり、それに続く会議は1988年に予定されております。

1988年の会議には電子時代における知的所有権にまつわる問題を把握する出発点になる一つの基本論文がＮＡＣのメンバーのために用意されております。目下問題として認識されているものには、(1)保護されるものとされないものは何で、それはどの位の期間か、(2)違反とされるもの、あるいはされないものは何か、(3)実施にはどのような機構を使うのか。これらの問題をあつかう方法として、ある程度の改正ともっと強い許可制を保ちながら契約や著作権制度にどこまでも依存する案が提案されました。

この会議の目標は、(1)この分野でのＮＡＣ組織の知識を深め、(2)はっきりした問題について解決策を示し、(3)ＮＡＣグループの構成員はその結果を受け入れ、(4)もしそれが妥当なものであるなら、その勧告をＮＡＣの結論として、ＬＣを通じて適当な議会の委員会に進言すること、であります。

ごく最近迄、多くの資源共有のデータベースは書誌レコードを保持はしていても機械可読形の印刷物のような伝統的な著作権を有する作品を持ってはいませんでした。権利と使用は概して契約に基づいていましたが、著作権法の役割は重要ではありませんでした。状況は変わりつつあり、著作権法の全面的な適用はまだにしてもその重要性は高まっております。

米国の著作権法の下では、データベースは編纂物と見なされ、セクション103で保護されております。この観点によれば編纂物とは以前に存在した資料に選択・調整・配列を加えた作品と定義づけられております。著作権を主張できるものは、オリジナリティがあること、それには人間の手が加えられ、最少限の選択・調整・配列が含まれていなければならないとされております。個々の書誌レコードにオリジナリティがあり、それにより著作権があるとする考えには異論があるでしょうし、単独のレコードには十分に創意に富む著作性はないかもしれません。何故なら、カタロガーがどんな特殊な目録をしようが、同じレコードになるように作られているのが目録規則だからです。このことは多分個々のレコードに著作権をないもの

にするかも知れませんが、レコードの集積物、即ち、その編集物であるデータベースの保護は可能であります。

他の権利に関する問題は、著作権を侵害するものは何かということであります。データベースを作成する機関が複製や編集物の一般に公開する権限をその権利は包含いたします。権利が無視されれば違反となります。複製権については、データベースの全体又はある個所の大部分の複製は違反行為であります。

国際的な場で、データベースのレコードの著作権がもつ意味の例証として、国外の商業ベンダーなどによるLCレコードの使用と頒布を観察して、LCはいかにそのレコードのデータベースを保護する努力をしているかを取り上げてみます。

1985年の4月1日より、国内外で頒布されるLCレコードのマークテープのすべてにコピーライトの注意書きがつき始めました。この処置は、LCの整理部、著作権課、総務課（General Counsel's Office）によるもので、LCレコードの著作権を国際的に明確にする目的からであります。米国における国立図書館として、たしかにLCのレコードは公のものでありますが、国境を越えた所には、我々が作成したデータに対して保護を欲するものであります。その注意書きは次のようになっております。〝LCが製作したこのテープのレコードは米国外では LC が著作権を有する、(c)1985″

国際著作権会議の決議に基づき、日・米は互いの著作権を認めております。従ってLCのマークテープについて、仮にLCのマークレコードのテープが日本のデータベースに取り入れられても、このレコードの使用は完全に保護されているわけです。LCと受入機関との承諾及び他の協定レコードの使用の範囲を決めることになります。レコードの使用の中には検索されたレコードに変更を加えず項目を同定するためにレコードを探すことを含みます。その中には、許される使用として、主題文献目録の部分としてそのレコードをプリントすること及び目録レコードを引き出すためにレコードの中のデータを細工することなどです。著作権告示で考えられている著作権は受入機関がこれらのレコードの頒布を他の日本の機関や組織に行うことを禁止しております。

同じような制限は、LCと国立国会図書館との話し合いで来年から始まるジャパンマークの米国内での変換と頒布についても当てはまります。紀伊國屋をその頒布エージェントとして、国立国会図書館は使用の詳細な協定書を案文しました。LCはそのテープの完全な形での唯一の頒布機関になるので、他の顧客はテープを複製、コピー又は出版しない限りそのテープを利用し、テープからレコード

を再配布することは出来るのです。

　書誌データベースの考案者と貢献者に対する報酬方法は今後のネットワーク活動ために確立しておかねばならないことは申すまでもありません。自発的なライセンス協定又は法律的に強制された認許は報酬の二つの方法であります。裁判所はデータ交換のフォーマットと形態について、著作権を有する必要な要件について明確な判決を行うことが期待されております。レコードが国際的規模で交換されるので、その状況はますます複雑になってきております。

ローカル処理と中央処理

　ローカルシステムの普及は今迄手作業で又は中央処理機関を通して行ってきた多くの伝統的な機能を実行する図書館にとって恩恵となっております。小型コンピュータが図書館にもたらす威力と効率は計りしれないものがあります。もし図書館界がローカルシステムのもたらす影響を注意深く見つめるのをおこたるなら、小型コンピュータが図書館にもたらす勢いにおされて、その有害な面を見失うことになります。図書館の必要に合うようにすれば、ローカルレベルで行った方が能率のよい業務はたしかにあります。雑誌の受付、収書、閲覧業務などは容易に思いあたります。

　しかしながら、目録業務は図書館の中でも最も費用がかかるので、参加館が全国及び地域のデータベースに目録データを送るのは資源共有のために当然のことであります。オリジナルであれコピーであれ、目録作業そのものによって図書館のユニオンカタログの指定は目録化された項目と一緒に蓄えられ、目録データ共有の費用効果だけでなく、ＩＬＬのシステムを通して、項目それ自身の共有の費用効果を可能にするのであります。

　今迄述べましたように、技術は効果的なローカルシステムを可能にしております。技術は又、システムの結合、即ち、コンピュータとコンピュータの間で、目録と所蔵データをローカルシステムから全国資源へのアップロード、あるいは全国資源からローカルシステムへのダウンロードの双方を可能にしております。光ファイバーと他の技術進歩はこれからもますます、通信コストを引き下げるものと思います。

　経済が不安定な昨今、米国の図書館には費用の観点から書誌ユーティリティの役割を疑問視しているむきもあります。ＬＣのマークデータは LC や他のソースから入手でき、目録ローカルシステムを使用すれば、書誌ユーティリティサービスの使用に比べて、格段の通信費用を節約することが出来ます。加えて、もしローカルに取

られたレコードが共有にはなっていないとすれば、目録またはフォーマットの基準に従う必要がなく、その分、費用の削減になります。この後者の特点はしばしば自館独自性の保持と呼ばれております。

　資源共有のもとにここ数年進めてきた成果を、あえて台無しにしてしまうことは余りにも視野の狭いことであります。通信コストや標準に従うコストはたしかに高くつきますが、オリジナルカタログを何遍も繰り返すことの方が、結局は高くつくことになります。目録作業の全コストは如何なるものかは、自館製作の目録が確立された目録基準に従い、全国の目録の蓄積に貢献し、大きな修正なしに交換できるかどうかを長期にわたって検証することにより出て来るものであります。

一つの統合された情報ネットワーク？

　比較的最近の関心事に統合情報ネットワーク構築の問題があります。資源共有のための実行可能なネットワークの確立をめざして図書館界がいかにＬＳＰを利用しているか私は述べて来ましたが、ＬＳＰネットワークのみが情報へのアクセスを目的とするネットワークではありません。一つの学術研究のネットワークは目下形づくられております。それはＩＢＭや、ＡＴ＆Ｔのような大企業と、連邦政府では米国科学財団（the National Science Foundation）のようにネットワーク環境に大きな影響を与える機関の援助を受けております。

　これらを推進する目的は、全米のスーパーコンを結んで〝スーパーネットワーク〟と特徴づけられるものを創造することにあります。この結合はＮＳＦNet（The National Science Foundation Network）の根幹をなし、同様に多くの構成ネットワークを全米に結ぶものであります。これらの中には ARPANET、BITNET、それに NYSERNet[6]があり、Internet を構成すると共に、ARPANET をささえるために国防省が開発した TCP／IP（Transmission Control Protocol/Internet Protocol）として知られる一連のプロトコルに制御される下部機構であります。TCP／IP は LSP／SNI プロトコルのように OSI に基づくものではないので、二つの独立したネットワーク組織は互いに交信できない恐れがあります。このようなことは情報を求める全国民のためにあってはならないことです。国民の多様な情報の要求に応えるためには一つの論理回路上の情報ネットワークがなければなりません。

　学術ネットワークを支える機関には NSF の他に、EDUCOM（高等教育機関の500以上で構成するコンソーシアム）があります。その

ネットワークの目的はこれらの高等教育機関を結びつけ、キャンパス間で共有される情報検索を可能にすることにあります。いうまでもなく、大学の一構成員である学術図書館はキャンパス内で結ばれているため大学間の LSP ネットワークの参加資格を有するものであります。従ってどのネットワークに属していようと、その構造は交信できるようになっていなければなりません。

　目下、ネットワークのために計画されている一つのプロジェクトがあります。それは端末の前に坐った研究者は図書館の所有する情報だけでなく、ネットワーク上の情報にアクセスできるようになることであります。しかし、これにも増して大事なアプリケーションは電子メールであるように思われます。一方、既に述べたように LSP は資源共有と他の図書館機能を支える生産本位のネットワークであります。

　開発中の二つのネットワークを結ぶための準備作業が双方で始まっております。それによって二つのネットワーク間の相互作業即ち交信が可能になるはずです。異なったグループの代表者間の意見交換がいくつかの局面で行われており、今後も続けられるでありましょう。LC のスタッフと TCP／IP ネットワークの代表者の間で話し合いが現在も継続して行われておりますし、これらの会合によって、各グループの現在行っていること、それに計画中のものの意図についての情報交換を行っております。それによって学術ネットワークの提案者は、ネットワークを成功させるために必要な分野、例えば、著作権、管理、基準などで図書館が蓄積してきた膨大な経験を活用することが出来るのであります。

　NSF は1990年代半ばの早い時期に OSI プロトコルに移行することを計画しております。それが実現するまでに、OSI／LSP と TCP／IP ネットワークを結ぶ方法のいくつかが LSP の参加者によって探究されるでしょう。RLG と OCLC は彼等のシステムとインターフェイスできる TCP／IP ネットワークの可能性を調査中であります。LC は NSFnet のノードになっている NACO 機関に TCP ネットワークを通じて典拠レコードを送らせ、ＬＣデータベースの典拠ファイルに加えることを検討中であります。今後の話し合いは、NACと EDUCOM が12月に合同会議を開く今年の後半に予定されております。

結び

　最適なアクセスを達成するために、協力はデータベース形成のすべてにわたって必要なのであります。この議論で最も大切なことは

データベースの創作方法について協力がなければならないことであります。データベース管理者は情報を集めることに十分時間をかけ、他のデータベース管理者と協力しなければならないのであります。情報を仕入れることは、まず今自分がやっていることを他に知らせることから始まります。もし、自分の進みぐあいを他に知らせる努力をすべての人がすれば、努力の重複が避けられるだけでなく、一貫性のための標準化が促進されることになるのであります。

　我々の窮極の目標は世界書誌調整の理念の実現でなければなりません。ということは、1件の目録はただ一度、それも理想的には、その発行国で機械可読形に基づき目録化され、全世界で使用されるよう、出来るだけ、完全に、正確に、かつ迅速に生産されなければならないということであります。

<注>
(1) この論文は1988年7月6日の〝技術と保存による図書館資料へのアクセス〟と題する米・ソセミナーにおける筆者の〝データベース──コンピュータ環境における情報の書誌調整の諸問題〟と題する提出論文の一部分に基づく。
(2) 一貫性（consistency）の辞書の定義は、〝すでに行われ、言葉で表わされた調和の状態、即ち以前からの慣習と一致を保持する状態〟（Webster's New World Dictionary of the American Language, David B. Guralnik, editor in chief. New York : World Pub. Co., c1970) p.303
(3) 1987年会議の議事録は L C の Network Planning Paper. no. 16に Intellectual Property Rights in Electronic Age(1987)として刊行された。
(4) 1988年会議の議事録は Network Planning Paper. no.17として刊行予定。
(5) N A C は L C 主宰のもとに1976年に始まった。それは主要な図書館、文書館、情報産業と業界団体、地域又は全国の図書館ネットワーク、書誌ユーティリティ、データベース販売業者、国立図書館、その他の情報サービス機関の代表者よりなる連絡機関で、その主目的は、①全米ネットワークにおける L C の役割についてLCの館長に勧告する。②図書館及び情報サービスの全米ネットワークの発展を促進し、その活動の中心の役割をはたす。③ネットワーク活動について、図書館資源協議会（the Council on Library Resources）に働きかける、さらに、④全米図書館・情報科学委員会（the National Commission on Libraries and Infor-

mation Science)に意見を伝える討論会を提供する。過去12年間、NACはネットワークの問題について広範囲にわたる勧告を行って来た。

(6)　ARPANETは1969年、国防省の Advanced Research Projects Agency（DARPA）によって設立された最初の広域パケット交換ネットワークである。1984年にARPANETは二つに分割され、一つはDODの操作に必要なMILNETで、もう一つはARPANETの名を引き継いだ研究ネットワーク機能を果すものである。BITNETは、高等教育における広範な目的のコンピュータネットワークで、現在、約400のキャンパスを、1,200以上のコンピュータで結んでいる。NYSERNetはニューヨーク州の教育研究ネットワークである。

米国におけるネットワークの発展をとりまく問題

Rowland C. W. Brown

成立ち

　米国の図書館協力は長い伝統を持っており、すでに“ネットワーキング”が私達の日常語として定着する前から盛んでした。相互貸借、シリアルズ・ユニオンリストの作成そして定期便による資料の巡回集配はMARCやOCLCを知る前から健全な図書館協力活動として行われていたのです。OCLC、研究図書館グループ（RLG）、西部図書館ネットワーク（WLN）はMARCの開発における米国議会図書館（LC）のリーダーシップのもとに、次のステップへの新しい技術を応用し、これまでになかった図書館書誌情報処理のネットワーク化に、コストと便益ならびに資源の共有を殆ど想像できないほどにもたらしました。協同と技術の結合の結果として生まれるこの活動は規模がもたらす経済性により可能になりました。このことはあとでもう一度触れることになります。

　米国ではOCLC，RLGそしてWLNの同時的発展が見られ、これは「図書館協力の黄金時代」と呼ばれてきました。しかし図書館協力のネットワークは単に彼らのオンライン目録を利用させるだけの図書館共同体（コンソーシアム）からOCLC，RLGあるいはWLNのように数千の図書館を相手に高度に組織され、専門のスタッフを擁する総合（マルチ）サービス機関までさまざまです。ネットワーク化はさまざまの形をとります。ある機関は政府出資、またあるものは非営利の会員制、そして商用ベースのものまでと言うようにです。進歩し続ける技術の選択可能性はこうしたひろがりを一層大きくし、また相互接続の機会を広げます。

　図書館協力のもとに強く結ばれてきた図書館では技術導入が資源共有、総合目録やシリアルズ・ユニオンリストの形成、共同分担収集そして資料保存の推進を可能にしてきたのです。このような図書館相互を結ぶ電子化されたネットワークの有効性は強固な基盤の上に成り立っているもので、技術革新によってもたらされるさまざまの新しい代替の選択によってゆらぐものではないのです。それはネットワークのカルチャーとしての支援基盤であって技術的な側面としての基盤以上のものなのです。技術適用の機会であることや経済的な便益性は、ただ相互協力の努力を支え強化するに過ぎないことなのです。しかしこの逆もまた真なのです。永く続く相互協力の伝

統と完全にコスト依存ではない資源共有の目標のないところでは、常に変化していく技術の選択可能性がネットワークの理念を犠牲にしてコストの正当化という祭壇に捧げてしまうのです。

　大規模書誌情報ネットワークの運用が開始されたとき、一次的な経済利益はナショナルライブラリに次いで、それに続く同様の機関からの直接利用可能な膨大な量の書誌情報をベースにした共同分担目録作業でした。かつてのようなオリジナル目録作成、資料整理の遅れ、全国目録入手の遅れはもはや問題でなくなりました。オリジナル目録は今も費用のかかる作業ですが、個々の参加館が作成する量は急速に減ってきています。お金のかかる遡及入力についても同じく劇的なほどに影響を受けました。

　共同分担目録の直接の副産物はILLに及ぼす効果でした。目録作業を通じて所蔵の記号が書誌レコードに付与されているので図書館はもはや所在・所蔵について推測に頼る必要はなくなりました。これまでと違って地域または全国の大規模図書館に集中するのでなく、あらゆる種類のまた大きさの図書館が相互貸借に参加してきたのです。電子化されたメッセージ伝送による高度のオンラインILLは地域から全国へ、そして国際的に広がりをもつネットワーク化の自然な発展でした。

　多くの国内図書館からのテープローディングや目録の追加があり、1,800万レコード以上に及ぶ巨大かつ急速に増え続ける国際的なOCLCのデータベースの中で、国内図書館の目録情報が占める割合は累積のみならずカレントな目録でさえも、25乃至30%に過ぎないというのは興味深いことです。これはいかに有効に共同分担目録が大規模に行えるかを示しています。このことは、図書館がデータの相互入力義務を無視するさまざまのローカル・オプションを検討していることからも、しばしば見失われる点です。これらの活動は遡及変換入力やローカルシステム・サポートに対する州や財団の援助により支えられてきました。電子化されたネットワーク化の可能性と相互協力がCONSER、全米新聞プログラム、主要マイクロ資料の共同目録、そして将来ですが共同分担保存のような広範囲の全国プログラムを起こさせました。

　システム相互接続プロジェクト（Linked Systems Project）における議会図書館（LC）、RLGそしてOCLCの作業は、とくにそれが国際標準（OSI）に向かって進んでいますが、まもなく書誌情報ネットワークの領域では飛躍的な発展が明らかになることでしょう。同様に地域の、そして場合によっては全国の、あるいは国際的な学術ネットワーク化の発展がOCLCのような機関の努力を広げて、彼

らの書誌情報を超えた情報入手と伝送を容易にすることになるかもしれません。

もうひとつは州のデータベースをもとにオンラインで分散型の資源共有をさまざまの形で提供する州機関の活動です。ひとつの試みとして州で発展した活動を現存の全国ネットワークに統合することが考えられましょう。

将来

主要な書誌情報ネットワークが機能している今日の環境のもとでその主役たちの役割は変わりつつあります。相互の結び付き、分散と支援のありよう、会員の概念、そして管理において変化が求められています。こうした変化はネットワーク、図書館そして利用者に影響を与えています。大学での問題のひとつは図書館と学内計算機センターとの関係、さらに教育研究での電子化された情報の活用との関わりを探る限りでは、広く教育界との総体の関係の変化です。これは大学および研究の全国的な、また国際的な通信ネットワークの出現によりさらに複雑になっています。主要な書誌情報ネットワークはそれ自体変化を起こす力となり、また同時にそれによって影響を受けているのです。

私達の環境の中では技術変化のもたらすものに焦点を当ててみましょう。技術を考える場合、その前提として次のようないくつかの点があります。

- 技術は単に道具または目的のための手段である
- 技術は常に進歩する。技術は自動化の計画と経済性において時代遅れの主要な要因になる
- 通信、ローカル処理およびデータ蓄積装置の進歩が早く、投資及び運用コストの両面から見てネットワークの経済性を変化させる。オンライン化およびローカルネットワーク化への取組み方も変わる
- 図書館界とネットワーク化は技術を持てる者と持たざる者の間のギャップに直面することになろう
- 新技術の開発、採用、そして実施はネットワーク参加者の間の関係を変え得る
- 新技術は力、地位、そして統制に影響を及ぼし得る
- 情報市場には新しい役者が現れつつあり、これが市場環境をますます競争化させ、選択枝をより多くしている

大規模書誌情報ネットワークは繁栄してきました。しかし急速に変わりゆく環境の中で今なおそれぞれ変化を続けていますが、それ

は組織にとっては決して変則的なものではありません。図書館界はとくに、OCLC，RLG，WLN そして Utlas に影響を及ぼした、いくつかの主要な変化を体験してきました。
- 分散システムおよびパーソナルコンピュータの発達
- システム同士、あるいはコンピュータ同士の結合可能性
- 図書館員の間での自動化システムの知識の増大
- 情報・図書館の分野での民間の競争
- 州の機関、情報提供者それに全国図書館のような新旧の役者が新しい役割を求めていること
- 増大しつつある国際・広域図書館相互協力の重要さ

主要なネットワークはその伝統的な生産物（プロダクツ）とサービスが、これまでネットワーク及び利用者に貢献してきた技術、ニーズ並びにそれらの関係の基に築かれた一つの成熟の段階を経験しつつあります。

変わりゆく環境はあらゆる段階でその加速度的な変化についていくために柔軟性を求めるようになります。システムは今やローカルレベルに焦点があります。つまりキャンパス・ネットワーク、ローカルオンライン目録から大学内の情報ネットワークへのひろがりと転換、そしてお互いユーザ同士でつながる個人や研究室のワークステーションなどです。個々のユーザはますます、ユーザの手によってより使いやすく、より簡単に設計されたソフトウエアおよびインタフェースの中心になってきています。広域ネットワーク化が国際的なデータベースと世界規模の資源共有の潜在的可能性を持ったこの広がりのもう一方の極にあり、各国の間で全体計画と高度なネットワーク化が求められています。システム同士の結合は情報の利用者と提供者のすべてのレベルにおいて鍵となります。

主要な書誌情報ネットワークは相互協力と会員の概念を通じて形成され発展してきました。こうした基本となる参加と見返りは、ローカル・オプションが増して図書館が実利的な参加の呼びかけに直面するにつれ、疑問がなげかけられてきています。共同分担目録と全国レベルの資源共有が同時に問題になるという根本的な逆説があります。というのは、国際的なデータベースが伝統的なサービス、ドキュメントデリバリ、資料保存と保管の計画、資料収集計画、原文献の直接利用（アクセス）、そして研究者ネットワークに対して包括的な計画の裏付けを提供し得るからなのです。

実際、書誌情報ネットワークに関して次のような数多くの逆説、あいまいさ、そして二分論（ダイコトミー）があります。
- 顧客の関係をもつ売り手としてのネットワークと明らかに区

別される、一方の会員制度と相互協力
- 所属ネットワークの管理統制とマーケティング並びに販売の役目
- ネットワークと図書館の間で相入れない協議事項
- 国内及び国家間の主張
- 目録あるいは/および図書館業務要求に応えて形成されたデータベースが今やレファレンスやリソース・シェアリングを支援していること
- 図書館業務向きと図書館サービス向き
- 図書館と利用者
- 図書館とその設立母体（教育機関、政府機関、親団体）
- 図書館環境と情報環境
- コストに基づく価格と市場価格に基づく価格

これらの二義性またはあいまいさは必ずしも完全に両立し得るまでに解決されなくてもよいのですが、ただネットワークが認め対処しなくてはならないさまざまに変化する見方を示しています。ネットワークの管理者とメンバーは環境の変化とそれらの二義性に建設的に立ち向かう用意をしておかなくてはなりません。

結論

　将来の図書館ネットワークにとって最も重要な変化は次の三つからくるものと私は思います。ひとつはマイクロコンピュータや卓上ワークステーションの能力、応用としての利用の進歩に加えて光学方式などの高密度大容量記憶装置の急速な普及であり、これはネットワークの形態に新しい試みを引き起こすことになるでしょう。次はデジタル光通信や衛星通信の利用可能性が高まることです。これは書誌情報のみならずドキュメントや他の形態の原文供給について国際交換を可能にすることでしょう。最後は、といってもこれは決して他に比べて重要でないというのではありませんが、図書館情報システムはますます一般の人、つまり図書館利用者、研究者、教育関係者などにとってより広く使えるようになってきたことです。そしてこうした利用者達は国内並びに国際的な図書館及び研究ネットワークの両面に対しその形態、内容、構造そして範囲について主張し指示するようになるでしょう。私達の旅は今始まったばかりなのです。

日本における情報資源の形成のためのネットワーク

田 中 久 文

はじめに

　「図書館ネットワーク」という言葉は多様な意味を持っている。かつては図書館間のさまざまな協力活動のための網（Web）を意味した。その典型的な活動例は、相互貸借であり、資料の分担収集などであった。しかし今日ではこの言葉は通常、書誌ユーティリティを中心とした通信網とコンピュータを介した「図書館情報ネットワーク」と理解されることが多い。いずれにせよこれらの言葉で表わされることは、地域的な、あるいは全国的な広がりの中での情報資源の形成あるいはその共有・運用のための方策を意味している。そしてこれらの各方策を総合化することによって一つの体制（システム）が確立することになり、これが本来広い意味において図書館ネットワークと言うべきかもしれない。

　このペーパーにおいては、日本におけるこの言うなれば近代的な図書館活動（特に学術の領域における）の体制について、その大きな側面である図書資源の全国的な分担収集の現状とそこに内包する課題を述べ、更にこの数年急速に発展している「図書館情報ネットワーク」の特質について簡単に紹介した。

I　全国的図書資源形成のためのネットワーク
図書資源形成の背景

　日本の全国的共有資源としての図書資料は、次の３つの範疇の図書館群、すなわち、公共図書館、大学図書館及び唯一の国立図書館としての国立国会図書館（NDL）に所蔵されていると言い得る。それらの総蔵書冊数は約３億冊（1986年）で、その内、大学図書館はその50％を有している。

　日本においては数少ない例外を除いては研究図書館としての公共図書館は未発達であり、またNDLは何よりも日本の出版物の継承機関であり、その書誌センターでもある。日本は極東の離れ小島であり、逆説的ではあるが、それだけに海外の情報摂取に意欲的であった。特に学術研究においては、海外先進諸国の情報が大きな比重を占めてきた。このような意味において、日本における学術研究用資料はその主要部分が大学図書館に所蔵されてきたと言い得る。

　大学図書館は他の図書館群とは異なり、第一義的には多数ではあ

るが特定の利用者集団のための施設である。基礎的で教養的、一般的な広い領域の資料を利用する学生という利用者集団も居るが、高度な先端的、専門的な領域の研究者の必要に合わせて収集された資料が、その蔵書の主要部分である。今日のように出版物も多様化、大量化する一方、図書費が相対的に縮減されるような状況下においては、個々の大学での図書資料の収集は、総合性あるいはバランスのとれた収集から離れて、それぞれがかなり個性的にならざるを得なくなる。この意味では大学図書館は専門図書館の集合体の性格を持つようになってくる。

　一方、学術研究が多岐に発展し、また学際的研究が進んでくると、総合性を欠いた蔵書の不十分性がますます明瞭になってくる。そこで、国全体の図書資源の総合性を維持するための方策が期待されるようになる。第2次大戦後各国は国内における総合的な資源形成のため、それぞれの国の諸条件を踏まえ施策を立ててきた。米国においては Farmington Plan が1940年代に、 NPAC が1960年代から実施され、英国においては NLLST が1962年に、西ドイツでは Sondersammelgebietsplan が1949年に、 Zentrale Fachbibliothek が1959年にそれぞれ発足した。日本も遅ればせではあったが、1977年より着手し始めた。日本の場合、この動きは図書館界の自発的取り組みというより文部省による行政指導型であった点にその特徴があるかもしれない。

全国的図書資源形成の基本的考え方
1　資料に則した収集の考え方

　ある国立図書館の1人の管理者がかつて会議で、その図書館に「古今東西、森羅万象」の図書館資料を収集したい、と発言したことがあった。それが一つのレトリックであり、その意気を壮とするとしても、その可能性はどの程度のものであろうか。学術研究にかかわる資料に限ったとしても、国内で発生すると予想されるすべての需要に対してたとえ強大な国立図書館であっても、1館でそれを満たすことは容易ではない。またそれを実現した例が、少なくとも近代において、いずれかの国において存在したという事実を知らない。逆にこのことは近年ますます困難度が高まっていると言うことができる。それではどのような可能性が残されているのであろうか。

　まず日本国内出版物の資源形成の状況を見ると、新しい出版物は1986年統計で見る限り図書約37,000種、逐次刊行物約10,000タイトルで、この他、地方での小さい流通ものも約20％程度あると言われている。ＮＤＬにおいては納本制度に基づきこれら国内出版物の

70〜80％を収集できると言われている。このことはまことに賞賛されるべきことであり、日本における一つの文化遺産の継承機関としてその役割を果たしつつあることを力強く感ずるものである。NDLに取り残された出版物についても、地方の大学図書館あるいは公共図書館等で相当部分が収集されていると考えられるので、ほぼすべての国内の出版物が国内のいずれかの公共的施設に収集されていると言えるであろう——それらが共有資源としてより円滑に運用される体制を整備することは重要であるが。

　問題は外国の出版物である。学術研究の領域に限定しても世界各国の出版物を網羅的に収集するとなると、国内出版物の何十倍もの資金と労力を要することであろうし、そのことは現実的に不可能である。また可能だとしてもそれを一箇所に1セット集めれば充分であると言うものではない。その利用者は全国に分散しているのである。先端的な研究を進める科学技術の一部の分野については、必要なある形態の資料を集めることは比較的可能性があるかもしれない。しかし、人文・社会科学関係の図書を網羅的に集めることは不可能である。そこで、その対応策として第一段階に考えられることは、それぞれの研究者もしくはその集団において当面必要とされる資料を、可能な範囲でその必要の程度に応じて収集させることである。そこでは厳密な意味での体系性や網羅性に欠けることがあろう。またそのグループ間に相当の重複があり得るであろう。しかしその重複は必要な範囲のものと考えられる。

　この言わば laissez faire（自由放任）の結果として、全国的観点からの非体系的な不完全さをそのまま放置しておいてよいかは、また別のことである。何故ならば、研究者は、その laissez faire を享受しても、それで十分満足しているわけではないからである。しかし laissez faire の結果を総体として見ると、それなりにかなりレベルの高い収集になっていると考えられる。従ってまず最初に考えられるべきことは、これらローカルのコレクションを相互補完的な共有資源としてその相互利用のシステム化を図らなければならない。次に資源の網羅性を高めるために、資料そのものの「欠落部分」を整備することが必要である。しかしこのことも一つの国の努力では決して容易なことではない。そこでさらに必要なことは、国際的協力である。このように考えてくると、資源形成の一つのパターンが見えてくる。すなわち各国は国の責任において国内出版物は国の中央的図書館とその補助的機関によって網羅的に収集し、外国からの協力要請に応える。外国出版物については、それらを必要とする利用者集団において第一義的に収集し、何らかの中央的施策によりそ

の相互利用のシステム化と網羅性を高める付加的収集の努力を行い、最終的には出版国との国際協力に期待する、というものである。

2　資源形成の方法

　出版物資源の形成の方法としては、大別して2つのものが考えられる。すなわち、集中的(単一機関)形成と分散的(複数機関分担)形成である。そのいずれを選ぶかはそれぞれの国における既存の資源の状況や行政機構の状況その他の諸々の条件に従い、その最適化の道に沿って実現されるであろう。

　前者の集中型の最も成功した例は、英国図書館文献提供センター(the British Library Document Supply Centre)であろう。また分散型の典型的な例は西ドイツにおける分野別専門図書館である。BLDSCは科学技術の逐次刊行物を中心とした収集・提供機関として発足した。その最も特色ある点は資料収集のレベルの高さも当然ながら、その提供サービス体制の、伝統的な図書館のイメージにとらわれないユニークさにある。それはまさに図書館というより配送センターである。

　西ドイツは教育行政が地方分権下にあることもあって、「国立」機関が存在せず、従って州立大学の既存図書館の中から、工学、医学、農学、経済学の各分野別中央図書館を各一館ずつ選び、体系的収集と「超地域的」提供の役割を担わせた。フランスもこのような分散型を採用しつつあると聞いている。

　この2つのいずれが優れているかを論ずることは無意味である。むしろそれぞれ任務を背負ったセンター図書館がいかに機能するか、ということが重要である。日本では結果的に分散型を採用したが、その運用は西ドイツのそれともいろいろの面において異なっている。日本では高等教育が高度に発達しており、その機関は全国各地に散在し、その内容もかなりの程度に整備されている。従ってこれらを総体的に見れば、その資源形成はかなり高いレベルにあり、それをより高くする現実的方策は補完的機能を果たす機関を整備することであると判断された。BLDSCにとって back-up libraries とは BLDSCの「穴を埋める」ものであるが、日本におけるセンターは既存図書館の穴埋め機能を果たしているのである。

3　日本における大学の収集状況

　日本の大学進学率は米国のそれより低いが同年齢層の36％に相当し、国立大学は96あり、しかも全国各地に所在する。また大学生数の74％を収容する私立大学(4年制)も350を数える。

教員等研究者は124,000人で、大雑把に言って1人あたり平均年間248,000円（$2,000）（1985年度）の図書と153,000円（$1,180）の逐次刊行物の経費を使っていることになる。外国出版物についてだけ見ると、図書129,000円（$1,000）逐次刊行物123,000円（$950）で、研究者が1人10～11冊の外国図書と2～3タイトルの外国雑誌を購入していることになる[1]。個々の研究者の満足度は別として、共同利用を前提とした図書費としては低すぎる金額だと言えないのではないか。

　各大学について見ると、1大学平均270人の教員、研究者が居り、約31万冊の蔵書を持ち、年間図書11,000冊（内、外国図書3,000冊）を受入、雑誌2,500（内、外国雑誌850）タイトルを購読していることになる[2]。外国出版物はほとんどすべてが研究用であると言い得る。

　以上の数字は米国のそれより低いと想像されるが、受入資料の内で外国出版物の占める比率はかなり高いのではないかと思う。特に科学技術の領域では外国雑誌の占める比率は高く、人文、社会系では雑誌タイトル数の25％であるのに対し、49％に相当し、全外国雑誌に占める比は60％である。このような点から推察できるように、日本においてはこれまで外国出版物の収集に相当の努力を払ってきたし、それだけの情報資源の形成が図られてきたと言い得るであろう。

外国雑誌センターの成立と効果
1　外国雑誌センターの設置

　日本において外国出版物（この場合、逐次刊行物）の体系的な収集について、「意図的」な措置がとられたのは1977年からである。国立大学に直接的責任を持つ文部省は、それ以前から外国雑誌の値上がりに比して国立大学の資料費の相対的な低下により、多くの雑誌の解約を余儀なくされつつあった状況を見て、その年度から「外国雑誌購入費」という新規の付加的な予算を計上した。当初これが僅かな金額であったこともあって、当局はこれを全国立大学に配分したのでは効果を生まないと判断し、特定のいくつかの大学に重点的に配分し、そこで我が国に収集されていない重要な逐次刊行物の収集にあたらせた。当初その任務を負った図書館は次のとおりである。

　理工学系：　東京工業大学図書館
　医　学　系：　大阪大学中之島（医学）図書館、他にこれを補助するものとして九州大学医学図書館、1978年より東北

　　　　　　　大学医学図書館
　農 学 系： 東京大学農学図書館、その補助館として鹿児島大学
　　　　　　　農学図書館

　一方、当局は学術審議会において日本における学術情報流通体制の在り方全般について審議を進めた。その結果、1980年審議会は答申を文部大臣宛提出した。その勧告は次の点に集約される。
　① 一次資料の体系的、網羅的収集を図ること。
　② 一次資料の全国的所在情報データベースを形成し、その情報提供を行うためのコンピュータ・ネットワークを作ること。
　③ 大学研究者に必要な二次情報データベース検索のためのシステムとネットワークを作ること。
　④ 日本独自に必要なデータベースを形成すること。
　⑤ これらの施策を推進するための中心的機能を果たすため「学術情報センター」を設置すること。
　この勧告の一次資料の整備について、当局は当面外国雑誌を対象とし、それまで単なる予算上の措置に過ぎなかった外国雑誌収集を政策的措置に格上げすることになった。その後、計画がありながら実現されなかった社会科学系（一部、人文科学系を含む）も1985年に神戸大学、1986年に一橋大学と指定され、収集が緒につくことになった。また、1987年度に理工系の補助機関として京都大学が追加指定された。その結果、現在9図書館によって実施されている。
　文部省はこれらの各図書館に対し、雑誌購入は勿論であるが、製本その他必要な事務経費及び職員定員を特別に増加配分してきた。これらの館はいずれも国立大学であるが、言うまでもなく、公・私立大学のみならず広く他の公私の研究機関へもサービスするものとされている。

2 外国雑誌センターの収集の現状

　当初5図書館から出発したセンターは、10年を経過し9館に増加し、全部で17,604タイトルを予約するまでに成長した。（言うまでもなくこの数字は、それぞれの館が大学に附属する館として購入するタイトルを含まない。）これらの館は収集すべき資料をどのようにして選んだか。各センターに共通していることは、それぞれの領域での代表的な二次資料に収載されていながら、日本の図書館で受け入れられていないタイトルから選んだ、と言う点である。
　医学では当初 *Index Medicus, Current Contents* が、その後 *Excerpta Medica, Biological Abstracts, Science Citation Index* など

がその調査源となった。(3)　理工学では *CA, Ulrich's International Periodicals Directory, Journals in Translations*（*BLLD*）, *Index to Scientific & Technical Proceedings*（ISI）など(4)。農学系では農学系学会誌の引用文献調査の結果と *SCI, CC, Commonwealth Agricultural Bureau* データベース、*Aquatic Science and Fisheries Abstracts* など(5)。社会科学系では *Ulrich, Social SCI* など(6)。

それぞれの図書館で選択した結果には相互に重複が生じる。この重複は原則的には避けることとし、該当館相互に協議して分担してきた。その結果、1987年において図1の通り収集されている。

図1　外国雑誌センター収集分野別予約タイトル数

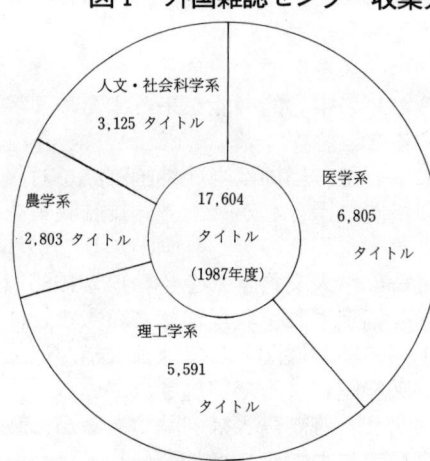

医学系：大阪大学、九州大学、東北大学の各医学図書館（1977年以降）
理工学系：東京工業大学、京都大学の各中央図書館（1977年以降）
農学系：東京大学、鹿児島大学の各農学図書館（1977年以降）
人文・社会科学系：神戸大学、一橋大学の各中央図書館（1985年以降）

　選定の経緯でわかる通り、これらの逐次刊行物はそれぞれの分野のいわゆる core journals ではなく、むしろ rare use のものと言えよう。その意味でこれらの資料は基本的に文字道り「補完的」なのである。このことは、これらの個々の図書館自体がその領域での逐次刊行物についての完結した総合センターを目指しているのではない、と言うことを意味する。これらのセンターは他の図書館よりは収集雑誌の点数は多いが、その大学内部の需要に十分応えるためにも他の図書館の相互貸借に依存しなければならない存在であって、その意味で基本的にはやはり一つの大学図書館なのである。この点が西ドイツの専門図書館とも異っている。

3　外国雑誌センターの提供サービスの現状

　前述の通り各センターはそれ自身総合的に逐次刊行物を揃えているわけではなく、かつ一つの領域を複数館で分担しているから、こ

れらの資料を広く共同利用するためには、言うまでもなくどのセンターが何を所蔵しているかの情報を整備することが不可欠の要件である。全国的な総合目録として『学術雑誌総合目録』欧文編1980年（ちなみに和文編1984年が発行されている。）が学術情報センターから刊行されているが、これは刊行年の間隔が長く、新しい収集雑誌の情報源としては十分ではなかった。今日では学術情報センター（NACSIS）でこのデータベースのオンライン・サービスが行われているが。このような理由から雑誌センターでは早い時期から各センターで受け入れた逐次刊行物についての受入れリストを共同で刊行してきた。第1回のリスト（1980年）から第5回（1987年）まで刊行され、これには各センターの全受入れタイトルが収録されている。これらのリストは言うまでもなく、全国の大学に配布されている。

　これらのセンターは外部に対しどれだけサービスをしているか。9センターで外部から受付けた文献複写件数の合計は、1987年度で約400,000件である[7]。この件数はセンターが受付けたすべてであって、その内センターとしての「補完的」資料がどの程度を占めているかは正確な全体的調査がないので不明である。一つの報告によれば、複写件数の中での補完的資料の占める割合は48％で、その「利用が予想以上に高い」という。[8]

　各センターのサービス状況については、かなりの差が見られる。これは各領域における情報利用の特性、大学界以外の機関における資源蓄積状況によると想像されるが、4つの領域のセンターで最も利用が高いのは医学関係である。日本の医学研究における大学の医学図書館の占める役割から、このことは当然とも言えるのである。米国の事情と異なり全国的な中心となる医学図書館がないこと、医学研究の中心は大学における医学部及びその病院であること、一般的に言って医学部ではその図書館の整備に相対的に熱心であったことがその背景として考えられる。工学・農学系では大学以外の部門における研究活動もさかんで、それに必要な資料整備もそれなりに行われてきたことにより、全国的に見た場合大学界に対する情報依存度が相対的に低い、と考えられる。

　英国のBLDSCは、外国に対しても高い満足度のサービスをしていることで有名である。1978/79年度にはＤＳＣが外国から受け付けた複写件数約520,000件のうち、日本が約7％（36,000件）を占めるとされている[9]。その後、1986/87では日本は"the largest user"になっている[10]。この間日本ではＤＳＣクーポンが民間の流通経路を通じて全国の機関において容易に入手できるようになったことも、

この利用の拡大に貢献したかもしれない。いずれにせよ、常々私自身ＤＳＣの経営力の巧みさに敬意を払っており、その柔軟な姿勢が日本の当局や図書館においても採用されることを強く期待するものである。

しかし日本の外国雑誌センターが、日本の図書館の対外国依存の軽減に全く貢献しなかったのであろうか。ここに一つのデータがある[11]。

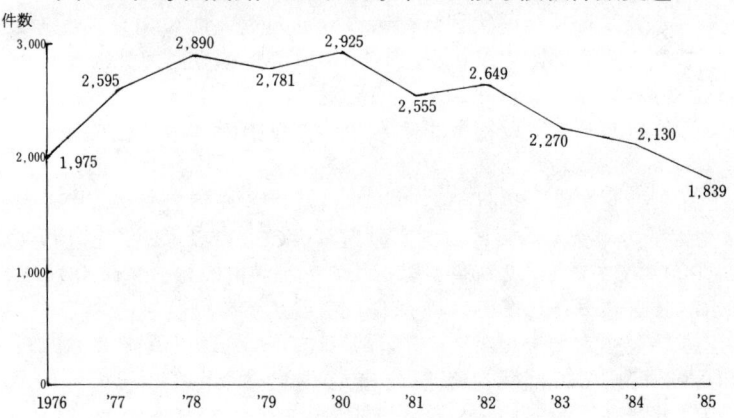

図2　医学図書館における海外への複写依頼件数変遷

日本の医学図書館は永年米国国立医学図書館の好意ある協力により複写サービスを受けてきた。多くの医学図書館員はこのことに感謝の念を抱いている。近年ＤＳＣを利用する館も増加しているであろう。これらの海外図書館への依存度は、大学の医学図書館について見る限り、明らかに外国雑誌センターの効果が明らかである。

5　今後の課題

外国雑誌センターの発足から10年を経過した。当局ではそれ以前に国立学術図書館の設置の素案が考えられたと聞いているが、広い支持を得られないままその企画は潰えた。そのような困難な状況下で、日本の学術資料整備の実を少しでも高めるための最もプラグマティックな方策として、当局は既存の資源の補完的機能を実現する道を選んだのである。これに要する資料購入費として年間4億6,400万円（$3.6Mill）(1987年度) が措置された。これはこの種の行政措置としては異例な効率的な方法であったかもしれない。その措置に見合う以上の効果があがりつつあると、私は確信している。言うまでもなく、そのためにはセンターとしての機能を併せ担うことになった図書館の積極的かつ献身的な努力があったことを忘れてはなら

ない。
　しかし一方、この補完的機能にもそれなりの問題点が存することも見逃せない。補完的機能が成立するのは、安定した根幹的機能が存在することが前提である。近年の出版物の値上がりに対し各図書館の予算の横ばい現象によってかなりの購読中止が行われるようになった。根幹が不安定になったのである。この状況を背景としてセンター・グループは、1986年あらためて他の国立大学で解約した雑誌のタイトルを調査し、必要な追加を行った[12]。補完的機能にとどまる限り、このような見直し作業は不可避なことであり、その結果センターでの収集に一貫性を欠くおそれが出てくる。従って今後は長期的展望に立って、「補完的」から、より「総合的」収集へと拡大を図っていく必要がある。
　補完的・分散的収集方式は、すべての構成機関の総合力によって完結するわけであるから、その各機関が所蔵する資料の所在情報が不可欠の前提である。その情報を蓄積、提供する役割を担っているのが学術情報センターである。最終的な目標はオンライン提供であるが、全国の図書館ネットワークが完成するのは時間の要することである。『学術雑誌総合目録』のオンライン検索サービスはすでに実施されている。これと平行してオンライン・チェックイン・システムもすでに実施されている。それと同時に有効なILLシステムが開発されることが望ましい。このようなシステムが展開すればする程、外国雑誌センターはその本来の機能を十全に発揮することになろう。
　国内での充足率が高まれば、国際的協力の必要は低下するであろうか。恐らく逆に高まってくると想像される。ローカルな出版物はその該当国でなければ、多くの場合収集不可能である。国の分野別の中央図書館（例えば米国のNLMなど）の存在する場合はともかく日本のようにそのような図書館が存在しないところにおいては、ILLの高度化のためにはその国における所在情報（ユニオン・カタログ）が必要である。このようなデータベースについては相互に提供できるならば、それぞれの国の書誌情報センター（Bibliographic Utilities）でサービスすることが可能であろう。あるいはすでに国際的通信ネットワークは発展しており、これによって相互に相手方のデータベース検索が技術的には可能となっている。一方、すでに日米間には電子メール・サービスも実施されている。このように情報技術は進展し、いろいろな潜在的可能性が高まっている。これをたとえれば、高速道路が整備されたと同じことである。問題はその上を走る自動車をいかに作り出すか、そしてそれらを走らせるための

メカニズムをどう作るか、という点にある。

　情報源は多様化している。電子出版などの新技術の問題は別として、我々が新しい情報の主要な根源としてきた図書、雑誌の他に、いわゆる grey literature の重要度が高まっている。これらの資料を体系的に収集している機関は世界的に見て未だ多くない。これらの資料収集は果たして体系的収集が可能だろうか。また、その十分な所在情報システムを形成するためには新たな発想が必要かも知れない。

引用文献
(1)　文部省学術国際局学術情報課編『昭和61年度大学図書館実態調査結果報告』、昭和62年3月。
(2)　同上
(3)　岩本　博「医学図書館員研究集会報告原稿」1986（未公刊）
(4)　今川敏男他「理工学系外国雑誌センター館としての10年ー現状と課題」（『大学図書館研究』30、p.p.91〜94、1987。）
(5)　尾崎達助「農学系外国雑誌センター館の現状」（『大学図書館研究』30、p.84、1987。）
(6)　山田幸彦「社会科学系拠点図書館の外国雑誌収集について――一橋大学附属図書館の現況と課題」（『大学図書館研究』29、p.p.63〜65、1986。）
(7)　外国雑誌センター館会議（昭和63年3月）資料（未公刊）
(8)　尾崎達助　同上、p.p.85〜86。
(9)　The British Library Annual Report　1978/79
(10)　The BLDSC Annual Report　1986/87
(11)　福留武士「外国雑誌センター館の活動」（『昭和62年度大学図書館職員講習会テキスト』p.58）
(12)　今川敏男　同上、p.p.94〜95

II　日本における図書館情報ネットワークの特色
図書館情報ネットワークの発展

　日本における図書館情報ネットワークは、社会や産業界における類似の領域の発展に比べて甚だ遅れて発展し、まだ4年の歴史を有しているにすぎない。それでは図書館業務の電算化が遅かったかと言うと、必ずしもそうではないが、その電算化はきわめてローカル性の強いシステムとして導入されてきた。これは、日本の図書館業務の処理態様が全国的規模において標準化が進んでいなかったこと、目録作成が漢字処理の技術的困難さのために当初の機械化のメニュ

ーから外され、貸出手続や受入・支払などの会計処理など、どちらかと言うと事務的な側面での機械化が主要領域であったことがその主要な理由であった。目録作成——この図書館サービスの最も基本的基盤をなす作業——が機械化の対象となったのはNACSIS（学術情報センター及びその前身）が設置され、当面は日本における唯一の米国型の書誌ユーティリティ機能を果たすようになって以来と言うことができる。

学術情報ネットワークの設置

このNACSIS（昭和61年度創設）は大学界における情報流通のための多目的ユーティリティとして設置された。従って、NACSISにとって書誌ユーティリティ事業はその主要な機能の一つではあるが、それ以外に二次情報データベースによる情報検索サービス、データベース作成などを行う総合的「大学共同利用」サービス・センターである。従ってNACSISは、大学の研究者や図書館員が、二次情報検索により求める研究に関する報告が、世の中に「存在」するかどうかを知るとともに、その情報を収載する資料（出版物）がどの図書館に所蔵されているのかの「所在」を確認し、資料の入手（document delivery）（近い将来、高速ファクシミリにより）を図ることができるという、一貫した情報サービスをおこなうことができる手段を提供するようデザインされたものである。

そのような情報の通信路をNACSISは専用回線により提供する。この通信網はまた、国内のいくつかの地区に置かれたスーパーコンピュータやその他のコンピュータ資源を各大学からリアルタイムで利用することができるようにしている。また、付加価値サービスとして研究者の端末機間の電子メール（メッセージ交換）が行える。この回線は現在日本列島の北から南まで幹線と中継点（Nodes）を設置しており、将来年次的にそのNodesを介して幹線に接続する各地の大学への支線を展開する計画である。日本の通信料金は米国に比べて高く、全国の大学間のデータ通信料を個別的に支弁するよりも一元的にディジタル回線を借り上げた方が経済的なのである。この通信網は図書館を含めた大学間の研究者その他の関係者が大学の活動にかかわる各種の情報処理・交換を行うための多目的学術情報専用VANであり、ユーザはこのネットワークをきわめて経済的に利用できる。

NACSISの目録システムに参加する図書館は、それぞれの目録情報をNACSISからダウンロードにより自前のコンピュータ（それが大学のコンピュータ・センターであれ図書館の専用コンピュータ

であれ）のファイルに取り込み、それを OPAC として学内 LAN あるいは構内電話網を通じて各研究室から検索できる。またその研究者が該当大学の OPAC で発見できず、全国総合目録（NACSIS ファイル）を見たい場合は、切り換えて NACSIS に接続する。このようなシステムの最終的な姿にまで発展している大学は未だ多くはないが、各大学のコンピュータ資源等の条件が許せば、これを実現することはそれ程困難ではない。

　NACSIS 通信網の今一つの特徴は多種メーカーのコンピュータ接続も可能としていることである。日本においてはメイン・フレーム・メーカーは IBM を含め数社が相拮抗した市場占有率を持っている。従って大学間ネットワークを構成するためには何よりもこれらの異機種間接続が基本的条件になっている。

　以上のように日本における図書館情報ネットワークは、BU（Bibliographic Utility）と図書館との独立したものではなく、より多くの目的をもつネットワークの一つの利用形態をなしており、図書館とそのユーザである研究者等とが共有するユーティリティである点が大きな特色をなしていると言うことができよう。

　北米及び欧州には国内的あるいは国際的なアカデミックの研究ネットワークが存在するが、日本の学術情報ネットワークは将来これらの外国のネットワークと接続することが計画されており、1989年1月にはワシントンの NSF に、先ずネットワークの回線を伸ばすことができた。当面この回線は NSF に置かれる端末から NACSIS のデータベースにアクセスが可能とするほか、CS・NET と接続し研究者間の電子メール交換が可能となる。さらに近い将来このネットワークを通じて米国内の大学から直接 NACSIS データベースを検索できるようになろう。

NACSIS 目録所在情報システムの入力状況

　1988年12月現在の NACSIS の目録所在情報システム（CAT）に参加している大学は78（国立62、私立16）であり、入力件数は図書のデータ約125万件（書誌レコード65万件）である。なお、逐次刊行物のデータについては約123万件（書誌レコード14万件）。1988年度中に参加大学は90に達する予定である。

"学術情報システム"と大学図書館
―期待と問題点―

大 野 公 男

はじめに

　北海道大学における私の職務は、理学部において量子化学の研究と教育に従事することで、附属図書館長に併任されたのは僅か3年半ほど前のことである。もともとは物理の教育を受けた者で、図書館学や図書館の管理にはずぶの素人であり、これらの分野の専門家の前で報告をするのは忸怩たる思いをせざるを得ない。この報告は図書館員の立場ではなく、図書館の一利用者の立場からのものであることを初めにお断りし、お許しを願っておく。数年前までは日本の大学図書館は全く個々にその業務を行ってきたといってよかろう。唯一の例外は図書館間の貸借（ILL）だが、その方法たるや他館の冊子体目録――しばしば数年から10年も古いもの――または電話で所在を知り、郵便で申し込み、郵便で現物が送られてくるという古典的なものであった。前講演者が述べられたように約10年前から学術雑誌については拠点図書館の制度が発足し、雑誌の収集体制については相当改善がされてきたが、ILLの方法についてはやはり旧態依然としていた。

　"学術情報の爆発"すなわち、1960年代の中頃に起った学術情報の量的な拡大と質的な多様化に対して、個々の大学図書館では対応する方策が全く立たなかった。当然急速に発展中であった計算機と通信技術の利用が考えられ、図書館業務の機械化とネットワーク化が討議されたが、大学図書館側の反応は鈍かった。現に1973年に出た学術審議会の第3次答申では、第2図書館システムという言葉が登場する。その意味するところは、従来の図書館の慣性が余りに大きいので、そのネットワーク化はあきらめて、別に新たにネットワークを作ろうということであったと思われる。

新しい"学術情報システム"

　第3次答申から7年後、1980年に出された学術審議会の答申では、第2図書館システムという考え方を捨て、既存の大学図書館、計算機センター等をネットワーク化し、かつその中心となる機関として"学術情報センター"を設置しようという提言を行った。その機能は、(1)連絡・調整、(2)計画、(3) 1次情報の所在を含むデータベースのサービス、(4)研究・開発、(5)教育・訓練である。

このセンターはいくつかの過程を経て、1986年に正式に発足した。政府の経費節減・予算圧縮の厳しい状況の下にもかかわらず、このセンターは着々と発展しつつある。大学図書館との関係についてみると、1988年3月末の時点で、61の大学図書館が学術情報センターに接続して、共同して書誌・所在情報のデータベースの構築に当っている。61図書館の内訳は国立が49、私立が12である。国立大学図書館の接続数は今後1年間にさらに11増加して60になる予定で、総数95の国立大学の60％以上がこのネットワークに参加することになる。一方公立大学の数は52だが参加館の数は0、私立大学334校で参加館12というのは淋しい。参加図書館の数が急速には増加しないのは、設備費と通信費がかかり、経費の効率的利用という点に問題があるためと考えられる。このうち通信費については1987年から大きな変化が起こっている。学術情報センター（NACSIS）が、東京大学から大阪大学までの間にディジタル回線を借り上げて、学術情報VANの建設を始めたのである。1988年初めには、この学術情報VANは北は北海道大学まで南は九州大学まで延び、さらに1989年には、新潟、群馬、筑波、千葉、神戸、鹿児島の各大学に広がっていくことが予定されている。このVANにつながる各大学間の通信料は大学が負担しなくてよいので、その経済的影響は極めて大きい。

　NACSISにおけるデータベースの構築の現況については、安達氏および倉橋氏から既に報告がなされたが、その中で触れられた図書目録の遡及入力について、それが終るまでにどの位の年数が必要かということについて、極めて粗っぽい推定をここで試みてみたい。1988年6月末における学術情報センターの図書総合目録の所蔵登録件数は60万件である。これは日本の大学図書館の蔵書総数1億5千万冊の0.4％に過ぎない。これを構築するのに要した実質的な作業期間は約1年であるから、最も単純に考えると250年という途方もない長い年月がかかることになるが、この計算ですら正しいとは思われない。大学の蔵書は1年間に約670万冊ずつ増加するからである。ここで言っている遡及入力の終了とは大学図書館の蔵書のすべての書誌・所在情報が学術情報センターのファイルにおさまることであるが、幸いなことに学術情報センターの図書総合目録書誌・所在データベースは、ある書誌が登録されていると、所在情報を比較的簡単に（書誌を登録するに要する時間の数分の1ないし10分の1程度の時間で）付加することができるように設計されている。従って独立な書誌情報の遡及入力が終了する（正確には大部分が終る*）というのは大きな意味を持つ。その作業に要する年月の予想を試みたい。

　大学図書館の1億5千万冊の蔵書中、独立な書誌（以下タイトル

と呼ぶ）がいくつあるかを、極めて大胆な仮定を用いて推定してみると430万という数字が得られる（注参照）。同上の仮定を用いて大学図書館が毎年受け入れる図書670万冊の独立なタイトル数を推定すると約10万となる。一方最近6ヶ月間に学術情報センターで入力されているタイトル数から推定すると、年間の登録タイトル数は約30万であって、これらの数値を用いると、"終了"までの年数は23年ということになる。以上の計算に含まれている仮定は非常に大胆なものであり、因子2位の範囲で変わるかも知れないが、この程度の年数で、書誌の遡及入力が一応"終了"するというのは、大学図書館にとって明るい希望と言えよう。なお、以上の推定は現在行われていてデータが得られるオンライン方式による入力のみによることを仮定しており、現在計画され既に部分的には実行されているバッチ方式による遡及入力が併用されれば、さらに大幅に"終了"までの年数が短縮されよう。

このようにして数年前まで個々別々だった大学図書館はネットワーク化されつつあり、図書・雑誌の事務処理も次々に電算化され、今やカードレスの時代となって、図書カードの作成（日本では過去においては手書きが多かった）と配列に要する人力が大幅に減少する途が開けた。研究・教育に携わる人々に必要又は有用な情報を発見し、提供するという大学図書館の本来の使命に向かって大きく前進する基盤が整いつつあると言ってよかろう。

"学術情報システム"の将来の課題

ここでは一大学教官として、"学術情報システム"や図書館の未来に対する期待や問題点を述べてみたい。

現在の時点では、学術情報センターおよび各大学図書館にあるデータベースを検索しうる端末の数が極めて少ない。条件の良い大学においてさえも、我々は各学部の図書室まで行かなければ検索ができない。一方各研究室には、各種の目的に使用するミニ・コンピュータが数多く存在する。これらの研究室にある端末からデータベースの検索ができればどんなに便利になるかわからない。そのためには、少なくとも二つの条件が満たされる必要がある。一つは学内回線網の整備であり、もう一つは同時継続の端末数の増加にホスト・コンピュータが対応できることである。日本の多くの大学で電話回線網には余裕がなくなっているので、学内ローカル・エリアネットワーク（campus LAN）の建設が不可欠であり、現に東京大学、京都大学、東北大学に予算措置が講じられ、キャンパスLANが建設中である。他のいくつかの大学からも強い希望が出ている。対応でき

る同時接続の端末数は、現在学術情報センターで約350、大学図書館では最大のところでも100程度なので、大幅な能力のレベル・アップをしなければならない。

　第2の問題として1次情報の入手の問題がある。ほしい1次情報の所在が判っても、それが他大学図書館の所蔵であった場合、なるべく迅速にその資料を入手できるようにするシステムが当然望まれる。望ましいのは、すべての1次情報を光ディスクに収納しておいて、オンラインで各大学に送り、そこでハードコピーをとる方法であろう。筆者はこの分野の専門家ではないが、実現は可能であることが技術的には分かっており、問題は実用化にあると聞いている。現在の時点では高額の費用を要するであろうが、こういう新技術の普及度がある程度に達すると、急速に費用も低下するのが普通であるので、その普及が望まれる。

　第3の、より基本的な課題としては、書誌情報の〝深さ〟すなわち詳しさの問題がある。まず雑誌に発表されている論文について述べる。現在は *Current Contents* 等で、読みたい論文の出ている雑誌名、巻、号、発行年を知り、雑誌の所在情報データベースで検索するという方法が普通であろう。この際、キーワードまたは文のタイトル中に現われる術語を使った検索式を使って検索ができれば能率は著しく向上しよう。

　キーワードまたはタイトルだけでは情報が不十分となると、人間が論文の内容を調べてデータベースを作る以外に方策はないように思われる。その対象は当然比較的狭い分野に限定される。一つの例をあげよう。筆者の専門は量子化学と呼ばれる分野であるが、この分野では日本の研究者グループが中心となり、大学院生および少数の外国人研究者の協力を得て、量子化学文献データベースが作られている。現在1978年から1987年までの量子化学のいわゆる非経験的計算の載っている文献約12,000を収録したデータベースが作られており、今後も継続する計画である。このデータベースは冊子体としても刊行されているが、同時に全データと DBMS が MT に収められ、提供されている。これを計算機に入力しておけばオンライン検索が可能である。この種の専門分野別文献データベースの数は今後も増えていくことが予想される。

　図書については、このデータベースの〝深さ〟の問題はより深刻である。例えば〝菊と刀〟という書名からその本の内容を推察するのは不可能だし、特に人文・社会科学分野の図書には、書名からだけで内容を知ることが難しい図書が多いように思われる。そこで、これはと思う書名があったとき、さらにその図書の各章、できれば

序文が画面に表示されるようになれば極めて便利なことは疑いをいれない。この実現は極めて大規模な事業となり、必要な経費も多額にのぼろうが、将来的には実現の可能性はかなり大きいと思われる。

　以上〝学術情報システム〟の今後当面するであろう問題について、思いつくままにそのいくつかをあげてきたが、いずれの問題についてもその解決には国際間の協力が必要になろう。現在通信とコンピューター技術において先頭を切っているのは、アメリカ、ヨーロッパ諸国及び日本である。アメリカと日本の、学術研究の中心である大学、そしてその大学において学術情報の流通・保存に責任を持つ大学図書館が、互いに連携・連絡し、数多くの共通の課題の解決に協力していくことは極めて重要と考える。

おわりに

　研究というのはいうまでもなく新しい知識を得ることである。従ってある知識が人類にとって既知であるか否かを予め知ることは、研究を始めるに当って基本的に重要なことである。一方実用のためにある知識を得たい時には事情が異なる。例えばある物質の性質の値を知りたい場合には、文献で調べたりするよりも、実験をしたり、計算をしたりして値を知る方が時間的にも早いし、経済的であるということはあり得ることである。しかしそうして得られた知識は、人類の持つ知識の総量を増やすことにはならない。これが研究と単なる情報の取得との基本的な相違である。現在までに人類の持っている知識を能率的に知ることは、後者にとっては単に望ましい条件に過ぎないが前者にとっては不可欠の要件となる。

　大学図書館をそういう観点で見てみると、到着すべき目標は無限のかなたにあるように思えるが、それを行いうる機関はまた大学図書館しかあり得ないと思われる。

　（注）　日本の大学図書館が所蔵する独立なタイトル数の推定

　日本の466の大学図書館の中で、旧帝国大学とよばれる7大学の図書館の規模が飛びぬけて大きい。これら7図書館の蔵書数は、全大学図書館の総数の約6分の1に達する。

　　仮定A　7大学以外の図書館の蔵書はすべて重複とみなす。
一大学内の重複率は大学の規模によって異なり、大きければ大きいほど重複率は大きくなろうが、北大の場合約1.3である。

　　仮定B　7大学の大学内重複率は1.3とする。
7大学間の重複率の推定は困難な問題だが、ここでは以下の方法を

とる。年間で最小の購入数の大学での購入のタイトルの重複率を7と仮定する。次に少ない購入数の大学で購入したタイトルの重複率を6とする。以下同様に仮定して、全体として平均の重複率を求めると4となる。

　　仮定C　7大学の大学間重複率は4とする。
以上の仮定A、B、Cを用いると、日本の大学図書館蔵書（総数1億5千万冊）のうち独立なタイトル数は430万、1年間の受け入れ図書（総数670万）のうち独立タイトル数は10万となる。

科学技術情報の交流と専門図書館の協力

宮 川 隆 泰

専門図書館とはなにか

　日米両国は、歴史的にみて専門図書館が比較的早くから発達した国である。米国では今世紀はじめから、日本でも部分的には第一次大戦後から、本格的には第二次大戦後から専門図書館の活動がはじまっている。

　ここで専門図書館とはつぎのように定義されている。

　日本の定義：「専門図書館とは、特定分野についての情報資料を収集・整理・保管し、利用者にたいし情報提供するために設けられた官公庁、特殊法人、民間企業体、大学、学協会、独立調査機関などの内部の専門組織、ならびに上記サービスを主たる業務とする独立機関をいう。海外ではこれらをinformation center, information services, special libraryなどと呼ぶ」（専門図書館協議会調査統計委員会）[1]。したがって、政府機関や地方自治体など公的機関内に設けられている資料担当部門や民間企業体の情報管理部門、さらには特定主題分野に専門化している大学の学部図書館や大学附置研究所図書室など、広い範囲の施設が専門図書館の中にはふくまれている。

　米国の定義：「ここで専門図書館とは、情報を収集・管理、提供し、原則として各種の媒体と方式によって専門的な利用者にサービスを提供するために、(a)個人、企業、団体、政府機関その他のグループによって維持されている図書館、もしくは情報センター、もしくは、(b)特定の図書館内の特殊コレクションあるいは部門別コレクション、を指す」（専門図書館協会規約第2条第1項）[2]。

　日米両国とも定義の表現はやや異なるが、内容は類似している。それでは現実には両国で存在する専門図書館はどのようなものであろうか。同一の基準でこれを比較できるデータはないが、両国の専門図書館協議会作成のデータをもとに、専門図書館の設置母体の構成をみると、以下のとおりである。

　まず日本では専門図書館協議会（1952年設立）の加盟会員数は670（1988年3月末現在）である。専門図書館協議会（以下専図協と略す）は、個人加盟ではなく機関加盟を原則としている。この専

図協では、この会員機関をふくめた全国の専門図書館の活動について、3年置きに実態調査を実施している。その最新の調査（1987年12月現在）によれば、日本の専門図書館の総数は2,116であり、その種類別構成は第1表のとおりである。これによると中央各省庁や地方自治体の附属機関が設置する資料室・図書室が全体の36％、民間企業内の資料・情報管理セクションが28％、大学および同附置研究所内の図書館などが22％、学協会・団体などに設置されているものが13％となっている。

つぎに米国専門図書館協会（Special Libraries Association）（1909年設立）によれば、その会員の所属機関の分布は第2表のとおりである。米国では日本とちがって個人加盟が原則であり、本表はその会員の組織別構成である。日本とは基準がちがうのでただちに比較することは適当ではない。しかし米国専門図書館協会の会員構成は、半分が民間企業体であり、約20％が大学研究機関、公共団体と政府機関が25％となっている。

日米両国の専門図書館の活動を相互に比較したことがないので厳密なことは言えないが、この表面的な比較からみる限り、両者のあいだに本質的な相違はないと判断しても差支えないであろう。

第1表　日本の専門図書館の設置母体別構成比

(1987)

設置母体	館　数	構成比（％）
1．立法・行政・司法機関	38	1.8
2．各省庁附属機関	161	7.6
3．公共団体・政府機関	48	2.2
4．地方自治体	511	24.1
5．大学附置研究所	454	21.5
6．学協会・団体	276	13.0
7．民間企業体	599	28.4
8．外国政府機関	29	1.3
合　　計	2,116	100.0

資料：専門図書館協議会『専門情報機関総覧』1988年版より

第2表　米国専門図書館協議会会員の所属組織構成比

所属組織	構成比（％）
1．民間企業	49.0
2．大学・研究機関	18.0

3．公共団体		15.0
4．政府機関		10.0
5．自　営		5.0
6．その他		1.0
合　　　　計		100.0

資料：David Bender

専門図書館と大学図書館の協力関係

　日本では、図書館の館種を超えた相互協力関係はまだ未発達である。これは本来の機能の相違に加えて、行政制度上の制約があるためである。したがって館種を超えた図書館ネットワークはまだ形成されていない。現実に大学図書館と専門図書館の協力関係は、ごく少数の特定の分野もしくは特定の機関のあいだで部分的に行われているにすぎない。専門図書館の側からみると、相互貸借はレファレンスなどで業務上利用している外部機関としてもっとも多くあげられているのが政府系情報サービス機関（日本科学技術情報センター、日本特許情報機構、ジェトロ他）と国立国会図書館で、そのつぎに大学図書館があげられている（第3表）。ただし大学附置研究所が大学図書館を利用するのは当然であるので、これをのぞくと、各政府機関や民間企業体のうちで、なんらかの形で大学図書館と関係をもっているところは、前者で3割、後者で2割となっている。今後この必要性が高まるかどうかは、相互協力の内容が不明なので、いまの段階では判断できない。

　アメリカにおいて大学図書館と専門図書館の協力関係がどのように展開されているかは、興味ある問題であるが、その実情把握は今後の課題であろう。

第3表　大学図書館を利用している専門図書館数

(1987)

設　置　母　体	大学図書館を利用	％
1．立法・行政・司法機関	0	0.0
2．各省庁附属機関	50	31.0
3．公共団体附属機関	7	14.6
4．地方自治体	78	15.3
5．大学附置研究所	342	75.3
6．学協会・団体	52	18.8

7．民間企業体	124	20.7
8．外国政府機関	5	17.2
合　　　計	658	31.3

注：利用比率数は各設置母体別専門図書館数に対する大学図書館利用比

資料：『専門情報機関総覧』1988年版より作成

日米間における科学技術情報の流通について

今回の会議の主題は「グローバルな情報流通に向けての日米大学図書館協力の強化」である。ここで米国からの国外へ向けての情報の流れと、日本から外国へ向けての情報流通を比較すると、米国は長年にわたって科学技術情報の諸外国への供給者としての役割を果たしてきたのにたいして、日本は近年ようやく科学技術情報の重要な発生源として国際的に認識されはじめたのである。これにしたがい日本からの科学技術情報の外国への提供について、最近は国際的な関心が高まってきた。

外国におけるこのような日本科学技術情報の収集と利用についての努力は、1980年代に入り組織的に行われるようになった。アメリカを例にとると、米国商務省科学技術情報サービス局（NTIS）やエネルギー省技術情報センター（DOE/TIC）などの連邦政府機関は、すでに1980年代のはじめから、通産省、JICST、国立国会図書館などの日本の公的情報サービス機関に対して、米側の日本情報収集努力への協力体制を確立する可能性を何回も打診していた。NTISは1981年より東京に日本科学技術情報収集の専任者をおき継続的に収集活動を実施してきた。また図書館と情報サービスの分野でも、1983年1月にマサチューセッツ工科大学（MIT）で日本科学技術情報に関するワークショップが開かれたのが最初で、その後いくつかの機関で同種の会議がくり返して開かれている。

一方、1980年代に入り、米国産業の国際競争力低下と対日貿易赤字を背景として、米国議会において、日本に対する経済的、技術的競争力をいかにして回復するかという問題が討議されるようになり、1984年3月には米国議会下院科学技術委員会で日本の科学技術情報の入手可能性についての公聴会が開かれるにいたった[3]。その後この種の公聴会は数回開催されている。さらに1986年6月には日本技術文献法（Japanese Technical Literature Act）が制定され、連邦政府が日本技術文献の収集・評価・翻訳などを本格的に行うことになった。こうして日米間の科学技術情報流通の問題は、経済的・政治

的交渉事項に増幅されてしまったのである。

　米側がここで提起している問題は、日本で発生している科学技術や経済産業に関する情報が、米側からはアクセスしにくいという点である。しかし、ここではどのような分野のどのような形態の情報が、どのような利用者にとってアクセスしにくいのか、ということは明らかにされてはいない。本来このことが明からにされないと、この問題についての対応策をたてることはむずかしい。しかし、現在のところ問題は一般論の次元で討議されていて、特定の専門分野の情報、あるいは特定の形態の情報、さらには特定のユーザーのニーズに対応する情報というふうに具体的に論じられてはいない。米側からみてアクセスしやすい日本情報もあるであろうし、アクセスしにくいものもあるであろう。ここではきわめて一般的な次元での論議であることを前提として、日本の専門図書館の立場からみた問題に対する認識と、対応策の現状について述べておきたい。

　日本情報が外国からアクセスしにくい第1の理由は言語障壁である。この言語能力の不均衡を改善することが、問題を根本的に解決するうえでもっとも基本的なことであるが、これには長い時間がかかる。翻訳は有効な手段であるが、これはあくまでも次善の解決策でしかない。

　第2は特定の形態の情報について、日本側にそれらを収集、管理、提供する制度がないものがあることである。たとえば博士論文の索引・抄録のデータベースや、いわゆる「灰色文献」のデータベースは日本ではようやく最近部分的に作成されはじめたばかりである。それらは包括的・遡及的な検索にたえ得るものではない。

　第3の理由は、、日本の科学技術情報が国際的に利用可能な情報ネットワークのうえに、まだ充分のっていないことである。

　このような状況に対しては、日本側でも近年かなりの改善の努力を重ねている。いま商用データベースを例にとると日本で制作されている各種のデータベースのうち、第三者に有償で提供されている商用データベースは、425件である（1987年10月1日現在）[4]。これらは大部分日本語で日本国内専用のネットワークを通してサービスされているのであるが、ここ数年のあいだに英語化された件数、オンライン形態もしくはオフライン形態で外国に向けて提供され始めた件数も、次第にふえてきている（第4表）[5]。しかしながらこの件数を、海外から日本国内に輸入されて国内で商業的に利用できる外国製データベース件数と比較すると、両者のあいだにはまだ著しい開きがある（第5表）。

第4表　海外に提供されている日本製データベース

（単位：件）

言語＼年・提供方式	1987 オンライン	1987 オフライン	1987 計	1988 オンライン	1988 オフライン	1988 計
日本語	5	2	7	22	6	28
英語	10	6	16	17	3	20
日本語・英語	3	2	5	28	7	35
合計	18	10	28	67	16	83

注：1）オフライン形態には、磁気テープ、フロッピーディスク、CD/ROMによる提供をふくむ。
　　2）調査時点、1987年3月1日、1988年7月31日。
　　3）調査対象は海外に有償で商業用に提供されているデータベースのみである。
資料：データベース振興センター『データベース白書』より作成。

第5表　日本における商用データベースの輸出と輸入

（単位：件数）

	1982	83	84	85	86	87
日本へ輸入される外国製データベース	334	552	725	1,008	1,187	1,370
日本から輸出される国産データベース	n.a.	n.a.	n.a.	n.a.	28	83

資料：データベース振興センターおよび日本データベース協会の資料より作成

　これらは科学技術、経済ビジネスなどすべての分野における文献型、ファクト型の商用データベースの全体に関するものである。また、この中には政府機関相互間や学協会相互間の国際交換によるものは含まれていない。したがって、この数字は日本をめぐる情報交流のごく一部分を示すものである。しかし、いずれにせよ、日本から外国の各種データベースのアクセスと、外国から日本の各種データベースへのアクセスとのあいだには、まだ大きな格差があることがわかる。
　日本側関係機関・民間企業ともに国産データベースの対外提供体制の強化を進めているので、このような状況は今後一層改善されて

いくであろう。ただ実際にこのようにして外国に提供された日本製各種データベースが、どのように外国の利用者に使われているのかは、詳細にはわかっていない。海外でのニーズを具体的に把握し、これに適合する対応策をつくり出していくことが今後の課題である。また日米両国の専門図書館協議会は、これ迄も相互に交流を行ってきたが、今後これを一層緊密なものにしていくことが重要である。

〈注〉
(1)　専門図書館協議会編『専門情報機関総覧』1988, 1988年5月, 東京

(2)　Special Libraries Association, Bylaws, revised as of August 14, 1974, Article II, Membership.
(3)　The Availability of Japanese Scientific and Technical Information in the United States, Hearings before the Subcommittee on Science, Research and Technology of the Committee on Science and Technology, House of Representatives, 98th Congress, 2nd Session, March 6, 7, 1984, USGPO, Washington DC, 1984.
(4)　通商産業省『データベース台帳総覧』昭和62年版.
(5)　Database Promotion Center : Database Services in Japan ; The Outline of Database White paper 1988, TOKYO.

閉会の辞

黒 田 晴 雄

　1988年10月3月から4日間にかけて開催されてきた第4回日米大学図書館会議は、予定のプログラムを終了し、ここにその幕を閉じることになりました。日本側実行委員会委員長として、日本からの参加者一同を代表して、本会議の準備をして下さった米国図書館協会日米図書館連絡委員会の皆様、特に、米国側実行委員会委員長のWelch博士に心から感謝申し上げる次第です。また、本会議を主催し、この美しい、そして、建築学的に記念すべき素晴らしい建物を会場に提供して下さったJohnson Foundation に感謝の意を呈します。本会議に財政的援助を与えられた、米国図書館協会ならびに日米友好基金にも感謝いたします。また、日本からの参加者が本会議に出席するにあたっては、文部省をはじめ、日本電子工業振興会、洋書輸入協会その他の各方面からの財政的援助があったことを申し上げ、日本側の参加者として感謝の意を呈したいと思います。

　本会議の初めに行われたプログレスレポートで、Welch博士も山崎教授も述べられましたように、第3回の会議が開催されたのは1975年でありますから、それ以来実に13年の長い年月が経過しております。この間に、アメリカでも日本でも、大学図書館をめぐる状況にはさまざまな変化がありました。日本においても、大学図書館へのコンピュータの導入が活発化し、学術情報センターと連結して書誌情報データベースをオンラインで共同作成する作業が軌道に乗り始めました。資源の共同利用を目的とする本格的な図書館ネットワークの形成に向かって一歩づつ前進しています。また、学術情報の流通システム全体の整備も急速に進行しつつあります。13年ぶりに、開催された本会議で、両国の図書館の現状や図書館が抱えているいろいろな問題が紹介され、討議されたことは、今後の両国の大学図書館相互の協力を推進するための基盤を提供するものと信じます。

　今回の会議では、テーマをかなり具体的なものに絞り、また、各講演者の論文をあらかじめ参加者に配布したことによって、実り多い討議ができたように思います。私は、本年4月から、山崎教授の後を継いで東京大学附属図書館長に就任するとともに日本側の実行

委員会の委員長を勤めることになったのでありますが、それまでの期間に、山崎教授とWelch博士との間で、本会議の進め方について検討を重ねてきて下さいました。本会議の成功は、お二人のそのような努力のたまものであります。

　本会議では、日米双方の参加者の間でかなり率直な意見交換が行われました。意見が一致したところが多くある一方、双方の見解がかなり明瞭に対立したところもあります。両国の状況の相違が浮き彫りにされたところもあります。私は、本会議での率直な意見交換を通じて、両国の図書館関係者の相互理解が一層進展したと信じます。

　各ワーキング・グループの報告にまとめられた事項の中で具体化できるものについては、今後、本会議の日米双方の実行委員会がその実現に向けてしかるべき努力をすることになりましょう。また、本会議を通じて両国の図書館人が旧交を暖め、あるいは、新しい知己を得たことは、今後の両国の図書館の交流、協力にとって大きな意義をもっています。

　本会議を閉会するにあたり、この4日間にわたって熱心に討議された参加者の皆様全員に深い敬意を表するとともに、会議の準備ならびに運営に多大の努力をされた米国側の関係者の皆様に、重ねて厚く御礼申し上げる次第です。また、最後になりましたが、会議の期間連日にわたって通訳を勤めて下さった方々に感謝致します。

閉会の辞
―第4回日米大学図書館会議を顧みて―

Theodore F. Welch

　私の任務として、ここに第4回日米大学図書館会議の閉会を宣言致します。閉会を宣言するにあたって、この会議を無事に開催できたことを皆様とともに喜ぶ気持ちと、この理想的な環境にもっと長く浸っていることができないのが残念だという気持ちとが混じり合った、複雑な感慨を抱いております。

　過去の日米大学図書館会議に比較してこの会議では、対話が改善され、多大な進展があったことを、会議の共同議長としてうれしく思っております。討議への出席者各位の活発な参加、達成された相互理解のレベル、率直で的を絞った対話、そして、問題の所在を明確化し、その解決策を提示した点で、この会議はまさに今後到達すべき方向の道しるべとなるものであります。最初の会議以来この20年間に、日米両国図書館の関係はいろいろな面で成熟しました。疑いもなく、それにはさまざまな要因があります。世界経済のリーダーとしての日本の台頭、米国も含めて全ての国々が日本に関してもっと知る必要が生じていること、増大しつつある日本の学術的、技術的データベースを日本が提供し始めたこと、これらが両国の大学ならびに専門研究図書館の代表者が真の相互協力関係を確立すべく、今週ここに真剣な気持をもって集まった大きな理由であります。過去20年間に両国は、優れた情報源へのアクセスと研究の発展や社会的、経済的発展の間には深い関係があることに気がつきました。1975年に京都で開催された第3回会議以来10年余を経て、再びその間の進展を互いに報告し、関心を分かち合うことになったのです。Wingspead で開催される書誌サミットとしては2回目になるこの会議を援助され、また、そのために多大なご尽力を賜った、ジョンソン財団、日本の大学図書館国際連絡委員会、米国図書館協会日米図書館連絡委員会のメンバー、それに、日米友好基金に厚く感謝申し上げます。1972年の会議、すなわち、一連の日米大学図書館会議の第2回目の会議もジョンソン財団のお世話で、Frank Lloyd Wright 設計の Prairie Home の建築で有名なこの Wingspead 会議場で開かれました。

　今回の会議の立案と実施にたゆまざる努力を尽くされた日本側実行委員会委員長の黒田晴雄博士とその先任者の山崎弘郎博士に感謝

申し上げます。日本語の論文の英訳を担当してくださった Hisao Matsumoto 博士、Warren Tsuneishi 博士に、私達一同を代表してお礼申し上げます。また、米国側の論文の日本語訳を担当してくださった日本の方々にもお礼申し上げます。

この3日間の集中的な審議に、40以上の国公私立大学、それに、議会図書館、国立国会図書館、三菱総合研究所、米国専門図書館協会、学術情報センター（NACSIS）、研究図書館グループ（RLG）、オンラインコンピューター図書館センター（OCLC）等の多数の専門諸機関から、合わせて80名近い代表が参加されました。

今回の会議では、以前の会議とは少し会議の形態を変えました。全体会議の論文数は少なくして、部会討議に多くの時間をあてました。このことによって、交流を深めたり、深く討議すべき問題をはっきりさせることに時間を費やすことができました。したがって、二つの全体会議で発表された13件の印刷され翻訳された論文の内容は、2日半の間に行われた8の部会に振り分けて討議されました。両国の代表の多くは日米両国語を話しますので、直接に、あるいは、同時通訳によって議論が進行しました。

初めて日本を訪問した1954年以来私が持っている印象ですが、日本では「人的ネットワーク」が、過去20年間の日本を特徴付ける専門的ならびに工業的発展の重要な基盤となっています。図書館対図書館の関係について見ると、情報をめぐる全般的環境の中で図書館が有効に機能するために必要な相互依存を反映する方向にようやく動き始めたばかりです。

米国では、議会図書館と二つの主要な米国書誌情報機関、すなわち OCLC と RLIN（RLG's Research Libraries Information Network）が関与する電子ネットワークが、電算機を基盤とする図書館サービスの未曾有の発展の要であります。米国における図書館間の関係も、近年急激な変貌を遂げました。

この会議の重要な成果の一つは、日米の大学図書館のリーダーや書誌情報システムの専門家の間に人的な結びつきができたことです。この会議を媒介として築かれた「人と人」の相互理解は、今後継続される議論や技術交流について合意の達成に寄与するでありましょう。本会議の参加者の皆様は、日本で開催されることになるであろう第5回の会議を計画すること、ならびに、それまでの期間に特別な話題に関する会合を持つことを強く支持されました。かつて日米大学図書館会議は3年毎に開かれました。私も定期的に会議を開催すべしという意見に賛意を呈します。

この会議の参加者の多くは、米国における主要な日本コレクショ

ンを代表しています。日本における米国通貨の価値の急激な下落のために、これらの学術的コレクションの継続・発展の速度は、大抵の所で、年間数千冊のレベルから数百冊のレベルに低下してしまいました。米国で研究する価値がある3000以上の出版物が毎年日本で出版されています。昨年それだけの数の出版物を購入する目標を達成できた米国の大学は一ケ所だけです。最近系統的な収書がますます困難になりつつある現状を見ると、日米の図書館が互いに、可能な範囲で、それぞれの国における日米双方の出版物の収書活動を支援するように努力することが望ましいと考えます。米国の図書館では、日本の出版物の選書（入手）ならびに取扱いについての有資格者の不足に悩んでいます。特定主題についての図書館員が求められた場合に、日本の図書館員が米国の図書館に協力することが可能ならよいと思う次第です。このことは、日本の図書館員にそのような需要についての情報を流すこと、ならびに必要に応じて米国の図書館にスタッフを、多分短期で、派遣することを含みます。（求めに応じて米国の図書館に図書館員を送り出す場合には、その図書館員の経歴に不利にならないような配慮が必要でしょう。）この会議で人的交流の増大が論じられたことをうれしく思います。

　データベースの形成に関した議論は、書誌レコードのデータベース（出版物目録あるいは図書館目録データ）と科学・技術ならびに学術的定期刊行物、特許、研究報告、企業ならびに経済関係データ等のデータベースとを区別して扱う必要があるために、議論の進展がやや少な目でした。

　データベースの形成やそれによってもたらされる資源共有に関連したさまざまな問題について専門図書館との関係を日米両国がどのように考えるかは、今後の重要な課題だと思います。将来の会議では、両国の大学図書館の間でいま行っているような対話の中に専門図書館に関連した問題も組み込まれるべきでしょう。

　私は、第2回日米大学図書館会議（1972年）における日米両国の代表がここ Wingspead 会議場の土地に植樹をしたことを覚えております。残念ながら、地図が保存されていないので、その場所を特定できません。しかし、多分この会場の外の広い土地のどこかで、16年以上も前に植えられた木が真直ぐに高く成長していることと思います。そこにあるはずです。私もその植樹に参加しました。その時にそして今回われわれが共有した理念も根を大地に張り、両国図書館の協力の花を一杯に開くであろうと固く信じている次第です。その中にはこの会議の結果だとはっきりとは分からないものもあるでしょう。しかし、われわれの今回の努力と関連したものが多く含

まれているであろうことは明らかです。

皆様有難うございました。これで会議を閉会致します。

最終コミュニケ

　第4回日米大学図書館会議において、日米両国の図書館関係者は、両国が世界における学術情報の流通において果たすべき役割を認識しつつ、共通する各種の課題について討議し、それによって両国図書館関係者間の相互理解が一層進んだことを高く評価した。
　参加者は両国の大学図書館の協力関係を強化するための方策として、以下に示す共通の結論に達した。

(1)　日米両国の図書館の協力関係を一層推進するには、適切な時期に第5回日米大学図書館会議を日本で開催するのが適当である。その開催時期、主題等については、今後、日米両国の関係者の間で検討する。ただし、参加者数は第4回会議と同程度とする。

(2)　第5回会議を有効に開催するために、次回の会議までの期間に、必要に応じて小規模な、専門的主題についての会合を持つことが望ましい。ただし、その種の会合については、日米大学図書館会議に関する両国の委員会が責任を持つ必要は必ずしもなく、他の機関によって開催される会合等を利用することも可能であろう。また、両国の委員会の代表者が適当な機会を用いて相互に接触し、次回の会議について意見交換を重ねることも有効であろう。

(3)　CJK書誌情報データベースの国際流通の促進は、東アジア各国における言語処理に最も適した形に開発されたシステムの尊重を基本原則としつつ実施するのが適切である。各国は独自の標準文字コードを開発する自由を保有すべきである。ただし、それらの標準によって作成されたデータの国際流通を図るために、相互の連絡窓口を整備することが望ましい。また、両国が自国の標準文字コードを維持するとともに、それに変更が加えられた場合には速やかに連絡窓口を通じて通知することが望ましい。

(4)　酸性紙の劣化による資料の消失に対する対策を確立することは緊急な課題である。この問題に対する一般社会の認識の向上、出版社に対する中性紙使用の要請、脱酸処理技術の開発、マイクロフィルム・マスターの作成の推進、光ディスクなど新技術の利用について、日米両国の図書館関係者が、それぞれの国内で努力すべきである。また、保存に関する技術開発状況、およびマイクロ

フィルム・マスターの作成などについての両国間における情報交換を促進することが望ましい。

(5) 近年、日米両国の大学図書館における相手国出版物の体系的収集が困難になりつつある現状に鑑み、両国の図書館が、日米両国の出版物の収集活動に対して、可能な範囲で、相互に支援するよう努める。

(6) 日米両国間の書誌情報データベースの相互利用を促進し、また、書誌情報データベースの質的向上のために、書誌情報データベースの作成に関する情報交換、協力を一層推進することが望ましい。

(7) 日米両国間での学術情報ネットワークの接続が進行しつつある状況を踏まえて、両国間の図書館ネットワークの接続について、その必要性およびサービス範囲、接続方式等について、それぞれ両国において検討することが望ましい。

(8) 著作権は保護されなければならないが、図書館における複写サービスが円滑に行われるよう、現行の著作権法が適切に運用されるべきである。

(9) 大学図書館以外の重要な特殊専門図書館との協力については、データベースの形成および資源共有等の共通課題に関し、今後の会議において考慮されることが望ましい。

著者紹介

<u>Theodore F. Welch</u>　ノーザンイリノイ大学図書館長。元ノースウエスタン大学図書館開発担当副館長及び同大学日米関係研究センター理事。氏は現在ALAの日米図書館連絡委員会及び、国際関係連絡会議（1987～1988）議長である。又、OCLCの大学図書館諮問委員会（ACCUL）の委員長にも選出されている。氏の著作には『Toshokan; Libraries in Japanese Society, 1976』『日米大学図書館セミナー（高等教育における図書館技術に関する日米セミナー議事録）』『Encyclopedia of Japan』の中の日本の図書館事情に関する27項目にわたる記事がある。氏は図書館情報学に関して東京大学より博士号を取得しており、日米にまたがる図書館界に広く活躍している。

<u>山崎弘郎</u>　東京大学工学部計数工学科教授。前東京大学附属図書館長。機械制御学会及び電子工学会会員。著作『日米大学図書館セミナー』、『センサー工学の基礎』『センサー工学』。氏の最近の図書館の研究は、カード目録の遡及変換である。

<u>John W. Haeger</u>　研究図書館グループ（RLG）プログラムプランニング担当副社長。元アジア財団（サンフランシスコ）企業担当部長及びポモナカレジ（クレアモント、カリフォルニア州）中国科長。最近の編書に『宋代中国の危機と繁栄』があり、その他『Journal of Asian History』、『Journal of Asian Studies』、『Journal of American Oriental Society』に寄稿している。氏の図書館の業績は電算化の分野に多い。

<u>菅原　通</u>　早稲田大学図書館学術情報システム課長。日本図書館協会、日本学校図書館協会、日本図書館研究会、日本図書館学会各会員。専門は資料組織論。最近の著作に『学校図書館入門　第2巻』の第4章「図書の分類」がある。

<u>高橋和雄</u>　国立国会図書館資料保存対策室長。日本図書館協会会員。氏の専門は図書館資料の保存で、よくこのテーマで講師を務める。氏は国立国会図書館報に「米国議会図書館及びカナダ国立図書館における大量脱酸性施設について」の報告がある。

<u>渋川雅俊</u>　慶応義塾大学研究教育情報センター事務室長。日本図書

館協会、三田図書館情報学会各会員。三田学会企画委員会、私立大学図書館協議会研修委員会、及び電算化委員会各委員。著作『図書館情報学概論』（東京　勁草書房　1983）、『新図書館学ハンドブック』（東京　雄山閣　1984）、『図書館情報学ハンドブック』（東京　丸善　1988）

Patricia Battin　資料保存・利用委員会会長。アメリカ図書館協会会員、図書館振興財団理事、EDUCOM評議員。氏の最近の著作は保存と管理に関するものが多いが、図書館の業績では図書館管理、図書館員教育、保存などである。

安達　淳　学術情報情報センター助教授。氏はNACSISのオンライン目録システムネットワークの設計、実行に携わった。氏は又、文部省の学術調査官でもあり、情報処理学会、電子工学会、情報通信工学会に所属している。専門は情報システムの自動化。

倉橋英逸　東京大学附属図書館事務部長。日本図書館協会会員。国立大学図書館協議会及び大学図書館国際連絡委員会事務局長。最近の著作『日米大学図書館セミナー』所収「日本における図書館技術とサービスの発展」、『大学図書館研究22（1983）』所収「学術情報システムにおける目録」、『図書館情報学ハンドブック』（東京　丸善　1988）

Henriette D. Avram　1983年以来議会図書館（LC）の整理部次長。アメリカ図書館協会会員。米国規格協会（ANSI）情報システム規格委員会（ISSB）及び国際規格調整委員会（ISSC）委員、国際図書館連盟（IFLA）委員,図書館振興財団統合システム計画（LSP）政策委員。氏は又、全米情報基準機構（NISO）の国際関係委員会及びLCのネットワーク諮問委員会（NAC）の会長でもある。氏の図書館電算化、ネットワーク、基準、書誌調整等の著作は100編に近い。

Rowland C. W. Brown　1980年よりOCLC会長及び筆頭理事。アメリカ図書館協会、オハイオ図書館協会、専門図書館協会、情報科学学会、高等教育協会各会員、氏はハーバードのロースクール卒業の後、ワシントンで長年弁護士として活躍する一方、MITのスローンスクールで上級経営管理コースを修得した。氏は実業と教育の多方面にわたる業績でいろいろな賞を受けているが、その中には氏の指

導力に対して与えられた Phi Delta Kappa Education 賞の他に Anti-Defamation League と MIT から与えられた賞がある。

田中久文　学術情報センター事業部長。日本図書館協会、三田図書館情報学会各会員。主な著作には「大学図書館における機械化の現状」「計画中の学術情報システムのその後」があり、『日米大学図書館セミナー』の編集者の一人。氏の目下の研究テーマは、学術分野の情報サービスである。

大野公男　北海道大学附属図書館長、理学部化学科教授。日本化学会、日本物理学会会員。東京大学物理学科卒。フロリダ大学、及びテキサス工科大学の招聘教授を務めたことがある。

宮川隆泰　三菱総合研究所情報管理部長。専門図書館協会理事、日本データベース協会会長。『三菱社史』（1979-1982）の編集に従事。氏の図書館の研究テーマは、専門図書館間のネットワークである。

黒田晴雄　東京大学附属図書館長、理学部化学科教授。日本化学会、物理学会会員。国立大学図書館協議会会長及び大学図書館国際連絡委員会委員長。氏は専門の物理化学について280以上の論文を発表しているが、図書館管理及びネットワークにも強い関心がある。

（編者）
Warren M. Tsuneishi　議会図書館の地域研究部長。国際東洋学図書館員協会会長。研究図書館グループ東アジア委員会における議会図書館代表。長らくALAの日米図書館連絡委員会のメンバーであり、過去の日米大学図書館会議に全て参加した。
第1回日米大学図書館会議議事録である『University and Research Libraries in Japan and the United States』（ALA 1972）の編者の一人であり、第2回会議の議事録にも論文を発表している。MA 及び MLS（コロンビア大学）、政治学の PhD（イエール大学）取得。

Mary Frances Grosch　ノーザンイリノイ大学の上級司書でビジネス、経済分野のサブジェクト・スペシャリスト。アメリカ図書館協会会員。セント・ノーバート大学で芸術史専攻。MBA 及び MSLS（イリノイ大学）取得。